Facets of Hellenic Life

John Scarborough
University of Kentucky

Houghton Mifflin Company · Boston
Atlanta Dallas Geneva, Ill.
Hopewell, N.J. Palo Alto London

Maps by Richard Sanderson

Printed in the U.S.A.

Library of Congress Catalog Card Number: 75-29704

ISBN: 0-395-20368-6

Contents

Preface

Facets of Hellenic Life is a volume somewhat different from a
Greek history book. I composed it in response to the many questions given to me in six years of teaching a survey course in Greek
history to college sophomores. Generally after the first month of
class, it becomes apparent that the usual Greek history books fail
to give answers to the questions students most often ask about the
Greeks. Their questions rarely are of the "who" or "when" sort, so
often detailed in ancient history textbooks, but often are about
"why" or "what." Questions recur year after year; and I think I have
gained a good sample of students' interests since my classes have
been large and have represented a random selection of majors typical
of a medium-sized college or university.

Students' questions, their predominant natural concerns about
Greek history, can be summed up by six topics. (1) Ordinary life,
the day's routine in Athens, is present throughout *Facets* but does
not, however, bulk large in one place since students can find many
inexpensive and well-written books on this subject. (2) Magic
and disease, are subjects not found in many books (except as
scattered and incidental matter). They are covered specifically in
Chapter 9 of *Facets*. (3) Life in the military is connected in students'
minds with the perennial popularity of Alexander the Great and his
campaigns. Many volumes give good accounts of the military career
of Alexander, but rarely do they describe tactics, strategy, and
attitude of soldiers. Year after year, my explanation of tactics at
Granicus and elsewhere seems to excite a myriad of questions. For
this reason *Facets'* treatment of warfare and military life is carefully
detailed. (4) Greek attitudes about sexual and moral behavior concern students. They want to compare similarities and differences
between the Greeks and us. I have attempted a general answer in
Chapter 7 under the rubric of "Proper Conduct and Sexual Mores."

(5) There is a great curiosity among students about Greek religion. Greek politics and Greek religion were part of the same package because the *polis* ("city-state") was bound up with religious and mythical values, a difference that intrigues modern students accustomed to a separation of church and state. Religion will be found scattered throughout *Facets,* with some specifics in Chapter 6, "Greeks and Myth." (6) Since most students grow up in cities, there is widespread fascination with the farm, the home of the vast majority of people in Greek antiquity. Chapter 2, "The Plow and the Mind," describes the land and the people it bred.

Queries also emerge about philosophy and law, although not in the numbers of the six listed categories. Both are difficult subjects, and in *Facets,* I have written a separate section on the philosophies through Hellenistic days, but have left Greek law in the context of conduct (it appears with sexual morality in Chapter 7).

For readers craving more "straight" history Chapters 4 and 5, "War" and "More War," should be perused before the remainder of *Facets.* The history of warfare among the Greeks runs like the proverbial thread and is easily summarized by chronology. War can be used as a kind of mirror in the measure of any society, and with that notion in mind I have designed these two chapters to be more than Greeks fighting from Homer to Ptolemy.

Translations from original sources are my own, and are cited in the usual manner of classical materials.

My debt to the numerous scholars in Greek history is apparent from the bibliographical listings. Another type of debt may not be apparent, but is important. Several students have given generously of their time and criticism to make *Facets* more understandable to the beginner in Greek studies. To the classes as a whole, I owe constructive comments on content and style, as well as suggestions on "what they would like to read in such a book." To Damian Barthle, Carl J. Post, and Park Rommel, I have appreciation for formulation and enunciation of themes and ideas, as they emerged in the chapters on the *polis,* religion and mores, and the military, respectively. Barbara Nutoni, Jan Prickett, and Lawrence Schneider read chapters and offered many points of modification for clarity and content. My able teaching assistant and graduate student, Michael Sweeney, read the entire manuscript and contributed numerous criticisms and corrections that have enriched the book. My colleague, Richard Williams, called my attention to several deficiencies in the account

of the Greek trireme, and the improved accuracy of this section is
due in large part to his cordial suggestions and corrections, backed
by evidence from the sources.

My wife, Lysa, has consistently performed the thankless and necessary task of reading for style. More than that her support often
rekindled my enthusiasm. If *Facets* succeeds, it will be due to
Lysa's encouragement that I write about not only the facts but
also the spirit of Greek civilization.

1

Greeks in Settlements

When Greeks talked about their way of life, they always shaped
their descriptions in reference to the *polis* (usually translated rather
weakly as "city-state"), the institution that colored every aspect of
their lives. The *polis* (or *poleis* in the plural) was contained in a
definite geographic area usually about the size of a United States
county. It had one major town, and the collected settlement was
most often walled, enclosing a fortified citadel (the original *polis*,
which later became the *acropolis*) and the marketplace (*agora*).
Each *polis* had its *acropolis*. Attica, a peninsula in eastern Greece
and the most famous of the Greek *poleis*, had its urban center at
Athens and Athens' port city of Piraeus; since Athens was the most
well known of the Greek states, her *acropolis* became known as the
Acropolis. The citadel at Corinth was known as the Acrocorinth.
   The *polis* made Greek culture different from that of the surrounding barbarian peoples, who did not share the institutions of
the *polis* and who, most essentially, did not speak any dialect
of Greek. This feeling of uniqueness was shared by Athenians,
Spartans, Thebans, Corinthians, and the citizens of the hundreds of
other *poleis* scattered throughout mainland Greece, western Asia
Minor, southern Italy and Sicily, southern Gaul, and North Africa
(notably, Cyrene on the coast of Libya). It was not city life that
marked the *polis* as novel, since urban centers had flourished in

Persia and Carthage was an offshoot of the renowned merchant cities on the coast of ancient Phoenicia. Farmers took refuge in fortified spots all along the Mediterranean seaboard and inland, and this distinction was worth little in the Greek sense of self-esteem. Other civilizations had kings and warrior-chieftains similar to the traditions of several *polis* institutions, and trade functioned effectively in the non-Hellenic centers of Persia, Egypt, Phoenicia, and Carthage. Even with all these similarities, Greeks from the individual *poleis* proclaimed a superiority of inner spirit and outer form, an arrogance that Plato's *Republic* and Aristotle's *Politics* summarize. Although both philosophers used Sparta as their model, they gained their real-life experience from the workings of the *polis* in its Athenian form.

The common farmer tilling fields outside the fortified center, who could take refuge there in the event of invasion or attack, and the city dweller making his living from trade or one of the crafts both reflected this pride in a unique existence. The citizens of the *polis* included both the farmer and the city dweller. Even though the citizens lived both inside and outside the walls, the government of the state generally concentrated in the town. Involvement in the day-to-day operation of the government (established by the constitution, which might or might not be written down) determined membership in the citizen body, and in each *polis* the whole citizen body *was* the state. Consequently, the name of the state came from the citizens in it, not from the town or territory. Greeks writing about *hoi Athenaioi* ("the Athenians") meant the people of the state as well as the geographical area. As Thucydides put it, "Men are the *polis* and not walls or ships without men in them" (*History of the Peloponnesian War,* VII, 77).

The ruling class in each kind of *polis*—whether it was an aristocracy, oligarchy, or democracy—comprised the citizens. In addition to the citizens there were some classes of people that did not have membership in the state. At the bottom were the slaves, and dependent lower classes were only slightly better off. Groups of resident foreigners (*metics*) and those foreigners who lived in the surrounding territory (*perioikoi*) were always found in the *polis*. The ideal Greek, however, was the man who was loyal to his *polis* while being geographically free; as Aristotle said, "That man is intended by nature to be an animal that lives in a *polis*" (*Politics,* I, 1253a3). (This is the famous—and usually mistranslated—"political animal" mentioned so commonly in political science textbooks.) The ideal Greek is also one "who is meant for political associations and intended by nature to live with other men" (Aristotle, *Ethics*, I, 8. 6).

Sources of History of the *Polis*

Much information about Athens' historical development is found in the works of the historians Herodotus and Thucydides, in those of her playwrights and poets, and of philosophers like Plato and Aristotle. Aristotle and his pupils compiled the *Constitution of Athens* (a collection of facts about Athenian history) in the fourth century B.C., and it remains a fundamental document for understanding Athens and her government. Less information and more legend have survived about Sparta. Scattered bits of reliable data about Spartan institutions are embedded in the writings of Plato and Aristotle and in Plutarch's *Lycurgus.* Xenophon's *Hellenica,* an account of Greek history from 411 to 362 B.C., provides solid information on Spartan and Theban dominion in the fourth century B.C. Sparta and Athens figure prominently in historical sources, particularly since the two *poleis* became stereotypes for oligarchy and democracy, opposing systems of government. In addition, it is Thucydides, one of the greatest historians of the West, who describes the war between these two states. Sparta and Athens led a Greek coalition against Persia earlier in the same century, and that struggle is documented by Herodotus, another excellent historian. (See chapter 10 for further discussion of Herodotus and Thucydides.)

Compared with sources for Athenian and Spartan history and institutions, material for the rest of the *poleis* is meager at best and nonexistent for most, with the exception of coin-issues that signal rich and varied economic, artistic, and mining activities. Thebes' history has a moment of brilliance in 371 B.C. when—to the surprise of everyone, including the Thebans—the Theban light infantry defeated the supposedly unbeatable Spartan phalanx at Leuctra. A scant ten years later, Theban fortune ebbed at Mantinea with another victory over Sparta—at the cost of Thebes' great general Epaminondas. Xenophon ends his *Hellenica* with that victory in 362 B.C., and chance references in Herodotus and Thucydides help somewhat for an understanding of the history of the fifth century B.C. The controversial *Hellenica Oxyrhynchia* gives some details of Thebes' Boeotian League. Herodotus' sources knew something of early Corinthian development, tyrannies, and colonization. Thucydides and Xenophon provide good material on Corinth for the period of the Peloponnesian War (431–404 B.C.) and slightly later. Depth and life for Thebes and Corinth, compared with that for Athens, is lacking; but along with Argos, Megara, and a host of other *poleis*, Thebes and Corinth had a powerful impact on Greek history and the eventual demise of the *polis*.

The Early *Polis*

Kings ruled in Greece when homeric bards were consolidating the *Iliad*, but by the time historic accounts begin, kings had almost vanished. Sparta kept nominal kings until the third century B.C., but their role was to command the Spartan army in the field. There may have been a king at Argos until *c.* 700 B.C., but in most other states kings were forced to give up power to an aristocracy based on birth. Sometimes violent revolution accompanied the change, but a peaceful transition was more usual. Weak kings in early Athens lost their military rights, but preserved their religious function as priests of local cults. Later, even these religious duties were transferred to officials who were elected or appointed for a year; the title *archon basileus* survived as the name of the magistrate who performed ancestral rites for the state. The title of king (*basileus*) aroused little emotion, suggesting a normally peaceful evolution from kingship to the several later forms of government.

The *basileus* was chosen from a hereditary "royal" family (the homeric stereotype). His duties were to lead in war, act as high priest of local cults, and settle disputes; he consulted a *gerousia* ("council of elders") for advice. Also present in pre-*polis* Greece was an *ecclesia* ("assembly") made up of all males over eighteen who were able to serve in the local army. The *ecclesia* probably voted Yes or No on questions given by the *basileus*, and it rejected or accepted candidates for that office.

Political control passed to the nobles, an exclusive class, well set apart from their fellows. Herodotus tells of the Bacchiadae, rulers of Corinth in early seventh century B.C., who married only among themselves. Everyone in the family claimed descent from Bacchis, an earlier king of Corinth. In contrast, Attica had other settlements besides Athens; the aristocracy there comprised a number of families claiming various lines of descent but all calling themselves

Eupatridae, families with fathers in the nobility. Other family names, like the Hippeis ("horsemen") from Eretria in Euboea, describe traditional agricultural wealth rather than family descent. Aristocratic power there was based on large landholdings as well as family claims.

Social organization in early Greece was grounded in the concept of patriarchy, and the smallest social unit was the family. All male and unmarried female progeny of one male composed a family, often run by a grandfather. The group included the grandfather's wife, all of his sons and their wives and children, his grandsons, and so on. Once the patriarch died, the family broke up into smaller units, with sons becoming heads of new families. Groups of families sometimes traced their descent from a common male ancestor and formed a larger social unit than the family. This superfamily, or *genos* ("clan"), was in turn a unit of a *phratry* ("brotherhood") known from homeric stories. The *phratries* were organized followers of particular nobles.

The population of a given area came to be organized into *phylai* ("tribes"), commonly based on distant ties of kinship but more usually on territorial units. Thus Greek political life included two types of social organization: locality and kinship. The twentieth century is most familiar with locality as a political unit, as in township, county, or state. But organization by kinship has modern parallels in the clans of Scotland or tribes of American Indians. For the emerging *polis,* the two types of social organization were inseparable.

The aristocracy in the developing *polis* probably originated in families who chanced to hold the most land in the years just prior to 800 B.C. Gradually the limited monarchy was transformed into an oligarchy ("rule by a few"), and military and executive functions were taken from the *basileus* and given to individuals from the aristocratic class. The *gerousia* became a council of nobility drawn from the most powerful clans, while the *ecclesia* declined in influence because fewer of the ordinary men could afford to go to war. Under oligarchic rule, contacts with the world outside the limited *poleis* slowly revived, and the first waves of Greek colonization began under aristocratic leadership.

In the seventh century B.C., many *poleis* faced the crisis of overpopulation. Hesiod's *Works and Days,* a sharp and telling curse against the corruption of the aristocratic class, held up a mirror to a time when the poor and practically landless classes were growing, while the power and numbers of the nobility remained static. A population that lived from the soil had to have land for farming and crops, but the noble's horses, status symbols of growing wealth, took many acres for grazing. The rich began to live closer to the fortified places within the *polis*, and the *agora* swarmed with traders plying golden delights from foreign lands. These same merchants brought the idea of coined money from Asia Minor, and although true coinages were not part of the *polis* economy until after 650 B.C., power and wealth could now be measured in other terms than land. Change marked the age in which the *polis* became a way of life for Greeks, change that included economic shifts, war and its use as an instrument of state policy, and the reorganization of political life in the *polis*.

Tyrants

Political motives, coupled with ever present social and economic problems, hastened the ouster of the crusty oligarchic governments. Throwing out the rulers was no easy matter, usually requiring an armed revolt led by a tyrant (*tyrannos*). The latter first behaved like a king, but soon the term meant a special kind of monarch with no hereditary claim to power who simply seized the reins of government through his own efforts. The first tyrants were welcomed as leaders opposing the old oligarchic class, but they shortly became leaders of a ruling clique of their own and were condemned as being ruthless and without compassion. Sometime before 650 B.C., Cypselus of Corinth, backed by popular support, expelled the Bacchiadae by killing the nobles and confiscating their lands. There were several reasons for the violence: agrarian discontent was common in Attica and Boeotia around 600 B.C. and it was most likely paralleled by conditions around Corinth; the economic growth from colonization distributed benefits unevenly and widened the gap between the rich and poor; soon there were considerable numbers of wealthy men who did not come from aristocratic lines, and they wanted some political power; and the old nobility constantly squabbled among themselves, adding to the confusion.

The change in Greek warfare also contributed to the collapse of aristocratic rule in the *poleis*. By 750 B.C. Greek armies were organized into the block formation called the phalanx, and its soldiers now included heavy infantry within tight formation. The *hoplites*, or heavily armed infantry, came from newly risen classes in the *polis*; although they were new landholders of nonaristocratic origins, they were able to equip themselves with body armor, shields, and greaves (curved plates of bronze or leather to protect the shins). Economic growth and the success of the phalanx, particularly against the unorganized battle formations of barbarian peoples on the fringes of the colonies, made the phalanx—and the men who fought as *hoplites*—an important political factor in the rise of tyrannies.

The "Age of Tyranny" (*c.* 700–500 B.C.) produced man-made written law, which was immensely important for the *polis* and the way its inhabitants conducted themselves. The Greek concept of law (*nomos*) provided links with venerated and limiting traditions and gave the *polis* a sense of inner cohesion and identity. The laws of Sparta and Athens were "common" only in that their origins were human as opposed to the laws given by the gods in the contemporary societies of the Near East.

This period also witnessed the introduction of true coinage, an idea borrowed from Lydia in Asia Minor. Lydians made coinage in gold, silver, bronze, and electrum, but Greeks generally produced coins in silver and bronze. The major silver coin was called a *drachma*, a given weight of silver, while the bronze piece was known as an *obol*. Attic coins bore the image of Athena, patron goddess of the *polis*, on the obverse (head), and Athena's owl on the reverse (tail). Since wealth in precious metals was measured by weight rather than value (or "backing" as in modern economic systems), Greeks knew great wealth in terms of *talents* (about sixty-six pounds each) and the subdivisions of *minas* (sixty *minas* being equivalent to one *talent*) and *drachmas* (one hundred *drachmas* equaling one *mina*). To put such coin-weights into modern equivalences is impossible, since the Greeks conceived their money in ways closely connected with farming and traditional practices. Early *obols* were simply "spits" of metal, and six "spits" made a *drachma*, or a "handful." Thus the "handful of spits" (*drattomai*) was what could be grasped. The smallest coins used in Attic marketplaces were worth one-eighth of an *obol*, with larger units of one-fourth, three-eighths, one-half, and three-quarters of an *obol*. These little bits of silver or bronze were so small that shoppers carried them in their mouths. Reliable coinage was important for far-flung trade, and the various *poleis* competed for dominance of foreign and domestic markets through their coinages. Acceptance of standard weights of metal also meant that commerce flourished, since capital and wealth were measured in other terms than real estate. Such capital, which derived from stocks of precious metal, aided the development of specialty items like olives and wine, which became the mainstay of Athens.

Athens and Sparta underwent their most crucial development before 500 B.C., and by the time of the Persian wars (499–479 B.C.), each had evolved into a mature *polis*. The history of Athens to 500 B.C. was packed with stress and tension, but carefully timed reforms and changes generally prevented open bloodshed. On the other hand, Sparta enjoyed an externally quiet history once a radical militarization of Spartan society solved her first near-fatal problems with the Messenians.

Athens: Her Ideal

Attica, the small peninsula jutting eastward into the Aegean Sea, was large by Greek standards, comprising approximately one thousand square miles. About 700 B.C., the nine *archons*, elected officials who held office for one year, replaced the traditional kings of Athens. Their names and functions showed the beginnings of Athenian methods for dealing with internal political problems. First was a chief *archon*, who acted as head of civil affairs and property rights. Then came the *archon basileus*, who supervised ancestral ceremonies and religious rites. The third official was the *polemarch* ("general"). The *thesmothetae* (the fourth through ninth *archons*) were learned in the law and made records of precedent. The Council of the Areopagus, drawn from the aristocracy and ex-*archons,* debated and executed the law. The *ecclesia* was also present, but it played a minor role, again indicating the aristocratic base of early Athens.

In the seventh century B.C., Athens had serious economic troubles. Pottery finds reveal that Athens lost her dominion in trade and artistic innovations to Corinth. Aristocratic rule harshened, and the lot of the poor farmer worsened through the decades. Although indebted farmers retained their land through a custom that prevented land seizure, they fell into increasing arrears to a few wealthy families, and most produce went to the money lenders, leaving the free farmers on the level of serfs. If a free farmer became landless through some abnormal quirk, he could be enslaved for debt, and some former farmers were sold as slaves in foreign ports to pay for part of an incurred liability. In turn, the political machinery of Attica, run for the profit of the few enriched families, did not govern well, and bitter feuding erupted among the top clans. Finally the Athenian aristocracy realized the need for reform to check growing unrest and increasing political chaos.

Broad changes were necessary to stem the threat of civil war, and the wiser leaders of Athens displayed the quality of compromise, a hallmark of Athenian history. In 594 B.C., the respected noble Solon was elected sole *archon* and given wide powers to effect solutions to the ominous problems, which seemed to forecast open bloodshed. A remarkable man of varied talents, which included writing elegiac poetry, he carefully separated the needs of Athens from idealistic desires, and made basic but moderate reforms. To the cry of "abolish debts," he replied by cancelling agricultural debt and instituting a fund to rescue Athenians sold abroad for debt. He made it worthwhile to raise olives and grapes, correctly forecasting Athens' role as a trading mistress. At the same time, he forbade the export of wheat from Attica, which provided a food supply (not adequate for long) for Attica's growing population. Olive oil and wine soon were packaged in glowing pots and shipped throughout the Mediterranean, and the Attic economy functioned on a base of commerce and silver coinage. Aristocrats were sharply limited in the display of luxury goods so that the gulf between rich and poor would not be so obvious. The rich craved jewelry and imported delicacies just as before, but Solon ordered them to use such items in good taste. In keeping with the new commerce, he inaugurated an Athenian "devaluation" with a switch to coins and weights of the Euboic standard, which was about one-third lighter than previously.

Political reform divided citizens into ranks according to income. Wealth was quickly assessed by farm production, and four classes emerged. First in prestige were the "men of the five hundred bushels" (*pentakosio medimnoi*), followed by the "horsemen" (*hippeis*) whose farms yielded three hundred *medimnoi* ("bushels"). In the third class were the "men of the line" (*zeugitae*), with property worth two hundred *medimnoi*. The remaining Attic citizens were grouped as "workers" (*thetes*). Political office was reserved for the first two classes, but all citizens could exercise a voice in the assembly and the law courts (*heliaea*). To put the *ecclesia* on surer footing, Solon established the Council of Four Hundred, a standing committee from the *ecclesia* that he charged with preparing business for de-

ANCIENT GREECE

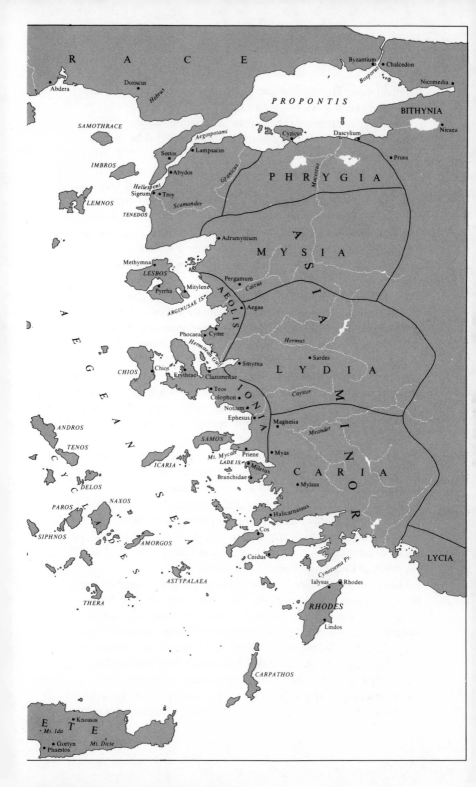

bate and vote. The *ecclesia* also acted as a court of appeals for decisions handed down by magistrates.

Solon gave considerable thought to the relations between the individual and the *polis* and enunciated principles that became the keystones in Western concepts of government. The rule of the *polis* had to be founded on justice, since wrongdoing anywhere in the *polis* affected all citizens. Reflecting current philosophical thinking, he believed the world had a built-in law that resulted in order and regularity, which the will of the gods supported. With the reforms, he wedded the concept of ethics to Athenian politics, even though control still remained in the hands of the rich. Provided the aristocrats governed well and in the interests of the *polis*, they were qualified to rule.

Solon's reforms did not prevent tyranny in Athens, although they delayed it. Factionalism broke out repeatedly among noble families, and one ambitious aristocrat finally managed to seize full power after two previous failures. The new tyrant, Peisistratus (who ruled in Athens from *c*. 546 B.C. until his death in 527 B.C.), did not tamper with Solon's reforms, which had weathered the great internal struggles unscathed. Instead, he wielded power lightly and increased Athens' power and influence abroad. He maintained extensive commercial and diplomatic contacts with foreign rulers through peaceful agreements. He also encouraged the development of the arts in Athens to abet their growing power and reputation, respected throughout the Greek world. Under Peisistratus and his two sons, Hipparchus (assassinated in 514 B.C.) and Hippias (deposed in 510 B.C.), a broad program of religious and cultural events encouraged patriotic duty in Athens. The Acropolis gained new temples, and the *agora* was organized to function as the urban center of trade and the gossip of politics. The *polis* sponsored local festivals, and the famous mysteries at Eleusis received official recognition.

The tyranny neutralized the old clans and their political machinery. Some prominent members of the old nobility were in exile, hoping to interest somebody with an army so they could regain power. In the meantime, the Attic people attached their political loyalties to the *polis* and its functions as a whole, rather than to the narrow clans. Thus by the time the exiled Alcmeonid clan inveigled the king of Sparta to take the field against Athens—in the name of deposing a tyrant—the political mood of Athens opposed the return of aristocratic rule. In 510 B.C., when the tyrant Hippias went into exile at the Persian court, Sparta's choice for the new Athenian oligarchy was left to rule Attica. Dissension, however, erupted almost immediately among the restored noble families, and Cleisthenes, one of the Alcmeonids, gained power in 508 B.C. To maintain his power and to insure that clan bickering would not block smooth government in Athens, Cleisthenes remolded the political mechanics of the *polis*, making the people the base of power. He did not go about his program for long-range idealism, but, rather, hoped to retain the people as the foundation for his own political control.

To break clan power, Cleisthenes had to abolish the old organization of Attica, in which citizens belonged to one of four Ionian tribes. He replaced them with ten tribes based on residence, in contrast with the old system of tribal loyalties based on kinship and religion. The *demes*, the smallest units of the *polis*, provided the footing of the reformed Athenian political system. Attic *demes* were like modern wards and functioned in a similar manner, and those who appeared on the *deme* lists were citizens. There were about one hundred seventy of these units of local self-government, and they included the villages and small populated centers scattered around Attica, as well as subdivisions of Athens. Each *deme* elected a Demarch, who supervised the *deme* assembly; the assembly kept a roll of citizens and a record of real estate and mortgages, and it conducted lesser judicial matters. From this base, the *demes* were organized into *trittyes* ("thirds"). While the number of *demes* in a *trittys* varied, three *trittyes* made up one of the new tribes, and thirty *trittyes* made up the ten reordered tribes. The *trittyes* in a tribe did not represent a particular area: citizens from Athens, the countryside at large, and the seacoast were part of one *trittys*. Each tribe was supposed to be a cross-section from the Attic population, but in reality the city *demes* became the dominant bloc in the Athenian assembly. Assembly votes were taken by tribe, and the urban tribes always were more closely knit than the other tribes, which had many members who were rich or poor farmers.

The reforms of Cleisthenes did away with the Council of Four Hundred and instituted a Council of Five Hundred. The new council was chosen by lot, with fifty members elected annually from each of the ten tribes. The council prepared business to be laid before the *ecclesia,* which met every ten days to pass measures into law, and shouldered responsibility for financial and diplomatic matters. To help the council work more efficiently, it was divided into ten committees, each of which was composed of fifty members representing a tribe. Each of the ten committees was chosen by lot to run the assembly for one-tenth of the Athenian year, either thirty-five or thirty-six days. Each day a different committee chairman was chosen by lot. During the time it directed the *ecclesia*, the committee was called a *prytany*, which also came to be the unit of time for one-tenth of the year.

The *archons* remained as executive officials, but Cleisthenes instituted a new treasury board, the Ten Receivers (*apodectae*), who supervised distribution of income to the two treasuries (the treasury of Athena, run by the "Treasurers of the Goddess" and the state treasury). The *demes* elected the members of the *heliaea*, and the old Council of the Areopagus was left to "guard the laws." The nine *archons* were elected as before from the first two classes, a limitation dictated by reality. Athens did not pay for performance of political duties, and only those members of the upper two classes could afford the honor of being an *archon*. Military districts were also reorganized along the new tribal lines. By 502 B.C. each tribe elected a *taxiarch* and a *hipparch*, who commanded the infantry and cavalry respectively. Another "reform" was ostracism, a negative popularity contest. Once a year, the people met together in the *agora* to determine whether anyone was becoming dangerous to the *polis*, or whether anyone might be too powerful in the near future. If a quorum of six thousand voters from the *ecclesia* were available, the man who got the largest number of votes was obliged to go into exile for ten years. The practice received its name from the potsherds (*ostraca*) on which voters wrote the lucky fellow's name.

Underlying assumptions in the Athenian system were quite different from those of other *poleis*. With further reforms—in 487 B.C. *archons* were chosen by lot, by about 460 B.C. the remaining power of the Council of the Areopagus was taken away, and about the same time, the state made payment to those who served in political office and on the juries—the development of democracy in Athens solidified. The rule of the people was considered capable, but there were limitations: no women, no slaves, and no resident foreigners could vote. The voting citizen was male and over eighteen. By 450 B.C. the assembly of voters had unrestricted power. The votes taken in the *ecclesia* were binding and came in theory from all forty-three thousand citizens (estimated for mid-fifth century B.C.), but usually only five thousand to six thousand voters showed up for the meetings every ten days. The formal mechanics of Athenian politics were useless without popular support, which came from the backing of leaders, the demagogues, who commanded respect from the mass of voters. The demagogues were known for their wisdom in politics. The voters listened when they got up to speak in the *ecclesia*. The citizens brooded over what the demagogue said on a given day in light of their own information on an issue—information they gained through gossip in the *agora* or at the frequent dinner parties.

There were several checks on runaway mob rule. The *prytany* exercised the first control over issues debated in the full *ecclesia,* since it first screened any business presented. The full council reviewed public accounts and costs for public buildings and religious festivals. The council was itself checked by the rule that one man could not serve for more than two years in his lifetime, and then not for two years in succession, even if his marked token popped out of the voting machine. Further, a check on legal innovations that managed to wiggle through the council and be passed in the *ecclesia* was the writ of unconstitutionality, which determined whether a new law was contrary to ancestral custom. If a law passed in the *ecclesia* was found to go against the customs of the *polis*, then the person who originally introduced the law would be fined very heavily. An additional check came from the fact that although the voting age was set at eighteen, membership on the juries was limited to citizens over thirty. Consequently, decisions of the people's juries were more "conservative" than measures of the *ecclesia*.

The magistrates were men of the town chosen by lot. Under Pericles about seven hundred magistrates were elected from the citizenry each year, which meant that every voter eventually served as a magistrate at least once during his lifetime. Only two major offices, requiring specialized skills, were elected by popular vote: the city architect and the Board of Ten Generals. Consequently, the leading general functioned as demagogue. The most famous general-demagogue was Pericles, who was continually re-elected general from about 461 to 429 B.C. As leader of the people, Pericles directed state policy and exercised considerable influence over the various magistrates.

The jury lists also implemented justice directly; after state pay for jury duty was introduced (a kind of social security), there were plenty of willing citizens. Juries were always large and came in odd numbers—at least 201 or more to prevent tie votes and bribery. The judge simply conducted the proceedings, without any authority, and the accused pleaded his own case. Two votes were necessary: one for guilt or innocence, another for the penalty.

The ideal of democracy in Athens shows similarities to and differences from modern concepts of democracy. The regular election of officials was similar, but otherwise Athenian democracy was quite different from the modern representative system in the United Stated. *Archons* were chosen by lot—democracy at its most literal—but the lot did not always mirror the will of the *ecclesia*. Direct participation in the political life of the *polis* was normal and expected of all citizens who sat in the *ecclesia*. Elected officials—*archons* or those on the council—did not have the power of legislation, which was always in the hands of the *ecclesia*. Consequently, although the assumptions of the Athenian ideal were at variance with those of Sparta, or most other *poleis*, the initial matter of citizen participation was the same throughout Greece. The way the *polis* defined "citizen" caused variations in the systems. Athens chose to include as many voters as possible, attracting them into political participation, while more severely limited systems—such as those for Sparta, Corinth, and Thebes—chose to give greater responsibilities to fewer people. All *poleis* sought internal stability, and as long as Athenian democracy was expanding in wealth and power, democracy functioned effectively even with an empire. Once Athens met her humiliating defeat at the hands of Sparta in 404 B.C., the democracy contracted in power but remained Athens' government until 267 B.C.

Another basic difference between Athenian democracy and modern versions of the democratic system is the important one of religious connections. In classical Greece, religion and the state were inseparable. Art, literature, and all cultural life emerged from the incorporation of religion into the very heart of the *polis.* Tragedians wrote ageless plays to educate and explain man's role in relation to the gods, and artists and poets took their images from religion and its mythical vehicle. The Greek *polis*, including democratic Athens, was a religious unit, just as it was an incorporation of political, social, economic, geographic, and military values. In Athens, democracy gave birth to an inner pride unrivaled in Greece, but it also gave rise to an unrealistic optimism that led to military disaster abroad and scapegoat hunting at home. In 399 B.C., condemned by the democracy's jury for teaching the people of Athens how to question,

Socrates drank hemlock. The charge was corruption of the youth, together with the vague accusation that he had introduced new gods into Athens. (See chapter 8 for further discussion of Socrates.)

Sparta: The Stable Oligarchy

A clear stereotype remains of Sparta and the ideal she represented in classical Greece, since Plato's *Republic* made her the model for stable government. Aristotle also chose Sparta as the state with the most stable constitution, and he compared Spartan justice favorably with his other ideal, the system of Carthage. Xenophon, the exiled Athenian mercenary and adventurer, was an open admirer of Sparta. Thucydides, the Athenian general who wrote the brilliant history of the Peloponnesian War (431–404 B.C.), often believed Sparta possessed the greater talent of the two *poleis*. Most sources, however, resemble Plutarch's "biography" of *Lycurgus,* put down in the second century A.D. It is myth bound with history, stereotype encrusted on fragments of facts.

To solve her population problems, Sparta uniquely chose conquest as an answer. Other *poleis* reduced population through colonization or commerce, but Sparta founded only one colony in southern Italy, Tarentum (*c.* 705 B.C.). Sparta gained respite from land hunger by launching a series of wars against her western neighbors, the Messenians. After a long and bitter struggle, victorious Sparta became the strongest state in the Peloponnesus and the most respected *polis* in the Greek world by 500 B.C. Although the conquest of Messenia enabled the Spartans to gain more land, military success created as many problems as it had solved. Sparta controlled much land from which came great wealth and power, but survival of the *polis* depended on her keeping the newly subjugated peoples cowed and isolated. The new lands also made it imperative to define the "citizen" who would rule the conquered lands.

For students of Spartan history, the basic questions of what happened when are subjects of much controversy. Some scholars assume that the so-called Lycurgan reforms of the Spartan constitution occurred before the Messenian uprisings against Sparta (variously dated as beginning anywhere from 640 to 620 B.C.). Other specialists in Spartan history believe the reforms came after the Messenian wars. Strong evidence supports both views, while a third opinion would throw out Lycurgus altogether, in the belief that he is a figment of

Spartan legend, a name who could give Spartan customs the status of having had an "inventor" or "founder." The tendency for founders to emerge in legend is rather common in Greek local traditions (Theseus of Athens is a good illustration), and many scholars think Lycurgus may have been someone the Spartans invented for themselves. The following summary, however, employs the basic opinions of W. G. Forrest in *A History of Sparta;* he believes that the figure of Lycurgus has some historic foundation, and that the reforms in the Spartan constitution came before the Messenian wars.

The threat of revolution confronted Sparta some decades before it became serious for other *poleis*. She was the first Greek state to devise a constitution, and first to recognize the changes that had resulted from an expanding economy and population. The Spartan system can be characterized as an arrested revolution, which gave the constitution its unique stamp in Greece. The source materials give a fairly uniform picture of the system, and it seems to have been well known and widely accepted as "historical" in classical Greece. Plato's *Republic* took the Spartan ideal and utilized it to illustrate the best kind of *polis*, and a similar ideal lurks behind Aristotle's *Politics*. The major hero in Xenophon's *Hellenica* is the Spartan, Agesilaus; Xenophon also eulogized Sparta in several minor works. In addition, Plutarch inserts "fragments" of earlier source material within *Lycurgus*, including the document known as the Great Rhetra. In the tradition, Lycurgus is the Spartan leader who devised both the system and life-style that enabled the Spartans to keep military control over lands, whether they were newly won by force of arms or held for many generations. The Great Rhetra ("enactment") stipulates that the people of Sparta were divided into tribes and *obai* (most likely "villages") and that the *gerousia* (the usual Council of Elders, in this case men over sixty years of age) included two kings. Through some quirk of history, Sparta inherited a dual kingship, and the two kings served the state as military commanders. The role of the *ecclesia* was to ratify decisions reached by the *gerousia*. The Great Rhetra emphasizes the important concerns that lay beneath a Greek constitution: religious rites, an assembly of citizens, and a council.

Connected to the *obai* were the Spartan fighting units, the *lochai* ("brotherhoods") or, as Lycurgus supposedly labeled them, the *sussitia* ("men who ate together"), numbering about nine thousand men who were members of the heavy infantry of the Spartan phalanx and always ready to march; this number produced a field army of about sixty-five hundred soldiers. These nine thousand men were the citizens of Sparta, the Equals who governed all and supervised the land. The conquest of Messenia made it impossible for the nine thousand Equals to supervise the land directly. The citizens had to leave their lands in the care of a class they could trust; this seems to have been the function of the obscure Spartan *perioikoi* (those who "lived around"). The *perioikoi* had certain citizen rights and occasionally fought with the Spartans, but they could not vote in the assembly. Below the two classes of citizens and quasi citizens the Helots existed, much like medieval serfs—but in reality having fewer rights and privileges than their historical look-alikes had under the umbrella of medieval Christianity. Generally, Helots were the peoples conquered in war and subsequently reduced to slavery. Keeping the Helots in check, especially in Messenia, absorbed the energy of the top two classes.

Plutarch's *Lycurgus* summarizes traditional Spartan life. The Spartan male was subjected to rigorous training beginning at age six or seven, when the *polis* took the boy from his mother and placed him in a pack of boys and adolescents led by a young man who had not yet attained full rights. Brutality and craftiness were constantly present in the group, with loyalty to fellow Spartans and the *polis* pounded home day after day; yet they also learned something about writing and the arts. The purpose of the reforms was echoed in the groupings of young men when Sparta broke the tribes apart and organized the military divisions around the *obai,* similar to Athens' later *deme* system. The boy now turned man gained a seat in the Spartan *ecclesia* and enjoyed the rights of being an Equal. The duties of a citizen were light and consisted of eating meals with his boyhood comrades in the *sussition* (the singular of *sussitia*), fighting in the army on call, and running his lands. Life was not onerous for the Equal, who took great pride in his status. Although women had no legal rights, they ran the *polis'* economy and lands while the men were off belaboring Spartan subjects or aiding Spartan allies somewhere in the Peloponnesus. The hardened ladies were known to mean "Come back victorious with your shield or on it" quite literally, although their seductiveness to foreign visitors became a watchword throughout Greece.

In spite of the Greek "knowledge" about Sparta, the economy, arts, and learning went on unabated, just as they did in other *poleis.*

Spartan pottery retained a high quality and wide distribution until *c*.550 B.C., when Attic ware gradually displaced it. Through diplomacy, Sparta maintained many ties with the outside world long after her rigid system separated her from the mainstream of Greek political life. The oracle at Delphi, a widely respected opinion source for all *poleis*, was openly pro-Spartan on most occasions. Sparta had numerous contacts with tyrannies in the seventh and sixth centuries B.C., but she later distrusted tyrants and by the end of the sixth century B.C. stood for their expulsion.

The great Messenian revolt began about 640 B.C. as a result of Sparta's overzealous expansion in the northern Peloponnesus. She had suffered a decisive defeat in 669 B.C., and Argos, her rival and sister Dorian *polis*, extended power over the northern coast of the Peloponnesus (all of Greece south of Corinth) at Sparta's expense. The blow to Spartan prestige brought Messenia into rebellion, and the hatred of her Helots almost consumed Sparta. When the last bits of revolution had been quelled, about 620 B.C., Sparta had learned two lessons about her own survival: (1) she was unable to conquer more lands in the Peloponnesus, and other means for dominion were necessary; and (2) she had to drain most of her military effort into the constant repression of a slave population.

After 600 B.C., foreigners (citizens of other *poleis*) were unwelcome in Sparta, and she slowly built a strong alliance system in the Peloponnesus. As leader of the alliance, Sparta promoted a policy that was both antityranny and pro-oligarchy, as her intervention in Athenian politics in 510 B.C. illustrated. After 546 B.C. Sparta had isolated Argos and became virtual mistress of the entire Peloponnesus. The *poleis* south of the Isthmus of Corinth were her dependent allies (except for Argos), and the reorganized Peloponnesian League resulted after Sparta mismanaged affairs in Athens in 510 B.C. By 506 B.C., the league was divided into two parts: the allied states had one vote, the Spartans the other vote. Corinth, Megara, Elis, Tegea, and the other *poleis* of the league had to vote yes with the Spartans or the alliance did not act.

Loyalty to Sparta and the Peloponnesian League was rather remarkable, but Sparta took scrupulous care to respect the internal independence of allied *poleis*—although she made pointed her preference for oligarchic governments throughout the Peloponnesus. Sparta gave some cohesion to a part of the politically fragmented Greeks, and a common feeling for defense emerged. When the Persian wars broke out in 499 B.C. Sparta was the strongest *polis* in Greece, and many states outside the Greek world sought her help. Sparta's short answer ("Too far") to most requests for military aid outside the Peloponnesian cocoon became a standard trademark; the laconic saying (from Laconia, around Sparta) was terse, nipping, and without reply. Spartan policy hinged on three points: opposition to Persian meddling in Greece, retention of her own position as the dominant *polis* in Greece, and open support of conservative governments (with frequent propaganda blasts from the oracle at Delphi), which meant stability as opposed to innovation and chaos, an appearance Athens' burgeoning democracy gave.

By 500 B.C., Athens and Sparta had developed governments that fulfilled the basic demands of each *polis.* The aims of both emerged in the surrounding of revolution or threat of violence, and the solutions offered, though opposite in method, were alike in purpose. Athenian democracy and Spartan oligarchy satisfied enough of the citizen body to insure peace. Athens envisioned a future in which the franchise would be extended, while Sparta looked ahead through the eyes of a limited body of citizens, barely numerous enough to arrest the ambitions and hatred of a subjugated class. Athens developed a constitution somewhat later than Sparta, but hers was the product of a series of reforms reaching back to Solon. Although the democracy suffered setbacks, the form persisted for two hundred and fifty years. Spartan oligarchy became weak and flaccid with foreign involvements, and her system buckled under the pressure of empire after 404 B.C. With her ignominious defeats at the hands of the upstart Thebans in 371 and 362 B.C., Sparta retired to her cocoon to nurse dreams of a glorious past.

Thebes: The Federation, the City, and the Farm

Thirty-five miles due northwest of Athens lay Thebes, dominating the southeast plain of Boeotia. From Mycenaean days, the plain had been home to a population living in various fortified places while making a livelihood in farming. (See chapter 2 for a discussion of the Mycenaeans.) Excavation has revealed that while Mycenaean lords held Thebes, neighboring Orchomenos was supreme over the plain.

Trade was important to the area. Cylinder seals from Mesopotamia, dating from about 1350 B.C., have been found with a mixture of Mycenaean potsherds, Linear B* tablets, imported ivory objects, and military remains similar to the swords and daggers from the great citadel of Mycenae. Archaeological finds have proven that Orchomenos had a special relationship with the Near East; this may explain Greek traditions describing a Phoenician (Cadmus) who founded Thebes five generations before the semilegendary Trojan War.

With the collapse of Mycenaean culture and the arrival of new waves of invaders from the north (the Boeotians), Thebes became the major settlement on the plain, but she was never strong enough to conquer or rule the other *poleis* that rivaled her. The many settlements warred frequently, and the collective power of Boeotia was normally so fragmented that Thebes and her neighbors had to bow to the Persians marching south against the Greek coalition in 480 B.C. Sparta and Athens never forgot the affront, although Theban hatred for Athens had been engendered earlier over a quarrel concerning control of Plataea in 519 B.C. The Plataeans, situated on the borders of both Thebes' and Athens' power, became loyal allies of Athens after many years of fighting with Thebes. It was the decision to bow to Persia that cost Thebes her predominance in Boeotia, however, and a confederacy led by Thebes broke apart. During the wars between Athens and Sparta, Thebes recovered her power at the expense of a number of the *poleis* in Boeotia; the new Boeotian Federation included Thebes, who claimed half the plain and four lesser *poleis*. Thebes and her subject allies elected four of the eleven officials (*boeotarchs*) who ran the Boeotian Federation.

Thebes was unhappy with the peace settlement between Athens and Sparta in 404 B.C., and she joined Argos and Athens in a long, drawn-out war with Sparta and her allies. With Sparta victorious, Thebes again lost power through her military miscalculations, and Sparta detached the other *poleis* of Boeotia from Thebes in 387 B.C., even going as far as installing a garrison in the citadel of Thebes. The Thebans soon drove the Spartans out of Boeotia (378 B.C.) and decisively ended Sparta's dominance of Greece on the battlefield of Leuctra in 371 B.C. Epaminondas, the great Theban general and military tactician, led the jubilant Boeotian Federation until he was

* Linear B is a form of early Greek dated ca. 1500 B.C. that has appeared on tablets found at Mycenae, Pylos, Knossos on Crete, and several other sites.

slain in 362 B.C. in the battle of Mantinea, another Theban victory over the Spartan *hoplites*. Both Leuctra and Mantinea were won through the use of the *peltasts*, lightly armed soldiers who were able to maneuver much more rapidly than their unwieldy enemies. Watching the strategy and tactics of the new Theban army was young Philip of Macedonia, hostage in Thebes while Epaminondas and Pelopidas, his equally gifted second-in-command, were making their bid for hegemony in Greece.

The Boeotian Confederacy was one of the few successful efforts in Greek history to build a federal state. Representative government in such a state, more or less balanced among its members, was more applicable, to the Greek way of thinking, in the oligarchic frame- work than in democracies like Athens. The theory of democracy taught total citizen participation, while the federal system of the Boeotians was founded on a practical need for a semblance of unity within a geographic pocket with no dominant power. Voting rights were based on property ownership, determined in a census of *hoplites*. In the *poleis* of Boeotia, one-fourth of the properly certi- fied citizens served on the *boule* ("council") and the remainder in the *ecclesia* of each settlement. In the federation, Boeotia was chopped up into eleven parts. Each of the eleven areas contributed one *boeotarch*, sixty councilors, some judges, an eleventh of the money in the federal treasury, and one hundred cavalry and one thousand *hoplites* to the joint army.

By Greek standards, Boeotia was lush and green. Thebes stood as the citadel on a plain blessed with fertile fields that fed horses and gave regular grain. The grumpy Hesiod did not trouble to hide his knowledge of the usual Boeotian farm: reliable land that produced good soldiers for the citizen phalanx, soldiers who clearly understood the need for discipline and unity against the corrupt upper classes. Unlike Attica or the Eurotas Valley, the part of Boeotia surrounding Thebes was well forested, even in Roman times. Fresh water bubbled forth from a number of springs, making the *polis* a place not only for refuge but also for enjoyment on dry summer days. Again Hesiod mumbled his begrudging thanks to the Theban traders who made it possible to sip imported wine in the shade. The lot of the Theban was fairly good, and the life of farmers throughout Boeotia was noted for good soil, excellent wine, and solid government. Even with the democratic experiments in the time of Epaminondas, the citizens of Thebes and her subject communities acted as before.

Corinth, the Trading Mistress

An all-weather highway enables the modern traveler to drive to
Corinth from Athens in an hour. The road skims through tortured,
rocky countryside, along the clear, blue Saronic Gulf on the south.
The roar of Volkswagens and Mercedes trucks has replaced the
clatter of donkeys and shuffling of sandaled feet along the formerly
twisting, angular roadway that once served travelers from Athens to
Corinth. Fourteen miles northwest of Athens lies Eleusis, famous for
its mysteries and shrines. From Eleusis, the footsore pilgrim views
the magnificent panorama of the island of Salamis, which seems to
float in the sea. Twenty-six miles from Athens on the road to Corinth
is Megara, famed in classic times for her woolens and as the mother
city of Byzantium. A characteristic white mussel-stone was used in
her public buildings, both on the twin citadels of the *polis* and in
the thriving mart below. Bits of the ancient harbor of Nisaea are
still visible, reminding the observer of the ancient rivalry between
Corinth and Megara. Upon Megara's request, the Athenians built
long walls to connect Megara with her harbor (in 461 B.C.), but
Megara later suffered from Pericles' decree barring her from Athenian
ports (432 B.C.), an act that helped precipitate the Peloponnesian
War.

After crossing the Corinth Canal, a project envisioned in both
Greek and Roman times but not completed until 1893, the road
descends into the modern town of Corinth, fifty miles from Athens.
The site of the ancient city, Old Corinth, supports a population of
about fifteen hundred people and lies four miles southwest of the
modern settlement. Modern excavation has laid bare many of the
ruins of Roman Corinth, over which the impregnable Acrocorinth
broods, towering 1885 feet above the ancient city. The Roman ruins
lie close to the modern village, which has a cooling square sheltered
by venerable plane-trees. Some of the finest reproductions of classical Greek pottery are to be found in the shops on the edge of the
square.

Early myths spoke of Corinth as the home of Medea, Sisyphus, and
Bellerophon, but the homeric tales probably mean Ephyra, closer to
the coast. From the beginnings, Corinth had a different quality from
the other *poleis*. Here traders and craftsmen were held in greater
esteem than soldiers. The rest of the Greeks told the story of
Sisyphus, doomed in Hades to roll a stone up to the top of a moun-

tain, and then to watch hopelessly as it rolled down the other side. In Corinth, however, Sisyphus was accounted a wise leader in preclassical times, godlike in his craft and inventiveness. He was the grandfather of Bellerophon, whom Athena favored. The goddess gave Bellerophon instructions in how to tame the winged horse Pegasus; and Corinthians were proud of inventing the bridle and bit. The temple dedicated to Athena of the Bridle was famous in classical times and possessed a wooden statue of Athena with hands and face of marble.

Mycenaean settlements vanished with the invasions of the thirteenth century B.C., but Dorians refounded the site at Corinth sometime after 850 B.C. The family known as the Bacchiadae ruled in Corinth until about 650 B.C., when Cypselus the tyrant ousted it. Under the Bacchiadae, Corinth became a trading center. Because the population of the *polis* was growing, colonies, Corcyra and Syracuse in particular, were founded (both *c*. 730 B.C.). Traditions recorded Corinth's increasing influence in shipbuilding and trade. Ameinocles of Corinth became known because he built ships for Samos in 704 B.C., and Corinth fought the first recorded sea battle against her colony Corcyra in 664 B.C.

Scattered finds throughout the Mediterranean of Corinthian pottery from this period indicate the dominance of her trade routes and markets. The manufactured articles themselves show that Corinth exported luxury items: the numerous *aryballoi* held perfumed oil, while the Corinthian *alabastra* contained expensive perfumes for noble ladies and courtesans. Highly decorated, double-handled *skyphoi* ("drinking cups") were also a major export; Corinthian potters distributed their ware in Syria, Sicily, southern and central Italy, and eastern Spain. Drinking was a well-known pastime in Corinth, and Corinthian drinking vessels advertised their owners as aristocratic connoisseurs of fine wine.

Meanwhile, Corinth established her rule over the isthmus, began building an impressive harbor at Lechaeum, and provided a market for the exchange of goods, getting wealthy from the collection of tolls. Her fleet cleared neighboring seas of pirates, a lesson Athens later recalled.

Cypselus devoted his rule to developing trade and diplomatic contacts further. Delphi, the oracular shrine to Apollo, looked with great favor on Corinth, and Gyges, King of Lydia in Asia Minor, was on particularly close terms with Cypselus. In the Corinthian Treasury at Delphi, visitors saw the six magnificent golden bowls Gyges sent; King Croesus added six silver vessels and a lion of gold. Since the Lydians were not Greeks, they could not have their own treasury at Delphi, and so they dedicated their offerings to Apollo in the name of their closest Greek friends, the tyrants of Corinth. The wealth of Cypselus was more prominently displayed at the Temple of Zeus at Olympia. Here the tyrant contributed a golden statue of the god.

Cypselus was succeeded by his son, Periander (traditional dates, 629–585 B.C.), later known as one of the Seven Sages of Greece. Under his rule, Corinth reached her height of prosperity, especially reflected in export of bronzes and beautiful pottery to Egypt and the northern ports of the Black Sea. As a friend of Thrasyboulos, tyrant of Miletus, Periander fought wars in his behalf. The Corinthian ruler believed in war as an instrument of diplomacy, and he resubdued the rebellious island of Corcyra while serving as arbitrator for a series of disputes among other *poleis.* Periander was given credit for making *polis* games part of a continuing tradition for Greek states. Some two hundred years earlier, the Olympic games had been set in motion, and the tyrant next door, Cleisthenes of Sicyon, had instituted the Pythian Games at Delphi. So Periander founded the Isthmian Games, held every two years in honor of Poseidon. The best athletes from all of the Hellenic world would gather, as well as assorted curio sellers, prostitutes, charlatans, spell casters, professional gamblers, and the gawking citizens of Corinth and her neighbors. All enriched the coffers of Periander, who sponsored the games under the guise of honoring Poseidon. The age of the professional, hired athlete was not far off. In the period after Alexander the Great (d. 323 B.C.), the games continued, with each *polis* buying gymnastic experts much as it paid mercenary soldiers.

As in Athens, the promotion of civic patriotism took the form of a religious festival. Periander invited Arion of Lesbos to come to Corinth and write choral odes for the annual celebration honoring Dionysus, god of wine, rebirth, and the green of spring. Orgiastic revels in the country were dignified through Arion's dithyrambs, choral pieces that became the predecessors of the Athenian chorus in tragedy and comedy.

A long list of Corinthian inventions and innovations were also credited to Periander's reputed wisdom. His architects erected a massive Temple to Apollo with monolithic columns twenty-three feet high and five feet wide at the base. The stone used, rough-cut porous limestone covered over with a red-yellow stucco, was local. His architects also designed the first pediments for temples. These pediments were triangular spaces created by the sloping roofs and the friezes, and the spaces provided frames for sculpture in the round. Later artists would perform remarkable works in this limited space, well illustrated in the Parthenon marbles, now in the British Museum. Corinthian architects became famous throughout Greece for their skill—all to the credit of the beneficent tyrant—and when fire destroyed the Temple to Apollo at Delphi in 548 B.C., the rebuilding commission was handed to Spintharus of Corinth.

The tyrants established a stable coinage in silver, proving a vibrant prosperity. Corinth used coins from Argos (thirty miles to the southwest, down the road from Corinth, past Mycenae) in the first half of the seventh century B.C. The tyrant Pheidon of Argos had brought the concept of coinage from Asia Minor and had the small bits of metal stamped with signs that told the world of his power and the prestige of Argos. Cypselus used the older coins for a time, but he later issued his own in a new style. Under Periander the Corinthian coins bore the image of the winged horse Pegasus, a favorite emblem for the *polis,* on the "heads" and an indented swastika on the "tails." Like the Athenian coins that were called "owls," the coins of Corinth were known as "colts" from the image of the winged horse, proclaiming the legend and traditions of the *polis* of Bellerophon. The trade routes Corinth governed can be traced by the colts that appear in great numbers in southern Italy and Sicily. The *polis* lived on imported wheat, and the trade lines to the west became increasingly important, just as Athens' sea-lanes to and from the Black Sea became necessary for her survival.

The tyranny was thrown out about 582 B.C. when Psammethicus, the nephew and successor of Periander, was assassinated. In his later years, Periander had developed the tyrant's usual vices, murdering his wife and banishing his son. In spite of the fact that he consolidated the Corinthian commercial empire, laid a road (the *diolkos*) across the isthmus for dragging ships, and founded two new colonies, Periander became feared and loathed. The new government officially damned the memory of the tyranny, causing the corpse of the assassinated Psammethicus and all the bones of his ancestors of the Cypselid house to be cast beyond the borders of the *polis*. Even the formerly friendly oracle at Delphi issued a reminder of a prophecy that forecast disaster for any sons of Cypselus.

The new constitution in Corinth was that of an oligarchy. At the top was a limited board of magistrates, assisted by a council (probably a *gerousia*). An obscure assembly (the *halia*) had a right of deliberation. Eight districts of the *polis* were represented on the board and in the council. The eight districts probably rotated the election of members to the board, so that the remaining seven elected members to the council.

Oligarchy favored the landed interests of Corinth. Under the tyrants, settlement in and around the towns had been officially discouraged, and the tyrants had not extended the franchise to the *metics* "resident foreigners," most of whom were involved in the lucrative crafts. As in Sparta, the *perioikoi* were allowed a quasi citizenship, but the old Dorian elites retained their rule, with real power measured in terms of land. The oligarchy controlled the wealth, which derived from markets, shipping, and far-flung trade, and wealthy citizens built ships, even selling them to Athens for the nominal sum of five drachmas (since Corinthian law prohibited giving ships away). Corinthian citizens manned the *triremes*, fought in the phalanx, and supervised the trading vessels, but the majority of the wealthy derived their income from land, in the Doric tradition. Corinth chose to retain the Dorian exclusiveness and preferred the order of an oligarchy.

Her bustling market drew merchants from the marts of the East, who sometimes settled in the *polis* to ply their trade or sell transshipped goods. Other traders came from Greek Sicily and southern Italy, bringing grain and timber, iron and tin from Elba and Cornwall, fish from the Adriatic, and sometimes gold and silver sneaked through the Carthaginian fleets that guarded the alleged Punic control over western trade. With her port and *diolkos,* Corinth cut the distance from Tarentum in Italy to Piraeus, Athens' port, by two hundred miles, which allowed the skittish Greek shippers to avoid the treacherous seas south of the Peloponnesus.

The Corinthian market was the largest in Greece and received public buildings during the tyranny. A courtyard and stairway leading down into the clear spring below, the Lower Peirene, added to the pleasant mood, and a basin collected the spring water flowing from two lions' heads made of bronze. The spring was open to all travelers, and the lower spring was famous for juicy gossip and pastimes pleasing to all tastes. Another spring, the Upper Peirene, flowed on the Acrocorinth; the long path leading to the top of the fortress was festooned with colorful hawkers of perfumes, aphrodisiacs, and other products of use to the pilgrim toiling his way up to the most famous shrine in Corinth, the Temple to Aphrodite. The mountain was sacred to the goddess of love, and after the traveler had paid his respect, he descended the path—which had taken him two hours to climb—back to Corinth, where he further enjoyed the worship of the goddess with the prostitutes who served Aphrodite as priestesses. The House of Aphrodite, one of the few such establishments in the Greek world, gained huge amounts of money for both the *polis* and the cult. Although the path up the Acrocorinth became lined with rich shrines to other female deities (we hear of dedications to Demeter and Persephone, Isis, and Hera), the temple atop the citadel remained to Aphrodite. Now only a few insignificant marble blocks greet the visitor, recalling the time when Corinthian prostitutes, known throughout the world for their variations, taught their skills. When the Apostle Paul arrived to preach in Corinth, his thunderings against the pleasure-loving and bloated population bit hard into the major source of local income.

Corinth served as headquarters for the Greeks in the Persian wars, and her citizens participated in the battles, although not prominently. More important, however, were the gradual Athenian dominion over trade routes, first in the east and north (which did not threaten Corinth's lifelines to the west), and Athens' attempts to bottle up Corinth. Corinth could not prevent the Athenians from annexing Megara in 457 B.C.; she finally pushed Sparta into war with Athens through Athens' miscalculation of the quarrel between Corinth and her rebellious colony Corcyra. (However, Pericles may have engineered Corinth's fury through the presence of Athenian *triremes* at Corcyra, *triremes* that did not offer battle but simply blocked Corinthian reinforcements.) Corinth's economic fortunes continued to fall, as they had before the war. Athenian pottery, in the form of beautiful Red-Figure ware, ousted Corinthian pots from both Western and Eastern markets. Colorful packaging sold Athenian oil and wine rather widely, and, like the earlier Black-Figure ware that had provided real competition for Corinthian pottery, the various pots became sought for their beauty as art objects. Rich Etruscans bought huge quantities of them for tomb decoration.

The great Athenian armada, launched in 415 B.C. against Syracuse, would have destroyed Corinth had it succeeded in taking Sicily from Corinthian markets. Naturally, Corinthian troops were dispatched and her ships outfitted, all in the name of her alliance with Doric

Sparta and the Dorian Syracusans. The Athenians met disaster
at Syracuse in 413 B.C. and Corinth's links with the West were restored, but her prosperity continued to decline even after the end of
the war (404 B.C.). She increasingly relied on her resident industries—
bronze foundries, the prostitutes of Aphrodite, perfume mixers, and
sculpture and painting shops. In the age after the death of Alexander
(known as Hellenistic), art became part of the trappings of Greek
culture, transplanted and advertised all the way from the Indus
Valley to Spain, and Corinthian artists were sought and coveted.
Corinth became a pawn in the complicated political struggles between Macedon and the rising Aetolian and Achaean Leagues, and
her prosperity continued through exports of terra-cotta roofing
tiles, building bricks, wooden doors, woolen rugs, armor, and shields,
which she traded for wheat and wood to build ships. Corinthian shipwrights designed and built the larger flagships of the Hellenistic monarchs, ranging from moderately heavy "fifteens" to the totally
cumbersome "forties," used only as barges or for massive displays of
wealth. (See chapter 4.)

When the Romans destroyed Corinth in 146 B.C., they ended *polis*
independence with an impressive orgy of destruction. In razing the
city, they destroyed one of the finest theaters in Greece, which
seated twenty thousand people in public meetings as well as plays.
Even though resettlement came a century later, the Italian colonists
little appreciated their surroundings of faded glory. They did, however, recognize the artistic quality of the tumbled remains of private
houses, public buildings, and accompanying statuary, and transported shipload after shipload of "Greek" art back into the maw of
the imperial aristocracy of Italy. Corinth became an important administrative center under the Romans, sitting on the major east-west
trade route as before, but her memory of independent fame slowly
grew hazy and had generally disappeared by the time Pausanias (*fl.
c*. A.D. 150) compiled his *Description of Greece*.

2

The Plow and the Mind

The setting for life on the Greek farm is and was unlike the rich agriculture of neighboring Italy, or the stories of fourfold and more returns from the Nile Valley far across the Mediterranean. The Greek peninsula is an extension of several mountain ridges that rise from the windswept plains of central Europe. The lofty, jagged mountains chop the few plains of Greece into tightly segmented and isolated pockets of level land. The spurs of the mountain chains march down into southern Greece, separating the Peloponnesus into three parts. Other mountains advance to the south and east, disappearing under the Aegean Sea for a distance to re-emerge as islands set like jewels in the diadem of the sharp blue waters.

Men in Greece and on the islands wrung every bit of produce they could from the limited farmlands. Historians are not sure how men learned to farm in terraces on the barren and stony hillsides of Thessaly and Arcadia. Greeks raised olives and grapes from earliest times, and no Greek would be without olive oil or wine. They were the staples of life, visible signs of the hard-won understanding of the harsh peninsula—an understanding that molded human existence into habits that survive even into modern times. The plow formed the mind of Greece, and a definite tension surfaces continually in Greek culture—the tension between the struggle to overcome the poverty of natural resources and bitter awareness of the restricted solutions to man's perpetual desires for security and health. In the

civilization that the Greeks created, the struggle did not turn inward
to consume, but burst outward in shrewd and childlike attempts to
admit the reality of cramped lands and meager productivity, coupled
with questions about the inner man and the outer cosmos. Greek
culture endeavored to put man into a ranging totality of known
factors—on the farm or in the most Greek of institutions, the *polis*.

The Mycenaeans and the Dorians

Little is known about Greek history and culture before the emergence
of the *polis*. Greek bards later recited and sang tales of clever pirates
and traders who had brought gold into Greece and then buried it
with their ruling elite. These people lived in stone fortresses, constructed of mammoth rocks that only the Cyclops (the mythical,
one-eyed sons of Earth and Sky, known as excellent craftsmen)
could have lifted into place. Modern archaeologists and scholars have
named these people the Mycenaeans after one of their largest
fortress-citadels, located at Mycenae and brooding over the small
plain of the Argolid. The Mycenaeans arrived in Greece sometime
around 2000 B.C. and settled in the Peloponnesus, subduing native
peoples who had tilled the soil for centuries before. Subsisting on
taxes taken in kind from the farmers, the warlike Mycenaeans extended their rule over most of Greece and the Aegean Islands. The
Mycenaeans possibly set up a loose federation, governed from
Mycenae, and they established fortresses at Athens, in Thessaly, and
Boeotia, as well as Tiryns and Pylos within the Peloponnesus. Crete
later came under Mycenaean dominion, and the new rulers took
what they had formerly imported. The clay tablets on which the
Mycenaeans kept their records gave lists of material wealth, in Linear
B. The lists give names of animals and slaves as well as probable
sacrifices to gods demanding blood renewal for planting and the
harvest.

About 1200 B.C. disaster struck the Mycenaeans when a new
warrior folk invaded Greece from the north and proceeded to loot
the citadels. Soon the invaders, the Dorians, replaced the Mycenaeans
as rulers in the Peloponnesus. The Dorians also spoke Greek. But in
contrast to their Mycenaean predecessors, the new warrior stock became integrated with the native populations; the period between
the end of Mycenaean power (*c*. 1200 B.C.) and the formation of the

fully developed *polis* (*c.* 750–700 B.C.) contained the origins of Greek civilization.

Homer and the Farm Ideal

The pottery of the period (*c.* 1000–750 B.C.) reveals cultural development and the combination of intellectual frenzy with poignant restraint, as do parts of the *Iliad,* a long poem composed, according to tradition, by Homer sometime around 850 B.C. Many of the folk memories of Mycenaean warlords seeking glory in arms appear in the poem, though it is set in another time. The values are those of farmer-warriors of aristocratic mien who do battle in the name of a society seen only in the faintest outlines. The farmer is seen quite clearly, however, in the portrait of Odysseus (Ulysses in the Latin translation), the major figure in the *Odyssey*, the sequel to the *Iliad.*

Although the princely activities of Achilles and Hector dominate Homer's tale of the war before the ramparts of Troy, it is Odysseus and his down-to-earth calculation that eventually win the war for the Greeks; however, the reader is not told this: the audience of knowledgeable and attentive aristocratic Greeks was supposed to know what happened between the end of the *Iliad* and the beginning of the *Odyssey.* As the character of Odysseus shows, the hard-headed aristocratic farmer can plow a straight furrow, and, according to Homer, he knows his tenants and slaves just as he understands the men under his command in war.

His meals are simple, as befits a hardy man of war. He dallies when a proper feast is set before guest-friends; there is time to sing of deeds and glory, war and life. Yet under the heroic veneer, the glittering exterior of the hero who hurls his life in a continual taunting of death, is a man with the simple thoughts of productive lands. The homeric heroes long to return to a home where ruling takes place alongside farming and judging the disputes of the daily swarms of common people who come to the feasting halls of the local lords. Bubbling noise and constant chatter mark Odysseus' household, and Homer's supple lines show the common folk enjoy an easy freedom with Queen Penelope. Rustic familiarity pervades. Dinnertime is utter confusion as all present—foreigners, relatives on both sides of the marriage, farmers, and their occasional slaves—are invited to share in the king's larder.

The Greek Farmer: Hesiod

Homer remained the font for the Greek ideal of warriors and aristocratic farmers, but Hesiod's acerbic *Works and Days,* written about
700 B.C., provides a better portrayal of the reality of Greek farm
life. The developed *polis* lurks in the background, and the poet's
most bitter lines are aimed at the bribe-accepting kings who cheated
him of his rightful inheritance of land. Hesiod despises the kings of
the nearby *polis* Thespiae (in Boeotia, near Thebes), in marked contrast to Homer's respect for the kings leading the Greek forces
against Troy. Another difference between the heroic ideal in Homer
and the crusty verse in Hesiod's poem is the relation of gods to men.
In the *Iliad* and *Odyssey,* the gods move with grace and have some
direct influence on the affairs of the battle-harrowed heroes, but
Hesiod's gods control the seasons and give his time the crude cast of
iron.

Greek farmers had a detailed and instinctive knowledge of soils and
the way crops could best be cultivated. Soils were mixed, the best
combinations being red with white soils, and heavy with light. Soil
exhaustion had been clearly defined by the time of Theophrastus
(370–c. 288 B.C.), who writes that farmers had practiced crop rota-
tion from ancient times. "Fat" soil took more seed than "thin" soil,
and less sowing was required for rich earth than poor. Homeric
farmers knew that deep plowing was necessary, and the Thessalians
had invented a spade (*mischos*), which they used to turn over the
thin topsoil to get at the richer subsoil beneath. Fertilizers were
commonly used, and Homer provides the first reference to heaps of
manure collected for distribution in the fields. Later the sophisticated
polis gathered and sold its sewage to farmers in need of fertilizers for
soil renewal.

Careful plowing was most important for successful farming. Farmers
continually worked and cut up the fields left fallow to eliminate
weeds. Greek farmers knew that constantly working the soil made it
lighter and that somehow such soil held more water. They plowed
their fallow land at least four times a year, and sometimes more,
with lighter soils exemplified in northwestern Peloponnesus. As with
the Biblical fourth plowing, the soil was chopped up with a hoe or a
weighted mallet. The first plowing of a field to be sown came when
the "Pleiades, Atlas' daughters, are setting," and the harvest was best
when the same stars were rising. Winter wheat was sown, as Hesiod

writes, "In the fall when the annual crane's call from the cloud signs the winter's coming rains." The harvest came "with the white petals of spring" (*Works and Days,* 248). Planting came just before the full onset of the winter rains, and the farmers distributed seeds on the ready fields on both wet and dry days. A sickle harvested the wheat. If the stalks were long and tall, they were cut halfway, but if they were short, they were cut close to the soil. Horses, mules, and spare oxen threshed the gathered grain and stalks on a circular cobbled area. Homer's description (*Odyssey,* XI, 128) shows that Greeks tossed and winnowed with a small cradle, made like an oar (*liknon*). The winnowed grain and chaff were piled in a large basket and tossed into the wind to blow away the chaff.

Hesiod's *Works and Days* combines practical agricultural advice with instructions of immediate value on the farm. In his choice of a wife, the farmer should seek a woman who is about nineteen, who will not spend too much time in front of a mirror, and who will be loyal to him in the incessant gossip sessions with other women. The poem gives information on what wood to use for making plows, what crops to raise and how to rotate fields from crop to crop and from season to season, and how to spend the small leisure time available (with good wine from Phoenician Byblos enjoyed in some leafy glen during the heat of summer). The mood of the poem is harsh. Farmers were neither to trust strangers nor to do favors for those who have wronged or insulted them. With luck, a farmer had neighbors who would not steal his ox or entice his slaves away in times of bad harvest. Looming over everything is the poet's sensation of change. He looks back to a time of free farmers, unshackled by debt to either larger landholders or wealthy city dwellers. Bribe-accepting kings were part of the coming age when the *polis* became the dominant form of government and rural values chashed with far-flung trading ventures and increasing wars among the *poleis.*

The *Polis* and the Farmer

A few areas of Greece were able to keep their time-honored farm customs intact as the new age burst around them. The plains of Thessaly, north of the main centers of Greece, continued to produce lush grain and became famous for a special breed of horses. Laconia, dominated by Sparta, raised wheat and barley, but by 650 B.C. the population had grown so large that Sparta launched a conquest of her western neighbors in Messenia to supply more land for her aristocracy. This decision permanently altered Spartan life and forced a deep cleavage between Spartan ideals and those pursued by other Greek *poleis.* To the north, the *polis* of Corinth, located on the narrow band of land connecting the Peloponnesus with the rest of Greece, solved the problem of her expanding population by colonizing distant shores; this solution was used by other *poleis* as well, such as those that dotted the western shore of Asia Minor and the large islands off the eastern coast of Greece. The resulting trade—manufactured items from the *polis* for grain from the colonies, who were fully independent from the mother *polis*—benefitted both sides and provided an even greater impetus to find new markets. Greek ships sailed as far west as Cornwall in England, and to Egypt and the coasts of Syria and Palestine.

In Attica, however, a third solution was devised to solve growing discontent from farmers, who felt ever more pressed by shrinking acreage and the growing political and economic power exercised by an increasingly closed aristocratic elite. Solon, a great statesman who became a compromise leader of Athens in 594 B.C., is credited with reforms that eventually led Athens to be a commercial empire in the fifth century B.C. The open recognition that Attica could not raise enough food to feed her increasing population averted the brewing civil war between poor farmers and their equally poor countrymen living in the expanding urban center around Athens. Although land redistribution was not one of his carefully tendered reforms, Solon did abolish debts. He told farmers to cultivate olives and grapes, excellent crops for export as olive oil and wine, and he forbade citizens of Attica to export wheat or other cereal crops. Commerce soon became the lifeblood of Attica, and Athenian oil and wine, packaged in glowing large pots decorated by master artists (the famous *amphorae*), drew large imports of wheat from Egypt and the southern shores of the Black Sea.

Life on the Attic farm changed little, even though Solon's reforms remained in effect for several centuries. The farmer was still considered poor, and he remained suspicious of the manners displayed by slick city-bred folk. The farmer's voice in the Athenian assembly was muted since he often could not make it to the meetings when important votes were taken. He still had to walk to town. His voice was stronger in the smaller meetings of the *demes,* the local subdivisions of Attica. Here his rustic speech and crude allusions to goats and plowing were appreciated as all grumbled about Athenian arrogance. He had to get up at dawn each day to till his small holdings, aided by a slave or two and a necessary ox; the routine of plowing, plowing again, seeding, weeding, and harvesting changed little through the decades of Athens' vaunted democratic imperialism. To be sure, he owned his own land, but the Attic farmer was subject to the normal whims of weather and seasonal variation. Planting too soon or too late gave the same poor results as they had with Hesiod, and if a small farmer was unable to find hands to help in the harvest, then much of the wheat would be ruined.

His diet was still frugal, even in the days when Athenian aristocrats dined on imported luxuries. Farmers relished good wine, much as Hesiod coveted imported wine from Phoenicia, but simplicity was the general rule. They brought out goat cheese, skimmed from the top of a brimming bucket of milk, for the arrival of friends. Bread, baked either on the farm or bought cheaply nearby, was broken (or more correctly, snapped) at mealtimes. With a small portion of heavily watered wine, tasting bitter to the delight of the Greek palate, the cheese and bread made a complete meal. On feast days, there might be a little meat, though Greek farmers did not crave meat and more usually chose fish when they could get it. Bread provided a reliable staple in their diet, as it was untainted by preservatives and contained all the essential nutrients of natural ground flour. The "loaves" of bread were made into flat plates, scored into fourths so they could be broken easily after they hardened. After a couple of days, the bread became brittle and virtually unspoilable. An Attic farmer always talked of eating a meal as he "quartered"— that is, cracked the chunks off the loaf.

The Attic farmer lived well, if seasons were kind and war did not disrupt his year, which happened all too often during the great war between Athens and Sparta (431–404 B.C.). His life was not tied to money, although he needed a little from time to time to buy replacements for the broken iron tips on his plows and to buy luxury items that the women in his household desired. A variety of foodstuffs was available, ranging from barley bread, and the less common loaf of wheat, to the cheeses made from the milk of sheep or goats, the vegetables and fish brought into local markets from Boeotia to the north (eels were a Theban specialty), and salted or pickled pork. On special occasions, donkey flesh was parceled out, and goat meat was known as being fit for the nobility. However, sheep were valued for their wool and were rarely sacrificed or used for food. Beekeeping was a trademark of Attica, and for its sweetness the Greeks considered the honey from Attic hives most excellent, compared with the bitter honey from Pontus on the north shore of the Black Sea. Geese and chickens were commonly found on the farms, and the Greeks considered goose eggs something of a delicacy. Ducks, however, were rare, while Greeks fancied pigeons and recommended pheasants for marriage feasts.

If he chose, the farmer could eat an assortment of vegetables. The list Theophrastus gives is extensive, including lettuce, cabbage, the ever present onions and radishes, beans, beets, celery, cucumbers, asparagus, leeks, and lentils. Fruits added variety to the plain diet. Theophrastus notes dates, figs, pears, plums, apples, almonds, and quinces, and the herb list included garlic, mint, savory, rue, sage, and parsley. For reasons embedded in the psychology of the farm, most farmers passed up this miscellany and preferred the dull (or so thought the city snobs in the works of Aristophanes and Theophrastus) diet of cheese, watered wine, barley bread, and fish. Pickled pork was put aside for times when everything else was gone.

Rural Stereotypes

Attic comedy sometimes provides an idea of Athenian stereotypes about farmers. Aristophanes wrote *Acharnians* in 425 B.C. as part of his own personal opposition to the war against Sparta. During the war the lot of farmers had worsened, particularly after the great plague carried away many people, who had been jammed into Athens in 430 and 429 B.C. Athenian strategy was sound: have everybody take refuge behind the walls while the Spartans ravaged the countryside. Athens' navy kept the sea open for foreign grain supply, but the farmers' fields were burned for several successive seasons. Many of the farmers, forced to remain in Athens for an extended period, longed to return to the simple pleasures of rural life. Their lives in the city were made less than calm by the continual jokes at their expense. A rustic stood out from sophisticated city folk by his typical warm cap, and his speech and mannerisms quickly identified him as uncouth and ignorant. Often the rural peasant was asked if he was "bringing a weed into town," an allusion to contamination from the countryside. A certain odor wafted before the unfortunate man as he made his way in the bustle of traders in the *agora,* and the city slickers could spot the farmers in their midst as "pigs and goats speckled on front." The buffoonery in *Acharnians* is gentle, but an underlying bitterness, similar to that in modern ethnic humor, becomes apparent.

Horses

Traditionally, the best Greek farms boasted of their fine horses, but most farmers did not have horses. Only the very rich could afford them, and the wealthy aristocrats raised them more for prestige than for warfare or help in plowing. In the ages before the horse collar had been invented, the yoke of oxen was much more practical for pulling a plow. Hitching a narrow-shouldered horse to a heavy plow would merely choke the animal. Thus horses had limited uses in ancient Greece; the horses pulling chariots in the homeric poems had little military value, since the heroes dismounted from their chariots and fought on foot. The terrain of Greece also made it rather awkward to use the horse in battle formations, because frequent rocks hurt their hoofs (horseshoes had not yet been invented). When the Greeks did raise horses, they were no larger than modern ponies, according to the famous Parthenon frieze. They were marks of wealth, prestige, and political influence. In Thessaly, to the north of Greece, horses were well pastured, and smaller herds could be well fed in Spartan Laconia and Messenia. The tradition of aristocratic values connected with the horse reaches back into homeric times, and Greek nobility stabled horses whenever possible. The *Odyssey* records a stud farm in Elis (in northwestern Peloponnesus) maintained by an aristocratic family related to the ruling clan of Ithaca, home of Odysseus. Horses later became the trademark of the class of large landholders, a fact often mirrored in the names of the wealthy families—names like the Hippeis of Attica and the Hippobotae of Euboea (the large island just off the eastern coast of central Greece)—suggesting economic and social distinction. In the fourth century B.C. Aristotle noted that the mounted nobility of Thessaly was the governing class because it could keep the common rabble in subjection (*Politics,* 1289B). But even with the lengthy history of aristocratic horse breeding, the cavalry played little part in the incessant warfare of the *poleis* until the fourth century B.C. Battle was conducted by heavily armed citizen-soldiers of the *poleis,* fighting on foot in the organized block of men, the phalanx. Citizen-farmers filled the ranks of the phalanxes, while the aristocrats swirled around the flanks on horseback. The nobility treated their horses with such painstaking care that they were useless except on an even, rockless plain. (Chapters 4 and 5 provide more detail on cavalry.)

Although classical Greek sources loudly proclaim the glory of the *polis,* with its attendant architectural, artistic, and literary achievements, most citizens in all *poleis* were farmers. The simple and geographically limited life-styles clearly etched in poetry starting with Homer reflected their values. The *polis,* the most Greek of institutions, was first a settlement of farmers who had a center for defense, which often became an urban hub. Athens was the city for one of the largest *poleis,* Attica, which covered roughly one thousand square miles. Most of Attica was farmland, but (as is typical in all periods of history) the population of Athens produced writings about themselves while the farmers remained generally mute.

3

Who Bought What, and Why

Popular accounts of classical Greek life generally emphasize the opulence of city dwellers or the spare and stripped style of living within the Spartan ideal. While the majority of the *poleis* were economically self-sufficient, their farms were not exceedingly wealthy or prosperous, and the rural population had little interest in luxury goods. Athens, however, chose a different course than was typical for a Greek *polis*, and after the beginnings of the fifth century B.C., she existed on the base of commerce and trade. A stable coinage, an excellent fleet (in the fifth century B.C.) to protect commercial routes that brought timber and grain, and an expanding political influence made Athenian commercial life very different from most other Greek states, with the marked exception of Corinth and, earlier, Aegina. Greek emporia (trading centers) had flourished even earlier, but generally among the Aegean Islands or Greek settlements in Asia Minor. Commercial centers that grew rich before Athens' heyday included Miletus and Smyrna (both in Asia Minor) and Samos and Chalcis among the islands (the latter on eastern Euboea).

Farms in Attica did not produce enough to feed the growing population of the *polis*, so foreign wheat became increasingly necessary for survival. Attic olives provided some exchange, as did Athenian pottery and wine, but it was the fabulously rich veins of silver from the state mines at Laurion that gave Athenians ready exchange. Importation of grain left many who lived in the urban center of Athens and her port, Piraeus, free to engage in other activities than farming. The men manning the fleets and supervising the growing commerce of Athens provided the means for Athenian imperial democracy in the fifth century B.C.

Yet only a small fraction of Greeks had ever traveled beyond the boundaries of their home *polis* before the outbreak of the war between Athens and Sparta (431–404 B.C.) that eventually embroiled the entire Greek world from the Aegean Sea to the island Sicily. The war destroyed the *polis* as an important political force, although it took the conquests of Philip II and his son Alexander of Macedonia to convince the Greeks of that fact. Even though the *polis* lost its political power after the Macedonian triumph, it remained the conventional social structure of Greek life throughout the Hellenistic Age—usually given as 323 B.C. (the death of Alexander) to 30 B.C. (the death of Cleopatra VII, the last Ptolemaic queen of Greek Egypt)—and had an important place in social and urban values in the eastern half of the Roman Empire.

Before the end of the fifth century B.C., economic life was uncomplicated except for the minuscule percentage of people in the top rungs of wealth or political power. After the whirlwind career of Alexander the Great (whose military career spanned the years 336–323 B.C.), both economic activity and political surroundings changed very rapidly. Increasing commercial specialization became normal as new sources of luxuries were sought from greater distances. In the fourth and third centuries B.C. great fleets of ships plied sea-lanes to India, Ceylon, and points beyond to procure spices, silks, precious stones, and items of artistic merit. Only the very rich could afford such things when they reached the trading centers of the Hellenistic world, like Alexandria in Egypt, the island of Delos in the Aegean, and Greek cities in the west like Syracuse in Sicily. The vast majority of the people were still farmers, having little to do with the comings and goings of commercial flotillas. Except for the small daily purchases of farmers and common folk in the local *agora,* the economic history of classical Greece, and its Hellenistic counterpart, usually centers on the rulers and the wealthy. Sometimes the wealth of a *polis* might be more evenly distributed than expected, but the gaudy country homes, with statuary and attendant slaves, were the trappings of the ruling classes.

Homer, Pirates, and Phoenicians

The emergence of Greek civilization from the mysterious Dark Ages (*c*. 1000–850 B.C.) is depicted in two poems written by Homer. In the *Iliad* and the *Odyssey* are allusions to a society somewhere between the unsettled stages of early wanderings and the beginnings of *polis* life. The homeric heroes thrived on raiding, and there is little doubt that the most doughty practiced a kind of piracy that brought honor with success and dishonor with an empty hold. The Greeks had little to give in a trading venture, and they took what they wanted when they could get away with it. They were quite successful as pirates, but they had little interest in exchange. The ubiquitous Phoenicians filled that role well, hailing from the ports of Sidon, Tyre, and Byblos, which in turn were fed by caravan routes coming to the eastern Mediterranean from the limitless reaches of Asia.

In Homer's *Odyssey,* the manly Menelaus wandered for eight years, ranging from Phoenicia to Cyprus and Egypt and as far west as Libya, "gathering together much property" (*Odyssey*, IV, 90–91). He also boasts that he was the most successful pirate ever to live, although others might have approached his level of stolen wealth. Odysseus likewise proudly lists how he came to possess the booty from his lengthy wanderings. Coming to Egypt, he stayed put for seven years, also "gathering together much property" (*Odyssey,* XIV, 285–286) until a slippery Phoenician trader tricked him, planning to sell the hero in some port in the west. With the help of Zeus, Odysseus proves even more crafty than the lowly Phoenician, and he foils the plan. Noble pursuits included piracy, and Homer's characters looked down on genuine traders. Merchants were not at all respectable and were constantly accused of "being greedy and grasping for gain" (*Odyssey,* VIII, 164), which was somehow less honorable than piratical raiding. The merchant was considered dull and unimaginative, coming and going away in a ship containing benches that seated sailors who were mere traders. They thought only of the cargo or the profit they were carrying home.

The seedy reputation of the trader lasted throughout ancient times. It may have had its origins in the rapacity of the Phoenician merchants who dominated commerce in the eastern Mediterranean and the Aegean Sea in early Greek history. The Phoenicians were hated for their dishonesty, and they were all too well known for their slave trade. They usually employed kidnapping to procure good quality slaves for the lavish courts of Near Eastern monarchs. Homer's *Odyssey* echoes these common tales, where the poet casts the traders from Sidon and Tyre as men who traveled with "flashy objects without number held in their black ship" and claims that although the Phoenicians were acknowledged as excellent seamen, they "gnaw at the goods of other men" (XV, 415–416). The Phoenician's chains of gold, fastened together with amber beads, attracted the attention of the women who were about to be hauled away. Luxuries like silver implements, dyed cloths and rich carpets, ivory carvings, and occasional performing monkeys intrigued the women, who, in Greek tales of Phoenician treachery, were always curious to a point of disaster. The foreign merchants were well known as sophisticated lovers, since Homer recalls one instance where a trader seduced a beautiful woman with the "embrace of sensual passion" (*Odyssey,* XV, 420–421). The woman was more than willing to accompany the merchants on their return voyage, and the traders supplied stories of knowing her lost family that made the bait even sweeter. White slavery was not the only line of profit for these wide-ranging, skilled seafarers. They carried wine from Thrace, together with magnificent vases and intricately designed bronze swords. Caria and Lydia in southwestern Asia Minor supplied them with carved ivory figurines, and they gained copper from Cyprus.

They normally carried manufactured articles as outgoing cargoes, with the hope of eventually trading them off for stocks of precious metals. Herodotus (*Histories,* IV, 196) gives the method of exchange that the Carthaginians followed (they traced their immediate history back to Phoenicia) on primitive coasts beyond the Pillars of Hercules (the modern Straits of Gibraltar). The merchant vessel cast its anchor just offshore and sent goods to be deposited on the beach. Lighting a fire to announce their arrival and the presence of the articles for trade, the Carthaginians went back to their ship. The natives came down to the beach and put the amount of gold they were willing to give beside the goods, and then they in turn went away. The merchants investigated the gold and determined whether it was enough. If it was, they took the gold and sailed away. If not, they went back to their ship and waited until enough gold had been deposited. No direct meeting took place between the buyers and sellers.

Ships that went to India found natives there like the ones in the far West, and eastern routes were later prized for the enormous stocks of gold and bronze that could be bartered in the old-fashioned way. The absence of contact ensured the safety of both parties, and the tradition long remained in Greek culture that the market enjoyed a truce of the gods.

Gold and Amber

Gold and amber were highest on the list of desired raw materials in the early trading fleets. Phoenician merchants sold their slaves to other kings, like those of Mycenae, in exchange for gold and amber gained through piratical expeditions. Most of the gold went into the coffers of various kings in the ancient Near East, although some of it purchased more manufactured goods in the East for new trading ventures. Profits were enormous. Amber (fossilized pitch) was a material favored for royal jewelry. It made its way from the distant major deposits along the southern shores of the Baltic Sea, coming overland in stages from tribal collections in northern Germany to emerge eventually in the civilized markets in the eastern Mediterranean. Until Greek sailors rounded the coast of Spain and tapped English tin mines directly, sometime in the fifth century B.C., amber from the Baltic came overland to Greece or was diverted down the Danube, where ships could carry it.

Other ancient amber routes knifed across central Europe into Italy, where Bohemian tin may have joined amber as an article of commerce for Phoenician-Carthaginian merchants. Although amber later went out of fashion in classical Greek history, it was the ultimate status symbol in women's jewelry among early Greeks, much as it had been in the ancient Near East. Modern aristocrats take pride in mink or sable coats, and it was a fine lady indeed who wore an amber necklace in Mycenaean Greece. The famous amber discovered in the excavations at Mycenae is not true amber, however, but electrum, a natural alloy of gold and silver. In classical Greek, the word *ēlectron* means both amber and pale gold, and Greek sources do not distinguish between amber and electrum. The legendary status of amber as a symbol of wealth may have led to the early coinages in electrum.

Gold was in good supply in the ancient Near East, coming in part from Egypt. The Phoenicians opened the gold sources in Spain for consumption in the East, and Arabia may have contributed some gold to the flourishing market, but "Arabian" gold sources are quite uncertain. The Phoenicians broke the gold monopoly held before 1500 B.C. by the kings of the Near East. With the opening of the Spanish fields sometime after 800 B.C., the quantity of gold available for trade and artistic employment grew rapidly. In the Greek world, before the emergence of the *polis*-centered civilization, the Minoans and Mycenaeans derived their gold ornaments from a trickling supply from Asian and European fields. After the collapse of the Minoan and Mycenaean civilizations, gold mines seem to have been opened in Nubia (south of Egypt), and Old Testament writers tell tales of gold that came to King Solomon (d. 925 B.C.) from the southernmost parts of Arabia. Silver was in short supply in the Near East and virtually absent in Egypt, where the ratio of gold to silver was 1:2. (Normally, the ratio was somewhere between 1:6 and 1:10.) Rings of gold functioned both as portable wealth and royal adornment; a saying from the *Song of Solomon*, "Thy cheeks are comely with rows of jewels, thy neck with chains of gold," points to the usual and convenient methods of valuation and transport. These methods were much easier than a series of gold bars notched for fractions.

Mycenaean Greece produced the gold cups and costly baubles that were expected in a rich culture (although in all probability the wealth was derived from piracy). Goldsmiths resided in the Mycenaean citadels after 1500 B.C., and their best work compares favorably with any other objects anywhere in the world. They had mastered the technical problems of welding bronze to gold, as the justly famous gold cups found at Vaphio (in Laconia near Sparta) eloquently demonstrate. The finest Minoan craftmanship, combined with a native Mycenaean genius for adaptation, are characteristics displayed in the Vaphio cups. A plain gold inner liner is fastened to a repoussé shell (a raised, hammered design done on the reverse side), which is worked into a bold series of reliefs depicting leaves and bulls. The remarkable bronze daggers from Mycenae are similarly crafted. The principle bronze blades are inset with smaller bronze panels, which in turn are inlaid with delicate, detailed foliage and animal patterns in two varieties of gold: the normal "red" gold and the so-called pale gold of the art manuals (again, the alloy electrum). Added to this already incredible variety of *honed* effects are inlays of silver and ground niello (niello is an alloy of powdered copper, lead, sulfur, and silver and is black in color). Precious and easily worked metals were sought in Mycenaean times, so it seems, for artistic enjoyment and for display of artistic genius. The trinkets of the rich reflected the presence of artists in the Mycenaean citadels, and gold had value beyond simple exchange.

Perfumes

Perfumes and unguents were an important part of Phoenician trade, and they carried manufactured perfumes throughout the Mediterranean. It was the hardy Phoenicians who opened the Adriatic sea-lanes to commerce and exploited the headwaters of the River Po in northern Italy. In Illyria (generally modern Yugoslavia) the Phoenicians gathered the iris plant, from which orrisroot (the rhizome of three species of iris) and a high-quality pungent perfume were made.

Corinthian trade routes later followed the older Phoenician lines, and Corinthian merchants took silver from southern Illyria. The iris and the perfume derived from it became a staple of Corinthian commerce, and Corinth became a well-known center for its manufacture. Although the sources show many instances where Greek nobility prized perfumes, it is difficult to pin down specific evidence for given odors or for specific plants used in their manufacture. Until Dioscorides provides his lengthy list in *Materia medica* (in early Roman imperial times), one cannot examine just what was sold and what was valued.

Most brewers concocted perfumes in a mixture of fats, which partially explains the prominence of the flourishing salve and unguents trade in fifth-century B.C. Greece. The base for most unguents came from the natural fat of sheep's wool (*oisupe*, or lanolin), but it decomposed rapidly and had to be manufactured and used locally. Other fatty substances were favored for overseas trading. A good smell, so Dioscorides writes (*Materia medica,* II, 84), results from carefully combining "strongly scented wine" with the fat of calves and bulls, as well as their marrow, and then carefully melting and skimming them and adding palma, cassia, calamus, aspalathus, xylobalsamum, cinnamon, cardamomum, and nard. Later the brewer could add such expensive rarities as "the plumpest myrrh, diluted in wine for many years." The brewer also mixed goose grease with many of the rare items listed above to produce perfumes and unguents, but Dioscorides suggests that goose grease be mixed and heated "with old Lesbian wine."

In the Greek world perfumes were more commonly smeared than applied, and naturally, brewers made cheaper varieties from the ever present olive oil. Prattling women commonly sold such unguents in the marketplaces all over Greece, and personal hygiene received a boost, even though personal cleanliness was little practiced. As in the Middle Ages, the sweet smells of the ruling class distinguished it from the mass of poor, who could ill afford the expensive rarities that went into perfumes and unguents. Often the medical practice used the salves as healing unguents. Traders could reap great profits from exporting perfumes to distant ports. As with the best wines, there were many ways to manufacture fraudulently what smelled like the best unguents. The test was to wait for decomposition. If they stood the summer heat or winter cold (and did not harden like Etruscan wax), then they were worth the high prices. Otherwise, the merchant came and went as rapidly as he could.

Dyes

The Phoenicians originated trade in dyestuffs, providing Tyrian purple, which supposedly still means the richest and most royal crimson-purple dye possible. Yet attempts to reproduce the purples of antiquity (using the shellfish *Purpura murex* and *P. buccinea*) have yielded a dull shade of red-violet, much less beautiful than modern analine dyes. In ancient Greece, the most costly purple, coming from the murex, was worth its weight in silver. The finest cloth was dyed twice, first with the purple of *P. murex* and then with that of *P. buccinea*. Manufacturing the dyes was a tedious process; only the merchants who exported the finished cloth, or the vats of purple, made any profit from the dyes and dyestuffs. In alluding to the crude professions, the Athenian comedy writer Aristophanes (*c.* 450–*c.* 385 B.C.) mentions how the dye was made: the shellfish were crushed into a jelly and then subjected to lengthy boiling (*Acharnians,* 381, and *Ecclesiazusae,* 215). Since other fluids (such as urine) often watered down the dyes, the people involved in dye production were despised for their constant odor.

Nonetheless, purple cloth, well fixed and presumably rid of most of the offensive smell, fetched a fancy price. The Phoenician purple was especially valued, followed in later Greek times by the Laconian variety. Although there were other kinds (the Chian and Ionian), they never competed with the traditional Phoenician purple. Other colors were also exported, including green dyes made from malachite, a form of copper carbonate, or red and yellow dyes made from arsenic trisulfide and arsenic monosulfide. Cinnabar, the red mercuric sulfide, was used for some staining. Attic dyers used the cinnabar deposits found on the neighboring island of Ceos; later sources were Spain and Colchis, located on the extreme southwestern coast of the Black Sea.

The far-flung trade in dyestuffs had little meaning for the ordinary man or woman in either Mycenaean or classical Greece. Both sexes wore an outer garment (*chlamys*) that a limited number of manufacturers produced. As Xenophon relates (*Memorabilia*, II, 7.6), poorer citizens probably wore *exomides*, sleeveless vests common in the *polis* of Megara. Only dandies like the infamous Athenian fop Alcibiades wore fancy dress; widespread indignation followed when ordinary folk "put on airs" by donning outlandish robes from Corinth, brightly colored cloaks from Greek Asia Minor, and semi-tunics with intricate embroidery. Most Greeks dressed as best they could, hitching up their tunics and cloaks without much eye to fashion and pinning them wherever it was convenient. Wool was made into common clothing in the traditional Greek household, and girls were taught from an early age to be the providers of clothing for their future homes. Possibly the rough wool products were sent out to be finished, but only the rich dyed their clothes or had them washed or cleaned more than once a month. In fact, according to Theophrastus' witty lampoon, *Characters* (see chapter 8), the fellow who wants to become one of the upper class first begins to change his clothes when they are not quite filthy enough to be cleaned. What is even more ludicrous, this fellow of petty ambition "keeps his teeth white, gets a haircut often, and employs sweet-smelling unguents rather than oil" (*Characters*, XXI). Merchants made their profits from the established nobility and those who wished to be considered aristocratic.

Iron

Herodotus (*Histories*, I, 25) recalled the Greek tradition that the technique of welding iron had been imported from somewhere in the East sometime in the seventh century B.C. Glaucus of Chios, whose name was associated with the process, was supposed to have "invented the art of inlaying iron." The Chian's chief claim to fame was a large silver bowl to which was welded an inner bowl of iron, dedicated by the kings of Lydia at Delphi. An even earlier tradition, which appears in the *Old Testament* (I Kings, 7. 46), suggests that the Phoenicians were skilled in casting iron. Being traders, they probably took a stock of tools and implements with them when they sailed into uncivilized areas; however, such markets were quite limited, since local blacksmiths took the Phoenicians' models of iron tools and produced their own varieties. Scattered finds of Greek and Phoenician iron and steel tools in northern and central Europe indicate that trade in manufactured implements was very important. This trade was particularly important when merchants sought exchange for gold and silver, or other raw ores. By occasional deposits of tools that originate in Greece or the Near East, one can trace the trade routes that follow Phoenician and Greek influence in and around the Aegean and Black Seas, west to Spain and north around the Iberian peninsula, and eventually to England and the North Sea.

Iron tips for plows were made locally, and each culture produced its own kinds of swords and daggers, but finely made specialty tools were bought and sold well into the Hellenistic period. Sometimes fine surgical tools are found, although Greek methods for iron smelting were spotty at best. Smelting was usually done through direct extraction, a process in which iron ore is mixed with charcoal and then blasted, thus melting the iron ore; the melted iron ore seeps to the bottom of the furnace and collects in a mass covered with slag (the metal's waste matter). Since many impurities remained, re-smelting was necessary to produce finer grades of iron. The Greek furnaces could not reach 1225° C, the temperature necessary to make pig iron, so wrought iron, which only required a temperature of 700° C, was most commonly produced. Nonetheless, speciality items were known for their exceptional quality, and commanded good but limited markets. Plutarch (*c.* A.D. 50–*c.* A.D. 120) notes the special procedure required to temper small iron objects: "They immerse needles, small iron clips, and other delicate items in oil rather than in water, since they are afraid the cold of the water would distort their shapes" (*Moralia: The Principle of Cold*, 950C). Small objects from the Hellenistic East, such as delicately produced needles and scalpels, turn up from time to time together with drug boxes and cases for surgical tools.

Iron from India was highly esteemed, and was procured as soon as the Greeks had mastered seasonal sailing with the monsoons from Aden to India, as Volume VI of the *Periplus of the Erythrean Sea* suggests. (This document originated from texts in the Hellenistic period.) Ctesias of Cnidos, a Greek physician at the Persian court (*fl. c.* 400 B.C.) who composed an account of India and a rather fanciful history of Persia, knew of a kind of steel that came from India. This may be the seric iron that Pliny mentions (*Natural History*, XXXIV, 145), a fine steel produced in central Hyderabad and exported west by caravan to the Phoenician coast. The famous blades of Damascus were made from this particular steel, although it did not reach mainland Greece in classical times.

Spanish steel was widely purchased, since a secret method of tempering converted Celtiberian blades of iron into steel. This secret was apparently well-known in Roman times, for Plutarch notes that "the Celtiberians produce steel from iron by burying their iron in the earth," digging it up later and cleaning off the large accumulations of impurities (*Moralia: On Being a Blabbermouth*, 510F). Then they reforged and exported the blades. Good whetstones were in demand, and the best ones came from the Aegean island of Naxos, as in Pindar's line, "He was a Naxian stone among all the others, a whetstone ruling metals" (*Isthmian Odes,* VI, 73).

The sources show that numerous other articles were part of a constant commerce. Blacksmiths made everything from their own tools— like hammers, smalls and sledges, clawed pincers, and saws—to carpenters' tools that included hammers, beetles, lathes, planes, augers, spokeshaves, and gimlets. All blacksmiths battered out large nails, as they continued to do until the nineteenth century, but smaller nails for shoes required special care. Made of iron, as were the larger kinds, the smaller nails fastened soles. A brisk trade was carried on in the special knives, awls, tweezers, and clamps that were needed in a shoemaker's shop along with the wooden lasts. Plato indicates that such scenes are quite common through his simile of the shoemaker who smooths down "the puckers in the leather with the instrument such as men use to eliminate wrinkles on a last" (*Symposium*, 191A). The finest tools for the special professions were often inlaid with bronze and ivory work, and no doubt their exotic origin gained them good prices in foreign marketplaces.

The Slave Trade

Although a somewhat distasteful fact to modern apologists of classical Greek life, the slave trade flourished throughout Greek history, and passed its heritage of piracy and brigandage on to Roman times. It is impossible to whitewash slavery in Greece. With the exception of some of the deeper Greek thinkers, Greeks accepted the place of slavery within a structured society as natural. In the lofty thoughts of Plato's ideal laws and in Aristotle's arguments for justice and intelligence is an acceptance of slavery as normal. The economic life of ancient Greece rested on the institution of slave ownership. Thus it is fitting to consider why Greek culture thought of slaves as an integral part of everyday life, even while the various *poleis* struggled to define citizen rights and painfully created some of the most brilliant intellectual and artistic works in Western history.

In a cryptic statement that helps us understand Greek thinking on slavery, Thucydides writes that early Greeks and barbarians turned to piracy under their most powerful leaders to satisfy "their own greed and the wants of the poor" (*History*, I, 5). He then relates how, in his own time, various less cultured areas in Greece retained such customs, while Athens had laid down her arms and taken up "a more luxurious manner of life" (*History*, I, 6). Piracy (and sacking defenseless settlements) was beneficial to the community as a whole, especially in maintaining the weaker members of the early, semi-tribal units. Later the "islanders" (the Carians and Phoenicians) became infamous pirates, carrying on raids as before. As an activity, war was not distinguished from piracy. In both cases, gain came from outside the community, and stealing from foreign settlements was considered far from disgraceful. Only theft *within* the tribe was offensive, which helps explain the puzzling reference in the *Odyssey* (XIX, 395), to Autolycus the thief who was under the protection of Hermes.

Aristotle's *Politics* summarizes social and cultural assumptions about the *polis* at the end of the city-state's period of importance politically. Together with those of Homer and Thucydides, his statements about piracy and war provide a needed context for understanding the constant Greek slave trade. "The various manners of life . . . may be grouped into five classes: cattle and sheep raising, farming, piracy, fishing, and hunting" (*Politics*, 1256a8–1256b). He goes through an elaborate explanation to clarify his definition: these occupations are followed by men who earn their living from their own labor, not by those persons who make a living from small trading or exchange. He then argues that equitable combinations of the five are possible—and quite usual. Piracy can join with pastoral

life, and farming with hunting. After stating that property for sub-
sistence (which derives from the ways of life just listed) is given in
nature to every living thing, he writes that

> all animals must have been made by nature for the sake of
> men . . . thus the art of war is a natural way to acquire prop-
> erty. The skill of hunting is a part of the skill of war, and
> hunting should be employed not only against animals in the
> wild state but also against human beings intended by nature
> to be ruled by others, and who refuse to obey that intention.
> War of this kind is naturally just. [1256b11]

Thus slavery and piracy are merged with the concept of war, which
was a natural activity to most thinkers in classical Greece.

Sources rarely mention the slave trade by name, but there are many
accidental references to a flourishing commerce in captured or
kidnapped human beings who were sold as slaves. The Phoenicians
had a reputation for being utterly ruthless in their slaving raids.
Homer's "gloomy Tyrian merchant" (*Odyssey*, XIV, 416) often
enslaved supercargoes of citizens of distant lands. The Phoenicians
particularly valued young women and comely boys; Herodotus begins his *Histories* by writing that the Phoenicians were the "authors
of the quarrel" between the Greeks and barbarians (*Histories,* I, 1).
On one of their typical raids, the Phoenician pirates captured some
women from Argos in the Peloponnesus and apparently sold them
in Egypt. An unnamed Greek state countered with a raid against
Tyre, in which the Greeks stole the king's daughter (*Histories*, I, 2).
Although Herodotus relates the tale of pirate raids in the manner of
"this is what folks say," his manner suggests that these were typical
and current instances. He maintains that the piratical raids grew in
size and viciousness, leading eventually to the conflict between East
and West. Other women were stolen from Thebes, in Greece, and
sold in Libya by the Phoenicians, yet Herodotus' confusing narrative
(*Histories,* II, 54) shows that slave women from Thebes in Egypt
were shipped to Libya as well as to Thebes in Greece.

Other pieces of evidence support the idea that the slave trade continued and expanded in the period of the Greek tyrannies (*c.* 700–
500 B.C.). Herodotus again supplied disconnected, but rather
decisive, stories of the increasing demand for slaves in the organized
poleis of Greece. Greek slavers sold Greeks in response to special
desires in the courts of the Near East. "Panionius, a Chian, made a
living by very disreputable means. He bought boys of great beauty,

and castrated them and sold them in Sardis and Ephesus for enormous sums. The barbarians value eunuchs more than other slaves because of their perfect faithfulness " (Herodotus, *Histories*, VIII, 105). Ephesus, a Greek city on the western coast of Asia Minor, was a sort of headquarters for slave dealers in Greek eunuchs, who were greatly esteemed at the Persian court. This slave trade existed for at least two centuries before Herodotus penned his history (*c*. 450 B.C.). The Persians also desired other Greek slaves, including doctors like Democedes of Croton; he displayed his medical skill so well that Darius forbade him to leave. However, Democedes managed to slip away from court by a ruse. Perhaps the Greeks boasted too much about themselves, since a Persian queen said, "I most ardently desire Spartan, Argive, Athenian, and Corinthian men to attend me" (*Histories*, III, 134).

Castrated boys made up a good portion of the growing commercial wealth of sixth-century B.C. Corinth. Periander, tyrant of Corinth (*c*. 627–586 B.C.), captured and dispatched three hundred boys to the court of Alyattes of Lydia in Asia Minor, whose capital was at Sardis. Periander offended Greek sensibilities because he had selected sons from the Corcyrean noble families "to gain vengeance for an insult" (Herodotus, *Histories*, III, 48). Another tyrant, Polycrates of Samos (*c*. 535–518 B.C.), frequently enslaved his war captives. His fleet of one hundred *pentekonters* and forty *triremes* swept the eastern Aegean, making pirate forays that reaped easy harvests. (See chapter 4 for a discussion of Greek ships.) When the fleet of Lesbos was defeated and the sailors taken prisoner, Polycrates "put them all in chains, and these slaves excavated the entire trench that encompasses the wall of Samos" (Herodotus, *Histories*, III, 39). Polycrates commanded a large mercenary army that supplemented an unusual force of one thousand Samian archers, and his pirate fleet and army captured so many slaves that Samos soon had enough men to build public structures. Forced labor constructed the largest Temple of Hera recorded by Herodotus, and the slaves dug an impressive and lengthy underground aqueduct "through which water is carried by pipes to reach the city from a never-failing spring" (*Histories,* III, 60). Slaves also built a huge mole (or breakwater) to protect her harbor. Even though Sparta and Corinth went to war against Samos, Polycrates survived until his overweening ambition clouded his judgment. Hoping to rule an island empire, he entered into an agreement with one of the Persian satraps (provincial governors). The Persian proved treacherous, and captured, castrated, and crucified Polycrates, a death "unfitting to him and his lofty thoughts" (*Histories*, III, 125). Without a doubt, Polycrates' short-lived pirate empire reaped much wealth from slavery, and the majority of the slaves were Greeks. Formerly free citizens of Lesbos shared the fate of Samians who opposed the tyrant, and Milesians and other Greeks from coastal cities and island settlements suffered from slave raids.

Few slaves came from domestic sources, and the Greeks found that it did not pay to raise slave children. Exposed babies were so common that slave dealers had little trouble keeping their supplies at levels that satisfied continual demands. Girls raised to be prostitutes and courtesans were especially salable and slave dealers frequented spots where girl babies were commonly exposed. Slave markets dealing in eunuchs, prostitutes, and educated slaves who could teach the children of the upper classes reading and writing were organized throughout the Greek world, and they were well established and taken for granted when Strabo (63 B.C.–A.D. 21) wrote his *Geography*. Slave emporia had existed for many centuries on the islands of Chios, Samos, and Cyprus, at Ephesus in Asia Minor, at Athens, and later on the island of Delos. Syria, Pontus, Lydia, Thrace, Galatia, Egypt, and Libya were widely considered good areas for slave raids, and year after year each area contributed its number. Like Aristotle, Strabo sees nothing amiss with the slave trade as such, remarking that "the pirates continued their plundering raids and forays under the guise of slave trading." These were the Cilician pirates, who troubled the eastern Mediterranean in the first century B.C. He also describes the fantastic numbers of slaves exchanged at Delos, "a large and wealthy marketplace, able to receive and ship ten thousand sold slaves in a single day" (*Geography,* XIV, 5. 2). In the fifth and fourth centuries B.C. Athens held a special market for slave selling once a month, and tax revenues on slave sales were a good source of income for the state. The *polis* taxed citizens of other states 2 percent when they imported slaves, and it levied as much as a 2 percent surtax and an additional 2 percent export tax. The most enlightened Greek *polis* profited heavily from slavery, although Athenian law insured domestic slaves good treatment to the point that slaves "could not be insulted on their persons" (Demosthenes, *Against Meidias*, 47). But slaves in the state silver mines at Laurion received brutal treatment while slaves on the small farms in Attica often achieved informal status as one of the family.

Many human beings were brought to the slave markets through the "gentle" practice of selling children, which many barbarian chiefs used, or through tribal struggles beyond the borders of Greek settlements, which produced war captives. Since the *poleis* of Greece constantly waged war, most male slaves were Greek. The campaigning armies usually included several slave dealers among the camp followers; the victorious army herded its captives together and sold them on the spot (and distributed the gold and silver among the soldiers) or shipped them to a market for sale. Slavery was such a common risk in war that the Greek proverb "Zeus denies a man half his *arete** when the day of slavery arrives" (*Odyssey*, XVI, 323) became commonplace.

Generally, slaves were sold to the rich, who sought them for their specialized skills. Artful prostitutes, call girls, and courtesans were common in the aristocratic households of classical Greece, and an accepted part of ordinary sexual liaison for the young nobles. (See chapter 7.) In the Eastern courts, a sure way to prevent tainting blood lines of the royal families was to procure eunuchs as slaves. Prostitutes and eunuchs brought good profits to the slavers, who only sporadically dealt in slaves for hard labor. Condemnation to the quarries and mines was generally considered the equivalent of a death sentence. Because the lower classes in the *polis* were often subject to slave raids in time of chaos, they tended to support tyrants when the latter could insure stability and order.

The *Polis* As Trading Center

The influential states in the age of Hellenic achievement were also flourishing emporia. Sparta was a center for trade until her great conflicts with Messenia, while Athens and Corinth continued their commercial expansion, at the same time undergoing political changes. Both *poleis* lay across the principal East-West line of commerce, and a major cause of the war between Athens and Sparta was the fact

---

*Arete is one of the Greek words that cannot be captured well in an English word or phrase. In the works of Homer and Herodotus, *arete* normally means "manly" qualities or simple manhood displayed in war or the actual prowess of a soldier in battle. In those of Theognis and Euripides, *arete* means one's rank or status, usually within a noble class. Plato employs *arete* to connote excellence in a skill or art, as well as to suggest a man's high merit or moral character. It meant *all* these things to a Greek, plus a number of other things (like "service rendered" to Thucydides and Xenophon, and utter virtue to Euripides).

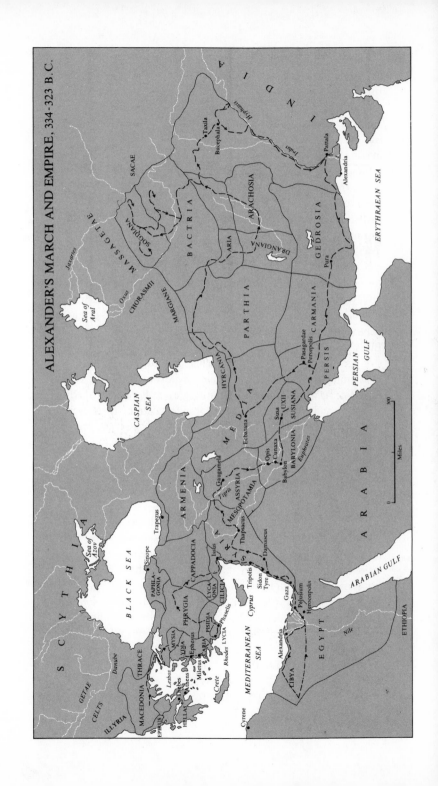
ALEXANDER'S MARCH AND EMPIRE, 334-323 B.C.

that Corinth badgered her ally Sparta into conflict with Athens over the control of vital trade routes. Yet neither Athens nor Corinth was a manufacturing center in the modern sense, although production of war materials in Athens made those merchants wealthy who began making shields and swords. Corinth subsisted on her control of the trade coming over the isthmus; anything that threatened that dominance threatened her economic life. Thucydides was correct when he succinctly wrote that the cause of the Peloponnesian War was "Athens' power and Sparta's fear" (*History*, I, 23), egged on by Corinth.

With the institution of a partial solution to land hunger and poor land distribution after Solon became sole *archon* (594 B.C.), Athens turned more and more to importing grain for her supply. Her state policy was to find grain that could be bought with Attic products—fine olive oil and wine. Egypt could not raise vines and produce wine of her own, so Athenian merchants found a good market there. Black Sea ports abutted on excellent grain-producing areas in southern Russia and eastern Rumania, and the beautiful pottery containing excellent Attic wine and oil grew more welcome as time went on. Athens' trading community grew as her contacts abroad widened, and a long list of luxury products coming from every known port in the Mediterranean suggests she had lively markets and quays. The Athenians did not consume all of the luxury items, although an occasional noble lived in a style that implied he was trying. Alcibiades, wearing a long Milesian cloak dyed purple, became a stereotype of the playboy nobility with much money but little sense of ethics or social grace.

Wheat fed Athens' growing population in the fifth century B.C., while other goods flowing into Piraeus whetted desires for artistic and exotic displays. After the middle of the century Attica's population grew alongside the increasing wealth of the Athenian Empire, but it is very difficult to determine exact numbers either for the population increase or for totals at any given time. In the *Oxford Classical Dictionary* 2d ed. (1970), p. 862, A. W. Gomme follows his earlier estimates from *The Population of Ancient Athens*, giving the following figures: in 480 B.C., the citizen total (men, aged 18–59) of Attica was roughly 140,000; but Gomme believes that the total population of Attica in 431 B.C. was 310,000—which includes 172,000 citizens, 28,500 *metics* ("resident foreigners"), and 110,000 slaves—and that that figure fell in 425 B.C. to 217,000 (116,000 citizens,

21,000 *metics,* and 80,000 slaves). For 323 B.C., his total population for Attica is 260,000 (112,000 citizens, about 42,000 *metics,* and about 106,000 slaves). This is a high guess, and in his *Athenian Democracy,* pages 161–180, A. H. M. Jones thinks Gomme's figures are grossly overinflated. Jones suggests 30,000 as the citizen total in the first quarter of the fifth century B.C., of which 10,000 would be heavily armed soldiers (*hoplites*); he also suggests that 20,000 *hoplites* were available in 431 B.C. Jones thinks Gomme's figures are, in part, "pure speculation, unsupported by any evidence" (*Democracy,* 162). With the exception of Thucydides (especially *History,* II, 13. 6–8), who provides *hoplite* figures for 431 B.C., the ancient sources allow various interpretations. Even the inscriptional evidence given by the *Athenian Tribute Lists* allows widely divergent guesses about population in the Athenian Empire. All agree—whatever their population guesses and figures—that the population of Athens increased enormously during the fifth century B.C.

Through Athens' bustling port passed silphium, coming from Cyrene and Carthage. Silphium was a mysterious medicinal plant that cured everything, much like the nostrums sold in state fairs. It commanded good markets in mainland Greece, and Athens was a central point in its general distribution. Figs and raisins raised by Rhodes were sent to Piraeus, pears and apples arrived from Euboea, dates and wheat flour came from Phoenicia, and Cypriot mustard and Paphlagonian almonds went to the dinner parties of the wealthy. Haggling masses of people jostled for positions close to the hawking merchants from far ports, who posted themselves in the closely packed marketplace. Each trader bellowed his wares, which rested before him on a rich cloth hailing from an unknown land; and the baubles of gold from India, iron trinkets from a place called the Land of the Chalybes, fancy Pontic swords, Syrian balm, and fine flax for nets from Carthage and Phasis excited even the casual onlooker. But the rich already possessed all these small bits of ostentation, and the merchant knew his great profits would come in ports far beyond.

An Athenian who strolled the four miles to Piraeus, the port of Athens, could see the heavily laden grain ships (*holkades*) slowly coming in from the Black Sea. Since these large cargo vessels were not oared, they were not beached like other large ships. The *holkas* (plural *holkades*) was broad (about 30 to 40 feet wide) and long (about 100 to 150 feet) and weighed 100 to 150 tons. Underwater archaeologists have uncovered hulks that sank with cargoes of olive oil and wine shipped in large jars of clay. In the same space grain would be carried on the return voyage. The *holkas* was towed into open water, where it slowly sailed along at five knots per hour with the wind. The Athenian might see an occasional oared merchant vessel (*eikosoros*), which could hold a cargo of three thousand jars of wine. But the traditional *holkades* were favored; these required towing and aid to get into port as well as out into the open sea.

Going north in the summer months, the heavy grain ships sailed the Aegean Sea and up the Dardenelles into the Black Sea. By late September, since the prevailing easterlies had begun to blow, they would be sent back into the Aegean. Ships returning to Athens from Sicily and the West also had to set out in early summer, returning with their load of grain from mid-July to mid-September by catching the Etesian winds blowing from the northwest. Vessels sailing south from Piraeus caught the Etesians to Crete, Egypt, Cyprus, and Syria, and they returned under the lee of Asia Minor to the Aegean Islands and thence to Piraeus. By modern standards, the trading vessels were small, single-masted and square-rigged. Thucydides mentions that the Athenians employed a very large "ship of ten thousand talents" in the siege of Syracuse in 415 B.C. (*History,* VII, 25). Since the talent and *amphora* both represented roughly a cubic foot of water (the Greek foot being about .97 of the English foot), each would have weighed from fifty-six to sixty-six pounds. Thus the vessel weighed about 280 tons (about 160 tons when empty).

After the surprising victory of the Greek coalition over Persian forces (by 479 B.C.), Athens sought to continue the struggle, even though Sparta thought the allies' ends had been accomplished. Athens had the finest fleet of warships in the eastern Mediterranean, and her lucky decision to devote new silver veins in Attica to ship-building meant a ready supply of new ships. Athens had cast her fortunes with commerce, and her continued prosperity depended upon a peaceful and pro-Athenian Aegean Sea. In organizing the Delian League, whose headquarters were on the sacred ground of the island of Delos, Athens proposed to continue the war with Persia; and she proposed to enroll as allies of Athens all those Greek states that would fight for complete freedom of Greek states, even of those on the coast of Asia Minor. Athens' fleet was to be the fleet of the new league, and financial support for the war effort came from *phoros*, a contribution in either silver or ships to maintain the league.

The thankless task of levying the *phoros* for each state fell to
Aristides of Athens in 478 B.C. He did the job so well that he is
known as Aristides the Just. It was a matter of time before Athens
turned the league into an empire, run by and for Athenian interests.
In the period of Athens' greatest power as mistress of a maritime
empire (446–404 B.C.), trade provided the glue that made subject
states generally loyal to Athens. The great fleet cleansed the sea of
pirates, allowing merchants from all the Aegean Islands to enjoy
fully the trade routes that had been closed too often in the past by
freebooters, or pirates. The supply of silver, derived from both the
tribute of subject *poleis* and Attica's own rich mines, provided a
standard of exchange that insured a reliable atmosphere of buying
and selling. The artistic pride Athens took in minting her coins
(generally called the "owls of Athens") gave her coinage a merit beyond the state's guarantee of fineness or weight. It also prompted
the whole empire to accept an Athenian decree of 449 B.C. com-
pelling all states within Athenian control to use only Athenian
drachmas. The inscription recording the decree includes heavy penalties for anyone using "foreign" coins, measures, or weights, and
orders such coinage to be turned over to the treasury and mint.
Local coins were shortly driven out of common circulation, and
archaeological sites throughout the islands yield very few coins
other than those of Athens during her dominion. The states did re-
sume their local issues after Athens began to lose her power after
412 B.C., but the Attic coins continued to be minted as "owls"
until 25 B.C., when the mines at Laurion were exhausted. Athens
had minted her silver owls for six hundred years, from the time of
Solon until the new empire of Augustan Rome—a remarkable history
for one kind of coinage.

Wood

Wood for shipbuilding was of primary importance to a state that depended on its fleet for basic food supply; hence, Athens carried on an
an extensive trade in timber. In many respects, Athenian foreign
policy was as wedded to access to good forests as it was to sources
of grain. In classical times, woods employed in shipbuilding included
fir, white pine, the cedars of Syria, and various pines that grew
around Aleppo in Syria. The keels of the *triremes* required a harder
wood since the vessels were beached so often; shipwrights made

them from oak or beech. Masts were constructed of white pine—called "silver pine" by Theophrastus (*History of Plants,* IV, 1 and 2; V, 7)—as were oars and yardarms. To the north of Greece, Macedonia and Thessaly were covered with fir, explaining to some extent why Athens usually attempted conciliation with the kings of Macedonia and the various rulers in Thessaly. During the Peloponnesian War, many campaigns took place in northern Greece, where the Spartans attempted to cut off the timber supplies that constantly refurbished the Athenian fleet. Thucydides writes that in 442 B.C. Athens signed a treaty with King Perdiccas of Macedonia (*History*, IV, 132). It stipulated that the Macedonian king would allow wood for oars to be exported only to Athens, and an inscription records how such wood sold to an ally of Athens had to be sent to Athens. Good Athenian silver and excellent wine would pay for the timber.

Fish

The Greek passion for fish promoted a lively commerce in imported seafood. According to *Deipnosophistae,* a collection, or miscellany, of lost authors gathered by Athenaeus (III, 116), Greeks gobbled up sturgeons' bellies cut into squares and pickled, and also sliced pike, pickled tunny, mackerel, fat swordfish, tunny hearts packed in jars, and sea perch from Pontus. They thought octopus a delicacy, and enjoyed almost all salted food, from whales to barnacles. Practically all Greek settlements had a flourishing business in some aspect of fishing. Fishermen knew the details of tunny migrations, breeding habits, and seasonal schoolings. All along the northern coast of Asia Minor cities had booming fisheries, but Byzantium was "the mother of tunnies, pickled in the right season, as well as of the mackerel from the deeps and fattened swordfish" (Athenaeus, *Deipnosophistae* III, 116b-c). The tunny rushed through the mouth of the Bosporus

> in great shoals, being but of small size and strength, and they are swept along the coast to Trapezus . . . and here fisheries begin, but they are not large since the tunny are not yet of the right size . . . when the tunny reach Sinope, they are in the right season for fishing and of the size and weight for salting.
> [Strabo, *Geography*, VII, 2]

At Byzantium, the tunny were so numerous that "they are easily taken even by hand, such is the force of the current and the narrowness of the bays" (*Geography*, VII, 2). Colchis, at the other end of the Black Sea, was famed for its high quality fishing nets and Sinope collected much revenue from her curing industry. Strabo notes (*Geography*, XI, 5. 6) that convenient salt deposits were invaluable for a city that made its living from salting and curing fish, and he says that Dioscurias (located on the coast of the Soviet Caucasian state of Abkhazskaya) possesses the best combination of salt pans and fish. The settlement of Olbia in the Crimea had a very large fish market, and the mouths of the great rivers flowing into the Black Sea from the plains of Russia made magnificent fishing grounds. At each mouth—of the Dnieper, the Danube, or the Don, which empties into the Sea of Azov—there was an abundance of salt. Even severe winters did not prevent fishing. "Fish are caught through the ice with a round net, called the *gangama*, in particular a large kind of sturgeon as large as a dolphin" (Strabo, *Geography*, VII, 3. 18). Not only did the Black Sea and Aegean provide seafoods for the rich and poor in the Greek world, but the Greek colonies in the West were active in fisheries. The Sicilian cities ran successful fishing industries; Syracuse, Messana, and Selinus were famed for their fish; and the Greek colony at Massilia (or Marseille) provided an abundance of "shellfish from a salt lake above the mouths of the Rhone," which also supplied "dug mullets for anyone who digs two or three feet into the murky water; the fish are prized because of their size and feed in the mud like eels" (Strabo, *Geography*, IV, 1. 6 and 8). Since eels were one of the greatest delicacies (most were caught in Boeotia in a fresh water lake), the mere resemblance of the mullets to eels signaled profits and consumption by the wealthy.

The fishing trade was divided into specialities, merchants who functioned as wholesalers and others who sold fish in the retail market. Jars made for transporting pickled fish employed many in fishing communities, since each jar had to be broken to enjoy the products within. The salted and pickled fish were the fare of the poor and often found their way into army provisions, as Aristophanes (*Acharnians*, 967) wryly notes. Greeks preferred fish from the salt water to those taken in fresh, with the major exception of eels from Lake Copais in Boeotia. Again, Athenaeus' miscellany lists many types of fish sold in the Athenian markets. Mussels arrived from Pontus and a kind of conger eel came from Sicyon. Crayfish from Eretria were preferred, and boar fish from Argos brought a good price. Smoked and dried fish were wrapped and sold in fig leaves. Fish vendors in the markets, the smelly fishmongers, were pictured in Greek litera-

ture as totally untrustworthy, a pack of cutthroats and sneaky
thieves. Amphis, who wrote *The Wandering Juggler* in the time of
Plato, notes that the fishmongers slurred their speech and dropped
unaccented syllables, so that one could not understand them:

> It is much more easy to gain a conference with the Board of
> Generals and get one's questions answered than it is to go up
> to goddamned fishmongers in the agora . . . should a
> prospective buyer lift up one of the fish on display and ask
> the vendor some question, the monger crouches in silence,
> pounding a polyp, paying no attention and pretending not to
> hear a word. The customer shortly lets loose his rage and
> merely gets back some unpronounceable and unintelligible
> jargon. [Amphis in Athenaeus, *Deipnosophistae,* VI, 224e]

Amphis notes that it was common to cheat by "rinsing the fish"
(Athenaeus, *Deipnosophistae,* 225c), which meant that the fish ven-
dor watered down his salt fish. An Athenian law expressly forbade
such practices, with no real effect. One part of the *agora* was customarily reserved for fish of good quality, while the market at
Piraeus sold cheaper kinds. Aristophanes recalls how an unwary
customer was bilked when he asked for change from a fishmonger
who "changed a *drachma* at the fish booth and put down three
mullet scales. I thought they were *obols* and put them in my mouth.
Egad! The awful smell! I spit them out" (*Wasps,* 788–792). Alexis'
comic verse records how the Athenians raved about Pontic salt fish,
which became a great favorite in the fourth century B.C. "O Athenians, you made the sons of Chaerephilus, the salt fishmonger, Athenian citizens since he began the selling of salt fish. On horseback, they
look like mackerels among the Satyrs" (Alexis, *Epidaurus* in
Athenaeus, *Deipnosophistae,* III, 119f).

Olive Oil

Olive oil was ubiquitous because animal fat was rare. Oil took the
place of petroleum for lubricants, of soap for cleaning, and of lard or
butter for cooking. Used in lamps, olive oil early became one of the
most important articles of commerce, as several references in the *Old
Testament* indicate. Since Attica could not support her population
by grain cultivation, olive trees were cultivated long before Solon
formally encouraged olive oil export (594 B.C.). The Greek cities on
the western coast of Asia Minor also had prosperous olive groves in

the river valleys running to the sea. In his story of the sixth-century B.C. philosopher Thales, who made a fortune by cornering the local market in olive presses, Aristotle reflects how olive oil had been known from earliest Greek history. Thales' story proved "that philosophers became rich when they wanted" (*Politics*, 1259a9). The oil of Miletus was renowned throughout ancient times. Several Egyptian papyri record how Milesian oil was imported into Egypt in the third century B.C. A vessel belonging to a man named Theon carried 101 half-jars and 255 large jars of Milesian oil, and a vessel of Aeropus brought 140 half-jars and 122 large jars of Samian and Milesian oil. Another ship came to Alexandria in Egypt, crammed with oil from Syria (C. C. Edgar, ed., *Zenon Papyri*, 59012 and 59077 . 267). According to the notice in Theophrastus' *History of Plants* (IV, 3. 1), the olive groves of Cyrenaica were very fruitful and the oil from the trees more abundant than normal. In the second and first centuries B.C., there was an important exchange center on the island of Delos, and the prices rose and fell with numbing irregularity. Olive oil was so common that it received little notice from writers and commentators. A modern author describing the process of toothbrushing in the American household each morning certainly would receive little attention, unless his treatment of toothpaste and the surrounding ritual was comic or a caricature.

Wine

Wine was a universal beverage in classical times, as it is in Greece today. Modern Greek Metaxa (a brandy liqueur) and Retsina are like the ancient products, since ancient Greeks sealed their clay wine jars with resin, which flavored the wine. In classical Greece, most wine was well diluted before it was drunk. The Greeks had been wine drinkers from the time of Homer, and they believed the god of wine, Dionysus, fled from Lydia to Thrace and founded viticulture. It was fortunate for the owners of the numerous Greek vineyards that Egyptian vines did not produce good vintages and that the inhabitants of the southern Russian coastal region found Greek wines much to their taste. Again, since wine was so common and used universally, evidence for wine trade and cultivation is sketchy from Hellenic times. Coins provide good indications of who shipped wine where. From the handsome silver coinages of Mende, Naxos, Thebes, Corcyra, Thasos, Chios, and Melos, which show either grapes and vines, or grapes and *amphorae*, clear signs of the wine-producing and wine-exporting areas emerge. In an Athenian legal squabble of the fourth century B.C., mention is made to how wine was transported from Cos, Mende, Thasos "and Peparethus to Pontus" (Demosthenes, *Against Lacritus,* 35). Wine-jar stamps, found in scattered sites around the Black Sea, usually originate from the islands of Rhodes and Thasos, but stamps from Cnidos and Paros are also fairly common. Lesbos had a long tradition of wine exportation. Strabo's confusing tale, dating from the time of Sappho of Lesbos (*fl. c.* 590 B.C.), told how Sappho's brother had a mistress who was a courtesan in the Greek trading colony of Naucratis in the Nile delta. Apparently Sappho hated Doriche, the mistress "of her brother Charaxus, a merchant selling the wine of Lesbos in Naucratis" (Strabo, *Geography*, XVII, 1. 33). Sappho denounced Doriche in her "poetry for bilking Charaxus of a good amount of money" (Athenaeus, *Deipnosophistae,* XIII, 596b–c). Naucratis was the special trading center of Greek products in Egypt—something like Hong Kong, which was China's Western post until very recently—and Hellenic traders brought wine, oil, fine vases painted by Greek master artists, and Greek weapons to it. Athenaeus (and Herodotus, *Histories,* II, 135) record that the port was inhabited by *hetairai* ("courtesans" and "call girls") of exceeding beauty with whom the wine merchants dallied before returning to Greece. Doriche was so skilled in her trade that she could afford to dedicate an offering at the Temple of Apollo at Delphi. The stories point indirectly to good profits in the selling of wine to Egyptians.

Naxos was made wealthy from her vineyards and was the center of worship to Dionysus. From this tradition, the colony of Naxos in Sicily minted her coins picturing clusters of grapes. Unlike modern wines, which are produced with full knowledge of bacterial action and alcoholic levels needed in decomposition, ancient Greek wine was put through a great many old wives' traditions in an attempt to gain stable and reliable vintages. The process of wine making was rather complicated, which explains to some degree the cost to the customers in foreign ports. Grapes were placed in a vat made of acacia wood and trodden by foot, with the whole village often joining in the merriment of the "wine stomp." After as much juice as possible had been squeezed out of the grapes by treading, the pulp and skins were placed in a woven sack made of reeds and twisted until the last vestiges of liquid had been squeezed out. The initial juice that trickled down from the untromped grapes, which were merely bruised by their own mass, was drawn off and processed into "rare" wine, as *Geoponica*, VI, relates, together with the account in the *New Testament, Acts*, II, 13. *Geoponica* is a tenth-century A.D. Byzantine compilation that the Emperor Constantine VII Porphyrogenitus (A.D. 913–959) directed; it contains a plethora of matter on illnesses of farm animals, wine processing and viticulture, useful plants and their cultivation, oil and wine presses, bees, and vermin. The sections on wine making were translated into Latin by Burgundio of Pisa (d. 1193 A.D.). Much of the collected data derives from Greek manuscripts dating back to the time of Aristotle.

Wine produced from lightly tromped grapes was next on the list of "good" wines, and it was esteemed with the initial juices for its characteristic of keeping well. A portion of the "new" wine was consumed at once, after receiving clarity through vinegar (*Geoponica*, VI, 15). The new wine had to be taken to wine cellars and stored there in cool earthenware. Pitch coated both the inside and outside of these jars, and they were sunk into the ground. The process required about six months of fermentation—the scum being skimmed off the top all the while—and then the wine was siphoned into smaller jars. Even so, the wine was filled with dregs, and had to be strained through a cloth or metal sieve. Straining the wine was part of the ceremony at a dinner party, and it took some experience to strain it without "spilling or roiling it, making the wine more turbid than before" (Athenaeus, *Deipnosophistae*, X, 420d). The worst wine, which was given to slaves, was created by pouring water through and over the pulp and skins that remained after the final pressing or treading.

Wine that was too acid never tasted very good with anything, and the Greeks employed everything possible to correct acidity in their wines. Sea water, pitch, resin, gypsum, and even burnt marble were mixed with wine, according to Cato the Elder (*On Agriculture*, 23). A writer of the Roman Republic (d. 149 B.C.), he used Greek sources for some of *On Agriculture*. Resin-mixed wine was especially common, and resin wine is drunk in modern Greece because it has that special bouquet. The Scythians, who lived north of the Danube, drank their wine undiluted; to consume wine "neat" was to invite "madness, caused by drinking unmixed wine in Scythian manner" (Herodotus, *Histories,* VI, 84). Normally, wine at dinner parties was served half-diluted with water, and as the evening wore on, the guests occasionally clamored for less and less water, "Scythian style" (Athenaeus, *Deipnosophistae,* X, 426 b–c). Old wine was prized, but the tales of the wine aged sixteen years, like the one described in Athenaeus (*Deipnosophistae,* XII, 584b), or aged ten years, which Nestor supposedly quaffed in the *Odyssey* (III, 388–392), were most likely wishful thinking. Old wine had a bouquet all its own, but fraudulently aged wine reeked of sea water or recent heating, so sneers Athenaeus (*Deipnosophistae,* X, 429c). Good wine, trans-shipped over the Mediterranean, was valued for its consistency and potency, and, as would be expected, a substantial number of moralizing pamphlets entitled *On Drunkenness* were available for morning-after reading.

The merchant's occupation never gained true respect in Greek society. His background was clouded by a tradition of piracy and greed, and the great writers and orators often apologized for their connections with trading ventures, even though they may have realized fat fortunes from them. The bustling markets of Greece did offer a fine variety of products, in both manufactured and local raw goods, but foreign articles were generally reserved for the rich, who could afford the high costs. Exotic goods are most noted in the source materials, and the merchant made huge profits from trading voyages that procured slaves with specialized skills, exotic and fancy frills to decorate the homes of the various nobles of the *poleis,* and rarities for the resplendent evening symposia that the rich threw for display. Common people were involved in the all-important trade of timber and grain in the period of the Athenian Empire, but Athenian silver and a half-century of economic stability in the Aegean had much more effect on trade than did growing numbers of common merchantmen. The fish trade reached down to the lower classes, but their fare was the poorest product left in the jars bringing pickled fish from Black Sea fisheries. Fancy and high-priced seafood went on the tables of the wealthy, who took pride in offering varieties of succulent cuttlefish and imported Crimean sturgeon. Olive oil was everywhere, although some traders made good livings by shipping it to Egypt, where Greek wine was also in demand, since Egypt could not grow excellent grapes of her own. The handbooks like Athenaeus'

Deipnosophistae list many kinds of wine, but most Greeks usually chose to drink wine of local vintage mixed with resin. The old wines were drunk at the dinner parties of the rich, which were characterized by much arguing about verbs and an occasional glance and pass at the flute girls hired for the evening. But most Greeks were unaffected by the busy trade so often noted in the sources, which were written by and for the upper classes.

4

War

The study of war is out of fashion as this book is being written. In the 1960s the United States became enmeshed in the Vietnamese struggles for identity, which have a history going back many centuries. Through a series of misjudgments and a fascinating ignorance of the European experience in Asia, especially that of the French in Indochina, the dogged determination of North Vietnam frustrated the preponderant military might and technical superiority of the United States.

Tiring of endless casualties in a "limited" war, growing expense, and seemingly stupid blunders (like using tanks in marshes and jungle), Americans lost patience, and public opinion soon made Vietnam something to be regurgitated and forgotten. Historians will ponder any lessons to be gained from the American disaster in southeast Asia, from executive-ordered wars to technical warfare versus infantry movements, for many decades to come. Yet the ultimate hope of no more war flies in the face of the total historical experience of Western man; the United States, whatever its form of government in the future, will certainly be at war rather frequently. Such is the nature of power. The first instrument of political power is war, and those who win wars—or have the power to merge military with economic penetration—stand as the great powers of history.

Whether or not military planners admit it, their initial introduction

to the art of war is derived from classical Greek concepts of tactics
and strategy. The great military academies of the twentieth century
still peruse the campaigns of the Persian wars, the Peloponnesian
War, the campaigns of fourth-century B.C. Greek states, and particularly the careers of Philip II of Macedonia and his even more famous
son, Alexander. Before the rise of the *polis*, fighting was on an individual scale, with heroes performing acts of valor for personal honor,
which was dimly linked to some larger cause. With the coming of
the *polis*, armies organized into fighting units called phalanxes, in
which tight blocks of heavily armed men fought shoulder to shoulder
against other tight blocks of similarly armed men fighting in the
same manner. Both massing of strength and probing of weaknesses
in enemy lines were limited, since the early Greek armies were so
much alike in character and composition. Thus tactics and strategy
were simple, circumscribed by Greek reluctance to engage in warfare.
The test of strength between two *poleis* was an enlargement of the
homeric single combat, and the soldiers of the phalanx fought as an
extension of the community.

At first glance, it seems puzzling that the *poleis*, with a common
culture calling itself Hellenic and generally the same religious and
linguistic heritage, should be at war so constantly. Throughout Greek
history as it unfolds after the time of Homer's heroes, incessant warfare among the numerous *poleis* runs as a thread, unbroken except
for a brief squelching by Philip II and Alexander the Great in the
late fourth century B.C., and finally stopped by Roman rule of
Greece after 146 B.C. One cannot explain this affinity for war in
Greek civilization with any of the stereotyped labels. Few Greeks
enjoyed war in the manner of a modern Patton, although many
classical Greek generals took great pride in their mastery of tactics
and timing. Greek culture—with the blatant exception of Sparta—did
not teach that valor in war gave a man true meaning, but rather that
success in war was most often the result of causes beyond man's control. Although Thucydides stated that wars come from the grave
misjudgments of very fallible political leaders, he affirmed a basic
Greek belief that most quarrels could be settled outside the bloodshed of a battlefield. Perhaps the best illustration of the Greek view
of competition comes in their athletic contests, a formal part of
Greek religious and political life from the eighth century B.C. Prowess in sports gave more publicity to the various *poleis* in times of
peace than did most military activity.

A sense of community based on a religious and ethnic bond, coupled with an understanding of political authority from within that community, provided a drive that created the Greek *polis* and its unique outlook on life. The goals of discipline and order were never quite achieved in political life, where tyranny and assassination were common; venomous hatred between clans formed a major part of the political activity within each *polis*. Sparta submerged her petty quarrels under the struggle for survival that became dominant after the early seventh century B.C. Here war and its accomplishments became the mark of manhood, in contrast to the philosophy in Athens. In Attica, wise leaders staved off the open bloodshed that threatened the state in the sixth century B.C., and a tradition of political concession prevented tyranny for fifty years.

War was the province of nobility, the class of the landed aristocracy; even with the introduction of the phalanx, the *polis* tended to employ only those soldiers who came from the upper ranks of society. A modicum of wealth meant the soldier could supply himself with armor and battle gear. The professional soldiers did not arise in large numbers until the Peloponnesian War between Athens and Sparta and the long campaigns that took place year after year. After the war ended (404 B.C.), the age belonged to semiprofessional soldiers, and it was not long before mercenary armies dominated Greek politics.

Homeric Warfare

The epic poems of Homer, which were known to all Greeks, provided models of warfare rather removed from phalanx formations. To be sure, Homer does indicate that something akin to organized formations provided a backdrop for his principle characters. The fine chariot of Achilles wends its way through the story, but the poet is little concerned with chariot tactics. He concentrates on the character of Achilles, the most brilliant warrior of the Achaean army— who is uncertain and whose thoughts are clouded with the passion of anger. Achilles thus voices his own reason for battle, with "I did speak saying I would never forget my anger until that moment arrived when the clamor of battle broke about my own ships" (*Iliad*, XVI, 61–63). As a chieftain supposedly following Agamemnon of the girt halls of Mycenae, Achilles has contempt for his commander, resulting from personal insult. Passion dulls his brilliance. Homer does not intend Achilles as a military model, but rather as a tragic hero who succumbs to the flaw of anger.

Although Achilles "remained wrought in anger, because he was best among them," the best "among the warriors was Telamonian Ajax" (Homer, *Iliad*, II, 768–769). The poet leaves the allusion of "men" and "warriors" (*aristos andrōn*) intentionally fluid, and Ajax proves to be the essence of a successful soldier throughout the *Iliad*. He doggedly fights without any divine aid (which Achilles enjoyed) and by grit and strength often carries a battle. He is a huge warrior who carries a shield heavy with oxhide seven layers deep. Although he is often compared to a wall, Ajax cannot single-handedly sweep the Trojans before him in a short burst like Achilles or Hector, the chief Trojan hero. Ajax is the doughty and unvarnished soldier, in contrast to the inspired brilliance of Achilles.

> Great Telamonian Ajax would not give ground before any
> man, mortal and eating bread, the spawn of Demeter, a
> man who could be severed with the bronze or crushed by the
> huge rocks cast at him. He would not give ground before
> Achilles, the breaker of men in battle by combat narrowed.
> [Homer, *Iliad*, XIII, 321–325]

When the Trojans had beaten back the Achaeans to their beached ships under the spirited attack led by Hector, Ajax led the weary defense. He sweats and grunts, and his sword arm grows tired and weary, and he seems without hope until Patroclus and his troops arrive to stem the attack. No glamor is attached to Ajax, and Homer never dignifies him with qualities of leadership. He is simply the best soldier of the Greeks, who fights and will fight until he drops from exhaustion.

Later periods of Greek history read Homer as though the poet intended the *Iliad* as an instruction book in the art of war. No attempts to deduce military theory from actual warfare came until the fifth century B.C., however, when some thinkers with sophistic leanings applied abstraction to war, as they did to many other subjects. The homeric combats do not lend themselves to technical analysis. Usually they consist of single-combat encounters between chiefs, who struggled in front of poorly armed followers. Sometimes phalanxes of Greeks and Trojans clashed, apparently in lines that fought shoulder to shoulder. Most interpretations of these sections of the *Iliad* suggest that later additions were made to the poem from the time of phalanx warfare and the *polis* organization of manpower. The occasional chariots appearing in the *Iliad* have little use other than to carry various lords in and out of the lines of battle.

The homeric chiefs came to the walls of Troy to aid Agamemnon and Menelaus, king of Sparta, in their quest to revenge Paris' abduction of Menelaus' wife, the fair Helen. Warfare in homeric times was securely rooted in tribal and clan ties, and revenge was a motive for war.

The Phalanx and the *Polis*

There is little connection between the duels of chiefs in Homer's writings and the warfare of the *hoplite* phalanx, which came into being along with the *polis*. Whether the *hoplite* forces created the new *poleis* or vice versa is a great argument among scholars. During the great wars that Sparta waged to enslave her neighboring Messenians, the poet and general Tyrtaeus (*fl. c.* 630 B.C.) composed stirring songs "which the Spartans recited from memory as they marched forward in time to the music" (Athenaeus, *Deipnosophistae,* XIV, 630f.). According to the *Suda* (a Byzantine literary and historical encyclopedia, compiled *c.* A.D. 1000), the poet came from Athens as a hobbling schoolmaster and "rekindled Spartan resolve, and he took Messene in the twentieth year of the war." In the traditions Tyrtaeus wrote stirring and lovely melodies, which were incorporated into the Spartan charging paean; the latter chilled opposing infantry with its high, shrill, and lilting strains. Instructions for the Spartan soldiers survive in a fragment of Tyrtaeus' writing:

> Every man should wear his shield straight up in the front
> ranks, swelling his heart with hate, and repel the swift-winging
> death spirits as ardently as he grasps the blazing instant of sun.
> [In addition,] the Spartan is disciplined by necessity in the
> labor of a heavily armed soldier, and should not be noticed
> beyond the missiles as he bears his shield. (Tyrtaeus, fragment
> 8, ed. Diehl).

The Spartan went directly up to his opposite in the enemy infantry and fought in close quarters, gripping the hilt of his swinging sword and probing with his long spear. The same fragment of Tyrtaeus tells the lightly armed, flanking skirmishers to "shower the enemy with your spears and remain close to the heavily girded men."

Although the poet Pindar wrote that "war is honeyed to someone not knowing it, but once tried, it is a thing feared" (Fragment 120, ed. Turyn) and Aristophanes wrote scenes where a saddened wife polished the warrior's shield, sooted in the corner during an era of peace (*Acharnians*, 279), the Greeks esteemed valor in war from *c*. 750 to 550 B.C. (This period is occasionally called the Archaic age of Greek history.) Artists decorated the magnificent pottery from Corinth and Rhodes with a myriad of scenes of warriors and blood. The Chigi Vase, a Proto-Corinthian olpe painted about 640 B.C. by a man known to art historians as the Macmillan Painter shows the prebattle preparations of suiting up in the armor of the day, as well as the actual march of lined soldiers. In an upper panel are two warriors, one putting on his greaves and the other adjusting his corselet. On the ground below them two shields are propped against two spears driven into the soil. Below this scene is a line of nine soldiers, each armed with a crested helmet, corselet, large round shield, and greaves. The shields of the *hoplites* bear heraldic symbols that include a Medusa's head, a flying eagle, the head and horns of a bull, what looks like a flying swan, and a partially obscured lion. They may all be devices from particular clans, as were the clan emblems that appeared on Athenian coinage in the sixth century B.C. The soldiers are sloping their spears, an artistic device indicating that they are marching. In front of the line appears a youthful flute player, who has tossed his head back and is playing the soldiers into battle. From the flute player's right arm hangs what appears to be his instrument case. Two opposing groups, four soldiers against five, portray the actual clash of the *hoplites*. Seven reinforcement soldiers stand by waiting with spears level at their sides, ready to hoist them to their shoulders when the time arrives to engage the enemy.

Tyrtaeus was not the only poet-statesman who urged his countrymen onward to martial exploits. Solon of Athens, sole *archon* in 594 B.C., had the task of averting a brewing civil war and wrote splendid lines that intensified Athenian growing pride and arrogance and distilled Athenian ambitions against Salamis and Aegina. "We march to Salamis, throwing off a burden of disgrace, fighting for that lovely isle" (Solon, fragment 2, ed. Diehl).

In the age when Greek civilization took shape, war was conducted to exterminate an enemy. Response to such an invasion was a war of survival, with little quarter granted or expected. Messenia was not the only state whose independence was eradicated. Greek states in southern Italy and Asia Minor fought each other with annihilation in mind, and several disappeared for good. Enslavement of any survivors was usual, as when Sparta made Helots of the Messenians. Pausanias records the harsh terms the Spartans gave to the conquered Messenians. The Spartans "demanded an oath from them that they would never revolt nor institute any change at all" (*Description of Greece*, IV, 14. 4), which meant that if they did revolt, they would forfeit the normal right of sanctuary in the temples. Further, "the Messenians were required to bring half of all agricultural products to Sparta." As a final insult, "at the funerals of the kings of Sparta as well as their governors, Messenian men had to come to Sparta with their women dressed in black mourning" (*Description of Greece*, IV, 14. 4). Sometimes simple slavery was not practical. To the north, the Thessalians took hostages from civilian populations and promised they would wage unconditional war against rebellion, which meant total massacre rather than slavery.

Within this setting of brutality, certain rules of conduct appeared that sometimes resemble personal codes of chivalry. Delphi's growing political and religious influence encouraged a modicum of decency in secular wars (as contrasted with sacred wars, which were fought to avenge the plundering of temples). Soon it became uncouth to raze towns and cities, and to pollute or poison an enemy's water supply was considered the height of crudity. War involved the general population more at this time than later in Greek history, however, and few conventions protected helpless civilians from plundering or raging armies. In battle, soldiers observed very few rules that could be labeled chivalrous. They callously killed unarmed and wounded warriors, and the defeated gained back only their dead, stripped of all armor and weapons—not the living captives, who would be sold as slaves. Gradually, given rules of decency applied here as well, again probably engendered by the Delphic admonitions. The dead of the conquered were to be neither mutilated nor denied proper burial, and the gods protected any truce held for burying the dead. Heralds and messengers, ambassadors and envoys were sacred to the gods. Other conventions of war are surprising, given the surrounding chaos and blood lust. Tradition records a custom that prevailed during the innumerable wars fought between Corinth and Megara; as Plutarch notes, "Corinth was constantly plotting to gain control of Megara" (*Moralia: Greek Questions*, 295B). The custom was that

> nobody harmed anybody working in the fields, and if anyone was captured, he needed merely to pay a certain known ran-

som. The captors gained the ransom after setting the man free, not before. The man who captured a prisoner took him to his home, shared salt and food with him, and sent him home.
[Plutarch, *Moralia: Greek Questions,* 295C]

Little softness remains in the accounts of the wars between Sparta and Argos, between Delphi and Crisa, north of the Gulf of Corinth (Crisa being destroyed in the First Sacred War, dated 595–586 B.C.), and between organized Thessaly and Phocis, Locris and Thebes.

In spite of their declining importance, the cavalry were the elite forces of the embryonic *polis.* Sometimes horsemen were employed with telling effect, as in the Lelantine War waged between Chalcis and Eretria (both on the island of Euboea) around 700 B.C. A religious ceremony fossilized at Eretria commemorated an earlier cavalry troop and military power that numbered "three thousand *hoplites,* six hundred horsemen, and sixty chariots" (Strabo, *Geography,* X, l. 10). Otherwise chariots did not appear except in religious processions and in the races at athletic festivals. The prestige of cavalry continued in the Peloponnesus, but lines of heavily armed foot soldiers that could withstand cavalry charge fought the decisive and sharp battles. The stirrup would not be introduced for a long time, and a cavalry charge against the wall of men in the front rank of the phalanx was sure disaster. All it guaranteed was the death of the horse and the vaulting of the rider.

The Chigi Vase shows how the *hoplite* parried and dueled with his nine-foot spear against his immediate foe, while he covered his fellow *hoplite's* unshielded side. Behind him, rank after rank of foot soldiers armored like the *hoplite* were ready to come into position, adding their weight and weaponry as support to the front line and impact on the enemy line. This kind of battle required skill with the spear and sword, firm discipline, and simple strength, and Argos excelled first in phalanx warfare, to be followed shortly by Sparta. An often quoted epigram, supposedly issued by the oracle at Delphi, reflects how good Argos had been in *hoplite* pitched battles. Megara had asked Apollo who might be better warriors than Megara. The god replied:

Of all the fertile soils, that of Pelasgian Argos is best, Thessalian horses are the best, Spartan women are the finest, the best men are those who drink from the waters of the lovely Arethusa in Chalcis. But even better than all these are the men who live betwixt Tiryns and Arcadia, wealthy in sheep, the linen-corseleted

Argives, prongs of battle. You Megarians are neither third, nor twelfth, nor in any account or numbering. [*Greek Anthology,* XIV, 73, with a short version in Strabo, *Geography,* X, 1. 13]

Citizens able to equip themselves with this full set of armor depicted in the Chigi Vase would provide an elite that replaced the poorly mastered cavalry. In the seventh and sixth centuries B.C., however, set and pitched battles between *hoplite* phalanxes were rather rare, except between Sparta and Argos. Apparently few other *poleis* had many *hoplites;* the motives and purposes of warfare involved the general population. The wars were lengthy and destroyed life and property. Every inhabitant took part as he was able to arm himself, and masses of ill-organized, lightly armed troops went into battle with an occasional sword, spear, bow, sling, or load of rocks to throw at the enemy. Certain *poleis* did quite well with archers and slingers, and these arms of the military became important in their own right in succeeding generations. Such warfare was utterly destructive, and it won battles at fantastic cost, but the experience it taught the Greek states in the art of war gained them far-flung overseas settlements and the crucial victory over Persia.

Hoplites were the normal heavily armed infantry of the classical Greek states. Once the effective and simple tactical unit, the tightly packed phalanx, had been devised, Greek warfare became extraordinarily rigid for about three hundred years. The phalanx was the best fighting formation of the seventh through the fourth centuries B.C., and with this unit Greek soldiers held their own even against Near Eastern kings. It was the well-tested and superbly oiled Athenian phalanx that defeated massive Persian forces at Marathon (490 B.C.) to everyone's surprise—including the Spartans, who had arrived too late to participate. The infantrymen within the *hoplite* phalanx were individuals who had sufficient property to equip themselves with armor, but who did not have the wealth to maintain horses. The development of body armor provides some evidence for the development of the phalanx, since the bronze-plated corselet seems to be Hellenic, and was not used in the Near East. The bronze-plated corselet, which was found at Argos (dated to *c.* 720 B.C.), consisted of a breastplate, backplate, and slotted attachments on the sides, and it is the first example of the full armor later typical of the *hoplite.* The grave of an Argolid warrior also produced a sophisticated helmet, complete with a crest. For two centuries *hoplites* wore bronze corselets, which went out of fashion shortly before the Persian wars.

Later additions included a helmet, with cheek and nasal pieces, and bronze greaves for the shins. The iron sword was short and straight. The spear was about nine feet long, and the warrior held it in his hand for thrusting. In addition, he fastened a heavy bronze or bull-hide shield, usually elliptical or circular, to his left arm with an inner armband, and he gripped it by a handle fitted into the inner rim of the shield.

Greek armies were armed alike and fought alike, and a battle was decided by weight of numbers. It was generally good practice to meet an invading army as close to the walls of the main home town as possible, since this would afford a haven of retreat in case of defeat. However, this often meant losing the best farmlands of the *polis,* and so the native force would advance to a point close to a known boundary and meet the enemy on a level area suited for phalanx combat. In rough or mountainous country the phalanx was helpless and could easily be scattered and defeated, so the opposing generals selected ground that would support the clash of phalanxes, front line to front line. With pushing and shoving, the phalanx battle was a tug-of-war in reverse, and the army that gave way first automatically lost. Once their lines had been broken, individual soldiers ran away from the battlefield as fast as they could. The sign of submission was a general asking the enemy commander for a truce to bury his dead. The lumbering formation was unable to pursue the losers, and cavalry was little used until the fourth century B.C. Yet losses of the losing army were heavy compared with the number of men killed or wounded in the victorious army. After breaking and running, the fleeing *hoplite* was vulnerable from behind, and many were killed in the rout before the defeated general asked for terms.

Training was important for performing the strenuous tasks required of *hoplites.* Only Sparta constantly promoted the rigor of exercise, with the result that her athlete-soldiers formed the best army in the Greek world by 500 B.C. It is no surprise to learn that Spartans were proficient in the sports pursued in the numerous athletic meetings held after 776 B.C. (the traditional date of the first Olympic games); the military as well as religious setting of those games was fundamental. Boxing, wrestling, throwing the javelin, and the other competitions were all part of primitive warfare and the basic art of survival. The earliest description of athletic competition comes from Homer (*Iliad,* XXIII, 262 ff.) in which horses and racing predominate; however, the contest is held in honor of

Patroclus, who has been recently killed. Throughout Greek history athletic competition has customarily been linked with lulls in war, both to display skill further and to employ idle energies. Prizes like "a fair woman of flawless working with her hands" (*Iliad*, XXIII, 263), exquisitely worked bronze tripods, gold, and the like appealed to soldiers from the time of Homer to Alexander the Great. Although little evidence survives for the existence of Greek games before Roman times, one inscription from Sparta records how ball teams were drawn from the *obai*, with at least fourteen members per team. This particular inscription trumpets how the team "won the competition for the Obai without drawing a bye" (*Inscr. Sparta Museum*, 400, in Harris, *Sport in Greece and Rome*). Dating from the first century A.D., the inscription registers a tradition going back much earlier into Spartan history.

The Growing Threat from the East

As the Persian Empire expanded its dominion into both western Asia Minor and Egypt (after 550 B.C.), Greek soldiers who had formerly been mercenaries with Egyptian and Lydian kings sought new patrons in the independent tyrannies of mainland Greece. The soldiers brought back with them techniques observed in the Near East, particularly the wise combination of infantry and cavalry, and skill in besieging cities. When the Persian king, Darius I, conducted his campaign into Scythian lands north of the Danube (*c.* 515-512 B.C.), he employed a fleet manned by Greeks and Phoenicians to transport supplies and men to the mouth of the Danube. The Persian king feared the Scythians, who threatened the growing empire, more than he did the disorganized Greek states, and he also had several scores to settle with the nomadic Scythians, who had, according to Herodotus, once caused havoc in western and central Asia Minor. "Darius collected an army to overrun the Scythians, to take revenge upon them" (Herodotus, *Histories,* IV, 4). The Persian army included Greeks from subject cities in Asia Minor, and they provided the Persians with their own skills. Mandrocles, an architect from Samos, constructed a bridge (probably like a pontoon bridge using barges) across the Bosporus. Darius I was so pleased that he gave Mandrocles "ten of everything" (Herodotus, *Histories,* IV, 88). Another bridge was thrown over the Danube, and the huge army of seven hundred thousand men, including cavalry, and six hundred ships with crews advanced deep into what is now the Ukraine of southern Russia. (Herodotus, *Histories,* IV, 87; however, Herodotus' numbers may have been inflated). Supply lines became too long and the Scythians harassed the Persian forces, with telling effect. Darius had to return to Asia without a settlement or conquest of Scythian country, but the Persians had established their rule over Thrace. The Greek states to the south were oblivious to long-range Persian designs for conquest in the West, even though Persia's motives had become clear some years earlier when a Persian force had enslaved a Greek settlement in Cyrenaica far to the west of Egypt. The Libyans and Greeks "paid no attention to Darius" (Herodotus, *Histories,* IV, 167).

The Scythians realized their danger after the Persian army departed, and they somehow managed to unite the warring tribes to the north in a defensive alliance. After making a raid across the Bosporus in vengeance for the Persian devastation of their country, the Scythians sent ambassadors to Sparta "to form an alliance. The Scythians agreed to invade Media [on the eastern end of the Black Sea] and asked the Spartans to march up country from Ephesus, and the armies would meet" (Herodotus, *Histories,* VI, 84). Apparently Sparta made no move, even though the Persians were conquering more states. Naxos in the Aegean Islands "requested" Persia to intervene in an internal squabble (*c.* 500 B.C.). The time was growing close when the Greek mainland would come under direct attack. Greece was known to be totally disunited, and the Spartans had proved their unwillingness to march beyond the Peloponnesus, where they had established dominance.

In the meantime, Greek states were learning from the military expertise brought back by soldiers and sailors formerly employed in the Near East. Cleomenes, king of Sparta (*c.* 520–*c.* 490 B.C.), became a master tactician by introducing ruthless and effective practices into Greek warfare. He coordinated a three-pronged attack on Attica in 506 B.C., and he violated the usual war customs by massacring troops from Argos "while they were taking a meal, following the Herald's signal, and Cleomenes killed an even greater number of Argives who had taken sanctuary in the Grove of Argus" (Herodotus, *Histories,* VI, 78). The Spartan king gained his victory (495 B.C.) at Sepeia, located near Argos, through a surprise assault, not a set battle. A good general could adapt the phalanx and use it flexibly, but most commanders chose to follow conservative, textbook battle plans in which phalanxes met in the traditional line-to-line clashes.

But Cleomenes could not capture the citadel of Argos, since the art of building fortifications had vastly improved after 550 B.C. The skill of defense had become stronger than that of offense, and Greek cities proved they could withstand lengthy sieges. Even the Persians, experienced and artful in sapping walls and using siege ramps for wall assault, could not take the final defenses at Naxos in 499 B.C., and they withdrew, leaving the Naxians inside their impregnable fortress. By 500 B.C., the walls of Greek citadels were usually about six feet thick, with chased (grooved) stone on both sides, and rubble stuffed in between. Like earlier Mycenaean walls, the Greek walls of the sixth century B.C. generally had no mortar, and the stones were cut precisely to fit, sometimes with curving sides and concave and convex thicknesses.

The armed forces of Greek *poleis* were quite small, by both modern standards and comparison with the masses of men the Persian Empire could raise for battle. The system of the Spartan phalanx, in which each soldier was both an Equal and a *hoplite,* exhibited its own peculiarities distinct from other Greek states. In the Battle of Plataea (479 B.C.) during the Persian wars, Sparta sent five thousand *hoplites* attended by five thousand *perioikoi,* divided into five groups by territorial origin. On the other hand, Athens organized her *hoplites* into ten tribal regiments, and divided the (generally insignificant) cavalry force into two units, each led by two cavalry commanders. Unlike Sparta, where the Equals served in the army from youth through the age of sixty, Athens required young men between the ages of eighteen and twenty and men over fifty only to serve as garrisons, and then only in time of great stress or war. Historians are uncertain about the actual size of the Athenian army, although Thucydides writes that Athens "possessed an army of thirteen thousand *hoplites* as well as sixteen thousand in garrisons and in Athens" (*Histories,* II, 13) in 431 B.C. Unfortunately, he muddles these statistics by adding that "this was the number of men on guarding duty in case of invasion, consisting of the youngest and oldest recruits and the *metics* who had armor." It appears that Sparta had a smaller army to put in the field but felt much more confident of its capabilities, while Athenian land forces were less reliable and more willing to guard frontier posts than engage in battle. The only standing military force in fifth-century B.C. Athens was sixteen hundred archers, hired as mercenaries from outside Athens. They performed duties similar to those of modern police departments.

The Persian Wars: Phase One

By 500 B.C. Sparta, her army, and her allies in the Peloponnesian League dominated southern Greece. As long as no other state threatened this informal control of the Peloponnesus, Sparta was content not to interfere in the affairs of other *poleis,* although a Spartan force was an important factor in expelling tyranny from Athens in 510 B.C. Meanwhile, problems between subject Greek states on the coast of Asia Minor and their Persian overlords had been building to the point of open revolt in 499 B.C. Because she had the best army in all Greece, the Greek rebels begged Sparta for aid. If we take Herodotus' tale at face value, the leader of the revolt, Aristagoras of Miletus, went in person to Sparta and laid out a bronze map "on which was etched the circumference of the whole world, the whole Sea, and all the rivers" (Herodotus, *Histories,* V, 49), which caused some wonder among the Spartans, who were unfamiliar with such charts or maps. Attempting to persuade the Spartans and their king, Cleomenes, to help the rebellious Greeks, Aristagoras spoke in glowing terms of the easy conquests and ripe plunder waiting for an army like Sparta's. The Milesian tyrant went on to contrast Spartan military ability with that of Persia. The Persians were called "cowardly," while Sparta "had attained the limits of glory in war." On the other hand, the Persians fought "with bow and arrow, a short spear, coming into battle dressed in baggy trousers and floppy peaked hats," and thus were easy to overcome. (The appearance of the Persian soldiers suggested a lack of training, unlike the rigorous exercises in Spartan athletics.) Furthermore, if the Spartans would seize Susa, they "would boldly challenge Zeus in riches" (Herodotus, *Histories,* V, 49). Cleomenes listened with great care to the plea and the colorful promises of easy wealth and quick victory. The Spartan king requested three days to think the request over and consult with the Spartan Elders. On the third day Cleomenes asked Aristagoras, "How many days' march would it be from the Aegean to the Great King?" The clever Milesian answered too clearly, "Three months' journey up country." The retort was sharp: "De-

part Sparta before sundown. For you are speaking nothing acceptable to the Spartans, requesting to lead them three months' journey
from the sea" (Herodotus, *Histories,* V, 49–50). Aristagoras shortly
tried to bribe Cleomenes to change his mind by raising his gift to a
fantastic fifty *talents,* but to no avail. The Spartan reply of "Too far"
was final; the disappointed Milesian then went to Athens to present
his plea.

The appeal went as before: booty could be had for the taking; the
Persians used neither the good shield nor the long spear, in contrast
to the Athenian helmet, spear, greaves, armor, and jabbing spear.
Added to his urging was Aristagoras' statement that "since Miletus
was settled by Athenian colonists, it would be fitting that Athens
should save that city, given the great power of Athens." The Athenians were persuaded, and Herodotus writes:

> It seems much more easy to deceive many people together
> than one man alone. He was unable to persuade Cleomenes
> the Spartan by himself, but was able to inveigle thirty thou-
> sand Athenians. Accordingly, they were persuaded to a fault,
> and voted to send twenty ships to aid the Ionians. These ships
> were the beginning of great troubles for Greeks and barbar-
> ians. [*Histories,* V, 97]

The city of Eretria contributed five *triremes,* and the allied fleet of
twenty-five ships came together at Miletus with high hopes of success. But local Persian levies poured into the defenses, and after
a signal defeat of the rebels and the death of a prominent Eretrian
general, the Athenians withdrew from the alliance and sailed home.
They gained some limited victories, however. "The Athenians sailed
to aid the Ionians with twenty *triremes*, marched to Sardis, captured
all of Sardis excepting the king's fortress, and afterwards withdrew
to Miletus" (Charon of Lampsacus, quoted in Plutarch, *Moralia: On
the Malice of Herodotus,* 861D). Although Athens had made a tactical and diplomatic retreat, Persia would not forget that Athens
had dispatched twenty ships to succor rebel Greeks.

Ships, Fleets, and Naval Power

Ships and fleets had become important in Greek warfare by 500 B.C.,
and Herodotus tells stories of the numerous seaborne expeditions
that preceded the great outburst of Greek naval power in the Persian
wars. The ancient bitterness between Greece and Phoenicia sharpened

even more when the Persian king sequestered the Phoenician fleets as a main portion of his armada. Sidon and Tyre came under Persian rule and contributed skilled seamen, who took part in the expedition against Scythia, and numerous Greek sailors from the cities of western Asia Minor also manned ships in the fleet.

The Phoenicians innovated from the form of the *pentekonter* more rapidly than the Greek states. After experimenting with *biremes* (in which one bank of oarsmen sat above another), more advanced Phoenician and Greek shipwrights began building the *trireme* in greater numbers after 550 B.C. But the most reliable account, that of Thucydides, makes clear that Greek states employed the *pentekonters* whenever they had navies, until "the expedition of Xerxes. Athens, Aegina, and some others possibly had some ships, but generally they were *pentekonters*" (*History,* I, 14). Herodotus' language is somewhat vague when he writes of ships, speaking of *triremes* to distinguish them from the normal vessels, which suggests that the *trireme* was in the distinct minority as a Greek warship before the battle of Salamis (479 B.C.). Previously, rulers like Polycrates of Samos (525 B.C.) had "a hundred *pentekonters* and a thousand archers" (Herodotus, *Histories,* III, 39), while Darius I had a fleet "of two hundred *triremes*" (*Histories,* V, 32); use of *triremes* seemed to be customary within the Persian-Phoenician navy quite a while before *triremes* became common in Greece.

Ships in the homeric poems were undecked and open, probably with various numbers of oarsmen. A galley pictured on a cup from Eleusis (*c.* 825 B.C.) shows that Greek ships had a pointed ram on the prow, indicating that sea battles were won by ships poking holes in the sides of their enemies. The oarsmen needed precise timing, and it was not long before someone added a deck where archers could be positioned (as in Polycrates' ships) to mow down the enemy. This early deck covered only part of the ship, running from stem to stern over the centerline but not from board to board. A space was left open along the sides, and the oarsmen rowed from that level, dangerously exposed to arrows and spears from an attacking ship. A little later, naval planners devised a logical solution: they added a lower deck for rowers' benches; when battle erupted, the oarsmen plied their oars below deck level. Some kind of panel probably closed the lower oar holes in choppy seas. Instead of using the oarlocks common in modern rowboats, Greek oarsmen worked their oars against tholepins shaped like miniature wooden pennants, as a cup in the Eleusis Museum shows. The oars were fastened with leather strapped loosely over the tholepins so that the oar would not be lost if an oarsman lost his hold.

Rigging consisted of a single, broad square sail; pottery after 600 B.C. shows how the sails were shortened. Sailors looped a series of lines around the sail and squinched it up around the yard, like a modern venetian blind being raised. Later sayings, such as those in Aristophanes' plays, delineate the normal practice of sailing and what ships did with their limited rigging. As the phrase "employing the sail's edge, with brailed sail" (*Frogs*, 999–1000) indicates, only the canvas at the end of the yard was used in a strong wind. If a squall was in the offing, the seaman was ordered to "slack the sheet out," but as the storm abated, the order was "to play out the ropes," and later, when the wind was moderate, he allowed the "brailing on the yardarm out a bit" until the sail extended to its full size everywhere (Aristophanes, *Knights,* 430–441). The wind was either astern or at the quarter, since Greek ships sailed with difficulty into the wind. A fourth-century B.C. work describes this limited tacking rather carefully. The oars "that steered" the boat (the two rudders) could not "counteract a powerful wind, but can when there is a weak wind." Sailors then "reduce" the sail in the stern exposed to the wind and the wind "moves the vessel forward, but the oar for steering converts it into a favorable wind fighting it, using the sea as fulcrum. Likewise the sailors fight the wind, leaning their bodies against it" (Pseudo-Aristotle, *Mechanica,* VII, 851b6 Morrison/Williams).

By 600 B.C. fleets of the maritime Greek states consisted of improved *pentekonters.* Shipwrights had straightened out the prow and eliminated an earlier sweeping curve. They swept up the stern into a series of wooden plumes, a design that looked like a huge parody of a hand fan. Both the ram on the prow and the stern ornament were chopped off defeated galleys and taken back to the victorious states, where they became trophies of war. The major warship had twenty-four oarsmen to each side, and two seamen controlled the two rudders on either side at the stern. The *pentekonter* was sleek and speedy, but it was neither particularly easy to maneuver nor very seaworthy. Again the logical innovation occurred. Shipbuilders realized they could place the same number of rowers on two decks, one slightly at an angle above the other, and thus shortening the length of the ship by one-third. The first piece of evidence of the

newer *pentekonters* comes from Phoenicia, under Assyrian rule
(*c.* 690 B.C.), but soon Greek ships were built in the two-banked
style. The double-banked *pentekonter* was more maneuverable and
gave enemy ships much less of a target to ram. Meanwhile, pirate
shipwrights had devised a version of the double-tiered *pentekonter*
that suited their own trade. Called the *hemiolia* ("one-and-half-er"),
the pirate vessel was designed so that some of the crew rowing in
the upper bank could leave their oars to board the luckless quarry.
The ship had a space between the mast and stern for stowing the sail,
and a dozen hands were available to load the spoils.

But it was not the double-tiered *pentekonter* that won the day for
the Greek allies in the Persian wars. Shipwrights apparently saw the
advantage of banking the rowers to gain power in a given stroke, and
the result was the *trireme* ("three-er"). The big advantage of the
trireme was that it allowed the oarsmen to row sitting down. Rather
than simply adding more men to each oar, Greek shipwrights chose
the three-banked arrangement. The third level of oarsmen was placed
at an angle above the second tier, along with an extended outrigger
that projected from either side laterally from the gunwales. The hull
of the *trireme* remained as in older *pentekonters,* and the added
power, speed, and ability to maneuver made the *trireme* mistress of
sea warfare after 550 B.C.

One of the most vexing problems in classical studies is the design
of the *trireme.* A widely accepted theory suggests that only one
opening accommodated the three oars, while another theory points
to a three-banked arrangement, following logically from earlier
developments from two-banked *pentekonters* (*biremes*). The three-
banked system has more weight behind it, both from the vantage
point of logic and evidence, and it is generally favored by modern
scholars (especially Lionel Casson). The account that follows thus
assumes that the *trireme* used three banks of oarsmen, positioned
one above another. The handbook *Greek Oared Ships* by Morrison
and Williams, cited under "Ships and Triremes" in the bibliography
to this chapter, conveniently lists the ancient evidence for Greek
warships.

From measuring dockyard facilities in ancient Piraeus, archaeologists have determined the dimensions and length of the largest
triremes. The ship was about twenty feet wide and about one hundred twenty-five feet long, about the same length as the earlier
pentekonter, with its twenty-four rowers and rudder man lined up

along a side. The freeboard of a *trireme* was about eight feet, and the ship had a draft of three feet, so that the vessel could be drawn up on a beach at night or transported overland on rollers. Thus the lowest bank of oarsmen rowed a foot and a half above the water-line, and the ports were fitted with sleeves of leather that kept the oar in place and the sea out. Inscriptional evidence indicates that twenty-seven rowers on each side sat on benches above and slightly forward of the seats below and worked their oars over the gunwale. The third tier sat on benches constructed on top of the gunwale, and the oarsmen sat slightly forward of the seats of the second bank. The space between all the rowers was about three feet, more or less set by the size of the human body. The rowers on the top tier worked their oars against tholepins set in the outrigger, which projected three feet from the side of the vessel. The strokes of the oarsmen on the upper bank required the most strength, since their oars struck the water at the sharpest angle. Since the hull swept up into the overhang, it squeezed some seats from the lower two ranks, but left some extra room on the top tier. Thus there were thirty-one oars-men on each side of the upper bank. Not including the two rudders, the fully manned *trireme* carried one hundred seventy oars. The *trireme* was arranged so that the oars for the three tiers were almost the same length, simplifying oar manufacture, and the ship could carry thirty spares.

The *trireme* carried a crew of two hundred, which did not include any marines or archers. In the heyday of Athens' maritime power (*c.* 480–400 B.C.), the ship had twenty-five officers and hands and five commissioned officers added to the one hundred seventy oars-men. Consequently, it was very difficult for an ordinary Greek *polis* to build and man one of these ships, or maintain a sizable fleet of *triremes.* A good fleet ran to about two hundred vessels, which meant about thirty-four thousand rowers, a rather steep number for most Greek states. As naval experts are well aware, it is extremely expensive to build ships and keep them seaworthy, and this fact was especially true before the huge steel and aluminum battleships and aircraft carriers came into prominence. In addition, military service in the land army generally had far more prestige, and naval duties were looked down on as second class. Men in the *polis* who could afford the cost of a suit of armor always chose the opportunity to march and fight, rather than sweat on a rower's bench. Athens did not often use slaves as rowers, since a large class of landless citizens (the *thetes*) was more than willing to serve in the fleet. Indeed, in the fifth century B.C., Athens rarely employed slaves in her navy except when all other manpower had been exhausted, and even then she did not draft slaves into the navy but promised freedom to those slaves who volunteered for service in the galleys. In general, the oarsmen came from the poorest class in the *polis*, the citizens unable to afford the cost of equipping themselves to fight in the *hoplite* phalanx. Other oarsmen were hired at good fees, with the highest salaries going to those rowing on the top bank, where strength and endurance were necessities. But no whips were ever used on the rowers. The officer who beat time to keep the strokes even and smooth never applied any physical coercion to the oarsmen.

Like the *pentekonter,* the *trireme* had a square sail set on a single mast. The sail was only employed for cruising, as in earlier pirate vessels, and the sail and gear were generally left ashore when the ship was about to engage in battle. The ship carried ballast in the hold, usually gravel, rocks, or sand, to counterbalance the superstructure of the top tier of oarsmen and the short outrigger. In combat, the *trireme* had two major weapons: its ram and the marines on deck. The Greek ram of the fifth century B.C. consisted of a large timber extending forward from the prow, sheathed in bronze with a top made of three prongs and added barbs. This ram was much more effective for tearing jagged holes in the sides of enemy ships than the *pentekonter's* single sharp ram. The Athenians became so adept at naval maneuver that only about fourteen marines were on board each *trireme,* their task being to toss enemy boarders off the ship. Other navies, like that of Corinth, relied less on ramming and had as many as thirty marines on deck for an aggressive boarding.

The *trireme* could, under full power, attain a limited, short-range speed of seven knots and still spin around in an incredibly small circle. Yet a navy based on *triremes* also had drawbacks. Great expense, large manpower expenditure, and the inherent lightness and cramped space on board the ships limited their use to those powers—like Persia and Athens after her lucky find of silver around 480 B.C.—who could pay for and man them, as well as have good field armies. The *trireme* was of no use in bad weather, and it could carry few supplies, requiring frequent ready bases. A fleet of *triremes* going off on a campaign had to hug coastlines, so that the ships could be beached and the men could cook, eat, and sleep ashore. So naval battles always took place within sight of land. The fleet of lightweight *triremes* could never mount an effective naval blockade, although it might bottle up an enemy fleet in a harbor.

Nonetheless, the simultaneous development of *triremes* and the heavily armed *hoplite* armies provided the two tools of war that preserved Greek freedom. The coordination of superbly commanded ships with the powerful *hoplite* armies of Sparta and her allies, together with the skill of Athens, enthusiastic after her victory at Marathon (490 B.C.), allowed the puny *poleis,* somewhat in disarray, to best the sprawling might of Persia. That tale of glory has been recounted ever since in Greek and Western tradition.

The Persian Wars: Phase Two

For a long time, it appeared that the Ionian revolt might succeed, even though Athens had decided not to continue her support. Persian forces were defeated in Cyprus, and the relief fleet was kept out of the Aegean until the Ionian Greeks suffered a series of misjudgments, allowing the Persian-Phoenician ships to arrive in great numbers. As long as the Greek rebels could maintain their fleet and stave off Persian armies (and the Greek soldiers were more than holding their own), the revolt stood good chances of success. The allied Greek fleets assembled in 494 B.C. at Lade, an islet just off the coast of Asia Minor at Miletus. The Persians were marching in numbers, and the Greek strategy was to man the walls of Miletus and collect their fleet, but not field a large land army. The Greeks practiced their maneuvers at sea, demonstrating their skill and ability to fight as a united fleet. Miletus

> gave eighty ships and held the east wing, next were the Prienians with twelve ships, and . . . the Myusians with three vessels. Next to the Myusians were Teians with seventeen ships, with the hundred Chian ships next in the line. . . . The Phocaeans drew up their three ships, followed in the formation by eight ships from Erythrae, and . . . seventy ships from Lesbos. Lastly, the ships of Samos were drawn up, taking the western wing with sixty ships. The fleet of the Ionians numbered all in all three hundred fifty-three *triremes.* [Herodotus, *Histories,* V, 8–14]

The "barbarians mounted a fleet numbering six hundred ships," and yet the Persians were in awe of the smaller fleet with its superior coordination and battle readiness. Persian threats seemed to make little impact on the determined rebels, who continued to plan for the coming battle off Lade. However, when the day of conflict finally arrived, the

> Phoenicians sailed against the Ionian fleet, and the Ionians drew out their fleet in a line to fight them. At that moment, the Samians hoisted their sails and steered home to Samos, excepting eleven ships whose captains refused to obey orders, and they stood firm and fought. The Lesbians, seeing the ships lying next to them in flight, also did the same as the Samians."
> [Herodotus, *Histories,* V, 8–14]

The few Greek ships left cut through the Phoenician vessels, sinking and disabling good numbers until they were overwhelmed. The Battle of Lade doomed the Ionian Revolt, although the Persian king's terms were quite lenient, except for Miletus. Then the king turned his attention west and began plotting revenge against those Greek mainland states that had dared to offer even minimal help.

The complex politics of the Greek states chanced to line up Athens, Sparta, and Corinth as the leading states in mainland Greece opposing Persian rule. Spartan foreign policy since *c.* 540 B.C. had been anti-Persian, and Athenian enthusiasm for giving aid to the Ionians in 499 B.C. had been wholehearted, although internal squabblings pitting pro-Persian politicians against those advocating war soon blunted the enthusiasm. Corinth was drawn into the struggle because Athens had fought a bitter war with Aegina and had hired twenty ships from Corinth at a minimum fee to help in the war. Argos, Sparta's implacable foe, had given volunteers to Aegina in her fight against Athens. Thus when Athens declared a truce in 491 B.C., Aegina's fleet was unavailable to the Persians, and Argos (already declaring herself ready for submission to Persia—what the sources called medizing) had been neutralized.

The Persian expedition of vengeance set out from Cilicia (in the most southeast part of Asia Minor) sometime in the summer of 490 B.C. and went from victory to victory. The Persians burned Naxos and deported the people, while in other Greek islands the Persians drafted men into service, collecting children as hostages. On reaching the island of Euboea, the Persians demanded surrender from both Carystos and Eretria (the latter sent five ships to aid the ill-fated Ionian revolt). Both resisted and were captured. The Persians burned the temples of Eretria and again deported the people (like the Naxians, probably to settle somewhere in northern Mesopotamia).

The Persian fleet thus obtained a base close to Attica, and supplies for the Persian army could be ferried easily across the narrow straits. Shortly, the Persians landed their troops at the bay of Marathon; Hippias, the exiled tyrant thrown out of Athens in 510 B.C., probably advised them in this action. He, in turn, expected some support from certain groups of Athenian nobles who were growing restive under the innovative constitutional reforms enacted in Attica after 508–507 B.C. The Persian forces probably numbered about twenty-five thousand at the most, even though Herodotus writes that they were "very great in number and well equipped" and that the Persian fleet contained "six hundred *triremes*" (*Histories*, VI, 95). The number six hundred seems standard in Herodotus to indicate large fleets. Later writers noted his vague statistics and enlarged the Persian numbers. For example, Cornelius Nepos, a second-rate Roman historian and biographer (*c.* 99–24 B.C.) wrote that "the Persians had five hundred ships, ten thousand cavalry, and two hundred fifty thousand infantry" (*Miltiades*, 4); these figures are completely unbelievable because of the easy deduction of transport of troops and horsemen in a fleet of *triremes* or updated *pentekonters*.

Calculating correctly that the plain favored their cavalry, the Persians deployed horse and infantry and waited for a possible attack from Athens, reasoning that if it did not come, the Persian army would march into the plain around Athens. The Persian fleet could then sail around Cape Sunion, no longer loaded with horses and supplies, and be ready for any Athenian ships at Phalerum or in the newly fortified harbor at Piraeus. Through this sound planning the Persians outflanked the Athenians and provided for the two major contingencies. But neither the Persians nor the exiled Hippias had counted on the resolution and military skill of Athens' leaders, especially Miltiades.

The Athenian assembly voted to make an advance to Marathon and sent a runner to Sparta (named Pheidippides in the sources), requesting immediate aid. According to the story, he covered the 140 miles in a single day. Unfortunately, the Spartans were celebrating the religious festival of Apollo Carneius and said they would march with the full moon, six days hence, citing a sacred law that forbade wartime operations while the festival was going on. Meanwhile, the Athenian army of ten thousand *hoplites* had marched to the northern foothills of Mount Pentelicus and had seen the plain at Marathon well-populated with Persian infantry, cavalry, and archers. The large force of horsemen controlled the plain, which was flanked by a dry September riverbed on the west and on the south by marshes. No line of infantry could possibly cross the plain openly, since the flanks and the rear of the phalanx would be exposed and attacked by the masses of Persian horsemen. Accordingly, the Athenians encamped in the higher broken ground, which protected them from cavalry attacks.

Miltiades, the commander of the Athenian forces, was an Athenian statesman who had made his mark earlier by opposing Persia and by suggesting that Athens control the northern Aegean ports for protection (in the decade of 490 B.C.). Since the ten generals shared the leadership of the army on succeeding days and four yielded their command to Miltiades, he led five of ten days on campaign.

Athens' problem was the timing of the attack, and Miltiades waited. Soon one thousand *hoplites* from Plataea arrived to reinforce the Athenians, but no Spartans. Some leaders advised staying put until the Spartan *hoplites* could help, but Miltiades saw his chance when some Ionian Greek soldiers snuck through a short message to the Greek army. It said, without explanation, that the Persian cavalry was absent. The Greeks prepared for battle, camping that night in battle order. Miltiades placed Athenians on the right and in the center and put the Plataeans on the left wing of his army. He then lengthened his front line to match that of the Persians, while he thickened the wings with additional ranks—in effect, thinning out the Greek center. Sacrifices were made to the gods, and the omens were favorable. Dawn came, and the Athenians and Plataeans advanced rapidly across the plain as the first light broke, shortly arriving within the range of Persian arrows. "They received the order to charge and advanced against the barbarians at double time," and the Persians thought them insane, as Herodotus observed. "They were rushing at them at top speed, having no cavalry, possessing no archers, being few in number" (*Histories,* VI, 112). The battle lasted a long time, though most *hoplite* clashes were usually sharp and rapidly completed. The two Greek wings, heavily armored and with longer spears than their Persian enemies, cut through the Persian ranks. The Greek center had collapsed under Persian pressure, and the Persians were pursuing when the two victorious Greek wings wheeled and attacked the Persian center from the rear. In the resulting confusion of closely struggling troops, the Persian cavalry, arriving belatedly, could not intervene. The Athenians and Plataeans "chased the Persians in their panic and flight, slicing them to pieces until they reached the beach. Calling for fire, they attacked the ships" and destroyed seven of them (Herodotus, *Histories*, VI, 113). Suspecting treachery, Miltiades marched the jubilant army back to Athens, giving the Persian fleet no opportunity for surprise. After sitting at their benches, resting their oars for a while, the Persian oarsmen (less-than-enthusiastic Ionians) were ordered to row east, leaving Athens intact and her army amazed at the favor of the gods.

Herodotus thus describes the belated arrival of the Spartans:

> Two thousand Spartans arrived at Athens after the full moon, hurrying to be in time, and they came to Attica after leaving Sparta. Having come too late for the battle, they wanted to see the Persians, and going to Marathon, they viewed the corpses. Afterwards they went home, having congratulated the Athenians on their achievement. [*Histories*, VI, 120]

The casualties mirrored the normal results of Greek warfare: the army that lost lost just about everything. Sixty-four hundred of the Persians were slain, while the victorious Athenians and Plataeans lost one hundred ninety-two men.

The Greek phalanx had proved its worth and would continue to demonstrate its superiority over the Persian methods of fighting in the war, which both sides knew would be renewed soon. Persian armor was meager, compared to the Greek bronze-plated cuirass. Greek spears were longer than their barbarian counterparts, and Persian archer contingents had made little dent in the phalanx charging at full speed. Most important in the Athenian-Plataean victory at Marathon, however, was the superb discipline of the *hoplite* phalanx, which kept its running line intact and had enough cohesion to wheel and charge the Persian center from behind at precisely the right moment. Miltiades had led a fighting force small in number, but well trained in infantry marching and fighting in formation. Of course, the phalanx fought with the zeal of men protecting their homes and temples against foreign intrusion.

Such glory was attached to Marathon that later sources raved of the bravery of the Athenians, contrasting it with the slovenly cowardice of the Persians (sources like *History of the Macedonians*, written by the obscure Pompeius Trogus in the time of Augustus and abridged by the even more obscure Marcus Justin in the third century A.D.). It was Athens' finest hour. Justin/Trogus wrote, "So great was the courage and daring of the Athenians as they fought that one might have believed there were men on the Greek side and a herd of cattle on the other" (Justin/Trogus, *Macedonians*, II, 9). Naturally, Athens was swelling with pride, especially since she had bested the Persians in the field without the help of the presumably better Spartan *hoplites*. This somewhat overweening attitude found its fullest and most eloquent expression in *Persians* (472 B.C.), Aeschylus' tribute to Athens and her new glory. He celebrated the later naval victory at Salamis (479 B.C.) in particular, but many passages could as well apply to the joy Athenians felt after their victory at Marathon. "Not for flight, did the Greeks thereupon raise their vaunted paean, but for the beginning of the fray, bursting with heart and courage" (*Persians*, 392–394).

Darius I realized that his newly regained control over the Ionian seaboard would be very insecure without the conquest and sub-mission of the Greek states on the mainland. After the signal defeat of his forces at Marathon, it was clear that such a conquest could not be achieved with a small army carried by sea to Greece. The Persian king immediately began preparations for a full-scale invasion— issuing decrees for the training of infantry, cavalry, and corps of archers and sequestering provisions for transports and warships. Supplies were collected and oarsmen drafted. Fortunately for the Greeks, the invasion had to be postponed because Egypt revolted in 487 B.C. and the Great King died sometime in the following year. Xerxes, his successor, reconquered Egypt in 485 B.C. and con-tinued the preparations for the invasion of Greece. The Persian fleet sailed without opposition in the northern Aegean, since Thrace was already under Persian rule. Earlier, the rulers of Thessaly had offered Persia the assistance of good horsemen for the coming in-vasion, and in 483–481 B.C. the Persians dug a canal across one of the peninsulas jutting from Thrace for the express purpose of giving the fleet a protected entrance to points south on the coast of main-land Greece. The *poleis* of Greece had ample warning of Persian intentions and time to prepare.

Athenian politics had in the meantime been varying from the yearly chaos of ostracism to calm appraisal of the coming battles for survival. In 493 B.C., Themistocles was elected eponymous *archon*. Under his urging, the new fortifications at Piraeus were begun. Elected *strategos* ("general") of his tribe in 490 B.C., he con-tinued to exercise an important political influence, which was tem-pered by his foresight of the coming whirlwind and fired by intense ambition. He manipulated enough votes to have his political opponents ostracized and emerged as the leader of Athens by the time a new vein of silver worth one hundred *talents* was discovered in the state mines at Laurion. In 482 B.C. debate in the assembly was finally resolved in favor of Themistocles' suggestion: build a fleet to make Athens' navy the strongest in Greek waters, numbering two hundred *triremes*. The keels for one hundred new *triremes* were soon laid down over opposition advocating that the new wealth be distributed among the citizen body of Athens. But swaying the assembly was a more important object. It was known that Aegina was ready to medize, which would put the Aeginitan fleet at the disposal of the Persians and neutralize the Athenian fleet. Athens, consequently, had to build more ships, both to meet the Persians and to protect herself from Aegina's moves of revenge. The new Athenian fleet was to be the salvation of Greece.

Greek *poleis* did not look to Athens for leadership against Persia, however, but to Sparta, whose prestige stood high. She had soundly defeated Argos in 495 B.C., and her Peloponnesian alliance was loyal and cohesive. Athens had too many enemies, her ambitions against neighboring states were too well publicized, and her victory at Marathon was thought to buy her time rather than to register her as a major land power in Greece. Xerxes had not sent tokens of submission to Sparta or Athens. Sparta had consistently opposed Persia, and Athens was slated for annihilation as a result of her victory at Marathon. The two states were marked for destruction, according to the replies of the realistic oracle at Delphi to inquiries. Delphi decided to remain neutral, and her warning to Sparta was cast most gloomily. "Sparta will, in necessity, be overthrown by the barbarians, or a king die," is Herodotus' summary of the Oracle's answer. He records it in full:

> You who dwell in spacious Lacedaemon will either be vanquished by men sprung from the seed of Perseus, or Lacedaemonia will mourn a king of the seed of Heracles. Neither the strength of bulls or lions can stand against him, strength pitted against strength. He has the might of Zeus and will not be stayed until he gains one of these things. [*Histories,* VII, 220]

The Oracle at Delphi had no illusions about the great size of the Persian forces, going so far as to compare Xerxes' army with the strength of Zeus himself. To the Athenians, the oracle was even more blunt and advised they flee before it was too late. "Go to the reaches of the earth, leaving your homes and lofty summits of your city fashioned like a wheel. Fire and swift Ares destroy it, driving the Syrian chariot" (Herodotus, *Histories,* VII, 140). The answer so stunned the Athenians that they asked for a second answer as suppliants to Pythian Apollo. The priestess' second reply was only slightly more encouraging and was couched in ambiguity:

> Pallas Athena is not able to move Olympian Zeus with entreaty and counsel of wisdom. Far-seeing Zeus, however, bequeaths a wall of wood to the Triton-born goddess, alone impregnable, which will save you and your children. Remain not waiting for the horsemen and foot soldiers coming in hosts from Asia, but turn your back and withdraw. Verily, a day will arrive when you can meet them. Divine Salamis, you will cause the death of women's sons, whether Demeter is either scattered or gathered in. [Herodotus, *Histories,* VII, 141]

Interpretation of this caused great debate, with some actually thinking the "wooden walls" meant that hedges should surround the Acropolis. Themistocles persuaded most Athenians that the ships recently built were Athens' wooden walls, and Delphi's shrewd assessment of Athens' sea power suggested that the battle site would be Salamis. To Argos, Delphi suggested total neutrality: "Hated by your neighbors, beloved by the gods immortal, rest your spears, guard well, and look after your head. The head will save the body" (Herodotus, *Histories,* VII, 148). Athens and Sparta would lead any coalition of Greek *poleis* against Persia, both from necessity and from prestige in arms. The two arms of Spartan *hoplites* and Athenian ships had to be coordinated.

In late 481 B.C. representatives of the *poleis* choosing to fight Persia met in Sparta, invited by Sparta and supported by Athens. The basic question was who would lead the alliance. Most states refused to serve under Athenian command, either on land or at sea, so the Spartans were given nominal direction of the allied fleet and firm direction of the land operations in the war. Argos agreed to a truce with Sparta if she could have half of the command, equalling Sparta; she was offered a third. Argos refused and did not join the allies. States within the alliance agreed to end wars among themselves, and the simmering conflict between Athens and Aegina was terminated. Envoys were sent to Greek states in the West and Corcyra agreed to help, but the Corcyrean fleet of sixty ships ar-

rived too late. The alliance asked Gelon of Syracuse to join, but he
found excuses for neutrality and even thought of submitting to
Persia should the war go badly for the Greeks. Gelon sent an observer to Delphi with money to be tendered to the Persians, along
with the tokens of earth and water symbolizing submission, if they
bested the Greeks.

In the spring of 480 B.C. the allied states met again at the Isthmus
of Corinth. Sparta and her league were the fonts of directive power,
but she did not seek to extend her dominion over the allied states.
For example, the command of the allies did not pass automatically
to Sparta, but was subject to the will of the assembled delegates.
The new organization called itself the League of the Greeks, modeled
after Sparta's Peloponnesian League. Thirty-one states were recorded
as fighting in the alliance, a small number compared to the total
number of *poleis*.

A call for help came from the rulers of Thessaly, who had the best
cavalry force in the Greek world. The league decided to send some
forces to Thessaly, just ahead of the invading Persians; but when the
Greeks arrived and joined the Thessalian cavalry, they found they
could not hold several passes at once. Shortly they retreated south,
giving the Persians Thessaly and all points south to the Malian
Gulf. But the allies decided to make a stand at the narrow pass
of Thermopylae, supported by the allied fleet of 271 ships at
Artimisium, covering the entrance of the Euboic Gulf. A vanguard of
about seven thousand *hoplites* positioned themselves at Thermopylae,
to be joined later by other Greek contingents. Although the Greek
navy took up its position without delay, the troops moved north
slowly, and the advance guard of the full army, commanded by
Leonidas, a king of Sparta, made the stand at Thermopylae. The
fleet and army met the full brunt of the Persian forces in this
single engagement in 480 B.C.

There is little doubt that the Xerxes' army was huge, but the
staggering number that Herodotus gives is beyond belief. "Thus
Xerxes, son of Darius, led 5,283,220 men to Sepias and Thermopylae" (*Histories*, VII, 186). Half a million men is within reason, a figure that the listings in the *History of the Macedonians*
support. "Xerxes had armed about seven hundred thousand of his
own men and about three hundred thousand of his auxiliaries," and
the fighting men taking part in the campaign were about half of
each (Justin/Trogus, *Macedonians*, II, 10). The size of the army

made transport difficult, and feeding almost impossible. Command of such an enormous force was ragged; Xerxes could not match the tightly coordinated command that the Greek league employed and that the Spartans implemented smoothly from long experience. Although the Greeks knew they were outnumbered in cavalry (after Thessaly medized, allied cavalry was of little importance), in infantry (the largest force of *hoplites* the Greeks could field ran to about forty thousand heavily armed infantry and about seventy thousand lightly armed troops), and in ships (the Greek fleet numbered about four hundred *triremes* and a smaller number of *pentekonters*), Greek leaders knew their forces would be effective fighting against larger numbers in enclosed or limited spaces. The strategic planning leading to the fighting at Thermopylae and Salamis was founded on this principle.

At Thermopylae, Leonidas and his three hundred Spartans, one thousand Lacedaemonians, seven hundred Thespians, four hundred Thebans, smaller levies from Phocis and Locris, and miscellaneous troops from around Sparta (possibly some Helots) faced the seeming sea of men that arrived and encamped north of the pass. A lone scout reported to Xerxes that he had seen a mere three hundred or so men guarding the frontal positions, who ignored him as he watched them. They were Spartans "who were in the middle of some gymnastic exercises, while some others were combing their hair" (Herodotus, *Histories,* VII, 208). When the Great King launched his attack, he saw his men mowed down by the Spartan formation defending the fifty-foot wide defile. Even when the Spartans retreated for a time and the masses of Persians chased them with much clamor, the Spartans calmly wheeled and mowed them down as before. Heaps of Persian corpses littered the entrance to the pass, and the praised Immortals, the best of Xerxes' soldiers, had been unable to dent the defense. Two days later a Greek traitor brought word of a mountain path that led around to the rear of the Spartan lines; Xerxes then sent men scurrying across the hills, causing the Phocian rear guard to withdraw. (Leonidas had known of the path, and had posted men to defend it.) The Spartans and remaining Thespians sold their lives dearly. When the battle was over, about twenty thousand of Xerxes' best infantrymen lay dead, while the Greek loss totaled about three thousand men slain. So great was Xerxes' fury that he "ordered Leonidas' head cut off and fixed to a pole" (Herodotus, *Histories,* VII, 238). The Greek fleet had also done well, although it was forced to retreat once Thermopylae had fallen. Storms had destroyed two hundred of the Persian *triremes,* and the Athenians had distinguished themselves by capturing or sinking another one hundred of the ships in several engagements. The Persian fleet still outnumbered that of the Greeks, but the naval battles at Artimisium proved Athenian mastery of naval maneuvers and Greek superiority in the narrow straits, where the larger numbers of Persian vessels bunched together.

The league decided to concentrate its fleet off the island of Salamis, while dispatching some allied commanders to fortify the narrow isthmus leading into the Peloponnesus. The Persian army ravaged Phocis and Locris, but a timely earthquake and storm at Delphi frightened them off. The barbarians found Attica generally deserted, and Athens herself had been abandoned through the wise advice of Themistocles and the urgings of the oracle at Delphi and the local priestess of Athena. The people of Athens had been sent to Aegina, Salamis, and Troezen, while those of military age were on the assembled *triremes* in the bay of Salamis. Xerxes' troops stormed the Acropolis and massacred the diehards who thought the "wooden wall" prophecy meant defending the shrine of Athena with hedges and shrubs. The troops set them afire with incendiary arrows and set the whole Acropolis ablaze, and Xerxes "dispatched a messenger on horseback to Susa," announcing his victory (Herodotus, *Histories,* VIII, 54). But the fleet remained intact and the people were free, though saddened as they watched, from Aegina and Salamis, the flames consuming their ancestral home. It was late in the fall, and the large Persian fleet and army would fare badly in the rugged winter from storms and lack of sure food supply, since occupied Greece was not fertile enough to feed and supply such an enormous armed force; as always, an army marched on its stomach. Xerxes decided to attack the Greek fleet as it lay pocketed in the straits, hoping for a final battle that would bring the Greek coalition to its knees.

The *trireme* now proved its mettle against the hordes of Persian ships. Some of the Persian fleet was made up of *triremes,* but they were manned by halfhearted seamen from Greek Ionia or Phoenicia who understood poorly the strategy of the Spartan admiral Eurybiades. His prestige united the varying leaders within the allied fleet, and his determination to engage the enemy made the Greeks fight as one under his command. Three weeks went by, and Xerxes hoped for disaffection among the Greeks while he reinforced his

fleet at Phalerum across the bay. Finally, a false rumor planted by
the resourceful Themistocles, reached Xerxes' ears that the Athenians were making ready to sail away to a new site to the west;
Xerxes, fooled by the ruse, judged the time ripe to attack.

The Greek fleet numbered 380 vessels on the morning of battle.
The 70 ships that the Corinthians manned held the northern section
of the channel, guarding against attack from the rear. The 310
triremes meeting the attack faced a fleet about three times as large as
their own, but the Greek crews were highly trained with their oars
and in the precision and timing of ramming and boarding. The new
Greek *triremes* had been stoutly built to stand the shock of ramming,
and they sat low in the water, light in construction and loaded with
heavily armed soldiers ready to board any floundering enemy vessel
and wreak final slaughter with spear and sword. But room to maneuver was a problem, and the Greek commanders had to get the
Persian ships to expose their broadsides.

The Persian fleet numbered about twelve hundred vessels; the
Phoenician ships were the best, being higher, larger, and faster than
the Greek *triremes*. These ships had rams, but they were not built
to withstand the shock of ramming. The Ionian Greek ships were
similar to those of the Greek league but equipped like the Phoenician
vessels, carrying archers who had orders to sweep the decks of the
more open Athenian *triremes*. Xerxes assumed that the solid wall of
advancing ships would simply cut through the less densely packed
Greek fleet and that the ranks behind the first line of ten ships would
would mop up the remainder, which would be thrown into confusion. But the left wing bunched up as it advanced into the straits,
and the Ionian vessels fouled one another. Consequently, the right
wing of Phoenician *triremes* shot forward out of the line. There was no
sign of the Greek fleet which encouraged the Phoenicians to row on
rapidly. The first lines of the Greek ships soon emerged from the
northern section of the strait, however. The Aeginitans rowed very
rapidly toward the left flank of the Persian fleet, which was being
slowly exposed, while the Athenian ships that followed backed
water and drew the right wing of Phoenician ships into the narrow
waters between the islet of Psytallia and the shores of Attica. A bold
maneuver thus pulled the Greek fleet into a crescent, with a front line
of seventy-five ships and three lines behind that, leaving the left
wing freedom to maneuver.

On the other hand, the Persian ships had been feinted into ranks
crowding the narrow waters, so that the full lines of the right wing

and right center could not support the extended right wing. The mass of about one thousand Persian ships "were jammed together choking the narrows in the hundreds, battering each other with prows of bronze, stripped of oars" in the resulting confusion (Aeschylus, *Persians,* 410–416). Themistocles waited until a swell had gone through the narrows, causing the Phoenician ships to lose their bearing and expose their sides for a little while. The lighter and lower Athenian *triremes,* not as affected by the swell, charged into the broken ranks. The heavily armed Athenian *hoplites* boarded ship after ship. Soon the water "was charged with blood, corpses, the littering wrecks of proud ships, and the beaches and rocks were glutted with the slain" (Aeschylus, *Persians,* 419–421). The Athenian squadron soon wheeled to cut into the Persian center and support the Greek right wing, which fought greater numbers of ships than were in the mutilated Persian right. The rout began:

> When the ships of Persians in the foremost rank were made to flee, then the largest number were destroyed. The vessels behind them, trying to gain the line of conflict, and hoping to give the king proof of their courage, ran into their own vessels flying from battle. Sailing away from the raging conflict, the barbarians made for Phalerum and were taken by the Aeginitans. [Herodotus, *Histories,* VIII, 89–91]

The Persians were rammed as they fled in files. The Greek naval victory at Salamis in 480 B.C. was complete, and the prize for valor was awarded first to the Aeginitans, and second to the Athenians. Xerxes saw that it was too late in the season to renew campaigning. He took the majority of his army home, marching them north and transporting them by ship across the northern straits of the Dardenelles, since bad weather had destroyed his pontoon bridge. But he left a large force in central Greece under the command of Mardonius. The war against Persia would be decided on land after all.

   In the campaigning season of 479 B.C., a consolidated Greek army under the command of the Spartan Pausanias, nephew of Leonidas, gathered at Plataea. It was a huge army by the standards of the *polis,* and supplying it soon became a problem. The Persian forces waited for the usual dissension to tear the Greek alliance to shreds. Already the Athenians and Spartans were in disharmony, and the Persians attempted to capitalize on Athens' discontent with offers of conciliation and enormous bribes. Although many citizens were strongly tempted, Athens refused, fearing a repetition of the previous devastation. The assembly began to voice shortened patience with the war.

The Greek army had five thousand Spartans, supported by five thousand *perioikoi,* and thirty-five thousand Helots armed as skirmishers. Eight thousand Athenians, five thousand Corinthians, fifteen hundred Tegeans, six hundred Plataeans, three thousand Megarians, and five hundred Aeginitans added to those forces. The number of *hoplites* from twenty-four *poleis* totaled thirty-eight thousand seven hundred, and the lightly armed foot soldiers numbered about seventy thousand, half of them Helots from the Peloponnesus.

According to Herodotus, Mardonius chose the forces he wished to remain with him for the coming campaigns. He selected the Persian Immortals, about ten thousand in number and the best troops Xerxes had, "a group of Persian cavalry counted one thousand, and Medes, Sacae, Bactrians, and Indians, both foot soldiers and horsemen. The whole number, including the cavalry, ran to three hundred thousand men" (*Histories,* VIII, 113).

The Persian cavalry raided the outskirts of the large Greek assemblage and captured supply trains, but both the Greek and the Persian generals played a waiting game. Finally, Pausanias lured Mardonius into believing that a Persian cavalry charge had disintegrated the *hoplite* formations; when the Persians entered a slight depression on the plain of Plataea, the Spartan phalanx advanced down the slope, smashing through the packed Persian infantry. Pausanias took revenge for the Persian massacres of Greeks captured during the previous year, and the victorious Greek army took no prisoners. The main Persian infantry had been annihilated. The threat of Persian occupation of Greece was stymied at the Battle of Plataea in 479 B.C., and, according to the tradition, the Greek fleet won a resounding victory at Mycale off Asia Minor the same day over the remaining Persian ships. The *hoplite* phalanx and new navy of *triremes* from Athens and Corinth had bested the army of the biggest empire in the world. Discipline and unified command preserved Greek freedom, which meant the freedom to do what Greek *poleis* had been doing for two and one-half centuries: to go to war with one another.

The Delian League and Athens' Empire

After the twin victories at Plataea and Mycale, Sparta believed the war was over, but Athens wanted to continue, citing the slavery of

Greeks in Asia Minor as an excuse. The Athenian fleet was well
experienced and properly manned, and enthusiasm for more victories ran high in Athens. Sparta decided to withdraw and went
home to her Peloponnesian cocoon, wary of Athens' growing power
but generally content with the fruits of her leadership in the years
from 481 to 479 B.C. Picking up the gauntlet of leadership, Athens
organized the new Greek war around the Delian League, which consisted of those states wishing to carry on the war with Persia. The
league's treasury was located on the island of Delos, sacred to Apollo,
and the League levied a *phoros* ("contribution") from each member
state. Most states gave money, but some—like Athens—gave ships.
The money kept the fleet in repair and in operation.

In the next thirty years Athens steadily subverted the league into
a democratic empire, run for the interests of Athens. Her superb
navy and skill in the tactics of *trireme* maneuver made her mistress
of the Aegean, and she sent ill-fated expeditions to Egypt and Cyprus
in hopes of extending her sway. War with brooding Sparta was
inevitable, particularly when Athens sought to extend her rule over
mainland Greece. Sparta's suspicion about far-reaching Athenian
alliances (namely, the ones Athens had concluded with some Greek
states in southern Italy and Sicily in the decade of 450 B.C.) surfaced
in the war that broke out between Athens and Sparta in 449 B.C.
Sparta was beginning to feel surrounded by Athenian power. On
land, the Spartan *hoplites* were victorious, smashing the more poorly
trained Athenian troops and their allied forces. The Athenians, on
the other hand, dominated the sea, and neither side could really test
the other's strength. Consequently, the Thirty Years' Treaty signed
in 446 B.C. recognized Sparta as the major land power in Greece,
while it left Athens' maritime empire intact. In hindsight, Thucydides
wrote that Sparta and Athens had together repulsed the Persians,
but soon

> both those Greek states that rebelled from the Great King and
> those that fought against him were divided between the
> Athenians and the Spartans. For these states appeared the
> most powerful in given respects: the one was strong by sea,
> the other by land. And for a short time the alliance held to-
> gether, but the Athenians and Spartans quarreled and waged
> war on one another or with their allies. The rest of the Greeks
> were drawn into this duel, even though they might have been
> at variance and even if they might have declared neutrality at

first. Thus from the Persian War they made war at one time, peace at another, either against each other or with their own rebellious allies, and they prepared themselves well in military matters and gained great experience in the school requiring scenes of danger.[Thucydides, *History*, I, 18. 3-6]

The peace of 446 B.C. was a breathing space before the final war, and both sides continued to wage war as Thucydides described. Athens had to contend with growing discontent from her "allies," those states now paying tribute (though it was still labeled *phoros*), and she had to suppress numerous revolts. Sparta faced grumbling within the Peloponnesian League, especially after the short, brutal war from 449 to 446 B.C. devastated some of her allies. Sparta's prestige had fallen and her fears about the Athenian maritime power, which seemed firmly entrenched, intensified. Athens went from glory to glory, and the years from 446 to 431 B.C. are often called the Golden Age of Greece. As leader of the Athenian Empire, Pericles wisely gave physical substance to Athenian pride by constructing new temples and public buildings and distributing the tasks and local honors as widely as possible among Athenian citizens. The fleet kept the seas open for the increased mercantile contacts Athens procured from all over the eastern Mediterranean, from the ports of the Black Sea, and in the West. This last encroachment finally threatened the life line of Corinth so much that she protested to Sparta. The open warfare in 433 B.C. between Corinth and her colony Corcyra soon widened as Athens joined Corcyra's side, leading Corinth to protest to Sparta once again. Meanwhile, a decree in 432 B.C. had barred the citizens of Megara from entering ports in the Athenian Empire, and she too registered her complaint with Sparta. The war that ensued in 431 B.C. between Athens and Sparta was one that everyone had known would come sooner or later.

The Peloponnesian War

This Peloponnesian War (431-404 B.C.) was destructive to both sides. It was fought with the strategy and tactics learned so well in the Persian Wars and wars that followed. The Athenians were now so expert in naval maneuvers that Phormio, an admiral, defeated a superior Peloponnesian fleet by shrewd tactics alone in the Battle of Rhium (429 B.C.). The Athenian flotilla of twenty ships mastered forty-seven Peloponnesian vessels by bunching them together in a tight circle and then circling round them with feigned attacks, contracting the circle even more. Finally the Spartan and Corinthian ships ran afoul of one another. Phormio calmly rammed the defenseless vessels. The Athenians lost no ships, while the fleet of Corinthian, Sicyonian, and Spartan ships lost twelve (Thucydides, *History,* II, 83).

In 430 and 429 B.C., however, Athens suffered from a plague that decimated the jammed city, cramped with refugees from the Attic countryside. The plague (which was a kind of typhus) demoralized many Athenians, especially when the pestilence carried off Pericles in 429 B.C. Political leadership in Athens slowly deteriorated through the war, although Athens continued to produce generals and admirals of genius to the very end. Unfortunately, Alcibiades, one of the finest strategists and tacticians of his time, was completely unscrupulous.

On the other side, Sparta was having troubles with her allies, and the "peace" of 421 B.C. made Athens and Sparta nominal allies, in effect to protect Sparta against her infuriated friends. But Athens grew arrogant, pursuing the tragic course of "might makes right" that Thucydides carefully and eloquently depicted in his portrait of Athenian ruthlessness in the sack of Melos (416 B.C.). Finally, Sparta found a navy, but at a price. Persia agreed to subsidize Sparta and ships to grind down Athens if Sparta would agree to Persian rule in Asia Minor. The last battles of the war exhausted Athenian resources, although after signal defeats she built new fleets and manned them. After a final disaster in late 405 B.C., Athens could float no more ships, her links with the grain route to the Black Sea were severed, and she sued for peace. Sparta emerged as hegemon (from *hegemon* ["leading state"]) of Greece, proclaiming freedom for all Greek states, as Athens had in 478 B.C.

The art of war had torn Greece asunder, the fragile unity gained in the Persian Wars totally demolished by the Peloponnesian War. The *hoplite* phalanx had evolved with the *polis.* In many respects, the stagnation of innovation in the phalanx armies mirrored the fossilization of political institutions in the various *poleis.* The oligarchy of Sparta fought the democracy of Athens; both *poleis,* shortsighted, failed to understand the danger to Greek freedom lurking from Persia even after the Greek victories of 480–479 B.C. The *hoplites* who had fought in the long campaigns of the Peloponnesian War soon found they knew little else as a living, and the age of mercenary armies was at hand. Greek mercenaries would still fight in the disciplined phalanxes, but their services would be rendered for pay. Only in the quasi-Greek kingdom of Macedonia to the north could the army be termed a citizen force, and its members fought for a king, not a *polis*. Also, although brilliant campaigns were waged on the seas, with spectacular Athenian victories in both the Persian and Peloponnesian Wars through her skills with ships, the navy proved less important than armies. For it was a Spartan army that defeated the Persians at Plataea, and a Spartan army that wore down Athens.

5

More War

The Peloponnesian War ended with Sparta completely dominant over Greece. Her prestige was great enough to save Athens from a sentence of *andrapodismos* (where all the adult males of a *polis* were killed and the women and children sold into slavery) proposed by an infuriated Corinth and a fearful Thebes. Spartans "said they would not perform the act of killing and enslavement on a Greek *polis* that had rendered such outstanding services during the times of great dangers to Greece" (Xenophon, *Hellenica,* II, 2. 20). Consequently, Athens was given terms of peace allowing her to survive, to the great relief of the beleaguered Athenians and the loud disgust of Sparta's allies:

> The Athenians were to tear down the long walls from Athens
> to Piraeus, and the walls of Piraeus. They were also to sur-
> render all their ships excepting twelve, receive back exiled
> citizens, assume the same enemies and friends as those of
> Sparta, and obey and follow Sparta on land and sea wherever
> she should lead. [Xenophon, *Hellenica,* II, 2. 20]

The Spartan admiral Lysander sailed into the port of Piraeus, the exiles came back, and the walls "came down to the music piped by some flutegirls." The Spartans and their allies thought "that day was the beginning of freedom in Greece" (Xenophon, *Hellenica,* II, 2. 20–23).

The great historian Thucydides did not live to complete his magnificent account of the great war between Athens and Sparta, although there are hints throughout his work that he did see Athens' vaunted democracy smashed and her imperial navy dispersed. Thucydides' history stops abruptly in 411 B.C., and Xenophon, a writer with an inferior perspective, continued the historical narrative. Xenophon took his *Hellenica* to 362 B.C., the date of the Battle of Mantinea and the collapse of Thebes' hegemony over Greece. Modern accounts of the confused fourth century B.C. in Greek history are ultimately based on Xenophon, although much more detail for the decade of 390 B.C. has come from an unknown writer called the Oxyrhynchus historian, so named because the papyrus containing these details was unearthed at Oxyrhynchus in Egypt. Xenophon is easy to read—most beginning Greek students cut their teeth on the more famous *Anabasis* ("March Up Country")—and his narrative sparkles with action, making excellent material for historical novels about Greek mercenary adventures in the fourth century B.C. He lacks depth, however, and does not seek causes below simple action. Where Thucydides' Greek is compact and stuffed with analysis of men's motives and the misjudgments of states at war, Xenophon's writing is smooth, clear, and concerned with surface events. Yet it is to Xenophon that modern students turn for a discussion of the change in Greek warfare that paved the way for Philip II and Alexander of Macedonia. The soldiers Xenophon describes were mercenaries hailing from every Greek state, fighting for a living, and owing loyalty to the richest and most successful general, who in turn fought for a state that could insure fat fees for national defense. As an expatriated Athenian who came to idealize Sparta, Xenophon became a professional soldier. In his lifetime (*c.* 427–*c.* 354 B.C.) he saw the shift from heavily armed soldiers to swifter, more lightly armed infantry (*peltasts*). He also witnessed greater use of slingers, archers, and cavalry in military operations, and he provides details about Greek armies that explain why Alexander's amazing expedition succeeded.

With the peace of 404 B.C. following the Peloponnesian War, many soldiers found themselves without either a home or a profession. It was impossible to return to ancestral farms that no longer existed, or to the farming life when a soldier had known nothing but war his whole adult life. The isolated life of the *polis* was limiting to men who had seen much of the world and who had tasted its varieties and pleasures. Although soldiers would continue to call themselves

Spartan, Athenian, Theban, Megarian, and so on, they felt little patriotism for the *poleis* of their fathers. They sought further wartime adventures in an age when war was more endemic than ever before. Sparta was soon at war with her former allies and eventually revealed a desire for empire, which had been the cause of Athens' troubles. Meanwhile, the Persian Empire was undergoing internal military chaos. In 403 B.C. a call for good Greek mercenaries came from Cyrus, the younger brother of Artaxerxes II, who had become the Great King in 405 B.C. Cyrus had befriended Lysander of Sparta, and their friendly cooperation meant victory for Sparta in the Peloponnesian War. Cyrus announced that the soldiers he was collecting were for an expedition into Pisidia, but in 401 B.C. he led them farther east in an attempt to wrest the throne from his brother. Xenophon enlisted, along with twenty thousand other soldiers.

Cyrus' army was weak in cavalry, even though he commanded some of the best soldiers in the world. His Greek mercenaries fought in the traditional phalanx and could hold their own against a determined cavalry charge. However, the Persian king, Artaxerxes II, had some excellent cavalry, and they determined the outcome of the Battle of Cunaxa (401 B.C.), forty-five miles from Babylon, where the land between the Tigris and Euphrates rivers is the narrowest. Here Cyrus lost his life in a desperate attack on his brother's bodyguard, while his Greek mercenary army, numbering some ten thousand four hundred *hoplites,* swept the enemy's left wing. Cyrus' center and right wing collapsed, and the Greeks found themselves part of a losing army. In the deadly quiet after the battle, when the victorious Artaxerxes proposed negotiations with the Greek mercenaries, a great unease swept through the army of mixed *poleis,* especially through the Spartans, who were ever suspicious of Persian envoys. Clearchus the Spartan, the commander of the Greek mercenaries, went with nineteen of his fellow leaders to confer with the Persians. The twenty generals and company commanders never returned, having been treacherously murdered by the Persians under a flag of truce. Rage replaced unease when the news arrived in the Greek camp, and it acclaimed new generals to lead the isolated army out of the barbarian heartland. Xenophon of Athens was one of those elected, and his account of the remaining ten thousand Greeks hacking their way out of Persia forms the adventure and action of *Anabasis.* The "march up country" had been the long journey to Cunaxa, and the continuation of the journey took the Greeks immediately east to the arrow-swift Tigris River. The army was constantly harassed by Persian cavalry and slingers. Crossing the river was impossible, since a strong Persian force held the opposite bank. Xenophon's army did not have the necessary catapults to clear the banks (as Alexander did later, when he faced the problem of crossing a river in the face of enemy cavalry). After discussing their plight, the Greeks struck north into the mountains of Kurdistan, which had never been quite subdued by the Persian kings. Once in Kurdistan, the Greek army was no longer pursued by the Persians, but other problems plagued it. Pack animals had to be found, provisions procured for the women, and a host of other matters resolved that most earlier Greek armies had taken for granted as they operated in the limited geography of the Greek homeland. Innovation and doggedness finally brought most soldiers in that lost army to the Greek port city of Trapezus on the Black Sea, but with about four thousand of their number lost from cold, hunger, unfriendly mountain tribes, and occasional collisions with Persian forces. So great was the joy when the advance of the army sighted open water that

> there was a tumult of shouting. Xenophon and his rear guard heard it and thought more barbarians were attacking in the front. They believed this since the inhabitants of the land they had just plundered were trailing the Greeks, and Xenophon's rear guard had killed some of them in an ambush and taken some prisoners, with booty taken of about twenty shields of oxhide, raw and still with their hairy coverings. The shouting became louder and louder, and some soldiers started running toward the front lines, where the men kept on shouting. The more men there were there, the greater the clamor became, and it appeared then something was there of great importance. So Xenophon mounted his horse, and taking Lycus and the cavalry along, they rode forward. Shortly, they heard soldiers raising their voices with 'The sea! The sea!' passing the clamor down the advancing column. Then everyone began to run, rear guard included, which drove the baggage animals and horses as fast as they would go. When everyone reached the summit, the soldiers embraced each other, eyes filled with tears, and they hugged their generals and company commanders. [Xenophon, *Anabasis*, IV, 7]

In the wars that raged in Greece during the fifth century B.C., no distinction was made between a *hoplite*'s pay and his ration. Thucydides makes it clear that pay for military service was uncom-

mon in Greece before the beginning of the Peloponnesian War, and
that payment generally concerned oarsmen in a fleet. Provisions for
the army were considered the same as money allocated for the troops,
and Thucydides called the entire monetary allowance *misthos* (see,
for example, *History,* VIII, 5. 5, and VIII, 36). However, when the
Spartan fleet had assembled at Miletus in 411 B.C., the Persian satrap
"gave pay for one month among all the ships, at the rate of one Attic
drachma a day per man" (Thucydides, *History,* VIII, 29). The crews
were pleased until they were informed they would receive only half
a *drachma* in later months. Shortly booty mollified the men. Thus a
new and widespread practice of pay for service came into being in
the last decade of the Peloponnesian War. Persia had employed mercenaries—including Greeks—for many years, and Persian gold sweet-
ened the shift in Greek military practice. Xenophon's army fought
for pay, as distinct from state provisions.

Until the mid-fifth century B.C., Athenian armies fought in the
name of their duty to the *polis,* just as citizens were expected to go
to meetings of the assembly or perform jury service as portions of
their civic and common loyalty: without remuneration. Under
Pericles, however, the state began "payment for service on the courts
of law" to citizens required for jury duty (Aristotle, *Constitution of
Athens,* XXVII, 3), and the "people gained a conceit for themselves"
(Aristotle, *Politics,* II, 1274a5). Even when pay for jury duty was
temporarily abolished in 411 B.C., soldiers were exempted from the
new rule. "Nobody was to receive pay that was not in the military,
and no more than five thousand persons should be part of the government of Athens, particularly those who served the state best in
their persons and wealth" (Thucydides, *History,* VIII, 65). The
oligarchic reforms were short-lived, state pay for patriotic duties
soon came back, and the ordinary payment for military service
embedded itself in Greek life. The new citizen army was made up of
"volunteers," soldiers who were out of a job at the end of a war
and who would seek new employers, as did the army commanded
by Clearchus the Spartan.

After that army reached Trapezus in late 400 B.C. and engaged in
sundry adventures, further skirmishes, short-term employment in
Thrace, and some exploits in Byzantium, most of the veterans described in *Anabasis* enlisted with Sparta. In 399 B.C. war between
Persia and Sparta was officially declared, although Spartan action
from 403 through 400 B.C. left little doubt that war was inevitable

between the two powers. By unofficially backing Cyrus' revolt with an army of crack Spartan mercenaries, Sparta made a cast for the empire she had wrested from Athens. In addition to the six thousand hardened soldiers who survived the Anabasis, Sparta collected three hundred cavalrymen from Athens, four thousand foot soldiers from the Spartan alliance, and one thousand more troops recently recruited and hired from among the "Laconians." Sparta had a large fleet, and she ensured her Eastern connections by an alliance with rebellious Egypt in 397 B.C. But Conon, a brilliant renegade Athenian, commanded the Persian ships.

Persia had greater difficulty than Sparta in paying her troops, and in 395 B.C. Conon weathered a mutiny of his fleet and Cypriot mercenaries at Salamis in Cyprus. According to the Oxyrhynchus historian (XV-XVI), the mutiny was caused because a rumor spread that Conon was going to pay only marines and sailors and not *hoplite* mercenaries, some of whom were from Cyprus. Earlier, the Oxyrhynchus historian (XIV, 3) records "pay given to the mercenary soldiers, being 220 *talents* of silver," a token payment from Persia to Conon's forces, which were fifteen months behind in their wages. The orator Isocrates (436–338 B.C.) confirms the delay (*Panegyricus,* 142), while Xenophon notes that the standard rate of pay at that time was 4 *obols* per man per day (that is, about two-thirds of a *drachma*) (*Hellenica,* I, 5. 7). Since each *trireme* had two hundred men, and the fleet may have contained about one hundred ships, the annual sum would total 4,800,000 *drachmae,* or 800 *talents,* an enormous sum even in a time of inflation. Soldiers and sailors for pay were becoming more expensive, as Thucydides' statistical summaries for the Peloponnesian War indicate. In 412 B.C. both the Spartan and Athenian sailors received 3 *obols* per day per man (Thucydides, *History,* VIII, 45. 2), while Persian wages were slightly higher—3.3 *obols* (*History,* VIII, 29).

At the same time, although payment to foot soldiers and cavalry was made irregularly during the Peloponnesian War, the *misthos* was always greater than that tendered to sailors or marines. Thucydides notes that in 430 B.C. the three thousand *hoplites* at Potidaea received two *drachmae* per day per man (*History,* III, 17. 4), while three Aeginitan *obols* was a known rate in 420 B.C. (Although here the correct term is *sitos,* which probably means something akin to "support" or "cost of military rations" [Thucydides, *History,* V, 47]). The *sitos* was three *obols* a day for a lightly armed *hoplite* or an archer, and six *obols* for a cavalryman; the rate is in Aeginitan *drachmae,* which were heavier than those of Attica. And some Thracian mercenaries were paid one *drachma* a day in 413 B.C. (Thucydides, *History,* VII, 27. 2). But the Greek *hoplite* mercenary who fought for the doomed Cyrus in 401 B.C. was proffered "three half-Darics a month instead of one Daric" (Xenophon, *Anabasis,* I, 3. 21), a half-Daric being higher than the usual wage. Since the Persian gold Daric was equal to twenty-five Attic *drachmae,* the daily wage for mercenaries in 401 B.C. was five *obols.* Generals received four times as much, while a captain of a company (*lochagos*) earned ten *obols.* The rate of pay, five *obols* a day, became recognized as a normal wage. The provisions for the army were added above such calculations and were furnished in the form in which they were used by the army.

Romantic notions to the contrary, the life of the mercenary was neither pleasant nor assured. His pay was often irregular, and his motives for fighting as a professional were not founded on avarice. Lofty promises to soldiers were common. Seeking the services of the crusty veterans of the anabasis, a barbarian chief "promised that he would give each fighting man a *stater* of Cyzicus each month, double that for the company commanders, and quadruple for the generals. And he promised as much land as they desired, teams of oxen, and a fortified coastal town" (Xenophon, *Anabasis,* VII, 2). The citizens of Byzantium had threatened to sell as a slave any soldier found within their walls, while the Thracian chief Seuthes held out some hope of food and booty:

> I promise to give the soldiers a Cyzicene *stater* every month, with the normal extra wage to generals and captains. You soldiers will take food and drink from the countryside—as you are doing at the present time—but I will claim all the booty for myself, so that I can sell it and thus be able to pay you. [Xenophon, *Anabasis,* VII, 3].

Later, at a dinner party, when Seuthes was well laced with strong Thracian wine gulped from horns, admirers gave him numerous presents, and Xenophon writes that he offered him "myself and my friends here, none who will hold back in battle." And he went on to promise Seuthes what they all hoped to gain from their coming campaign. They would "win many horses, many men, and many beautiful women, which will not be taken by force. They will come bearing gifts in hand" (Xenophon, *Anabasis,* VII, 3). Riches were to be had for the taking, or so the talk through the increasingly sodden evening indicated. Willing women and fine horses seemed to be the goals the Greek soldiers avidly pursued. Often, however, when a campaign ended, any pay received had been spent in local taverns or in badly conceived land purchases. The soldier might buy a tract of alleged farmland, find it hopelessly barren or encrusted with rocks, and be forced back into the growing ranks that Isocrates worries about. "In Greece, affairs are now such that it is much easier to gather a larger and mightier army from the wandering exiles than from men who inhabit their own *poleis*" (*Address to Philip*, V, 96).

The military and political chaos in Greece worsened as Sparta attempted to enforce her rule, and a myriad of states rebelled against her. Even Sparta was forced to admit that she could not gain soldiers except by hiring them from her allies. In 383 B.C. states asked by Sparta to contribute their usual troop allotments, according to traditional agreements, were most reluctant to do so. So Sparta made do with money:

> It was agreed after much talk that any state that wanted to do so could send money instead of men, at the wage of three Aeginitan *obols* for each man, and a state which usually sent horsemen would send money enough to pay four *hoplites* for each cavalryman. [Xenophon, *Hellenica*, V, 2. 21]

The force of ten thousand soldiers that eventually assembled did include some of the Spartan Equals, but very few in proportion to the whole force.

Still Sparta hung on to her old myth of invincibility. Her phalanx—growing smaller each decade, with fewer and fewer of the true Spartan *hoplites* fighting in the heavily armed lines—kept the creaky Peloponnesian alliance generally loyal. An Athenian effort in 377 B.C. to set up a Second Confederacy, hoping to avoid the errors of her first ill-fated Greek League, fizzled when Athens began to insist on hegemony. That brought back too many memories of Athenian ruthlessness to the island members, and the Second Confederacy faded from importance by 372 B.C. The major thorn in the side of both Athens and Sparta was the newly resurgent power of Thebes and her Boeotian League. In the wings waited Jason of Pherae, a Thessalian king who commanded the best cavalry in the Greek world and who also talked of war against Persia.

Another change in warfare was the longer campaigning season, brought about in part by the long war between Athens and Sparta, but also by the blunt fact that mercenaries were not tied to state customs or civic duties or even regular farming activities, as were most citizen-soldiers. With some surprise and irritation, Greeks soon recognized that famous military recruiters did not campaign in the customary season. Traditionally, war took place in the space of four or five months from spring to fall; the Greek commonly thought of winter as extending from the morning setting of the Pleiades (November 8) to the evening rising of Arcturus (March 6), a period of four months (Thucydides, *History,* VI, 21. 2). Summer warfare meant that the Greek mercenary *hoplite* usually received pay for only four or five months—but often eight if the mercenary captain did not feel bound by the ancient rule to campaign only in the "summer." Demosthenes, the Attic orator and implacable foe after 350 B.C. of growing Macedonian power under Philip II, grumbles that Philip did not observe these old, semichivalrous codes of seasonal campaigns (*Third Philippic,* IX, 48-50), implying that the Macedonian king fought unfairly. Mercenaries took employment no matter what the season. Isocrates adds his lament, saying, "Many of these men are forced by the lack of the mere necessities of life to enlist in the armies of the barbarians, and are being killed fighting for their enemies against their friends" (*Panegyricus,* IV, 168). The ordinary farmer or citizen lived in increasing fear of the wandering bands led by condottieri who plundered at will. The mercenaries, not finding a convenient war to fight in, often overran a neighboring town, "disgusting the *polis* as they beg their living from those passing by on the streets; and these poverty-striken men outnumber the men of the town who have any wealth at all" (Isocrates, *Areopagiticus,* VII, 83). Whole families of mercenaries roved about, and the recruiting captain often had to make provision for the women and children as well as pay the soldiers, as Xenophon suggested in *Anabasis.*

Peltasts

Meanwhile, the *peltast* formations had become increasingly important in the turbulent warfare of the time. *Peltasts* carried less armor than the heavily armed *hoplite,* but had more equipment than the lightly armed soldier, who had no shield. The *peltast*'s name came from the crescent-shaped shield he held in place of the round one that the *hoplites* hefted. Early vase-paintings show that the *peltasts*' shields were made of wickerwork and that the warrior carried two spears, one of which he cast from a distance at his opponent sometime before he engaged him. The second spear could also be hurled on a running charge, and the vase-paintings provide details suggesting that the javelin was thrown so it rotated rapidly. To do this, the *peltast* inserted two fingers under a small strap attached to the spear and cast it whirling. The origin of this mode of fighting was attributed to Thrace, and a distinct helmet was associated with the Thracian *peltast*. It was made of thin bronze and was peaked at the crest like a soft stocking cap. A short sword (*machaira*) completed his equipment; this was used for slashing, since it had a slight curve. Later a longer spear sometimes replaced the two javelins, but the *peltast* could be equipped with either the two lighter spears or the heavier thrusting spear. The light crescent-shaped shield was made from bronze, but the wickerwork shield dating from homeric and Archaic times was occasionally employed in the time of the Hellenistic monarchies (300–30 B.C.).

Peltasts were commonly used in the frequent wars before 500 B.C., especially when Greek settlers fought barbarians in the new colonies. In Thrace, Greek settlers quickly adapted native Thracian tactics, and the *peltasts* soon fought side by side with the traditional *hoplites*. Thracian archers proved their worth, but it was Xerxes' horde at Thermopylae that brought home the value of arrow showers to the Greek mainland. The shock tactics of *peltast* warfare were used in the Peloponnesian War, but the dominant troops were still the standard *hoplites*. After Athens' defeat in 404 B.C., the *peltasts* increased in number and importance—probably because their equipment was cheaper than the full armor of a heavily armed *hoplite*. Xenophon gives an interesting summary of the mercenary forces that Clearchus the Spartan brought into the service of Cyrus:

> The Lacedaemonian exile, Clearchus, came with one thousand *hoplites*, eight hundred Thracian *peltasts*, and two hundred archers from Crete. Likewise came Sosis of Syracuse with three hundred *hoplites*, and Sophaenetus of Arcadia with one thousand *hoplites*. Cyrus reviewed them all, counted all the Greeks, and they totaled eleven thousand *hoplites* and about two thousand *peltasts*. [Xenophon, *Anabasis*, I, 2. 9]

As shock troops, the mercenaries fought well, and Xenophon's comments on their pluck and mobility were not lost on other captains.

The first successful *peltast* commander was the Athenian Iphicrates (*c.* 415-353 B.C.), a prototype of the condottieri so common in the middle of the fourth century B.C. Rising from obscurity, he took the *peltasts* and welded them into a formidable fighting force. "He doubled the length of the spear and lengthened the sword and changed the sort of breastplates they wore, giving them linen ones in place of chain armor or bronze" (Cornelius Nepos, *Iphicrates,* 1). *Peltasts* had tried wearing bronze cuirasses, but they had become too weighty for swift maneuver. Iphicrates discarded the bronze armor in favor of a heavy linen shirt, and he drilled his troops in the precise manner of the *hoplite* formation. They could move rapidly, wheel to make flank charges, and defend themselves from rear attack.

The new troops surprised a Spartan contingent of six hundred *hoplites* in 392 B.C. Led by Iphicrates, the *peltasts* routed the heavily armed *hoplites* by harrying the unprotected flank of the phalanx, and by being able to wheel about quickly. Seeing that the Spartans were without good cavalry, Iphicrates boldly attacked them in the Battle of Lechaeum, near Corinth (392 B.C.), and "as some of the spears were hurled at them, a few of the Spartans were killed and a few were wounded. Shield bearers were commanded to carry the corpses back to Lechaeum, and these men were the only survivors of the Spartan contingent." The Spartan *polemarch* ordered the *hoplites* to charge "to drive off their attackers. But they were *hoplites* in pursuit of *peltasts* at the length of a spear's cast, and they did not capture anybody, since Iphicrates had commanded his men to fall back before the *hoplites* came within close range." The Spartans lost their line, "since each man was charging at his own pace," and then they turned around to retrieve their line. "The *peltasts* wheeled around, some casting their javelins from the front while others ran up along the flank, hurling their weapons into the side unprotected by the shields" (Xenophon, *Hellenica,* IV, 5. 15). Regrouped, the Spartans charged again with the same results, and the loss of even more of the *hoplites.* Even a cavalry reinforcement did not help, since the horsemen kept to the line as well, and the *peltasts* picked them off as they turned around. The immobility of the phalanx had been demonstrated. The Spartans lost at least four hundred of their best troops, while the mercenary *peltasts* lost very few. The skirmishers had become victors over the *hoplites.* It remained for a good general to put together the combination of heavily and lightly armed men and cavalry, to defeat a Spartan army in full battle array. As it was,

Iphicrates proved that *peltasts* were capable of breaking up the phalanx block, and he proved the fighting qualities of well-drilled mercenaries who were armed only with spears, a slashing sword, and a light shield half the size and weight of the one the *hoplites* used.

Horses in War and Sport

Even though cavalry and chariot riding formed a glamorous part of the homeric tales, the employment of cavalry in set Greek battles was very limited. There were many good reasons for preferring *hoplites*. Most of Greece was quite unsuitable for raising horses, and the stony ground made soldiers' mounts go lame. Xenophon wrote two tracts on cavalry, which review some of these problems, *On the Cavalry Commander* and *On the Art of Horsemanship*. He suggests getting the horse used to rocks by "making him stand on stones whenever he goes out of his stable. The horse will continually use his hooves on the rocks when he is cleaned and when flies are worrying him. The hooves of the horse will become rounded" (*Commander*, I, 16). Like *triremes,* horses were expensive, consuming huge amounts of fodder and, since most Greek wars took place in the summer, drinking with an enormous thirst. Only in Thessaly was the cavalry a major arm of the army; the Thessalian mounted knights used their prowess to keep the peasantry overawed and subdued. Sometimes horsemen were useful for scouting and reconnaissance, but the same task was better performed lightly on foot, especially in broken country. Generally, Greek *hoplites* standing firm in the face of the fiercest cavalry charge could rest assured there was little danger. Xenophon writes of this confidence, as he was seeking to buoy his mercenaries' mettle against fears of the Persian horse. "Nobody ever died in battle from a horse's kick or bite. A *hoplite* can strike with more force and with surer aim than can the cavalryman sitting precariously on his mount. He is as afraid of falling off his horse as he is fearing the enemy" (*Anabasis,* III, 2. 18-19).Ten thousand horsemen were, after all, merely ten thousand men.

The cavalry had no horseshoes, which would have allowed them to attack in and traverse rocky country, nor did horsemen have good saddles. This may not hinder riders who have been trained to ride bareback from very early childhood (as had the Mongols and certain American Indian tribes), but it was a definite hindrance for the Greek nobility. They bred horses for display, occasional forays within the *polis* (especially in those *poleis* of northern Greece), and for victories in the rousing races at the various athletic festivals. Horses and their care were the pursuit of the rich, and the winners of Olympic equestrian events include the names of famous Greek leaders. Along with the listings of Spartan kings, rulers of Cyrene, and tyrants like Myron of Sicyon and Hiero of Syracuse are many names from the rich and noble families of Athens. During the tyranny of Peisistratus (d. 527 B.C.), an Athenian noble exile had "the good luck to gain the Olympic prize in the four-horse chariot race." In the following games "he was victorious with the same mares, and he allowed Peisistratus to be proclaimed victor. Having conceded victory to the tyrant, the exile returned to Athens. Later he gained another prize with the same mares" (Herodotus, *Histories,* VI, 103). The celebrated Athenian dandy Alcibiades ran seven teams of horses in the Olympic games of 416 B.C. and took first, second, and fourth places. As a sport of the rich, horse racing had few peers. Diodorus Siculus, the author of *World History* (written *c.* 60–30 B.C.), writes about the efforts of Dionysius of Syracuse to win the four-horse competitions (what the textbooks called the *quadriga* races, since the Latin term used in later Roman races has become standard in physical education handbooks). In 388 B.C. Dionysius sent several teams to Olympia, along with experts in reading poetry to recite his poems, written for the occasion. The tyrant ordered a pavilion set up for the races, and it was festooned with richly embroidered hangings and gold cloth marquees. The Syracusan teams ran in the races but won no prizes. On the way back to Sicily, the ships carrying the horses and their drivers were wrecked. Sailors remarked that the disgrace to the Syracusan teams and the disaster at sea resulted from Dionysius' bad verse (Diodorus Siculus, *World History,* XIV, 109. 1, and XV, 7.2). Princes of the royal house of Macedonia also won races, and in 356 B.C., according to tradition, Philip II of Macedonia won a race on the same day his son Alexander was born. Only the very wealthy could afford to race, and only the wealthy in any *polis* could afford to ride in the cavalry. In the Olympic games, riding horses seemed rare. (An inscription from *c.* 450 B.C. records an arrogant Spartan claim to forty-three victories in four-horse races, but only eighteen on ridden horses, "such as nobody of the present generation ever equaled" [*Sparta Inscriptions, Inscriptiones Graecae,* V, 1.213 in Harris] .)

Boy jockeys were highly trained for the riding races, as the magnificent bronze jockey now in the National Museum at Athens shows.

Recovered from the sea near Artimisium in A.D. 1935, the bronze shows a boy skillfully perched on an absent horse galloping at full speed. The jockey has perfect balance, sitting still atop a hurtling mass of muscle and sinew, his left leg held against the flank of his steed while his right leg is slightly extended. Straps hold the spurs on the boy's inner heels, and he holds the reins in his left hand, which is angled up. His right arm and hand remain stiffly posed to balance the left. He has perfect control of his mount and exactly the right balance to remain on the horse as it thunders its way over the level course to the finish line. Boys made poor horsemen in an army, however, and the battle sites were not like the smooth hippodromes with the usual three *stades* (six hundred yards).

The virtual unimportance of horseback events in Greek athletic festivals suggests why troops of cavalry were trappings for the *hoplite* phalanx in war. Stirrups were nonexistent, and chariot warfare was totally useless in country without vast plains, such as those found in Persia or the barren expanses of Egypt. A ravine or gully smashed a cavalry or chariot charge as effectively as might the wall of waiting *hoplites,* with spear extended. Without the firm seat that stirrups provided, the charging horseman would fall off his mount if he missed his target. In *Through the Looking Glass,* Lewis Carroll provides a ludicrous image, in the scene where the Red Knight and the White Knight keep careening off their horses because they always miss each other as they hack away.

A Decade for Thebes

Some *poleis* began to put together the elements of heavy and light foot soldiers with cavalry to create an army. Thebes was particularly suited for the new methods, since the plain of Boeotia had long nourished fine horses. Just north of Thebes and her Boeotian Confederacy were the plains of Thessaly, famed for excellent horsemen for many generations, and over the northern ridges of Thessaly lurked the growing power of Macedonia. It was Thebes, however, that first noted and put into practice the lesson learned when Iphicrates' *peltasts* fought against the Spartans in 392 B.C. The Theban general Pelopidas took to heart Iphicrates' analysis of an army: "soldiers without heavy armor are like the hands, the cavalry like the feet, the phalanx like the chest and breastplate, and the general is like the head" (Plutarch, *Pelopidas,* II, 1). Pelopidas also noticed that the

Sacred Band, which one of his Theban colleagues organized into a
body of three hundred men armed like *peltasts,* fought best if the
members were kept together in a band "knitted by the bond between
lovers, a bond which cannot be broken and is indissoluble. The
lovers are shamed to be cowards in front of their dear friends, and
both stand firm in the face of danger to protect one another" (Plutarch, *Pelopidas,* XVIII, 2). Not all Greek observers approved the
open homosexuality of the utterly masculine Sacred Band, but most
acknowledged their fighting prowess as the shock troops of the new
Theban army. As the best fighting unit of its time, the Sacred Band
never lost an encounter until its total slaughter at the hands of
Philip II of Macedonia in 338 B.C. The Macedonian king was supposed
to have cried in anguish, "Those persons will die miserably who
believe these men did anything or suffered anything disgraceful"
(Plutarch, *Pelopidas,* XVIII, 5), as he viewed their mangled corpses
on the battlefield.

Theban cavalry was taught to fight in conjunction with heavily
armed *hoplites* and the more lightly clad Sacred Band and other
peltasts, as well as with the usual unarmored skirmishers. The most
important lesson was the coordination between infantry and cavalry,
a coordination that slowly emerged after Iphicrates' innovations
with his *peltasts* and after Pelopidas' inspiriting of the Sacred Band.
Thus in 371 B.C., when the full Spartan phalanx met the Theban
forces at Leuctra, ten miles south of Thebes, the Spartans fought in
the traditional phalanx block, while Thebes fielded a much more
flexible army. The level ground appeared well suited for the normal
hoplite clash. The Spartans were drawn up in the usual way, blocked
twelve deep on their right wing. The Boeotian army stationed the
Theban contingent opposite the Spartans, but the Thebans were in a
block fifty deep. This innovation was due to Epaminondas, commander of the Thebans, a man who was untried in battle but who
had studied carefully the many circulating handbooks on war and
specific battles. The battle began with the Theban cavalry throwing
back the poorly trained Spartan horsemen in a quick encounter.
Sparta failed to perceive the importance of skilled horsemen, even
though she had met many in her encounters with Persia after 399
B.C. The fleeing Spartan cavalry clattered into its own line, causing it
to break a bit and throwing it slightly off balance. The Spartans
hastily got their line back, but not before the Theban infantry
charged, led by the Sacred Band, itself flanked by the wheeling and

victorious cavalry. The Spartan *hoplites* held ground until the depth of the Theban formation bowled them over by sheer weight. Once the Spartans were overpowered, Sparta's other allies fell back. The Battle of Leuctra firmly demonstrated how rigid and fossilized the old phalanx had become. The short and sharp engagement at Leuctra in late August, 371 B.C., involved ten thousand men but

> all of the Spartan army of one thousand had been killed, and four hundred of the seven hundred Spartan officers fell. They sent a herald to the Thebans to recover their dead under a truce. Then the Thebans put up a trophy of victory and gave back the bodies under the truce. [Xenophon, *Hellenica*, VI, 4. 15]

Immediately Thebes sent word of her victory to Athens and sought further alliance with Jason of Pherae, the Thessalian ruler who had such fine horses. (Unfortunately, Jason was assassinated in 370 B.C.) Thebes was now hegemon of Greece and had the dynamic leader Epaminondas, ably assisted by the less colorful Pelopidas.

Sparta nursed her wounds as Thebes' rise to dominion in Greece became surer, and nine years later (362 B.C.) she challenged Thebes at the Battle of Mantinea. Thebes won this too, but Epaminondas was killed. The Greek world, exhausted by the ever increasing tempo of war, lacked any effective leader. Although the bulk of the armies comprised hired mercenaries, a small core of *polis* soldiers—such as the Boeotians and Thebans, or the Spartans at Leuctra—always fought with the mercenaries. The professional tone of warfare by the mid-fourth century B.C. is mirrored in the military instruction manual *On the Defense of Fortified Positions,* written by the otherwise unknown Aeneas Tacticus around 360 B.C. The budding mercenary captain could read Aeneas for points of strategy and tactics, hints at defense, and tidbits about how to use ships and horsemen and how to size up possible recruits. Tacticus clarifies the worst problem Greek states faced, internal civil war:

> In a *polis* where strife is common and the citizens hate one another, you must exercise extreme caution about the masses of people that go out to see a torch race or a horse race or other competitions whenever there might be sacred ceremonies in which the whole citizenry gathers outside the walls, and processions come out of the city under arms; this includes occasions where the people watch ships hauled up, and public honoring of the dead. On such an occasion, it is quite possible

for one faction to overthrow another. [*Fortified Positions,* XVII, 1]

Many times, the only element of stability in these Greek *poleis* was the hired mercenary force, which fought for order to keep regular payments coming in.

   The willing recruit who did not pass physical muster had the opportunity to become an attendant to one of the mercenaries, just like the slaves and servants who had served the *hoplites* on the battlefield in the fifth century B.C. The attendants' tasks were to carry provisions, weapons, and articles of comfort, to remove bodies from the battlefield, and to act as general servants. Xenophon notes that he "was deserted by the servant carrying his shield" in the heat of an encounter (*Anabasis,* IV, 2. 21); he also relates how a soldier "taking his shield from his attendant, fell fighting at that place. But his favorite boy remained by his side" (*Hellenica,* IV, 8. 29). This suggests that a number of camp followers surrounded each soldier either in camp or on the march. One of the primary reforms instituted in the Sacred Band of Thebes was the elimination of servants and sexual partners, to insure better discipline. Philip II of Macedonia was well known for the strict measures of discipline in his army. Two later sources preserve the tradition of his insistence on discipline in the ranks; both borrow their materials from much earlier authors. Frontinus wrote the crabbed *Strategems* in Latin sometime before A.D. 96, and the Macedonian rhetorician Polyaenus put down his hasily extracted *Strategems* in Greek about A.D. 162. Both reflect the change that Philip II brought to his army, the army that conquered Greece and propelled Alexander on his amazing quest for world conquest.

> When Philip was forming his first army, he commanded that nobody use a wheeled cart and he allowed cavalrymen only one servant to do the drudgery, while to foot soldiers he allowed only one of these calloused servants for every ten men. The lowly attendant was detailed to carry the millstones for grinding grain and to carry the ropes. And when the troops marched to their summer quarters, he ordered each man to carry flour on his back for thirty days" (Frontinus, *Strategems,* IV, 1. 6).

He did not only that, according to the tradition embedded in Polyaenus, but also "Philip got his troops used to continual exercise before actual battles by ordering them to march three hundred *stadia* [slightly over thirty-four miles] quite often, bearing their own arms and carrying their helmets, greaves, spears, provisions, as well as their own utensils for daily use" (*Strategems,* IV, 2. 10). Such rigor contrasted with the lax and flaccid troops of Greece. An army that marched with slaves, servants, and assorted camp followers could not hope to match the crack soldiers that Philip II trained in stamina and precision.

After Epaminondas' death, Thebes quickly lost her status as hegemon of Greece. No leader arose who could unite the quarreling Boeotian Confederacy against the continual sniping from Sparta, Athens, and the host of other jealous *poleis.* None of the other states, however, had either the financial means or manpower to proclaim a hegemony. With Jason of Pherae gone, there was nobody who could renew the wars that Greeks enjoyed so much. It would take a bit of time for recovery; Athens still had a good navy and controlled many points in the northern Aegean, as well as the essential shipping route to the Black Sea. It appeared that Athens might, once again, make a cast for power over her Greek neighbors.

Philip of Macedonia

While Epaminondas was leader of Thebes, one of the hostages taken from Macedonia was the young Philip II. He watched the planning of the remarkable new army, noted the careful training of both infantry and cavalry, and remembered how the citizen phalanx of the Boeotian Confederacy fought so valiantly in company with mercenaries. Upon his return to Macedonia, Philip must have pondered the victory Thebes won at Mantinea (362 B.C.) and the resultant decline of Theban fortunes with the death of Epaminondas, the great master of coordination. The young Philip also must have reflected at length on the Epaminondas' humanity, noting that even a great leader could not subdue hatred or the common callousness of Greek assemblies. He may have thus summed up Epaminondas' career, as did Cornelius Nepos some centuries later: "Before Epaminondas was born, and after he died, Thebes was under the constant dominion of other states. But as long as he led Thebes, she was the leading state in Greece. This shows that one man was worth more than all the citizens" (Cornelius Nepos, *Epaminondas,* X, 4). Philip recalled how treacherous Greeks were to one another, even within a given *polis,* and understood the value of utter loyalty to a leader, which Pelopidas' devotion to Epaminondas brilliantly illustrated. The concept of a citizen army, the coordination of the four arms of that army (light and heavy infantry and light and heavy cavalry), the trappings of Hellenism, complete obedience to a leader by his immediate inferiors, personal command of an army, and ruthlessness in seeking goals were the basic lessons Philip learned while he was at Thebes. He knew Epaminondas lacked the last, and Philip surmised—correctly—that a leader who did not occasionally display firm justice in the ruthless pursuit of power had little chance for long-range success. He planned from the beginning of his kingship to pick up where Jason of Pherae and Epaminondas of Thebes had left off. Philip meant to be hegemon of Greece, but he was in no hurry. Careful preparation and succinct timing were part of his cunning.

Philip became ruler of the Macedonians in 359 B.C., when he was twenty-four years old. Shortly he consolidated his armies, won a tough series of wars against marauding border tribes, seized rich gold and silver mines in Thrace, isolated the Greek colonists at coastal Olynthus, and maneuvered a place on the prestigious Delphic Council in Greece. Carefully calculating when a show of force would pay and when a mere compromise would serve his immediate ends, he coolly combined diplomacy, hard bargaining, pro-Hellenic propaganda, ruthless military policy, and rugged training for his troops to throw Athens off balance. Athens, with her navy, was the only *polis* able to oppose Philip, and for a time she seemed able to stem the Mace-donian king's conquests through her alliance with Olynthus. But Philip threw the ploy of peace treaties to Athens while marching past the ever more nervous Olynthians. Finally, when he judged the time ripe, he threw the treaties into the breeze and brutally sacked and destroyed Olynthus in 348 B.C., carefully timing his moves to keep Athens unsure of his true motives. Most Greeks were baffled by his military moves: having defeated a Phocian coalition in 352 B.C. (in the name of Greek freedom), he moved his army south toward Thermopylae, an apparent threat of invasion. A hastily raised army of Athenians, Spartans, Phocians, Achaeans, and Thessalians blocked his southward advance at the pass. Philip appeared, looked about and noted the size of the Greek army, made an announcement about his victory over Phocia "in the name of Apollo," and went home. "He returned to Macedonia, having enlarged his kingdom not only by his deeds but also by his respect for the god," runs the cryptic line in Diodorus Siculus (*World History*, XVI, 38. 2).

Not all Greeks were bamboozled. Athens produced the leader

Demosthenes (384–322 B.C.) to fit the time of grave danger. An orator of power and skill, he thundered his anger in the Athenian assembly in speeches like his *First Phillipic* of 350 B.C., in which he compared Philip with a boxer whose blows were parried too late, an athlete who had stamina, speed, and resilience. He urged the Athenians to attack Philip before he attacked Attica, a theme he repeated in the *First* and *Second Olynthiacs* of 349 B.C., pleas for strong aid to threatened Olynthus. Exasperated by the haggling and pussyfooting so usual in Attic politics, he blasted both the people and their leaders in a slothful democracy in his *Third Olynthiac* of the same year. "Now the politicians grasp the money and control everything, as you, the people, enfeebled and shorn of money and allies, play the role of their lowly servants, gushing with thanks for any festival funds they chance to disperse among you" (*Third Olynthiac*, LIX, 3–5).

Athens sent help too late, and Olynthus fell in 348 B.C. Philip's puzzling mercy—he sold all the Olynthians into slavery, while Athens had earlier killed all the men on rebellious Sestos, selling women and children into slavery—served to mollify many Greeks and gave Demosthenes' enemies a better fulcrum to pry under his growing influence. In addition, Philip asked Athens for alliance and a peace treaty through 348, 347, and 346 B.C. Peace was signed when Demosthenes made no opposition. With Athens as ally, Philip soon smashed the remainder of Phocis' forces. His victory gave him Phocis' power in the Delphic Council, and he then presided over the Pythian Games of 346 B.C. It seems that Demosthenes hoped Philip meant what he said (to be merely a "friend of the Greeks"); Demosthenes spoke for peace and at least diplomatic friendship with Philip, especially since the alliance was made under duress. Again Philip allayed more fears by going home after the Pythian Games. His policy was clear; he sought alliance with one state—Athens. He would dominate the rest through a cleverly timed tactic of divide and rule. Athens had prestige and the most perceptive leader among the Greeks. Demosthenes realized all too well the political truth that weakness invites dominion, and his ambition in Athenian politics would be coupled with continued and bitter opposition to Philip.

Although Athens was a nominal ally of Macedonia, many of her traditional enemies (like Thebes and Megara) were also allies of Macedonia and openly hostile to Athens. A feverish preparation for war against Philip or someone else characterized the years after the "peace" of 346 B.C. Feeling surrounded and isolated, Athens thought war was inevitable. In this gloomy military climate, Demosthenes adroitly played his political enemies off against one another, declaring them either stupid or soft or downright traitors while enhancing his own stature as the focus of resistance to Philip. Philip, however, chose to ignore the insults that the famed orator hurled his way, realizing that unless Athens actually mobilized a coalition complete with army and navy, his policies were in little danger. Demosthenes could bellow to his heart's content. Words did not match Philip's power or his magnificent army, heavily armed and absolutely loyal to the Macedonian royal house.

Open war came between Philip and Athens in 340 B.C., after Philip's unsuccessful siege of Byzantium. Although the city survived the Macedonian attack, Philip's threat to the grain shipments caused grave concern not only to Athens but also to Greece as a whole. Thebes dallied, unsure whether she should honor her treaty agreements with Macedonia and go to war against Athens, her traditional enemy. Meanwhile, Philip felt he could flout any threat from Thebes and moved south into Thessaly, menacing Boeotia and irritating Thebes, who complained about his meddling in Greek affairs where he had no real right or reason to do so. Finally, Demosthenes persuaded Thebes to fight for Greek freedom alongside Athens, a personal triumph for the orator as it was a decision of extreme courage by the Boeotian assembly. Of the remaining Greek states, only Corcyra joined Athens and Thebes. Athens immediately dispatched ten thousand mercenaries to help Thebes, in the last desperate gamble for Hellenic independence. Sometime late in the spring of 338 B.C. Philip destroyed this mercenary army by a ruse, and he concentrated his army at Chaeronea in western Boeotia for the decisive battle.

Under the personal command of Philip and his eighteen-year-old son Alexander, the Macedonian army was the finest fighting unit anywhere in Greece or Asia Minor. It contained a heavy cavalry, called the Companions because these men were personal friends or relatives of the king. At Chaeronea, the Macedonian cavalry was reinforced by the Thessalian cavalry, and both units wore armor and saddle quilting to protect the horses' bellies, "which gave a rider a safer seat and did not rub the horse's back," as Xenophon had described thirty years before (*Art of Horsemanship*, XII, 9). Each rider also had a shield, sword, and a special lance (*sarissa*) for infighting, and the unit fought in a wedge, a tactical formation that Philip invented. Light cavalry carried lighter armor, and bore a sword and two javelins for a skirmish. The Foot Companions led the heavy infantry. These men were armed like the Greek *hoplite*, except that they carried a pike twice as long as the *hoplite*'s spear, which was usually about six feet, six inches long. Philip had learned much from Epaminondas' battle tactics, and he adapted his whole army into a larger, more flexible modification of the Greek phalanx. Philip's phalanx was deeper and more open than the usual line of *hoplites*, ranking ten men in a file and giving each soldier a three-foot front. The innovative, longer spears varied in length, with the longest measuring about thirteen feet; this meant that three spearheads were presented by any particular file to the front ranks of the enemy. Philip also employed *peltasts* and other lightly armed foot soldiers as troops with the mobility to protect the phalanx as it shifted for position in battle. When the final clash came at Chaeronea on August 2, 338 B.C., Philip and Alexander led thirty thousand infantry and two thousand cavalry, the full strength of the Macedonian field force.

Against this citizen army, which was trained in precision and experienced from long, arduous campaigns under Philip, came the Greek army of thirty-five thousand foot soldiers and an assortment of horsemen. The Boeotian *hoplites*, numbering about twelve thousand, took up the Greek right wing, and the Theban Sacred Band held the extreme right. About ten thousand Athenian *hoplites*, with only one month's fighting experience in the previous twenty-four years, held the left wing. The remaining *hoplites*, including five thousand mercenaries, occupied the center. The entire Greek line crossed the two-mile wide plain of Chaeronea, well flanked on the right by a river and on the left by the acropolis of Chaeronea. Except for the Sacred Band, which was massed in its deep formation, the Greek line stood eight men deep, while lightly armed troops and *peltasts* linked the left wing with the hill of Chaeronea. The allied Greek cavalry, numbering about two thousand, was put in reserve.

"Once it began, [the battle] was desperately fought for a great while, and many men were slain on both sides, and for a time, victory appeared in the grip of each army" (Diodorus Siculus, *World History*, XVI, 86. 2). Philip's tactics were adopted after his time by Alexander and the Hellenistic kings who inherited the vast Macedonian conquests. At Chaeronea, Philip's main problem was to drive gaps into the solid line of Greek *hoplites*, which his horsemen could not attack directly. To gain this objective, he formed his army into a phalanx line that almost met the Greek left wing; his own left wing, led by Alexander and the heavy cavalry, was far distant from the Greek right, which was packed with the Thebans. His line advanced obliquely, and the Foot Companions clashed with the Athenians long before his center and left engaged the Greek center and right. He then issued an order to the Foot Companions to march backward, thus contracting the "retreating" phalanx into a porcupine of protecting spears while the remainder of the Macedonian center and left were advancing. The inexperienced Athenians fell for the ruse and ran without further thought after Philip's retreating right, causing the entire Greek line to shift to the left to maintain its massed formation. Soon a gap opened between the Greek center and the Theban right wing, and Alexander and his cavalry quickly charged into this opening. At the same time, Philip commanded his Foot Companions to charge the Athenians, whose line had become disjointed and overly extended by their reckless advance. The Macedonian Foot Companions smashed through the Athenians, killing one thousand and capturing two thousand more. On the Greek right, Alexander's cavalry had encircled the Sacred Band, which fell fighting to the last man. The cavalry destroyed the Greek right wing, the Macedonian infantry came into the gap caused by Alexander's cavalry, and the Macedonians wheeled and attacked the Greek center on its right flank, making the entire Greek line roll to its left. Soon the whole Greek line broke and fled. Philip's victory was complete, and he ordered the cavalry not to pursue the fleeing Greeks.

The old *hoplite* phalanx had been superseded by an army that used light and heavy infantry, and cavalry, skillfully combined and superbly led. Epaminondas had proved that lightly armed *peltasts* were effective alone against *hoplites,* and Jason of Pherae indicated how well-organized horsemen could devastate *hoplite* formations once gaps appeared in the long front lines. Philip had destroyed the Greek allied army piecemeal, chopping one section from another and then attacking the flank of the cumbersome phalanx where it could not adequately defend itself against a rapid advance. The old *polis* army was a matter of the past, a fact illustrated with tragic finality by the Athenian levy that fought with valor and courage so unsuccessfully against heavy Macedonian pikemen drilled by hard marching and experience. The new age belonged to the professional soldiers fighting in the Macedonian phalanx. Such an army carried its own flanking protection in a well-coordinated cavalry and in its initially loose and flexible formations.

Thebes immediately surrendered, while debate raged in Athens concerning the final defense of the city. The assembly sent Demosthenes to gain money and further supplies from Persia, and he took ship for the East. Wiser heads, however, prevailed over the urgings of the absent orator, and the general hopelessness of further resistance was transmuted into negotiations with Philip, who had sent an Athenian prisoner back with his terms. Philip's generosity of spirit won the Athenians over to the peace settlement, even though they had to dissolve the Athenian alliance and become Philip's allies. Philip "sent his son Alexander and his friend Antipater to Athens to make peace and establish amity" (Justin-Trogus, *Macedonians,* IX, 4). No Macedonians were to occupy Attica, nor were any Macedonian ships to put into Piraeus. According to Polybius, the Greek historian, Philip released Athenian prisoners without ransom, and the victors "honored the Athenian dead, giving their bones to Antipater to be returned to their homes" (Polybius, *Histories,* V, 10. 4). The Thebans did not fare as well. If relatives could not ransom captives, they were sold into slavery, and Thebes had to purchase her dead. Philip posted a Macedonian detachment on the Cadmea, the acropolis of Thebes, dissolved the Boeotian League, and reduced Thebes to a solitary *polis* without influence. He was as shrewd in dealing with defeated enemies as he was in calculating the weakness of battlefield opponents. Although he treated Thebes harshly, her fate was not as cruel as the one she had given to sister *poleis* who fought against the Boeotian League in earlier decades.

Athens soon rejected Demosthenes' vile taunts in favor of enthusiastic support of Philip and his new crusade against Persia. Athens even gave citizen status to Philip and Alexander, and a new hope for Greek unity was born in the Hellenic League, which Philip formed in 337 B.C. Again Philip shrewdly assessed Greek sentiments, since he took his army home to Macedonia in late 338 B.C. after issuing a manifesto proposing his plans for a Greek alliance. With the exception of Sparta, all the states he contacted accepted. The new Greek League, or League of Corinth, was ratified by delegates meeting at Corinth. Except for Sparta, all mainland Greek states and many island *poleis* became members of a quasi-federal organization calling itself "The Greeks." In 337 B.C. "The Greeks" and Philip, who was the leader of the League of Corinth, jointly issued a declaration of war against Persia.

Many Greeks recalled the union of 481 B.C. that defeated Persia, and the sense of a true crusade in the name of the Greeks sparked the preparations for the war. Polybius, (c. 200-118 B.C.), who also chronicled Rome's rise to power, wrote of this mood of zeal for "The Greeks" that Philip engendered. "He was the creator of freedom in Greece, and since he benefited all Greece, they chose him hegemon [in this context, commander-in-chief] on land and sea, an honor the Greeks had given to nobody previously" (Polybius, *Histories,* IX, 33. 7). Elsewhere in his *Histories,* Polybius writes of Philip's humanity in his quest for peace among the Greeks and for glory in the coming campaigns against the enemy of all the Greeks:

> Philip calculated upon the lack of manliness and utter sloth among the Persians, contrasted with the martial skill of his Macedonians and himself. Furthermore, he directed his eyes and grasped the magnificence of the prize the war proffered and took little time, once he gained the goodwill of the Greeks, to seize a pretext for war. It was in the name of revenge on the Persians for their bad treatment of Greeks.
> [*Histories,* III, 6. 12-13]

The best account of Alexander's campaigns, *Anabasis of Alexander* by Arrian (*fl. c.* A.D. 140), contains a number of reflections on Philip's abilities. Arrian has Alexander speak to his troops of his father's genius in first

> making you Macedonians hardy opponents of your enemies, so that you trusted your courage rather than the village defenses. He made you into city dwellers, gave you civilization with good laws and just customs. Then you became masters of the tribes that stole your goods, and then he added Thrace to the holdings of the Macedonian people. He captured the best coastal towns and opened the land to trade and allowed you to work the mines in peace. Then he made you masters of Thessaly, before whom you previously quailed in fright; and he brought down the Phocians, making the path into Greece broad and easy, while before it was narrow and full of danger. He also humbled Athens and Thebes, always waiting for their opportunity to destroy Macedonia. Thus rather than [his] giving tribute to Athens and following Theban orders, those two cities had to win from Macedonia the right to live on. Then he went into the Peloponnesus and created order there, and he

was declared overlord [*autokrator*] of Greece for the military
expedition against Persia. He gained this new glory and honor
for the Macedonian people rather than for himself. [Arrian,
Anabasis of Alexander, VII, 9. 3–5]

Alexander

Before the great expedition set out, Philip returned to Macedonia to
attend a wedding feast. In the drunken festivities, a disgruntled relative assassinated him. Alexander, the new ruler of Macedonia, was a
mere twenty years old; when the Greek states heard of the murder,
they thought the old days of anarchy had returned. Thebes rose
in revolt while Alexander was attending to the usual tribal incursion
on Macedonia's western frontier. At the head of his hardened troops,
Alexander swept down on Thebes, sacked it, and razed it to the
ground in 335 B.C. as a warning to the rest of Greece. The Persian
adventure would proceed as before.

Alexander inherited his father's throne without much contest since
he was already well known for his military abilities, having commanded the left wing at Chaeronea with distinction. He also inherited
an army, the "Macedonian people in arms," trained and experienced
in war, expert in conducting warfare in mountain country, and
unusually skilled in besieging fortified cities. Besides its magnificent
cavalry and infantry, the Macedonian army contained auxiliary units
of light cavalry, *peltasts,* slingers, engineers, wall sappers, surveyors,
and proficient organizers of the necessary commissariat. The Macedonian army had proved itself almost invincible against Greek *hoplites,*
the infantry of western Illyrian tribes, and even the famed Scythian
cavalry that had given the expeditions of Darius I so much trouble
two hundred years before.

In 334 B.C. Alexander's army of Macedonian and allied Greek
contingents arrived in force in Asia Minor, numbering about thirty-
two thousand infantry and five thousand cavalry. Opposing them
were about twenty thousand cavalry recruited from many of the
inland satrapies of Persia, augmented by an army of about twenty
thousand Greek mercenaries led by Memnon of Rhodes. The armies
met at the Granicus River, where "there was a profound silence for
a time as both armies stood without motion on the banks of the
river, as if in some awe at what was about to come." Shortly,
"Alexander leaped on his horse and called to his Companions to fol-

low and provide the models of courage and valor" (Arrian, *Anabasis of Alexander,* I, 15). The charge smashed into the Persian cavalry, and the more heavily armored Macedonian cavalry soon wore down the more lightly armed Persians. The Macedonian infantry followed, and the Persian horsemen fled, leaving the army of Memnon surrounded. Alexander declared no quarter to "Greeks who fought against him," and took only two thousand prisoners, who were "sent shackled to Macedonia to perform forced labor." Macedonian losses were light, considering the importance of Alexander's victory. "About twenty-five of the Companions on horseback were slain in the initial assault," and "about sixty of the other cavalrymen were killed and about thirty of the infantry" (Arrian, *Anabasis of Alexander,* I, 17). Alexander amply demonstrated his tactical and strategic genius—in many ways surpassing that of his father—at the Granicus. The Persian king, Darius III, now realized that he did not fight a young and impetuous king at the head of an experienced army, but a master of war.

Quickly Alexander marched east to meet the full army of Persia, which Darius III had collected to expunge the young upstart. The two armies collided at Issus, south of Cilicia in Syria, in November, 333 B.C. The Macedonian army had been beefed to full strength—forty thousand infantry and the five thousand cavalry. Darius III commanded a force of some thirty thousand Greek mercenaries, an equal number of Persian infantry and lightly armed troops that had been trained as *peltasts,* and a good number of horsemen. The battle was hotly contested, particularly by the Greek mercenaries who fought against the center of the Macedonian line, which was made up of heavy infantry. Alexander attacked the Persian line as Philip had assaulted the allied Greek line at Chaeronea. An angular charge with his right wing, a maneuver repeated from the charge at the Granicus, opened gaps in the opposing line, but ten thousand of the mercenaries broke through Alexander's encirclement. Shortly all the Persians broke through and fled, led by Darius III, and Alexander gained great treasures at Damascus, as well as capturing Darius' wife and mother in the abandoned Persian camp. Another great victory for the young king resounded back in Greece.

Continuing his march south, Alexander laid siege to Tyre, which fell in July, 332 B.C., thus gaining him the large fleet of the Phoenician cities. Taking his victorious army into Egypt, Alexander added that country to his conquests. The priests of Egypt hailed him as a god, and later in the same year as pharaoh. Turning east, he pursued the remaining armies of Darius III across the Tigris River in Mesopotamia and found the forces of the Persian king concentrated at Gaugamela (near Nineveh). Darius had inserted spikes in the plain to cripple Alexander's horses, and he leveled uneven portions of the seven-mile wide plain to make easy passage for his two hundred chariots, which were equipped with scythed outer hubs. Darius hoped these chariots would open gaps in Alexander's heavy infantry and thus allow the Persian cavalry to surround isolated pockets of the Macedonian army. The Persians assembled forty thousand cavalry, sixteen thousand heavy infantry, hordes of lightly armed foot soldiers, and the two hundred equipped chariots to fight Alexander's forty thousand infantry and seven thousand cavalry.

The Battle of Gaugamela (October, 331 B.C.) would decide the fate of the Persian Empire. Again Alexander employed a short, slanting line as he advanced against the massed Persian lines. Darius hoped to gain victory through envelopment by his superior numbers, while Alexander knew victory would come only if he could penetrate and break the Persian blocks of cavalry and infantry. A duel between Macedonian and Persian horsemen resulted as Alexander's marching phalanx obliquely came at Darius' line, threatening to chop it up, and Darius threw his Scythian horsemen into the fray. The Macedonians beat them off. In a short while the fearsome scythed chariots rumbled into action, but Alexander was prepared. "The phalanx joined shields together, and everyone clashed their weapons on their shields, making a great din, as Alexander had ordered." The horses shied away from the clattering and clanging, and "most of the chariots twisted around and bore down on their own lines with terrible impact, irresistible in its force," slicing through the startled Persian infantry. Other chariots made it to the Macedonian line, "but the soldiers divided ranks and opened gaps, and the chariots passed rapidly through the paths provided." Some of the horses "were dispatched by spear thrusts," but others managed the gruesome task they were sent to do. They dealt

> death to the Macedonians in a variety of ways, severing the
> arms of many, shields attached; and in other instances the keen
> and cleverly contrived scythes sliced necks, sending heads
> tumbling with eyes yet open in an expression unchanged, while

others were sliced through the ribs, and the mortal gashes
inflicted a rapid death. [Diodorus Siculus, *World History*,
XVII, 58. 2–5]

Diodorus' bloody scene has no parallel in Arrian, who avoids such
tawdry descriptions that appealed to readers of lesser taste. Arrian
writes of this same series of battle details with calculated restraint.
Some spearmen "grasped the reins of the advancing horses, dragging
the drivers down, and surrounded the horses and cut them down."
Some of the chariots did make it through, according to Arrian, "but
they had no real impact, since the Macedonians were under orders to
break formation, wherever the chariots attacked, and allow them
through the lines deliberately." This happened when the chariots got
to the Macedonian lines, and the thundering vehicles "and their
drivers suffered no damage at all" (Arrian, *Anabasis of Alexander*,
III, 14). The gory details in Diodorus Siculus (or *his* source) smack
of tavern tales told over wine drunk Scythian style (neat), while
Arrian's account gives a minimum of glamor to the carnage of battle,
spending more time describing the essential genius of Alexander's
planning and responses to threats like the sinister blades of scythed
chariots. As an experienced general, Arrian avoided the hazy glory of
bloodbaths that cost too many men.

Alexander won the battle at Gaugamela by casting his heavy cavalry
at Darius' strongest point. The Macedonians shoved their spears into
the faces of the Persians, who soon broke and fled, the Great King
fleeing in a chariot. Alexander pursued until nightfall, capturing the
royal chariot but not Darius. Meanwhile, his army captured the
Persian camp and baggage train. Thus the Macedonians understood
how the Persians used elephants and camels in war, since the camp
included several of the larger elephants, along with their Indian
mahouts. The new King of Persia, Pharaoh of Egypt, King of Macedon, hegemon of Greece, and King of Babylon, now styling himself
King of Asia, finally caught up with Darius III, but not before he had
been murdered by one of his own nobles (July, 330 B.C.). Alexander
gave his predecessor a gigantic funeral, and meted a horrid death to
his slayer, according to the ancient laws and customs of Persia.

The King of Asia had captured an enormous fortune, a bullion
store of about 180,000 *talents* (worth about $500,000,000) that
soon began supporting the commerce of the broadened Greek world.
The young king decided to conquer *all* of the Persian Empire, using
the logic applied to control the Macedonian homeland. In Macedonia,

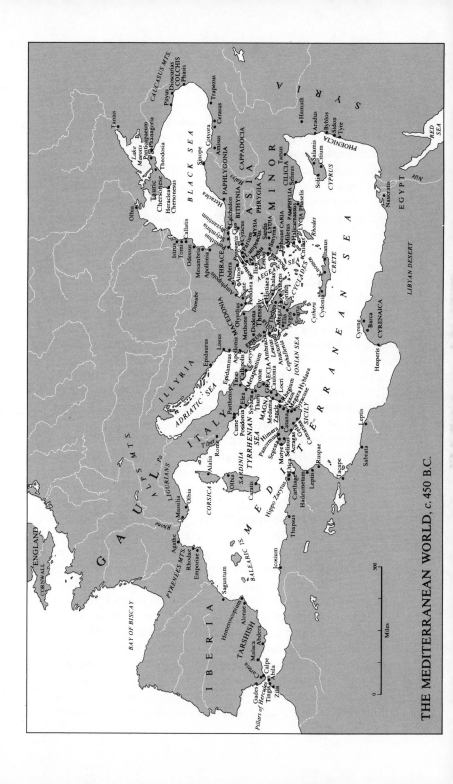

THE MEDITERRANEAN WORLD, c. 450 B.C.

the kings had conquered the mountain tribes surrounding the fertile plains; once the vigorous mountain peoples were subdued, they became good barriers against the warlike nomads beyond them. Alexander used this principle as he marched north into the strange and mysterious regions of the northern Persian frontiers. Names like Bactria and Sogdiana came within the ken of Greeks listening to stories drifting back to Syria, Asia Minor, and the Greek homeland. With growing wonder, they heard tales of Alexander's wanderlust, which seemed to drive him ever further east. Many assumed he had disappeared into the mists of the East never to return, and rumblings of potential revolt occasionally rose from Athens. Sparta had earlier been forced to join the Hellenic League after an abortive war against the Macedonian army that had been left in Greece. More stories followed. Alexander had passed through lofty mountains and a great pass into lush green lands near the great Indus River. By this time (327 B.C.), the Macedonians were merely a segment of the army swelled by Persian and even some Indian mercenaries, "world conquerors, bedecked with the tatters of Indian and barbarian booty, patched together badly" (Diodorus Siculus, *World History,* XVII, 94. 2). An elephant train was contained in the remodeled field army that ran into King Porus, one of the native rulers of the Punjab who had decided to fight the foreign invaders.

In early 326 B.C. Porus drew up his large army to prevent Alexander from crossing the Hydaspes River (now the Jhelum), a tributary of the Indus. The Indian king had about two hundred elephants, thirty thousand infantry, three hundred chariots, and four thousand cavalry trained to remain steady in sight and smell of the elephants. Alexander had one thousand mounted archers, but his cavalry were elephant-shy, so he only had the massed infantry to fight the elephant line. Attacking the flanks of Porus' army, Alexander managed to cause enough confusion that the Indian cavalry plummeted back into its own lines. Into the gaps came Seleucus, commander of the Macedonian phalanx, who engaged the elephants and their mahouts. The Macedonians picked off the mahouts and hamstrung many of the huge beasts. Wounded and lacking the urges that pricked them into trampling, goring, and picking up enemy foot soldiers, the elephants backed like huge ships into the Indian ranks, trampling friend and foe as they bellowed their way away from the Macedonians. Locking shields at Alexander's command, the phalanx broke the last resistance of Porus' army, and the Indian losses were extremely heavy. On the other hand, the Macedonians suffered the casualties of two hundred fifty cavalry and seven hundred infantry killed or badly mauled, more than the combined total losses in the previous battles since 334 B.C. The fear the elephants corps inspired was not forgotten, and Seleucus imprinted the need for elephants deep in the Greek military mind. In spite of the carnage, Alexander persuaded Porus to return; so Porus could be granted any request. He replied to Alexander's question, "Treat me as befits a king" (Arrian, *Anabasis of Alexander,* V, 19. 2). The volatile Macedonian was so taken with this answer that he granted Porus his kingdom, making him satrap in India of the vast empire.

Soon Alexander's troops refused to march further east; though he sulked in his tent for three days, his soldiers did not change their minds. They were exhausted. Turning south, Alexander's army sailed down the Indus on a fleet of one thousand ships built by shipwrights who had come with the army, under the common impression that they would reach the great Eastern sea. Finally returning to Babylon in 324 B.C., Alexander spent his energies reorganizing his far-flung realm and planning new expeditions into Arabia. The pace eventually took its toll, and Alexander became ill at Babylon from the effects of marathon drinking bouts and overwork. He died in Babylon on June 13, 323 B.C., at the age of 33. According to Arrian, the generals hovered around his deathbed, asking him to whom the great empire should fall. He replied, "To the strongest" (Arrian, *Anabasis of Alexander,* VII, 26. 3).

Hellenistic Warfare

Commonly tucked into general histories of the classical world as a postscript to classical Greek history is the complicated period of time labeled Hellenistic history, which followed the death of Alexander and continued down to the final Roman conquest of Egypt (30 B.C.). The label is a modern invention (to distinguish this period from Hellenic history), and its neat beginning and end points belie the plethora of cultural, military, economic, social, and political events that transpired until Rome came to the Near East. Political instability, cultural fermentation between East and West, and the ancient equivalent of imperialism generally characterized Hellenistic times. So it is difficult to unweave the threads of Hellenistic history; many modern histories of the Hellenistic successor states are too often Hellenistic telephone books: names and numbers. There *are* many names and many dates, as a cursory glance at volumes 7 through 10 of the *Cambridge Ancient History* will show.

Almost immediately, Alexander's generals began fighting for either a chunk of the empire or control of all of it. One general, Ptolemy, correctly sensed the drift of events and simply took Egypt for himself, defending it against all comers. By 305 B.C. his dynasty was firmly implanted in Egypt, and his line held power until the suicide of Cleopatra VII (30 B.C.). Other generals fought each other for the rest of the empire; however, Antigonus, the major contender for Alexander's mantle and one of the older commanders in the original Macedonian army, was killed at the Battle of Ipsus (301 B.C.). His son Demetrius Poliorcetes (so-called Beseiger of Cities in a Greek joke because he botched the siege of Rhodes so wretchedly in 305–304 B.C.) escaped, but the Battle of Ipsus proved that no one man could rule the entire Alexandrian empire. Thus by about 280 B.C. the huge empire was divided into three major kingdoms. Alexandria in Egypt had been founded and built as the Greek headquarters for the Ptolemaic kingdom, named for the slippery Ptolemy. A second kingdom, established in the heartland of Syria, was named after Seleucus, the phalanx commander at the Hydaspes River. The Seleucid dynasty ruled from Antioch, like Alexandria, a city that the Greek overlords had constructed. The third line of kings, called the Antigonid dynasty, descended from Demetrius Poliorcetes and ruled in the Macedonian homeland. It did well until Rome dismembered Macedonia in 168 B.C. In southern Greece, two leagues (the Aetolian and Achaean) fought between themselves and against the hated Macedonians for dominance. Athens retained some of the aura of an intellectual center and became the home of several new brands of philosophy. Sparta remained in her Laconian cocoon, rising briefly to challenge Roman power in Greece around 190 B.C. Rome's legions silenced Sparta's revival, especially after the whole Peloponnesian peninsula came under direct Roman rule in 146 B.C. The Seleucid kings gradually dwindled in power; by about 90 B.C. they were merely leaders of mercenary bands. Rome made Syria a province in 63 B.C. The citadel of Pergamon in Asia Minor broke away from Seleucid control shortly after 300 B.C. and grew rich until the kingdom was willed to the Senate and People of Rome in 133 B.C. Rhodes, the island and city immediately southwest of the peninsula, rivaled Pergamon as a champion of localism in Greek politics in Asia Minor.

Her navy kept the Eastern seas free of pirates until she incurred Rome's displeasure. By 100 B.C., Rhodian power was totally on the wane, and Rome had to clear the seas of freebooters at her own expense. She did so, but only after the pirate menace had become almost unbearable; one sweeping campaign (67 B.C.) took care of the voracious Cilician fleets.

Hellenistic political history is very complicated, and a proper study of the period should take each of the three major kingdoms—Ptolemaic, Seleucid, and Antigonid—into account. Even so, the constant marriage alliances, shifts of political agreements, and swift changes of political fortunes in each dynasty make the period varied and mysterious for those seeking simple themes and historical sense. Added to these kingdoms were the Greek kingdoms of Bactria and India, which soon fell away from direct Western rule. They form a fascinating but poorly known adjunct to Hellenistic history. (Some of the Bactrian kings are recorded only through their beautiful coins.)

Warfare in the Hellenistic period fossilized the innovations of Philip II and Alexander the Great. Each of the kings and their mercenary commanders read and pondered the tactics and strategy of the romantic march into the East, and each fought according to set patterns laid down by the great masters. The phalanx became heavier, a grinding block of heavily armored, porcupine-like men. It also became less mobile, as the flexible Roman legions proved after 197 B.C. and on numerous other occasions. Even the new device of elephants proved more of a hazard than a dependable addition to the armies of the Greek rulers of the Near East. They loom large in fictional portrayals of the time, but elephants did not live up to the expectations given them. They were part of more defeats than victories, but they were akin to status symbols for the Hellenistic military establishments. The handbooks record how Porus used his elephants as a screen for cavalry that had been trained not to bolt from their smell, and how an elephant advance guard could open up holes for infantry or delay an infantry attack. Alexander never used elephants, although he had at least one hundred of them on his return to Babylon. Hellenistic generals quickly learned how to fight one another using elephants or defending against them. For example, in the Battle of Gaza (312 B.C.) Ptolemy had no elephants but managed to cause his opponent Demetrius, who had a number of the beasts, grave disappointment by a kind of ancient mine field. Ptolemy stopped the hulking pachyderms by sowing hidden spikes connected by stakes and chains in the field of battle. The poor elephants stepped on the spikes with their vulnerable and very tender feet, making them—as was expected—crunch part of Demetrius' own line (Diodorus Siculus, *World History,* XIX, 83-84). And at the Battle of Magnesia (189 B.C.), where the Seleucid king, Antiochus III, contested Roman influence in Greece and Asia Minor, his elephants went into reverse and trampled his own men.

6

Greeks and Myth

The enormous popularity of J.R.R. Tolkien's works, especially
his *Lord of the Rings,* has once again demonstrated the deep attraction of myth and the worlds inhabited by mythical beings. A great
strength in Tolkien's writing is the unity of otherworld characters,
clearly identified with "real" things. Hobbits live just beyond the
ken of men, but their adventures contain manlike beings. Wizards
and good warriors loom as demigods, living within the natural laws
that apply to that universe which is somewhere close, yet distant
from ordinary and plainly mortal men. The last half of the twentieth
century has also produced a somewhat unique literary genre in the
same class as *Lord of the Rings,* which exploits the inner feeling that
scientific explanations via mathematics, physics, chemistry, or whatever do not quite include the fact that something else needs explaining, too. This type of literature, called science fantasy, uneasily
solders scientific logic to powers that are beyond ordinary men;
myths explain those powers to mortal warriors thrusting swords and
hurling oaths. Without the matrix of myth and the gods or powers
from whom they derive their purpose, neither Tolkien nor science
fantasy has little cohesion other than as a simple adventure yarn.
The best of the modern craftsmen in science fantasy know this, and
their myths give some of the best tales a gossamer beauty, even
though fictional myths live only in the pages of fiction and in the
minds of readers.

Much as science fiction makes a halting attempt to consolidate the ethos of twentieth-century society, so Greek mythology spoke to man's relations with the gods and the powers around him—some seen and others mysterious and brooding, known only to a chosen few who understood riddles and the arcana of times so distant that they were mired in folk memory. The purpose of myth has never been to tell historical facts or to relate the chronological development of a culture or a people, but rather to embody what a people most value, much as law will define and encrust what is most valued. Also within the canon of commonly accepted myth, a people devise further definitions in ritual and community observances, ceremonials that are often called religion. In Greek civilization, however, there was little separation between religion and myth, or between ceremonial and religion, since Greeks believed every action involved some kind of divine presence. Another way of defining Greek religious ideas is to assume that Greek myth allowed the gods to act in a very human way, while Greek religion provided divine attendance around the individual, especially if he were "heroic," like Homer's major characters. The homeric poems, the *Iliad* and *Odyssey*, provide the prototypes of the Greek gods and goddesses, and those images remained fairly standard throughout Greek history. Hesiod recorded some of the mythological riches behind the Greek view of the gods, but his contribution to knowledge of divine appearance was slight compared with that of Homer.

Even with this surface uniformity, which is surprising in the context of the constant warfare and strife between the *poleis* of historic Greece, each clan and settlement had its own deities. Both the small and locally important gods and the local representatives of the major gods entered every facet of life. It is this quality of Greek life that distinguishes it from most of Western society, and the literature that remains from classical Greece contains many more references to the gods or religion than would the total scope of literature produced in the United States. Another distinguishing feature is that a modern student of myth and religion might probe the historical antecedents of or attempt to deduce origins for a given belief; but the Greek knew that Apollo was a great god and did not speculate how unevenly he might be worshiped. In a similar manner, the earlier Minoans carved thrones on mountain tops for their gods, leaving the actual image of the deity to the imagination; this custom may have eventually lead to the anthropomorphic ("formed like

men," from *anthropos* and *morphe*) gods pictured in Homer. Indeed, the common double-headed axe that a god was to throw *was*,
in effect, the god, both in fact and in artistic symbol. (Later Greeks
chose to think of their gods as generally beneficent figures, uplifting
in spirit–a concept suggesting that men were not subject to perverse
divine will as such.) As a consequence of this anthropomorphism,
there was–with the exception of the commonly accepted great
deities of Olympus (the Olympian Twelve of the handbooks)–little
orthodoxy in Greek religion. Quite a variety existed in local cults,
especially in those of the patron god or goddess of each *polis.* In
these local cults, marked by a temple, lay the spiritual focus of the
state, which created an intense feeling of unity. In his *Origins of
Greek Civilization* (New York:Knopf, 1961), Chester Starr puts
this sense of unity, religious and political conservatism, and exploitation of limited forms in another way. "Only by imposing upon
themselves the tyranny of form and type and by restricting license
for the communal good were the Greeks able to master the threats
of anarchy" (p. 381).

Homer and the Gods

In the *Iliad* and the *Odyssey,* the gods are important for the flow of
the narrative and are wedded to the actions of mortals through the
tale of Achilles' anger in the great war with Troy. The gods talk
with men, sometimes in human guise, and they give advice and
direction to the various heroes during the conduct of the war. The
gods of the *Iliad* demonstrate a later Greek saying: "What are men?
Mortal gods. What are gods? Immortal men." Such deities, seen
through the poetic eye of Homer and later bards, were like immortal men and women in their form and action, but they had greater
power then mere mortals. Like men, they were influenced by very
human desires and emotions; although these were always larger
than life, they were recognized as basic human reactions. The gods
could be seduced, teased, pushed into childlike wrath, flattered,
and admonished. By making their gods into many variations of
manlike forms (what the textbooks call "anthropomorphic
polytheism"), the Greeks indicated their own opinions about the
world of nature and the inner world of the soul. Myth and religion
did not *explain* creation, nor did they give explanations for life in
any future world. Rather, in myth the Greeks expressed how much

they enjoyed life and how incredibly curious they were about it. On the other hand, the inner poetic reflection that permeates the myths in both Homer and Hesiod gave the Greeks a balance between the gargantuan excesses of Zeus in his more amorous moments and the gloomy, brooding introspection that characterizes both Achilles and Agamemnon in the Greek army before the walls of Troy, and additionally shows the poignant tragedy of Hector, the major Trojan warrior. From the glitter and gore of war and the blustering, uncouth, heartless god Ares, who *is* war, the poet leads his listeners to tender Helen, the wife of Menelaus of Sparta. She had been seduced by Paris, son of the Trojan king Priam, and she had decided to run off with the handsome prince in spite of her better judgment. The purpose of the war, so the poet intones, was to rescue fair Helen, and the assembled Greek nobility came to Troy seeking revenge.

Helen shows remorse and anger. Her ire first explodes against Aphrodite, goddess of love, for tempting her to do something she thought unwise; but her regret is Helen speaking within herself, a recognition that the decision was her own, even though the Cyprian goddess clouded her mind with passion for the male beauty of Paris, who was skilled with the bow and had no peer as a lover. In her mind and in her keen insight, she reflects that her flight to Troy was foolish; but now that the battles rage, she displays the dignity due from a queen, either of Sparta or of Troy. To be sure, Aphrodite offered her complete satisfaction in the sensual passions, but reason later brought her the realization that the price for Paris was too high.

The gods have full power over men, but one god may favor one mortal over another and sway a fellow god by argument, flattery, or divine strength. The strongest of the gods is Zeus, but he occasionally refuses to exercise his will, knowing that the consequences of his action are sometimes unpredictable or unpleasant. Homer notes that Zeus is not overtly ruled by fate:

> And when the god of the sun was astride the middle of the sky, then the father held out and balanced his scales of gold. In each pan, he set a fateful share of death, which renders men supine—one for the horse-taming Trojans, the other for the bronze-bearing Achaeans—and lifted the scales by the middle of its beam. Heaviest was the Achaean side, the beam and fates of the Achaeans lowering to the fruitful earth, while the Trojan side soared up into the vast vault of the sky. Zeus

thereby hurled a great bolt of crackling light, thundering down from mount Ida, and the fiery light descended among the men of the Achaeans. Beholding it, they became numb, the terror making their faces pale. [*Iliad*, VIII, 68–77]

Likewise, when the final contest between Hector and Achilles comes,

then the father held out and balanced his scales of gold. In each pan, he set a fateful share of death, which renders men supine—one for Achilles, the other for horse-taming Hector— and lifted the scales by the middle of its beam. Hector's side was heaviest, sighing down to earth. Under doom, Phoebus Apollo abandoned him. [*Iliad*, XXII, 209–213]

The gods have the power of weighing the scales and can twist and divert human actions if they want, but they cannot alter the basic natures of the men they advise, cajole, or fool with false advice. The choices in the *Iliad* are human ones. Divine interference does not change the meaning of the poetic purpose, which is to create a moving and clear depiction of man's flaws and his nobility. The weighing of the scales became an impersonal thing, a simple ceremony akin to compromises of differing opinions. Achilles' martial valor, Hector's final mistakes, Helen's flawed judgment, the craft of wily Odysseus, and Agamemnon's booming call to battle all foreshadow the fall of Troy.

The *Iliad* was the first Greek description of cultural and religious values to dominate in Greek civilization. The poem also marks the beginning of Western literature; many of the moral and ethical standards enunciated in the *Iliad* became marks of Western culture thereafter. The physical world outside men, the inner nature of men, and the relationships of gods to men form major themes in the poem. Homer took his tone from dim folk memories of the glory and grandeur of the days of Mycenaean warlords; but the embedded myths tell more about what Greeks in Homer's day (*c.* 850 B.C.) thought about war, the gods, and kinship and its obligations than they relate history. Homer makes a kind of catalogue listing the great Achaean powers fighting the Trojans, and archaeological excavations in Pylos, Mycenae, and Ithaca (an island off the western coast of northern Greece) have indeed yielded many finds of Mycenaean origin. But the reader who takes Homer's history literally will be sadly misled while being tantalized by remains that look "just like Homer's tale."

For example, the University of Cincinnati's lengthy excavations at the site of Mycenaean Pylos (on the western coast of the Peloponnesus) proved beyond much doubt that Pylos was a great Mycenaean fortress-citadel. There is a heated argument whether this is the site of Nestor's Pylos as related in Homer, but Linear B tablets also unearthed at Pylos show that the settlement was an important administrative and religious center. Likewise, in the late 1860s, European classical scholars chuckled when the self-trained German traveler and archaeologist Heinrich Schliemann went to western Turkey to dig up Troy, armed with the *Iliad,* many shovels, and grim determination. After doing some surveying in 1868, he began to dig at the site of Hissarlik in the summers of 1871–1873. He found Troy. In 1876 he discovered the royal tombs at Mycenae, and in 1884 he uncovered a huge palace complex at Tiryns, another Mycenaean citadel near Mycenae. The "Mycenae rich in gold" yielded a beautiful death mask, which Schliemann immediately called the face of Agamemnon. Later archaeological work at the sites of both Troy and Mycenae have led to speculation about which level of each site was really contemporary with the Trojan War, a term which some scholars believe to be a figment of poetic license. Professor Carl W. Blegen, from the University of Cincinnati excavations, thought level VIIa was the Troy of Priam's time, while continuing work at Mycenae has revealed a second series of graves (termed Grave Circle B, since the Schliemann digs had unearthed Grave Circle A); this discovery suggests a number of possible explanations that do not quite fit the facts in the mixed traditions of Homer's poems. What archaeologists have shown at Pylos, Mycenae, and Troy is that the Greek myths did preserve a dim memory of Mycenaean Greece.

There is little agreement among specialists about the origins or venerability of the various strands of Greek myths, but most general accounts reflect the opinions of the Swedish scholar Martin Nilsson. He has made arguments (especially in *The Mycenaean Origin of Greek Mythology,* with summations in his monumental *A History of Greek Religion*) for Mycenaean origins for the major Greek myths, as well as arguments for the Mycenaean origins of the Greek pantheon. Other specialists have accused Nilsson of a Nordic predisposition, but the Linear B tablets from Pylos seem to bear out part of his theories. Unfortunately, the names of the deities are listed as slaves on the tablets, suggesting that common names in Mycenaean times later became the names of gods and goddesses. It appears that the Mycenaeans brought a father god with them when they invaded Greece sometime around 2000 B.C.; this male figure, later identified as Zeus, retained his image, in contrast to the mother goddesses that seem more predominant in Minoan Crete and the cultures of Asia Minor.

The Greeks, unlike modern scholars, regarded their myths as a way to understand the gods, particularly the divine figures most closely identified with a locale or with a man who was later deified. The tales surrounding Heracles (Hercules) are good examples. According to the story, Heracles was king of Tiryns, but a vassal to the king of Mycenae. In the Heracles cycle the king of Mycenae seems like the homeric Agamemnon; he is cowardly and brimming with deceit, yet able to inflict impossible demands on the hapless Heracles. After the hero manages to get through his twelve labors, completed when he brings the great watchdog of Hades up onto the earth, he gains immortality. Such mythical cycles, which may have emerged from Mycenaean times, are packed with brutality and crudity. The hunt provides opportunities for great deeds indicating prowess, and heroes slay lions with a staccato regularity.

Homer, on the other hand, molds his gods and heroes into beings that are less brutal and more humane. According to an early version of the Heracles cycle, he had murdered a guest-friend and stolen his horses, but the homeric poets do not relate the tale, although they admit they are acquainted with it. Homer's ethic is that of *arete,* a Greek term that cannot be translated by a single English word. In one context, *arete* may mean the qualities of a dignified leader, while in another setting it connotes the noble who has excellent wine and willing slave girls who wait in the dark recesses of the great hall where the poets sing of his glorious deeds in battle; in yet another surrounding *arete* suggests the kind of man whose mere prestige commands and controls other men. *Arete* is remotely similar to the ideal of medieval knighthood, but the knight owed service to the meek in general, whereas the Greek with *arete* was bound by kinship obligations. This Greek ideal of manhood was wrapped up with mythical and religious customs; in Homer's time these customs were generally similar over the Greek world, especially the worship of the Olympian Twelve, who presumably resided on Mount Olympus. However, each *polis,* had a unique religious life, which often focused on chthonic (infernal) cults and on cults to local heroes. Thebes became famed for her veneration of Heracles, and Athens was widely known for

her cult to Theseus, whose resemblance to Heracles is quite remarkable.

Hesiod's Divine Genealogy

The Homeric poems are generally impersonal, mirroring Greek culture in the transition from the confusion of the so-called Greek
Dark Ages (*c.* 1100–*c.* 750 B.C.) to the time of the fully developed
poleis. Thus Hesiod of Ascra (a town above the plain of Boeotia),
who wrote the *Works and Days* and the *Theogony* about 700 B.C.,
was part of an embryonic *polis* culture, aristocratic in structure and
undergoing rapid change. His lines of poetry are personal and sharply
intense, often revealing a prevalent bitterness among the small farmers against the rulers of the *polis*. The rhythm and hexameter
of Hesiod's poetry, as well as his chosen vocabulary, are quite similar to those of the homeric poets, but the mood within the *Works
and Days* and *Theogony* is of an age quite removed from the strut-
ting nobility of the *Iliad*. Hesiod gazes back fondly to the good old
days, when hard work was rewarded and farm life was reasonably
secure (something of a perennial myth in all ages), while he looks
forward somewhat reluctantly to the time when the *polis* will insure
justice.

Where *Works and Days* is an encomium to labor, a muted fanfare
to farm routine and the varying seasons of the planting and harvesting year, *Theogony* is a divine genealogy documenting the Greek
view of the gods and their origins. However, it does not provide a
creation doctrine, although it takes for granted various creation
myths as being commonly known. Hesiod intends it to be an outline
of the cosmos, both divine and human, and the universe is pictured
as living in its own right, a viewpoint not far removed from the
beginnings of philosophical speculation. The major thread in *Theogony*
is an explanation of the cosmos, with minor themes of the human
and physical cosmos, the universe closest to men within this dominant idea.

Zeus' quarrel with Prometheus explains Zeus' control of the divine
cosmos, but the struggle gives fateful portents for men as well.
Prometheus gave the gift of fire to men but also bequeathed them,
according to mythology, the curse of women, which in turn makes
labor necessary. Divine, physical, and human spheres are woven
together as Hesiod relates "how the first gods and the earth came

into being, and rivers, and the sea without bonds with its angry swell, and the glowing stars, and the broad sky vaulting above, and the gods born of them" (*Theogony,* 107-111). Through brutal conflict, Zeus becomes king and father, but only because there is strife in the divine cosmos. After he wins dominance, Zeus reorganizes everything—the realm of the gods, the physical universe, and the kingdom of men.

In one sense, the entire *Theogony* wraps history in the idiom of myth. Hesiod believes that the present universe is to be understood as the result of growth and change. The poem's form is the genealogical table, myth is the vehicle, and hexameter provides the cadence and expression. In his extension of the beginning genealogies, the poet includes everything of importance in the worlds of the gods, of earth and sky, and of men. First the Whole comes from two primordial powers, Void and Earth. Then what we might call "creative energy" begins the process of gradually separating them. Hesiod calls this elemental creative energy Desire; Desire causes change through four generations, each generation leaving its mark in the cosmos. Earth and Zeus provide the beginning and end in the poet's development of the cosmos, with the cosmic evolution delineated through progressive generations.

Earth produces the first generation—the Sky, Mountains, and Sea, all parts of nature. Later come the Titans, followed by Zeus and the gods of Olympus, who in turn connect with the fourth and last generation, man. Hesiod sees the Olympian gods appearing like human beings but having immortality and greater power, and the cosmos as evolving from the opposition between Chaos and Earth into an order men can understand through Zeus and the gods. Zeus gains final victory more through political maneuver than through brute power or coalitions with other gods. The poet terms Zeus' underlying strength *metis,* meaning statesmanship coupled with wisdom and cunning. By Hesiod's definition, power or authority (Zeus) embodies wisdom; *Theogony* expresses this by Uranus (Sky) having a secret store of knowledge, even after Zeus has deposed him. As proof of this secret store, the poet offers the evidence of the oracles that Uranus gave to Zeus.

The Greek justification for the existence of the *polis* is wedded to Hesiod's account of why Zeus is not fated for destruction like Cronos (Time). Zeus avoids the fate of Cronos and Uranus because he sits above Good and Evil. Similarly, the state—which provides

law, order, justice, and peace for its citizens—is itself not subject to
law. The Father God melds within himself previously existing forces
of good. In his divine role, he creates forces of good from within
himself to supplement those already present in the cosmos. These
forces of good, which are the names of Zeus' children, are lawful,
universal forces subject to the will of divine law (Zeus). With his
offspring, so Hesiod writes, Zeus creates the potential of law. Metis
is wisdom, Idyia is the quality of knowing and remembering,
Nemeretes never makes mistakes, and Polynoe is a rich and full
mind. Even more children of the Father God populate the divine
cosmos. Protomedea becomes first in leadership, Leagora is the
gatherer of the people, Peitho is the art of persuasion, and Themis
is law. Since through his offspring Zeus is wise, all-knowing, infallible, rich in intellect, is able to lead the gods, harvest goodness in
gods and humans, be skilled and crafty in arguments, and be the
progenitor of law, he is able to be just and to dispense justice.

Zeus mates with Themis to produce the twins Time-for-the-law
and Fates-which-punish-injustice. Thus the supremacy of law is
firmly based on the union of force with law. Likewise, two more of
Zeus' children, Apollo and Artemis, are breathless beauty among
divine figures, "children lovely beyond all the sons of heaven"
(Hesiod, *Theogony*, 919–920). When Hesiod says Zeus also created
the power of art, he is speaking about the artists and sculptors in
his own time, who were honing the canons of beauty and proportion, especially in their depiction of the gods. Thus the Father God
also mates with Eurynome, mother of the three Graces, and with
Mnemosyne, mother of the nine Muses, siring the Muse Erato,
the essence of loveliness. This procreation, in turn, began the ob-
servance among men of festivals that promote art (the three Graces)
and began the refinement of the differences among the various arts
(the nine Muses).

Hesiod believes one of Zeus' most important tasks is the supres-
sion of evil in the cosmos. To accomplish this end, he honored the
dark and foreboding force of somber Hecate as the go-between for
men and gods, but she also is absorbed into Zeus' actions. Her dark
power, haunting men with ghostly hints at crossroads and having
the force of black magic, lies in unsettled death, which is the fate of
men who fail to observe the customs of law and of those who do
not receive proper burial. Prometheus is the bad mediator, and Zeus
gives his brothers, "Meneothius of overweening pride and insane

presumption" (Hesiod, *Theogony,* 517–519) and Atlas of violent skill and strength, repressed but constructive roles. The heroes, more of Zeus' sons or descendants of Zeus, fight monsters, which are the evil powers remaining in the world. Heracles acquires immortality by the success of his twelve labors.

The struggle between good and evil in the cosmos provides the artistic tension in the *Theogony;* the emphasis on the play of opposites underscores the Greek explanation of the universe in terms of causation, order, and unity. This explanation is a short step from philosophy, which soon explained the cosmos in terms divorced from divine will. *Theogony* mapped the pattern of Greek thought. Although the poet expresses order, causation, and unity in terms of myth and religious value, man is the central point of explanation and understanding. Hesiod may have inherited themes and motifs from Near Eastern sources, but his poem is essentially that of a Greek: a personal view of the world and the gods.

Even more personal is *Works and Days,* whose setting is the world of men, where rampant injustice robs their lives of goodness. Hesiod writes of his wicked brother Perseus, who connived with a "bribe-swallowing king" (*Works and Days,* 38–39) to cheat the poet of his rightful inheritance of land. In the standard Greek manner, he uses his personal bitterness and problems as a tool to generalize about the misery and injustice so widespread throughout the world. Hard work and a well-earned rest provide Hesiod's farmer with a full life, an ideal starkly contrasted to the life led by his profligate brother. Muttering that bribery and flattery gain too much for the swift of tongue, Hesiod gives an exhortation of work and its essential value: that it is self-rewarding and fits well into the just cosmos intended by the gods.

He then supplies the allegory of the two strifes, Good-models-of-conduct and Quarrelsomeness. Turning to myth, Hesiod shows how evil and the necessity for work first came to be. The first tale illustrating his point is the story of Pandora's box, a well-known one among his listeners. The sealed pot appeared to be packed with blessings, but when impatient Pandora opened it, she released all of the evils known to man. Only hope remained inside. Hesiod proceeds to describe the five ages of the cosmos: the ages of gold, silver, bronze, iron, and heroes, noting the increase in evil as he moves along. The myth of the hawk and the nightingale, a condemnation of violence and injustice, shows that, in the present, strife is unavoidable. In *Works and Days* the gods have become aspects of ethical forces, which have the power to restrain the change that might wash away the old standards completely. Yet it is in the *polis* that justice emerges. The king of the gods "does not fail to see what kind of justice the *polis* holds within it" (Hesiod, *Works and Days,* 269). In the kingdom of men, justice and prosperity result if men act justly and take frugality as the means of everyday life. Hesiod's axiom "Observe correct measure: proportion is best in everything" (*Works and Days,* 694) became a Greek proverb, and it formed a cornerstone in later Greek ethics.

Works and Days illuminates another way in which the Greeks used myth to explain things to themselves. Here the gods seem a bit more distant from the world of men than in the genealogy of *Theogony,* although they have an impact on men's action and ideals. But the myths within *Works and Days* reflect the pain and smarting that came from the personal mistreatment of a magnificent poet. As another example of the use of myth, the nightingale pleads for kindness and mercy from the hawk, but the hawk chastises and derides the smaller bird for her cries, saying that she must submit to the will of the stronger. This use of animals to act as men and women in mythical, yet very familiar settings, would be fully exploited by many poets, especially the ever popular Aesop of Samos (d. 564 B.C.). The problems depicted are ones that ordinary men met each day, but Hesiod makes his animals speak for the abstractions of power and meekness and the question of justice and force. But he, too, cannot ignore war as a current and positive necessity, although he discards the homeric warrior ideal. The gods existed and were involved with men, whether men knew it or wanted them to be; whatever the *polis,* the mythical tales about each of the gods were part of the common knowledge of Greek culture, especially the twelve Olympian gods.

The Gods of Olympus

In the days of the classical *polis'* expansion and prestige, the twelve Olympian deities were believed to be a kind of unit, "a kind of corporate body" (W. K. C. Guthrie, *The Greeks and Their Gods* [Boston: Beacon Press, 1962], 110). The man on the street uttered common oaths like "by the Twelve" (Aristophanes, *Knights,* 235), and before 527 B.C. the tyrant Peisistratus had erected an altar to the Twelve in the Athenian *agora.* Another altar to the Twelve existed at Olympia in the fifth century B.C., and legends suggest that Heracles founded that particular cult. In spite of the fact that Greek authors took the Twelve for granted, scholars have some difficulty in sorting out which twelve gods were actually meant. The usual roster contains the names of Zeus, Hera, Poseidon, Demeter, Apollo, Artemis, Ares, Aphrodite, Hermes, Athena, Hephaestus, and Hestia. Sometimes Dionysus replaced Hestia on the list, but the god of wine was a late foreign import; he became important once Athenian drama commemorated him in a theater dedicated to his veneration. As Guthrie puts it, "Hestia probably made way without much fuss, for as her name suggests, she was accustomed to stay at home when the other gods went out on holiday" (*Gods,* 111). The other gods and goddesses had become so standard in the fifth and fourth centuries B.C. that Plato could assume his readers would know the Twelve, even though he never describes them all in writing. Plato's student Eudoxus, who wrote treatises on astronomy, probably suggested that the Twelve were associated with the twelve signs of the zodiac, but Plato wanted his ideal state to celebrate "twelve feasts to the twelve gods" (*Laws,* VIII, 828B). To him, the Twelve were connected with the twelve months, and he gave the twelfth month to Pluto, writing that

> this god must not be disliked by men who are soldiers, but
> he should be honored as a god who constantly gives good to
> humankind, since—as I would say in full seriousness—there is
> no better method for the union of the soul with the body
> than through dissolution. (*Laws,* VIII, 828D)

Variation in the roster of the Twelve was not confined to Plato's philosophical substitutions, or to the addition of Attic Dionysus. Given localities venerated certain gods and demonic forces through the classical period. At Olympia, the Titans Rhea and Cronos and the river god Alpheius took up the positions of Hephaestus, Demeter, and Hestia. Other areas in Greece made their own substitutions from time to time, but there was general agreement about Zeus, Hera, Poseidon, Apollo, Artemis, Ares, Aphrodite, Hermes, and Athena.

The portraits of the major deities that the homeric poems gave to Greek civilization remained fairly constant throughout Greek history. But even though the general qualities of the gods were somewhat standard and endured a long time, the myths related about the gods suggest a cross-identification with divine forces quite unlike the pantheon led by the Indo-European sky god known as Zeus.

Tales woven into Greek tradition about Zeus seem, at first glance, to vary his realm from the "the expanse of heaven, alike in cloud and brilliant light" (*Iliad,* XV, 192), to the god of weather and the sky. The myths suggest that Zeus was not always what he represented to the Greeks, a dignified and venerable ruler, all-powerful and king of gods and men. Homer notes quite often that Zeus is the "son of Cronos," but the poet rarely speaks of Cronos, merely hinting that Zeus had banished him sometime before. Thus the Greek gods embodied at least two strands of religious thinking: one strand is well illustrated in the *Iliad,* where the gods are clearly Indo-European types, closely linked with images in Nordic and Sanskrit tales; the other strand is the mythological setting that the Greeks gave to the gods, a surrounding that all classes—from the philosophers to the common, unlettered poor farmer—took for granted. Everyone knew the stories. In fact, the tales have survived in Christian guise without conscious effort; but sometimes they are revived in their original form as trappings of modern national identities. This revival is quite true in modern Greece, where the stories of the old gods go hand in hand with a pride in the Greek heritage of philosophy and art.

The Greek myths do not humanize the gods as much as they connect them with the common mythical tradition that was prevalent in the eastern Mediterranean before the arrival of the Mycenaeans. Beginning with Zeus—whom all Greeks recognized as the primordial concept of the sky, which has life and being in itself—stories were attached to his origins that had little to do with his image as the hurler of thunderbolts, or with the Aristotelian idea of Zeus, "who does not rain to cause the crops to grow, but out of necessity" (*Physics,* II, 198b18). In *Theogony* Hesiod gives an introduction to the myths around the birth of Zeus (453 ff.) that were familiar to his listeners, but about which Homer is silent. Homer's Zeus was not quite conceived as a baby, and Homer did not connect his Olympian stature and dignity with the myth of his father's foreboding that his progeny would throw him out—although such stories linked vividly with the ageless struggle between earthly fathers and sons.

The setting of Hesiod's tale is the island of Crete, the cradle of a culture far older than that of the homeric warlords. According to his story, the generation previous to the Olympic generation was that of the Titans, daughters and sons of Earth and Sky (Gaia and Uranus). Most important of their children were Cronos and Rhea, who mated and had their own children. Gaia and Uranus, however, prophesied that Cronos would be overthrown by one of his own sons. To prevent this from happening, Cronos devoured his children as they were born, which made Rhea very unhappy. She went to Gaia and Uranus for help against Cronos' practice, and her parents sent her to Crete when she was about to produce another offspring. Here Rhea bore Zeus and hid him in a cave, and Gaia became Zeus' nurse. Gaia knew her son was somewhat simple, so she devised a ruse to fool Cronos. She gave him a stone wrapped up in swaddling clothes, and Cronos devoured it, thinking he was swallowing his latest son. The stone did not agree with Cronos' digestion, and he later vomited it up, along with some of his children he had eaten earlier. Thus other deities of Zeus' generation survived, among whom were Hera, Poseidon, and Hades. The crude tale did not detract from the nobility of the Zeus who was thought to be a ruler who would tolerate no rivals, but the story was well known and versions sifted from century to century in Greek history. The point of the myth of Zeus' birth and saving from Cronos' fear may be as simple as it seems on the surface; the new father god established an order in the cosmos unlike the barbarous and uncouth manner of the previous generation of gods. That made sense to the Greeks.

In the myths Hera was Zeus' lawful wife and the mother of Ares and Hephaestus, among other children. She may be the fertility goddess of earlier times, wedded to the newer male-dominant force of prehomeric Greece, but classical scholars heatedly debate about Hera's identity with the fertility and sexual cults of Asia Minor. To the Greeks, she was the goddess of fertility in women, the "guardian of the keys to wedlock" (Aristophanes, *Thesmophoriazusae,* 976). She was a force for successful childbirth, and the goddesses of birth (Eilithyai) were her children, according to both Homer and Hesiod. At Argos she was worshiped as a virgin queen, and in that *polis* there was "a spring called Canathus, where the citizens of Argos say Hera washes every year to renew her virginity" (Pausanias, *Description of Greece,* II, 38. 2). The literal acceptance of a major goddess in which wedded propriety is coupled with virginity has implications in the social life of the *polis.* (See chapter 7, "Proper Conduct and Sexual Mores.") In the literature of Homer, she is consistently hostile to Troy, while in the tale of Jason seeking the Golden Fleece of distant Colchis, Hera appears as his helper and guide. (The most accessible version of Jason and his Argonauts is in the *Argonautica* that Apollonius of Rhodes wrote about 250 B.C.) Hera is constantly condemning her divine husband and his roving eye, and most myths around her consider her rivalry with Aphrodite and her bitterness toward those goddesses with more sex appeal than she has. Again Greeks told her story in a kind of reflection of the plight of the matron, who could not compete with beautiful young women or comely slave girls.

Poseidon was god of the sea. In Homer, when the three brother gods, the sons of Cronos, drew lots to divide up the universe, Zeus received "the allotment of the expanse of sky," Hades gained the lot "of darkness and the mists . . . becoming the lord of men in death," and Poseidon drew "the sea gray blue to dwell in forever" (*Iliad,* XV, 185–192). The three gods had Earth as common ground, and Poseidon is also called Earth-shaker, the author of earthquakes. In addition, he was the god of horses and was worshiped as Hippios in Arcadia (in the north central Peloponnesus). Pausanius includes the myth explaining this form of Poseidon.

> They say that when Demeter was wandering in search for her child, Poseidon chased her, lusting to have sexual relations with her. Thus she transformed herself into a mare and grazed in the herd belonging to Onkios. But Poseidon perceived the manner of her trick and changed himself into a stallion and coupled with her. [*Description of Greece,* VIII, 25. 5]

The three-pronged trident was his staff; since he was lord of fresh and salt water, many Greek springs were attributed to the sharp blows of his trident. The most famous of these springs cleaved by Poseidon was struck in the rock of Athens' Acropolis, although other versions suggest a stamping hoof from the divine Poseidon-horse made the water flow forth. He was often thought to be the husband of Earth (*posis das*), a new form of the force of male fertility that permeated the earth. Horses with their massive organs suggested such an identity to the Greeks, and the myths surrounding Poseidon give him a procreative power not unlike that of Zeus. To sailors, his dominion over the sea was proverbial, and a lack of respect for his rule brought heavy penalties; Odysseus learned this to his expense (*Odyssey,* passim).

Demeter was the goddess of the harvest, the spirit of fecundity in wheat. Since she was the governing force of fruitfulness and of growth in plants, the Greeks thought she was connected with forces under the earth. Thus Demeter is the mother-in-law of the god of the dead, who is married to her daughter Persephone. The homeric

Hymn to Demeter first records the myth of Demeter's problems concerning her daughter. It starts thus: "I begin and sing of thickly locked Demeter, the goddess terrifying, and of her daughter slim in ankles, stolen away by Aidoneus as bequeathed by Zeus, All-Seeing, the Thunderer." Shortly Demeter is described as the goddess "of the golden sword and fruits glorious." The tale tells of Demeter's sorrowful search for her stolen daughter, who had in the meantime gone with Hades into the underworld. In her wanderings, Demeter came to Eleusis, where she appeared in disguise as an old woman. Later she revealed herself, and the people of Eleusis erected a temple to her. Meanwhile, Zeus wanted the earth to flower and crops to grow as before, but he had to get Demeter back to Olympus first. He promised to return Persephone to her, but her daughter had already eaten some seeds of the pomegranate in the underworld. Persephone could not remain above ground for the full year, and had to return to the underworld for part of the year. The myth served to explain the celebration of the Eleusinian mysteries as well as the Greek seasons, while the various festivals to Demeter celebrated her power of magic and black forces that could bring plague and famine. Later her identity with the underworld became a kind of oath; when a person thought that someone was of "the people of Demeter" (as in Plutarch, *Moralia: The Face of the Moon*, 943B), that person was consigned to the world of the dead. As a mother goddess, she had several husbands in the myths; in one story, her daughter was fathered by Zeus. Apparently Zeus was quite jealous of any other lovers. Homer (*Odyssey*, V, 125 ff.) relates how Demeter was lying in a plowed field with Iasion when Zeus hurled one of his bolts and killed him. The moral here seems to be that one should not become a lover to a mother goddess. Myth put death and spring, sexuality and the power of female fertility, and magic and winter into an understandable package. Women worshiped Demeter as their sign of fertility, much as she was the green of spring, the red-gold of autumn, and the biting frost of winter.

Most famous of the Greek gods was Apollo, who was especially suited for artistic depiction of the ideal. He was the epitome of male beauty and the great encourager of music, prophecy, archery, medicine, and animal husbandry. Herodotus writes that Apollo was famous for approving fair codes of law, especially those of Sparta. "You have come, Lycurgus, to my rich temple, honored by Zeus and all that live in the heights of Olympus . . . some also say that

Apollo gave to Lycurgus the laws now established in Sparta" (*Histories,* I, 65). Furthermore, the god supported the highest kind of moral and religious values, a characteristic Herodotus again reports (*Histories,* VI, 86). The oracle of Apollo at Delphi speaks of perjury as "the nameless son of Deceit, who has neither feet or hands, and he pursues with exceeding swiftness until he has captured and destroyed an entire people." The myths tell that Apollo was born of the Titan Leto, who "was gentle and kindly to men and the immortal gods" (Hesiod, *Theogony,* 404). Leto was also the mother of Artemis, but only Apollo was born on the island of Delos, where a great shrine to the god later flourished. According to the homeric *Hymn to Delian Apollo,* Leto was in labor for nine days bearing Apollo, because Hera "of the white arms" kept Eilithyia "the goddess of childbirth, sitting atop Olympus amid golden clouds." She failed to hear the cries of Leto because her ears were blocked by the "malice of Hera, since Leto of the beauteous hair was soon to give birth to a son strong and without flaw" (*Delian Apollo,* 95–100). The tale continues with Hera finally giving her consent for Eilithyia to go to Leto, but only after the other gods had promised her a huge bribe.

As Apollo was a god of incredible beauty, it is no surprise to learn that the Greeks thought he was endowed with good taste and a desire for grand variety in his love affairs. He conceived one of his more noted passions for Cassandra, daughter of King Priam of Troy. Hoping to win her, he gave her the eye of prophecy, but she still refused to give the god her love; so he made his earlier gift meaningless by making Cassandra's prophecies unbelievable to her listeners (Aeschylus, *Agamemnon,* 1202 ff.). But Apollo was most important to the Greeks for his oracular shrine at Delphi, from which issued a stream of advice of apparent good judgment in divine guise. It is little wonder that Greek tradition thought Apollo the father of Plato.

The name Artemis appears on one of the Linear B tablets as the owner of a slave, and this goddess may date back to Mycenaean times. In Homer, she is Apollo's sister, a "wearer of the bow, since Zeus created you like a lion among women" (*Iliad,* XXI, 483–484), and the Greeks believed her to be a protecting spirit around childbirth. Generally, she exercised her true power over uncultivated country, especially over forests and wooded hills where wild beasts were numerous, but even ancient mythographers confused her with

Hecate and Selene. It seems that the figure of Artemis was the remnant of very old sacrifical rites present in Greece before 2000 B.C., in which she was offered goats on altars. Some scholars think that Artemis received at least some meaningful signs of human sacrifice; during an obscure ceremony at Halae in Locris Opuntia, north of Boeotia, a man's throat was pricked to draw a few drops of blood. A rather sparse mythology was associated with Artemis, but as Artemis Orthia she was important at Sparta, where she was worshiped through scourging and offerings of cheese.

Likewise the name of Ares may appear on Linear B tablets, but his name may be prominent in Mycenaean times because it was a common one for slaves. He was the Greek god of war, but he never provided the ideal of a warlike leader who propelled troops into battle. Rather, Ares was the name given to the irrationality of war, the tone of rage and anger for bloodletting that resulted when everything short of war had failed. Ethical or moral attributes like those of Zeus or Apollo did not evolve in the god of war, and myth cloaked Ares as the force leading to violence or as the brutal, turbulent lover. Although Aphrodite was the wife of Hephaestus, she was often the paramour of Ares; Hesiod (*Theogony,* 934) tells how Ares fathered his attendants Phobos and Deimos (Fear and Fleeing), who were depicted in the homeric Trojan war saga. He was also the father of numerous doughty and occasionally uncouth warriors by various mothers, both mortal and divine, and one myth makes him the father of Eros. The majority of the myths about Ares provide a portrait of a braggart soldier, a bumbling and thoughtless luster after women, and a god who rages, childlike, at every problem. His principle sexual partner, Aphrodite, also had many warlike characteristics, as well as her better-known attributes as the force of sexual passion. Pausanius relates how the women of Tegea in Arcadia paid tribute to Ares

> in the market square, where the god was sculptured in relief on a tablet of stone. The women here call Ares Feaster of Women (Gunaikothoinas). . . . having at one time, when no man was around, slaughtered and sacrificed to Ares, giving nothing to the men as portions of the meat from the sacrifice. [*Description of Greece,* VIII, 48. 4]

Here the Greek tradition recalled how important women were in the magic of war, a function that may go back to the Stone Age. "In Sparta, they sacrifice young dogs to the bloodiest god, Enyalius," a rite associated with the occult practices around Hecate "of proper balance to avoid and cast out evil" (Plutarch, *Roman Questions,* 290D). Enyalius was a common name for Ares, and that name occurs on a tablet from Knossos in Crete, suggesting a muted link with an earlier Mycenaean or Minoan god. Although myth makes Ares a son of Zeus and Hera, he is most prominent in acts of war when he aids non-Greek peoples such as the Amazons, whose queen Penthesilea was his daughter. He remains the irrational force of war, avoided and shunned by the more rational gods and simply expiated by men.

Aphrodite, the goddess of love and the power of sexual passion and fertility, is often joined with Ares in Greek myth. She was born of the sea from the jagged and bloody remnants of Cronos' sexual organs, which were

> cast away from the firm land into the swelling sea, where they were carried for a great while. A foam of white around them covered and circled the remains of the flesh deathless, and within grew a beautiful female form. First she came close to sacred Cythera, and thereafter she came to Cyprus armored by the sea around. She came out of the sea, a goddess terrifying and utterly lovely, and under her divine and comely feet grass grew in profusion. [Hesiod, *Theogony,* 188–195]

Homer thinks, however, that Aphrodite was born of Zeus and Dione, and that she became the wife of Hephaestus, but in the *Odyssey* (VIII, 266–366), Ares appears as the consort of the love goddess. She is the mother of Aeneas by the Trojan Anchises, according to the homeric *Hymn to Aphrodite* (91–201). And in the *Iliad* Homer assumes her complete hostility to the Achaeans coming before Troy, since all those who heard the great lay would know that Paris gave the prize for beauty to Aphrodite, insulting Hera and Athena, the implacable foes of Troy. The favor she shows to Troy in the myths indicates her Eastern origin, much as the setting of Cyprus in Hesiod locates her major cult in the East. She also received veneration as goddess of the sea and seafaring, and she was an armed goddess, statues to her in Sparta and Cyprus girt for war. Her strongest historic cult center remained on Cyprus, although she replaced Ariadne on the island of Delos. As the goddess of prostitutes, she was identified with the Near Eastern Astarte, but only in Corinth was sacred prostitution practiced in her name. Generally, if Aphrodite was worshiped in the *poleis,* her cult was staid and rather prudish. The later sacrifice of pigs in her honor seems to mark the incorporation of the cult of Adonis (the consort of the Astarte-Aphrodite figure) from the East. But Greeks remembered Zeus' admonition to Aphrodite in the *Iliad:* "Not for you, my golden Aphrodite, are the things of war. Rather look with concerned care on the delightful things of wedlock, and the rest will be left to blustering Ares and Athena" (V, 428–430).

One of the Linear B tablets from Pylos lists the name of Hermes, but like so many other names from this distant time, the name may not be that of a god. However, he may be one of the oldest gods in the Greek pantheon or, by plausible argument, one of the youngest. One modern deduction of his name revolves around the concept of the *herma,* the spirit who lived in the stone or pile of stones that often rested by a road, for reasons lost to Greek travelers. Magical stones were quite common in many ancient cultures, and later artists pictured Hermes carrying a magic wand. Other traditions make him the divine messenger, and his emblem is the *kerykeion* ("herald's staff"), which became the caduceus in its Latin transposition. In addition to his staff, magical or otherwise, Hermes is shown in a wide-rimmed hat and heavy sandals; the god thus stands constantly ready for journeys. On the other hand, a strong tradition among the Greeks represented Hermes merely as a stone or squared pillar, with a bust at the top and an erect penis set halfway up the stone. The herms common in Greek literature are this kind of pillar, linking the tradition back to the concept of magical or divine stones.

Hermes was the son of Zeus and Maia, the daughter of Atlas. Maia was shy for a nymph and "dwelt deep in a shady cave" (the homeric *Hymn to Hermes,* 3–5), where the roving Zeus lay with her. The stories surrounding Hermes are lighthearted in comparison with the gloomy or bloody tales about others in the pantheon. From the moment he was born he was crafty, cunning, and lucky. On the first day of his divine life he invented the lyre by "making a singer of the turtle." Seeing the animal "feeding in the luxuriant grass before his house, waddling along," he had an inspiration. Soon he took the turtle, "cut off its limbs and scooped out the middle," measured some reeds and fit them into the turtle shell, and stretched oxhide over them. Then he "fitted a crosspiece on two of the reeds and on them stretched seven strings fashioned from the innards of a sheep." Adding keys, Hermes tested the strings and broke into snatches of songs, "like young men twit each other in song at festivals" (*To Hermes,* 20–61). Having produced the first lyre, he stole the cattle of

Apollo, denied the theft with laughing impudence, and was forgiven anyway. Other myths tell of his carefree outlook on matters of sex and fertility. He was the father of Hermaphroditus by Aphrodite, a kind of Greek pun about the god "who could not make up his mind." Another story makes him the father of Priapus, the spirit of the engorged penis; this was another way in which the Greeks poked fun at mortal men who could not govern their passion. In the *Odyssey,* Hermes is the guide for souls, which puts him in a unique class among the gods, most of whom are connected with either the upper or the lower world. With all these associations, Greeks made Hermes the god of merchants and everyone else who used roads, including thieves. A section of Plutarch's *Greek Questions* illustrates his non-moral nature:

> Why do the Samians allow anyone to steal from them and
> carry off their clothes when they are making sacrifice to Hermes,
> the Joy-Giver? Because they obeyed an oracle and changed
> their home from Samos to Mycale, and made a living from
> piracy there for ten years. Afterwards, they sailed home to
> Samos and conquered their enemies. [*Greek, Questions,*
> 303D]

At an unidentified Hermean festival, masters served their slaves while the feasting went on (Athenaeus, *Deipnosophistae,* XIV, 639b), a playful reversal of reality in Hermes' name. An extended function under Hermes was his favor to young athletes, especially those competing in one of the Pan-Hellenic games. Perhaps his identification with playful sex and male fertility evolved into a feeling about fortune or luck; since luck goes hand in hand with athletic competition, Hermes is later associated with the games.

A Linear B tablet from Knossos gives the name A-ta-na po-ti-ni-ja, which proves that the goddess Athena came from preclassical times. Her name, with the characteristic non-Greek ending -*na,* also suggests that her beginnings came long before the origins of the *polis.* Her fame in Athens has obscured the distribution of her worship throughout the Greek world, for Athens was the proud possessor of the blessing and guardianship of the virgin goddess. According to the myth, Athena sprang fully armed from the cloven head of Zeus and in effect had no mother. She won ownership of Attica from Poseidon by giving an olive tree to the Athenians, which was a greater miracle than Poseidon's causing water to flow from the barren rock. She is seen in both art and myth as an owl, and her epithet "gray-eyed

Athena" suits her vigorous character well. She was associated with
the power of windswept citadels and competed with Poseidon for
rule over the water. As an immediate product of Zeus, the primordial
force, she was a goddess of war, the female equivalent of Ares.
Homer puts the two of them together as he intones, "Ares, the rally
of warriors, and Athena" (*Iliad,* XVII, 398). Consequently, she was
venerated as the inventor of many instruments of war:

> First is the daughter of Zeus, bright-eyed Athena, who holds
> the dominion. She takes no joy in the things of golden Aphro-
> dite, but rather revels in war and the things of Ares, in conflicts
> and battles and in making famous skills. It was she who first
> taught mortal craftsmen how to fashion war chariots and battle-
> wagons all girt and fashioned in bronze. [But she also] is the
> teacher of soft maidens in the household, giving the skilled
> knowledge of the domestic arts to each one. [the homeric
> *Hymn to Aphrodite,* 10–15]

Crafts and warfare were her rule, and at Argos she was worshiped
simply "as *salpinx* ["Trumpet"]" (Pausanias, *Description of Greece,*
II, 21. 3).

Potters took Athena as their protectress, goldsmiths gave her
honor for their craft, and women blessed her for their spinning and
weaving. In Elis in the northwestern Peloponnesus her title was
Mother (*meter*), giver of the arts of motherhood. As Woman of Work
(Ergane), she was conceived by the Greeks as the force behind many
of the necessary tasks in the flourishing *polis,* particularly the *polis*
that had many craftsmen rather than farmers. The Athenians celebrated a festival called the Chalceia, or festival of the copper and
bronze smithies, in this context, much as Athenian women honored
her for their less glamorous—but equally necessary—skills. Good
health seems to have been important when the Athenians conceived of
Athena, and one of her titles "was Hygeia, the daughter of Asclepius
[the god of medicine] as some say, . . . Athena Hygeia" (Pausanias,
Description of Greece, I, 23. 5). Archaeologists have found a pot-
sherd at Epidaurus, on the east coast of Argolis (where the most
famous shrine to Asclepius was located), that suggests this form of
Athena was a running figure, armed with a shield that bore a serpent.
As the force of martial splendor and skilled craftsmanship in the
home and in the town, Athena could well make the people of Attica
proud of their patron deity. She found respect throughout the Greek
world, and she figures greatly in the mythical traditions.

The last deities on the list of the Twelve were not so widely venerated as the previous ten. Dionysus was a late importation from either Thessaly or Thrace who would be important in Athens as sponsor of the city's Dionysia, a festival in which the great tragic and comic plays were produced. (See chapter 10, "On the Poetic and the Sublime".) Hestia was a goddess of the hearth fires, and little is known about her private cult. Since she did not become a figure in the widely circulated conceptions of anthropomorphic deities, the mythology about her is quite scanty. The short homeric *Hymn to Hestia* was written to honor the eternal fire in the temple of Apollo at Delphi. Hephaestus is described in Homer as a wondrous blacksmith, strong of arms, but lame. He fashions Achilles' armor, Agamemnon's royal scepter, and the complicated necklaces of royal ladies. In Hesiod, Zeus charges the divine blacksmith to make the first woman. "The lame god well known molded clay in the form of a shy maiden . . . and the son of Cronos called her Pandora ("endowed with everything"), since all who lived on Olympus each gave a gift, a plague for men the eaters of bread" (Hesiod, *Works and Days,* 70-82). The son of Zeus and Hera, or of Hera alone (*Theogony,* 927), Hephaestus was banished from the realm of the gods because of his deformity. Mythographers made him the husband of Aphrodite, suggesting the union of beauty with craftsmanship.

Though there were minor variations in the lower end of the list of the twelve, the idea of the corporate unity of the twelve gods remained important to Greeks throughout classical times and well into the period of the Hellenistic kingdoms. The Twelve called specific associations into the mind of the Greek. Zeus was the supreme god, leader of the divine cosmos, ruler of the mortal world, and the giver of law and justice. Apollo was music and sage advice, Ares was war, Athena was (to the Athenians) the wise and firm guardian of the finest *polis* in Greece, Aphrodite was sensual passion and ideal female beauty, Hestia warmed the fires of home life and watched the hearth of the *polis,* Demeter endowed farm life with rebirth and the cycle of the seasons, and Poseidon was the surging power of the sea, whose winds were kind or frightening to seafarers. No greater testimony could be given for this enduring unity of the Greek ideal than the altars Alexander built in India to the Twelve. His troops had mutinied and would go no further into the depths of Asia, so he pondered "how he could best mark the endpoint of his expedition. He first built altars of the twelve gods, each fifty cubits [about

seventy-five feet] in height" (Diodorus Siculus, *World History,*
XVIII, 95. 1). The Greek gods literally stood at the edge of the
known world in 326 B.C. and were the political life line back to the
Greek homeland. For their corporate meaning and activity, the gods
were the *polis,* and they were more important in the life of the
Greek community than they were for individuals who might hail
from differing local traditions.

Hellenistic Religion

Myth and religion in the Hellenistic kingdoms (those kingdoms after
the death of Alexander) became amalgamated and permeated with
the welter of stories and religious practices of the Near East. Greeks
who accompanied Alexander went either as soldiers or as part of the
large camp following of geographers, doctors, prostitutes, bureau-
crats, and so on, but they were a small number of Greeks among
great numbers of natives. Alexander founded many cities along his
march, each with the external garb of the *polis* but ruled by a king.
Alexander's successors—especially the kings of Syria and Egypt—
followed this custom, and the cities came to house Greek minorities
that ruled the non-Greek majority. As an urban elite, Greeks gradually infused their habits and styles into the countryside, particularly
in Syria and Asia Minor, but native customs also came into the cities.
Ancient Near Eastern religions were even older than the traditions of
the Greek Twelve and had unchallenged loyalty from the mass of
natives. With the important exception of the Jews, the new Greek
kings allowed the old religions to go on as before, with a few modifications. In Syria and Egypt, they severely limited the political power
of the native priesthoods, but the Hellenistic monarchs allowed
their subjects complete freedom of worship.

Greek religion and its outward forms offered a number of attrac-
tions to barbarians outside traditions of the *polis.* The Near Eastern
cults had nothing quite like the Greek Panegyris, in which actors,
musicians, literary men, athletes, and dancers all displayed their
crafts in the name of a god in the setting of the world's finest architecture. Also, outside observers would note quickly that certain of
the gods in the Greek pantheon were more widely honored than
others. Large areas of the Hellenistic world worshiped Zeus, and
within a couple of centuries he became easily identified with the
chief god of many other religions. Within the customs of Greek

religion and myth there were means of satisfying the more personal religious needs that the long-lived state cults to the Olympian Twelve did not meet. Some individuals craved relief from a sense of guilt, others hoped for immortality, while some sought a union with the essence of divinity. The Greeks did have their own mystery religions, too. At Eleusis, the shadowy worship of Demeter and Persephone drew many thousands of converts hoping for a sense of rebirth through the great Eleusinian mysteries. On the fringe, Orphic cults preached doctrines of a new life of bliss after death and prescribed rituals of purity in this life that might insure later happiness. Seeking release from emotional tensions in a time when the individual felt a greater sense of helplessness than before, Greeks also practiced religions in private clubs (*thiasi*) that incorporated many of the surrounding customs.

Variety was characteristic of religion, as it was of everything else in the Hellenistic period. Hellenistic kings increased the number and magnificence of the public festivals, and the Greek priesthoods were prizes that citizens bought, in spite of heavy personal expense. (For example, at Priene in Asia Minor a major priesthood cost twelve thousand *drachmae,* as F. Hiller von Gärtringen records in *Die Inschriften von Priene* [Berlin, 1906], 174). The art of soothsaying was still in high repute, and the oracles at Delphi and Dodona received dedications from monarchs and cities. The common folk sought out oracles of every variety, from the charlatan on the street who claimed some inner knowledge to the famous incubation temples and sanctuaries of Asclepius, the god of medicine. Temple medicine grew in importance, in spite of (or perhaps because of) the growing numbers of Hippocratic doctors. Miracles of healing occurred regularly and they speak of a direct communion with the god in a dream of salvation from death or further disease. Several mystery religions other than the Eleusinian mysteries, like the Great Gods of Samothrace and the private religious clubs, rapidly increased in number. Macedonia adopted the Greek gods and incorporated them alongside the native spirit worship, a pattern common in the Hellenistic Near East as well.

In the new Hellenistic kingdoms, each dynasty fostered cults to particular patron gods. The Seleucids encouraged the worship of Apollo, while the Attalid kings at Pergamon chose Athena as their patron goddess. Ptolemy IV of Egypt (221–203 B.C.) spent much effort and money to organize a cult to Dionysus. Each of the new Greek cities founded by either Alexander or his successor kings chose one god or several deities from the Greek pantheon. At Alexandria in Egypt, the trinity of Zeus, Hera, and Poseidon were the gods of the Greek community, and Greeks were required to swear oaths in their names. On the other hand, although Alexander's conquests had given the Greek gods greater prestige over a broader expanse of territory, the settlement of Greeks in the cities of the conquered lands weakened their local loyalties to the outdated concepts of the *polis.* The veneration of the Twelve flourished in the old *polis,* since the Twelve embodied the spirit of Hellenic civilization in its local variations. The Greeks in the first generation of settlers, scattered in cities from the coast of Asia Minor to the distant Greek kingdoms of Bactria and India, would tightly grasp their mythical and religious traditions from home. But in the second generation of Greeks, now more integrated and intermarried with native stock, settlers would loosen their ties and take up customs more in keeping with their new homes.

The common people, both Greek and native, followed their personal religions without question, but this kind of lasting strength was confined to local objects. Family hearths functioned as before, but the state gods underwent some change in the new surroundings. In this matrix, the better intellects looked into philosophy for some personal guidance, while those uninterested in wrestling with philosophical or logical definitions inquired elsewhere. The lazy chose the misty area between religion and atheism by venerating Tyche ("chance" or "luck"), a vaguely conceived force that could be personally invoked; however, Tyche was subject to caprice. In an age of increasing personal uncertainty, others lapped up the answers of astrology and magic. Both astrology and magic came from very old lines in the Near East, but in the second century B.C. they gained an underground popularity that has endured. Astrology was revived in Seleucid Syria, where it took up with the continued study of astronomy, long conducted in Mesopotamia. The package of astronomy and mathematics provided for precision in astrology, and the illusion of numbers attached to observations impressed a fair number of the gullible, who did not expend the effort to understand the reason for the star charts or the mysterious calendars that linked men with the planets and stars. Astrology sifted into the teaching of Stoic philosophers. (See chapter 8, "Myth and the Womb of Philosophy".) And Poseidonius (*c.* 135–*c.* 50 B.C.) adjusted astrology for Stoic thinking and accepted the general validity of the shadier forms of oracle mongering. Magic exercised great attraction for those who lost all religious touch but who were repelled by the tight rigor of astrology. Magic promised results—quick, dependable, and repeatable. It had been part of Egyptian culture since its inception, and in Ptolemaic Egypt, magical treatises made their appearance in Greek. Galen (A.D. 130–200), writing at the end of a tradition of Hellenistic medical and scientific achievement, noted that "astrology [and magic] were the best sciences given by Egyptian sages for the practice of medicine" (Galen, IX, 911 and XII, 207).

King worship became normal in the Hellenistic monarchies. Traces of such tendencies can be found in the hero cults of classical Greece, like those of Heracles at Thebes and of Theseus at Athens. The old myths suggested a kind of bridge between the human and the divine, but Greek sarcasm greeted Alexander when he demanded in 324 B.C. that he be worshiped as a god ("let him be a god if he likes"). Such a precedent led to Hellenistic cults that worshiped dynastic lines and sometimes living monarchs. Ptolemy I stole Alexander's corpse while it was being carried back to Macedonia, brought the body to Alexandria, and established a cult to the god Alexander. By 285 B.C., the Alexandrian cult was firmly entrenched in Ptolemaic Egypt, and its chief priest was honored by having his name attached to all official documents. Ptolemy II (283–245 B.C.) founded a cult worshiping his father and mother as the *theoi soteres* ("savior gods"), and in 280 B.C. he instituted the Ptolemaieia, replete with festivals and games to celebrate the new cult. Thus it became the custom for the reigning Ptolemy to raise his predecessor to the rank of god. In Seleucid Syria, the dynasty deified its founder as Seleukos Zeus Nikator ("Seleucus, Zeus, the Victor"). Later Antiochus I (280–262 B.C.) was venerated as Apollon Soter ("Apollo, Savior").

The process of making divinities of living monarchs took a similar path. By the reign of Ptolemy IV (221–203 B.C.), the native priests at Memphis were required to deify ritually the new Ptolemy, giving to him the double crowns of upper and lower Egypt in the same ceremony. The new "god" was indeed a god for the Egyptians, as the Pharaoh had been a god, but Greeks living in Alexandria did not seem to take Ptolemy's godhead too seriously. The cult of Ptolemy

IV became common in his reign; the priesthoods directed the worship of the king and the royal line. These priests were usually of the royal family, while in the foreign possessions of the Ptolemaic Empire (the Ptolemies held small areas of Asia Minor and from time to time some of the Greek islands), the Ptolemaic governor was also chief priest of the cult. In Egypt the tradition of Pharaoh worship allowed the new cult to operate without much overt opposition. To the north in Syria, Antiochus II (*c.* 287-247 B.C.) formed a cult to himself, but only Greeks were allowed to participate in the Seleucid monarchy. The cult was somewhat popular as long as the king represented good government and some kind of economic stability for the Greek upper classes. But the initiative for monarch worship seems to have come from the common folk, who remembered Alexander with awe.

There is ample evidence to suggest why the idea took hold in the Hellenistic world. Soon after Alexander's death in 323 B.C., many of the Greek states instituted cults to several of the successor generals, who were fighting among themselves for power. An inscription records that Antigonus I received divine honors at Scepsis in northwestern Asia Minor in 311 B.C. (W. Dittenberger, ed., *Orientis Graeci Inscriptiones Selectae* (Leipzig, 1903-1905), 5). According to Plutarch, the Athenians made Antigonus and his son Demetrius gods in 307 B.C. (*Demetrius,* 11). Diodorus Siculus (*World History,* XX, 100) says that Ptolemy I was worshiped at Rhodes in 304 B.C., and according to another inscription, Cassander (one of the eventually unsuccessful generals) was venerated at Cassandreia (the old Potidaea in the Thracian Chalcidice) by 286 B.C. (W. Dittenberger, ed., *Sylloge Inscriptionum Graecarum* (Leipzig, 1915-1924), 380). The writings of Euhemerus (*fl. c.* 300 B.C.) nicely mirror the mood and inclinations of the time; he claimed he had found proof in documents that the gods were simply men who had died.

King worship, particularly as embodied in Alexander, signified a greater personification of power. Giving divinity to a monarch was not an act of craven obeisance but something akin to rendering in the "form of a man present blessings." Such king worship was quickly reduced to ceremonial and ritual—highly appealing in its own right, but only form and ritual. Thus, together with the deification of kings in the Hellenistic monarchies, Near Eastern rites (sometimes in Greek guise) had great attraction for Greeks in their

foreign settings. The veneration of Serapis and Isis in Ptolemaic
Egypt is an excellent example of conscious Hellenization of ancient
religious customs to fit the new cosmopolitan tone and demands
of Greeks in Egypt. Serapis was the halfbull called Apis, embalmed.
According to Egyptian myths, Apis joined the god Osiris after death.
The cult of Apis-Osiris had a long history at Memphis. Isis was a
goddess of fertility who mated with Osiris, becoming one of the
powers in the world of the dead (the Greek underworld). Ptolemy I
remodeled the worship of Serapis, infusing the old cult with new
images that would remind Greeks of Pluto and Egyptians of their
old god, now reborn. Serapis shortly became the god of Egyptian
sailors and was identified with various Greek healing deities like
Asclepius, Apollo, and Hermes. Ptolemy's fleets carried the cult to
the various ports on the Mediterranean; the veneration of Serapis
flourished in Athens seventy-five years later. Isis matched Serapis
in broad appeal and widespread popularity. Initiation into her worship included being reborn into a new life here on earth, and sailors
likewise established her new cult in far-flung seaports. Isis was
quickly established at Athens before Serapis, and she was worshiped
there before the death of Alexander in 323 B.C. Soon Isis cults were
found in Spain and Greek southern Italy. Her appeal is understandable in an age moving more rapidly toward syncretism (the cross-
identification of one major deity with another in a foreign land) in
religion and myth. Serapis became Pluto, and Isis was easily inter-
changed with Aphrodite, Artemis, and a host of other female deities
that flourished in Syria and Asia Minor. The great "sending of ships"
from Alexandria under the protection of Isis reminded many Greeks
of the mythical association Aphrodite had with Poseidon, or of
Athena's frequent association with water and the sea. Later the
Romans termed this "sending of ships" a *curris navalis.* Many of the
attributes of the Christian Virgin Mary also go back to the cult of
Isis and her "sending of ships," a lasting reminder of the syncretic
base of Christianity.

Remolded gods and the worship of kings were simply aspects of
the cosmopolitan age of wandering scholars and far-reaching merchant ventures. The Greek world had exploded into new and seemingly limitless vistas, but the grafted *polis* had become something
new as well. Worship of the king became worship of the state, since
the Hellenistic monarch was the state. His army and bureaucracy
kept the machinery of government functioning, and the Greek pan-

theon provided links with a common heritage. The age characterized as cosmopolitan is also defined as an age of change. Hellenistic religion blended old Greek gods with old Near Eastern deities, and worshipers raised supplications to gods of syncretic creation, from both the East and West. This amalgam is the underlying foundation of the acceptance later of a widely diffused monotheism, especially during the Roman Empire.

7

Proper Conduct and Sexual Mores

Sensationalist historical fiction commonly offers an unreal view of past social customs. In every society but our own sexual activity was somehow freer. These fictional accounts include the activities of homosexuals and religious cultists, as well as of the more usual men- or women-about-town who enjoy sexual activity without hindrance. Many historical novels about classical Athens assume that society was very open in the fifth and fourth centuries B.C., and that Greeks generally were not inhibited in their sexual conduct.

In defining "completely uninhibited," one may think of an activity that would cause no social, moral, or legal reaction; no sense of outrage would result. To us, a game of golf or tennis would thus be "completely uninhibited," while many of us react strongly to tales of wife-swapping clubs or to open avowal of homosexuality. If the notion that the Greeks were sexually uninhibited is true, then they had little or no moral, social, or legal indignation to prostitution, homosexuality, adultery, illegitimacy, or any other aspect of public or private sexual conduct. Yet one of the few universals on which anthropologists agree is that *all* societies—from the most primitive tribes to the most complicated and sophisticated cultures—have rules governing sexual behavior. Source materials from classical Athens

likewise make it clear that there was much less than total freedom in
sexual matters.

Archaeological and Literary Evidence

At first glance, the extant literary and archaeological materials,
including the marvellous vase-paintings from fifth- and fourth-century
B.C. Greece, appear to depict open sexuality. Each Athenian house
had a herm sitting at the front door. This bust of Hermes consisted
of a head on top of a flat stone slab, without any ornament except a
large, erect penis, which projected from its center. The City Dionysia,
the festival honoring the god of wine, erotic pleasures, and artistic
creation, had a procession in which the participants carried large
erect penises made of terra-cotta, while lustily singing "songs to
Phallos." In many passages of Athenian literature, especially the
comedies (which were a part of the City Dionysia), there were numerous phrases like "the erect penis" and "things of Aphrodite," which
always meant sexual intercourse. In Greek mythology, the gods and
goddesses indulge in veritable orgies of sex, with the notable exception of Athena, the patron goddess of Athens. Every now and again
the poets and compilers tell of the amorous Zeus spying a mortal
woman with whom he can dally, selecting the choicest with his roving eye. Tales of Zeus changing into mortal form—the swan and the
bull were his favorite disguises—generally crop up in modern accounts
that seek to justify the arguments for Greek sexual freedom, particularly the practice of sodomy.

Pindar (518–438 B.C.), a poet of genius who composed memorable
odes in honor of victors at athletic competitions, seems to show
what kinds of practices were offensive in the fifth century B.C.—or at
least to show what *he* found offensive. Certainly his personal life
was rather unrestrained, as he notes in *Pythian,* 12, written in 490
B.C. in honor of a favorite flute player. However, Pindar is less com-
fortable about open bloodshed and crudity among the gods. In
Olympian, I, he rejects the popular version of how Pelops, beloved of
Poseidon, was carved up and eaten at a feast of the gods. He offers his
own more acceptable substitute: a god raped a human boy. According to Pindar, the other stories were "artfully clad in resplendent
lies" (*Olympian,* I, 29). The occasional practice of older men taking
lovers among young boys offended him less than the folk legend of

brutal cannibalism among the gods. Sex replaced the perversion of bloodlust for Pindar; the ideal that the poet evoked reflected the general Greek admiration for the physical beauty of the young male.

Added to such archaeological and literary evidence are the hundreds of vase-paintings—the Greek equivalent of the sex manuals of the late twentieth century—drawn by skilled artists and intended for sophisticated and genteel households. They show blunt scenes of male and female masturbation, the varied and gymnastic poses of sexual intercourse, and an occasional depiction of anal intercourse.

One aspect of erotic Greek vase-painting gives a clear visual impression of what Athenian audiences thought was funny and ludicrous: the depictions of comic stage figures. In this case, since the Athenians were judging the plays presented in the festival of Dionysus, we are assured immediately that Athenians thought these scenes were humorous and acceptable on the stage.

On a *chous* ("small pitcher") that J. D. Beazley in *Attic Red-Figure Vase-Painters*, 2d ed. (Oxford, 1963), p. 1215 No. 1, dates to about 420 B.C. there is a scene of a man and a woman watching a cavorting actor on stage. The actor represents Perseus, and he is wearing tights (an artistic and stage convention that represented stage nudity) and an odd, zigzagging penis. The actor is carrying what looks like a curved knife blade in his left hand, while over his left arm is draped a *himation*. Another, more elaborate *chous,* dated to about 410 B.C. (Beazley, *Vase-Painters,* p. 1335 [No. 34]), shows Heracles riding in a chariot, preceded by a dancing comic actor. Heracles is distinguished by his club and headdress, goggle eyes, bulbous nose, and large mouth, and the hero is intently gazing at something in front of the four-centaur team pulling the chariot. The dancer is wearing tights and a very long penis, and he is prancing around as he leads the centaurs. A third *chous*, from about 410 B.C., which A. Pickard-Cambridge describes in *The Dramatic Festivals of Athens,* figure 78, pictures one seated actor wearing tights and an enormous penis and a standing figure, also in tights, who wears a coiled penis resembling a small shell. A fourth *chous* (Pickard-Cambridge, *Dramatic Festivals,* figure 81), from about 410 B.C., shows a running actor with a long, erect penis, tights, buttock padding, and a curling, wandering staff held in his left hand. Many more examples like these four portray poses and the expected stereotypes for comedies, which are liberally laced with obscenities and depictions of sexual acts.

Straight sexual scenes were also painted, but these are rarer than the exaggerated ones. An *oinochoe* (another variety of small pouring vessel with a raised handle) of about 420 B.C., shown in A. Greifen-hagen, *Antike Kunstwerke* (Berlin; Walter de Gruyter and Co., 1966), Figure 57, cited from Beazley, portrays a pair of lovers. The man displays an erect penis of normal proportions, and the woman is about to mount him while he reclines in a sloped-back chair. The whole mood is pleasant rather than comic. The Greeks felt no aver-sion to the picturing of sex or the sexual organs in the art of vase-painting.

The Greeks enjoyed erotic puns and the expected gross antics of stage characters (for example, in Aristophanes' *Lysistrata*); all of them make gestures that are intended as sexual and scatalogical innuendo and farce. On the stage, male characters often wore the large *phalloi* strapped to their waists, a convention that distinguished them from any female characters. (No women were allowed on the stage, so men had to play the women's roles as well.) The actors behaved in an utterly uninhibited manner. The sexual chase, a stock theme in Athenian comedy, always had the audience of men and women roaring with glee as they watched the men panting after the women (and vice versa) in the most ludicrous situations and poses. *Lysistrata* is rich with scenes and encounters that intensify the effect of sexual mirth, and even the names are sometimes sexual puns. For example, the name of one of the characters in *Lysistrata* (852), Kinesias Paionides, plays with the words *kinein* ("to move") and *paiein* ("to strike"), both slang terms for sexual intercourse. But sex-ual allusions are not the only lampooning device in comedy, as the *pappax* and *papapappax* ("explosive farts") in Aristophanes' *Clouds* (390 sq.) illustrate. All kinds of obscene parodies make up comic poetry, and sex takes its place among the many subjects Athenians found funny. The intent of the sexual costuming in the vase-paintings is clear to the modern observer, but many of the remaining obscene jokes and puns become apparent only from the texts and scholia (marginal comments) of the plays themselves. The sexual scenes pictured on many of the vases came from the comic stage produc-tions, and stage characters were *not* intended as realistic portraits of ordinary men and women. The comic hero (for example, Heracles in Aristophanes' *Birds*) was lusty and violent, something Athenian audiences found laughable, not admirable. The "normal" sexual scenes of the vase-paintings depict an ease with the actual sexual act, but within a proper context. Sexual athletics may form part of the

artists' armory, and the pots may have been decorative objects for
upper-class homes, but the pictured ease with the sexual act does not
mean that Greeks tolerated the whole range of sexual aberrations.
Sexual intercourse, in and of itself, was a part of life, both on the
stage and in ordinary living.

Literary evidence provides another aspect of Greek sexual attitudes. Herodotus (*Histories,* I, 199) relates the account of temple
prostitution in Babylon in a way that makes it clear the practice disgusted him, although it was well known that there were great
numbers of prostitutes in Thebes and Corinth. In writing about the
religious traditions of the Egyptians, Herodotus emphasizes that the
Greeks and Egyptians were the only peoples to make having intercourse in the temples an offense:

> The Egyptians were also the first to make it a religious practice
> that men should not have intercourse with women in the
> sacred areas; nor should men come into temples unwashed after
> intercourse [Furthermore,] most other countries, except
> Egypt and . . . the Greeks, have sexual congress in sacred
> precincts, and they come into them unwashed, believing them-
> selves like other animals . . . I cannot approve. [*Histories,* II,
> 64]

Writers like Herodotus may reflect their own feelings, but in reading the comic poetry or orations intended for public airing and aimed
to please an audience of citizens, one realizes that commonly
approved sexual standards appear in the orations, and sexual buffoonery forms part of the comic poetry. But even in the comic
writings, one may detect some shifts. Menander (341-289 B.C.) wrote
plays in the style known as the new comedy (classical scholars usually placed Aristophanes within old comedy), and his plots resemble
soap opera in content and themes. There are far fewer obscenities
than in the poetry of Aristophanes. Words are coy and euphemistic,
often lacking the acid bite of the rollicking puns of the old comedy.
Xenophon is most circumspect when he mentions delicate matters
pertaining to the other sex. Fourth-century B.C. authors prefer to
treat open sexuality as something outside the proper taste of their
reading or listening public.

The famous Attic orators of the fourth century B.C. (among them
Aeschines, Demosthenes, and Lysias) attacked each other with sexual
allusions that leave no doubt what proper conduct was supposed to be
for the upright Athenian. They praised the ways of the extremely

modest Athenian women. Lysias writes that his sisters and nieces lived in a manner so "well conducted that they were ashamed to be seen even by their own male kin" (*Against Simon,* 6-7). The historian Thucydides (*History,* II, 45) had earlier remarked on the enviable chastity and usual seclusion of Athenian women, making them fit wives for the finest men living in the greatest *polis* in Greece. Thucydides made his observation to illustrate the customs in Pericles' Athens; Lysias made his commentary to indicate an expected prudery among proper citizen men and women.

Prostitution

In spite of Herodotus' disgust at temple prostitution and the coy approach to the topic in the extant works of many Greek authors from the fifth and fourth centuries B.C., prostitutes were very common in all the important *poleis* of classical Greece. Proper citizens, however, did not take them for granted. In Athens, brothels (*kasalbia* or *kasaureia,* the latter found in Aristophanes' *Knights,* [1285]) were under the supervision of officials (*astynomoi*) whose task was to maintain public decorum and decency. An appointed committee of the larger decency board fixed the fees that patrons paid in the establishments, if the custom at Colophon (a Greek city in southwestern Asia Minor) had its Athenian counterpart. At Colophon, there was a law "that all girls who played the *aulos* for pay, all girls who were hired to play the harp, and all the rest of these kinds of female entertainers would receive a wage" (Athenaeus, *Deipnosophistae,* XII, 526c). The girls were organized into shifts at Colophon—early morning until noon, noon until dusk, and dusk to dawn—and the *misthoma* ("wage") went to the owner of the girls, who were assumed to be slaves. In Athens, the owner of the *"aulos* players and other entertainers" was required, since he was presumed to be running a brothel, to pay a *telos pornikon* ("prostitute tax"), "which the Council lets out every year to those men who buy it and who know exactly those persons engaged in running these kinds of businesses" (Aeschines, *Against Timarchus,* 119). The collection of this particular tax was farmed out to bidders, who collected the tax after they had paid the state. One may wonder how much the *pornotelones* ("tax collector") could squeeze from the *pornoboskos* ("brothel keeper"), since charges varied according to the wealth and appearance of the clothing of prospective clients. While one *obol* obtained entrance into the more seedy houses, many of the more accomplished prostitutes charged far more. According to Athenaeus (*Deipnosophistae,* XIII, 581a–c), the famous Athenian courtesan Gnathaena demanded one thousand *drachmas* from a richly dressed elderly gentleman for her services for a single night. He managed, however, to gain her for half that sum, five *minae.*

Prostitution was an accepted protection against adultery, a cheap way to avoid the legal complications of making love to a married woman. Diogenes Laertius (*c.* A.D. 200–250), the author of a series of biographical sketches about famous philosophers, sums up the custom well when he quotes from the sayings of the Athenian philosopher Antisthenes (*c.* 446–366 B.C.): "Once, seeing an adulterer hastily departing at a run, [Antisthenes] said 'Poor fool! You could have had that with no danger for an *obol!*'" (*Antisthenes,* VI, 1. 4).

Ancient Greek was rich in words that described the various kinds of *pornai* ("common whores") who plied their trade where large numbers of merchants and their customers might gather. (According to the Greek thesaurus *Onomastikon* [IX, 5. 34], that Julius Pollux compiled in the second century A.D., most of the Attic brothels were located at the harbor of Piraeus.) The lexicon by Hesychius of Alexandria (fifth century A.D.) offered even more definitions; his work is based on Greek glossaries that went back to the first century B.C. Hesychius writes that there were many *pornoboskoi* in the Potter's Quarters (sometimes called the Kerameikos), an area of Athens that extended northwest from the *agora* to the Dipylon Gate, from which led the road to Eleusis.

The Greeks had a sensitivity about prostitutes, and they drew a careful distinction between the common whores and the "better girls." The former were often known by the places where they walked or waited or the way they performed on the job. A *dromas* ("runner") took too little time with her charges, the *gephyris* waited for clients next to bridges (as her name implies) where prospects could not avoid her, and the *epipastas* ("fixture of the bedroom") was known for her meek behavior. Quite often, call girls wore special sandals that had nails on the soles spelling out *akoloythi* ("Follow me!") in the mud of the street. There was no doubt about their profession.

The *hetairai* ("better girls"), or courtesans, are very prominent in the sources. They were set off from the ordinary prostitutes, or brothel girls, by their education and the social respect they engendered among the upper classes. In a time when most proper women were supposed to stay home and cultivate the domestic arts, these women offered feminine companionship, especially on the intellectual level, as well as the expected sexual expertise. As a social institution, the courtesans thrived in Athens and Corinth because they offered a semirespectable alternative to adultery, a crime that could be fatal, on the spot, for the adulterer. The best courtesans were skilled in other arts as well, and they were often accomplished musicians or had read widely. *Hetairai* were part of Athenian life as early as the time of Solon (he was *archon* in 594 B.C.), and Solon attempted to impose some legal restrictions concerning courtesans:

> [Solon] . . . allowed a man caught committing adultery to be killed, but if a man raped a free woman, he was only fined one hundred *drachmas;* if he gained his purpose through persuasion, the fine was twenty *drachmas,* unless the act was performed with one of those women who sell themselves, the *hetairai.*
> [Plutarch, *Solon,* 23. 1]

The most talented and attractive of these women frequently became the mistresses of distinguished politicians, philosophers, and artists. Aspasia of Miletus became Pericles' mistress in about 445 B.C., after he had divorced his wife. Aspasia was intellectually gifted and well schooled in rhetoric and music, and she became good friends with Socrates. That association caused Socrates' students and followers to recall her fondly, and they used her story as a kind of ideal, even though there had been rumors that Aspasia induced Pericles to start the Peloponnesian War. Aristophanes makes sport of these idle stories in *Acharnians* (especially 526–527), while Plato idealizes her rhetorical abilities and musical talents. His dialogue *Menexenus* contains the alleged text of a "Funeral Oration" that Aspasia composed (236D–249C), and she "taught many fine orators . . ; there was one of them who surpassed all Greeks: Pericles, son of Xanthippus" (*Menexenus,* 235E). Another student of Socrates, Antisthenes of Athens, wrote a tract about her (Diogenes Laertius, *Antisthenes,* VI, 16).

Other famous *hetairai* pepper the careers of famous Greek men. The courtesan Laïs of Corinth was a lover of the philosopher Aristippus during the Peloponnesian War. Laïs the Younger was a lover of the painter Apelles and of the orator Hypereides in the generation following the war (Athenaeus, *Deipnosophistae,* XIII, 588c–589b). Hypereides was also famed for his association with the beautiful Phryne, whom he successfully defended in court by openly displaying her physical beauty before the awed judges (Athenaeus, *Deipno-*

sophistae, XIII, 590d). Phryne's story also included the sculptor Praxiteles, who took her as his model for the magnificent Aphrodite of Cnidos. Thaïs of Athens was mistress to Alexander the Great (Plutarch, *Alexander,* 28), and she later married Ptolemy I, the successor-general who became the first Hellenistic king of Egypt. Lamia of Athens was the notorious companion of Demetrius Poliorcetes, one of the more dashing successor-generals who fought for power after Alexander's death. When Demetrius conquered Athens (307 B.C.), he and Lamia made the Acropolis into their personal brothel (Plutarch, *Demetrius,* 27; Athenaeus, *Deipnosophistae,* XIII, 577c).

The tales about these six courtesans are merely indicative of the large amount of literature concerned with the lives of famous mistresses and courtesans. Most of the literature is lost, but Athenaeus preserves the fragments of a number of these books, especially those penned by Aristophanes of Byzantium (257–180 B.C.). A good example of this genre of Greek literature is the surviving *Dialogues of Courtesans* by Lucian of Samosata (born after A.D. 120).

Wives naturally resented the presence of the *hetairai,* but generally the courtesans existed as a social institution in classical Athens, side by side with the legal unions that produced legally recognized children. Sometimes wives displayed their discontent by turning to wine, like "the woman called Cleo who became a heavy drinker" (Athenaeus, *Deipnosophistae,* X, 440d). Hipparete, the wife of the brilliant and scandalous Alcibiades, decided to leave him, since he "indulged in sexual relations with native and foreign-born courtesans." Hipparete loved Alcibiades, but his lack of public decorum was too much for her, and she left him and lived with her brother. Soon she decided she wished to divorce him, so she appeared in person at the court, as Athenian law required women to do when they desired divorce. But the law also included a catch clause. If the husband appeared in court and took his estranged wife home with him—by force, if necessary— the woman's petition was voided. Alcibiades did not want Hipparete to divorce him, so he "came and seized Hipparete, carried her home through the *agora,* and nobody dared to take her from him or oppose him" (Plutarch, *Alcibiades,* 8. 3–4). She lived with Alcibiades until she died quite soon thereafter, presumably because of the *hetairai* she detested so much.

Sometimes, a married man (in this case, Apollodorus in 350 B.C.) became so enamored of his *hetairai* that he "bought the freedom of one, gave another away in marriage, all the while having a wife of [his] own" (Demosthenes, *For Phormio,* XXXVI, 45). When any man used the institution of the *hetairai* too blatantly, it was very troubling to the moral sensibilities of the time, and the sources are openly in sympathy with the long-suffering wives. Overuse of the *hetairai* also seems to have tarnished a man's public repute, since so many of the high-class call girls were slaves; perhaps the *pornoboskoi,* "who take from every possible source" (Aristotle, *Nicomachaean Ethics,* IV, 1. 40 [1121B]), procured them when they were very young. Aristotle compares such businessmen with small-time usurers, "who lend money in small sums for very high interest."

A youth with good moral training could easily resist the temptation to follow the good-looking young woman whose sandals tracked "Follow me!" in the mud, or to respond to the apple toss of the local prostitute. Throwing an apple to a prospective client was an invitation from the prostitute, something the young man might encounter quite often on his forays into Piraeus. If possible, young men of the upper class were to avoid the areas where the *pornoboskoi* had their shops. Foreign women were most prominent in the trade, and the practice of recruiting Athenian girls from poor families received much legal publicity. This publicity resulted in the girls losing their citizen rights if the acts were discovered.

Customarily, the upper-class youth was isolated from women of his own status, and the only girls he knew were the ever present prostitutes or convenient noncitizen women. Such women were widely known for their lack of restraint, which instantly distinguished them from Athenian females; the latter, haughty and aloof, were seen only on the occasions when their fathers chose to exhibit them before prospective husbands. The young man who wanted sexual experience before marriage had to be rather wealthy: local courtesans of the right training and expertise were expensive. Greeks by and large accepted the stereotype that only the rich could afford the pleasures the *hetairai* offered. The tradition reached back as far as Archilochus: "Twice the age of her apprentices/That wrinkled old madam Xanthe/ Is still regarded as an expert" (Fragment 80, Davenport). Otherwise, according to the same moral image, the noble youth spent little on sensual pleasures. He could borrow a slave girl from an older friend for free (however, only young men of the right class were allowed to do this). Or he could engage in an affair with a married woman of the right class, but this was quite dangerous in Athens. If the husband caught him in bed with his wife, he could, by law, kill him on the spot; or the adulterer was shamed in public by torture of the "offending parts."

The oration *Against Neaera,* which is attributed to Demosthenes, details how Attic law treated problems arising from prostitutes. The case that the oration describes is incredibly complicated, and it involves the action against Stephanus, who had lived with a foreign-born woman whom he introduced as his wife. An old enemy of Stephanus discovered the fraud and sought revenge on him in court, especially when he discovered that Neaera, the woman in question, was not only a foreigner but also had been a slave and prostitute in a Corinthian brothel. In fact, she was one of seven girls in the house of Nicarete, a famous madam of Corinth; this house was apparently well known to the members of the jury assembled to hear the case. The enemy charged that Stephanus had conferred citizenship on someone who did not deserve it, which offended the laws insuring the purity of Attic descent.

According to the prosecution, an Athenian profligate had rescued Neaera from her sorry plight in the house of Nicarete, bought her, and came to Athens with her. After a time, she ran away and lived in Megara for two years, where another Athenian, Stephanus, "discovered" and rescued her again. He, in his turn, agreed to live with her as her husband and to bring up her children as his own. On her return to Athens, her original owner saw her and brought suit for the recovery of his property. The decision of an arbitration board declared that Neaera was free, but that she had to return any goods she had stolen from her original master and that she should live on alternate days with Stephanus and her former owner. Having lost his case, the previous owner disappears from the background of the oration, and Neaera lived with Stephanus as his wife. Her husband proved utterly unscrupulous, making much money from Neaera's trade, which she plied as before. When any of her lovers threatened to expose the fraud of her improper background, Stephanus extorted the unfortunate men by hinting that he might bring suit against *them* for adultery. Stephanus presented Neaera's children as his own and contracted a marriage for her daughter Phano.

Phano's new husband, an Athenian citizen, later discovered the fraud and divorced her, whereupon Stephanus brought suit because the dowry had not been returned. He dropped the charges when the infuriated ex-son-in-law threatened to bring a countersuit against

Stephanus for giving him a foreign woman as a lawful wife. The family of the ex-husband rejected a child born of the union according to the law. In Athenian law, it did not matter who fathered the children of foreign women or prostitutes. Legally, they were all illegitimate, in the sense that they could not inherit property and could not participate in any of the religious cults of the *polis*. The ex-husband did not wish to be accused of perjury, even on behalf of his son, and in the face of his own family's rejection, he refused to take an oath swearing to the legitimacy of his offspring.

Meanwhile, Phano was practicing her mother's art in the house of Stephanus and (for unclear reasons) she caught the eye of the *archon basileus* Theogenes. For the second time, Stephanus gave his "daughter" away in marriage, but this time the indignation of the *polis* was too great to be stifled by bribery or threats of countersuits. The wife of the *archon basileus* had to be of pure Attic blood and she had to be a virgin at marriage, since she had official duties at some of the most solemn ceremonies performed in the name of the *polis*. Phano could not even be present at these rituals, since it was a flagrant violation of the law; since she was an adultress and a foreign woman, her presence at the ceremonies was an insult to the gods and a disgrace to the *polis*. Apparently, the notification from the Board of the Areopagus to Theogenes about his wife's status caught Theogenes unwittingly, and they fined him. Shortly afterward he dissolved the marriage, and the whole case was brought into court by an old enemy of Stephanus. He was charged with deceptively giving the appearance of citizenship to persons of the most infamous profession. As the author of *Against Neaera* puts it (122), "A man has the *hetairai* for erotic pleasures, the use of concubines to care for the body, and takes a lawful wife to bring up children and to be faithful as a mistress of his house." The text of *Against Neaera* does not include the jury's decision, but from the context of the prosecution arguments (which quote the laws in question *in extenso*), the probable verdict was expulsion or slavery for the woman and loss of citizenship and a heavy fine for the man.

Male Conduct

Although there were no legal strictures against Athenian males dallying with prostitutes or high-class call girls, there was a pervasive moral code against cavorting with the women who threw apples. However, it was not the laws of Athens but the everyday cultural myths implanted in the minds of the young men that gave the code its force.

The traditions of his *polis* taught a youth two moral models of men. On the one hand, parents and relatives urged diffidence in sexual relations as part of proper behavior; the ideal is expressed clearly in Xenophon's portrait of Agesilaus, King of Sparta (d. 360 B.C.), found in both *Hellenica* and *Agesilaus,* a middling encomium. On the other hand, the literary traditions around Heracles, a glutton in all things— including sex—embody another model of man. He was called "old fifty-a-night" (Pausanias, *Description of Greece,* IX, 27. 6). Even in antiquity, there was a lively debate over Heracles' prowess, since a myth told of Heracles' seduction of the forty-nine daughters of Thestius and of one maiden who refused. She was sentenced to be a virgin priestess at Heracles' shrine (Apollodorus, *The Library,* II, 4. 10). Apollodorus thought the story impossible, making the seduction into a lengthy fifty-night affair. The obscure Herodorus argues for a mere five days (Athenaeus, *Deipnosophistae,* XIII, 556). (This whole section of the *Deipnosophistae,* "Learned Men at a Dinner Party," is devoted to sexual myths.) In addition, Heracles was known as being "most avid after women" (Athenaeus, *Deipnosophistae,* XIII, 556); the list of sexual athletes in Greek tales included Aegeus, Theseus of Athens, the tragic poet Euripides, and Philip II of Macedonia. The king "took a new wife at the beginning of each new campaign he undertook" (Athenaeus, *Deipnosophistae,* XIII, 557).

Of the two ideals, the properly raised Athenian male officially followed that of Xenophon's Agesilaus, widely known for his resistance to sexual temptation. Under the surface of Athenian life, however, there are constant hints of the pleasures the opposite model proffers and of the quasi fame gained from sexual exploits. Through constant exposure, the youth had to struggle continually against "the women who are dominant over all the pests of the world" (Athenaeus, *Deipnosophistae,* XIII, 558).

Male Notions about Women

The usual male concept of women in Greece points up the mixture of the two ideals of presumed uninhibitedness and required circumspection. Women had no voice in anything, and men regarded them as property. The numerous legends contrasted male physical strength with female physical and moral weakness, and the Greek father thought it his duty to protect his daughters. Since it was believed that the generations of the Attic family were continuous through the male line, the father picked a correct husband for his daughter. Marriage was simply the transfer of property. However, the new husband could not use the dowry his wife brought with her; he was permitted to use only the interest that might be gained from the original capital. Divorce could take place only when he returned the entire dowry to the wife's family.

Generally the *polis* believed it was descended from a common male ancestor, and all citizens within the *polis* thought of themselves as part of a lengthy tradition of custom and social mores. Smaller kinship units came into being through the diverging male lines, and the ancient "brotherhoods" held great influence in Attica throughout the classical period. These men were the *real* citizens, and the religious ceremonies conducted for the health of the *polis* were always performed within this context. If religious matters concerned a noncitizen or someone not of the male lineages, then the whole ritual was aborted. Consequently, Greek biological theory (for example, in Aristotle, *Generation of Animals,* 775–776) was based on the belief that women played a kind of "greenhouse" role in the growth of the fetus in their wombs. In modern terms, this meant that women made no genetic contribution to the offspring they might produce. The Greeks believed not only this but also that the "female state is one, so to speak, of deformity, which is in the world of nature as a matter of ordinary occurrence" (Aristotle, *Generation of Animals,* 775a). Since women were considered deformed creatures, it was the male duty to regard women as weak (because they had less "heat," according to Aristotle) and to make sure they were held in seclusion, and locked up if necessary. Another result of this community attitude was the acceptance of infanticide; it could not be considered a crime because the father might judge certain female babies weaker than normal, in which case he could expose them. This brutal picture probably had a common counterpart: a local slave dealer, a specialist in training girls to be accomplished courtesans, would be informed of the coming exposure and would be conveniently on hand to receive the child. Although the *theory* of contraception was being taught in the late fourth century B.C. (for example, in Aristotle, *Historia Animalium,* 583a), there was no effective contraception in the Greek world; consequently, many such infants were cast out to the avarice of the slave dealers.

Greeks firmly believed in an essential dichotomy between men and women. Physical and moral stamina was much stronger in men than in women, and men could resist grief and tears in a way that was impossible for women. The stereotype of this dichotomy is marked in the opening scenes of Aeschylus' *Seven Against Thebes,* in which Eteocles, the sturdy king of Thebes, stands in stark contrast to the wailing and moaning of the chorus of panic-stricken women, who represent all ages. Like Agesilaus, the ideal man easily resisted sexual temptation, but women were regarded as moral weaklings. For example, in *The Library,* an uncritical collection of Greek myths that Apollodorus wrote down sometime in the first or second century A.D., Zeus and Hera consulted the Theban seer Tiresias because they were in heated argument over "whether the pleasures of sex were enjoyed more by women or by men" (III, 6. 7). The wise man of Thebes replied, "If the pleasures of sex are calculated at ten, then men enjoy one and women nine." Zeus was delighted, while Hera was so infuriated that she blinded the seer; but Zeus rewarded him with long life and further powers of prophecy. Apollodorus also notes that Tiresias changed his sex every so often, making him a prototype of the hermaphrodite in Greek stories. The tale of Tiresias' judgment, which favored women's ability to enjoy sexual intercourse over men's, became a great favorite among scholarly commentators in the medieval period. In marginal notes on Homer's *Odyssey,* for example, a scholiast quotes lines from this often repeated tale proving the moral depravity of women.

The initial scenes of Aristophanes' *Lysistrata* reinforce the stereotype of moral weakness among women. Someone hatched the idea of stopping the war between Athens and Sparta through a sex strike by an association of the women from the Greek states. The whole project was immediately thrown into doubt because the assembled ladies could not forgo sexual relations for that long a period. The women flatly state that they cannot do it until Aristophanes introduces Lampito, the manlike woman from Sparta. She leads the way by shaming her sisters into abstention; she is stronger because she resembles a man. Throughout the play the women are slaves of sexual longing and desire, and many of the delightfully ridiculous twists in *Lysistrata* turn around a few of the women who attempt to sneak off for "just a little" on the sly.

Young men were admittedly more interested in the sexual act than their older brothers, and men were urged not to marry until after age thirty, since "intercourse begun before the male seed has completed its growth" produced stunted children (Aristotle, *Politics,* 1335a8 [VII, 16. 8]). In the same passages, Aristotle likewise notes that "young women are more wanton, once they have experience with sex." The philosopher thinks the best age for marriage is thirty-seven for men and eighteen for women. Xenophon writes that children are not produced for sexual satisfaction, since "the brothels and streets are filled with those who would satisfy that need" (*Memorabilia of Socrates,* II, 2. 4). Oversexed wives are assumed and feared in the ideal marriage, contracted to beget children, which would suggest frequent pregnancies. But in an age when unwanted babies were exposed, the wise husband provided his sensual wife with an *olisbos* or a *baubon* ("instruments of self-satisfaction"), suggested by Aristophanes, in *Lysistrata,* 109, and Herodas, in *Mimes,* ed. Headlam, VI, 19 ff.

Homosexuality

A logical effect of isolating men from women was the practice of homosexuality and pederasty ("love of boys"). Even though it was argued that homosexual desire was natural among men and the desire was considered to coexist easily with a nature defined as heterosexual, Athenian law carefully circumscribed the practice of sodomy. Modern tastes might see this attitude as a kind of homosexual double standard, but Plato's *Symposium* puts forth the Greek point of view quite cogently, from the purely intellectual level. In *Symposium,* Pausanias' speech illustrates what Plato thought about relationships between men; and Alcibiades' attempts to seduce the character labeled Socrates lead to his becoming drunk, while the philosopher argues for a love higher than the sensual.

Whatever the upper-class intellectual might have believed, the law firmly protected young men against sexual abuse. In *Against Timarchus* (6–12), Aeschines reminds his audience that such rules dated back to the time of Draco and Solon. The well-known *paidagogos,* who accompanied their young masters going off to the schoolmaster's lessons, always carried a heavy stick, which W. K. Lacey, in *The Family in Classical Greece* (London: Thames and Hudson, 1968, pp. 157–158), thinks they used to "protect their charges." Adult Athenian citizens, enrolled in the *demes,* were forbidden to hold any diplomatic, judicial, or administrative offices if they had ever been catamites (Aeschines, *Against Timarchus,* 19-21). The orator in *Against Timarchus* cites the actual law in question verbatim, so that the listeners might not have any doubt as to its provisions. The orator goes on to say that catamites or ex-catamites were even forbidden to address the assembly. Men who procured free boys for sodomy were punishable under the law, and he who paid money for the use of a boy came under general charges of *hubris* ("wanton injury" in this context), which carried a death sentence as the ultimate penalty (Aeschines, *Against Timarchus,* 13-17). Lysias, another orator, tells us that sodomy was looked down on when the catamite was not a citizen, but that the practice in this particular instance was not illegal (Lysias, III, 4; 26; and 33). The law was probably like the one that applied to adultery: if such activity went on among noncitizens and slaves, it was not considered illegal, but among citizens it was considered illegal.

For the older gentleman, pederasty was expensive and carried some risk of blackmail by former lovers. The boy was not expected to like homosexual relations with an older man, but he could commonly provide an excuse for himself by saying how worthy (rich) his lover was. If the older man was of the right class or had prestige and money, then the relationship was tolerated, although there was a good deal of grumbling about making boys too much into little girls.

Plato attacks these practices in the *Laws,* where the philosopher sets down his belief that sodomy is less acceptable than heterosexual relationships outside marriage, provided they are conducted discreetly. His ideal (the best) law in such matters would be "that nobody would dare have sexual congress with any upper-class woman or one who is freeborn, except with his own wife" (Plato, *Laws,* VIII, 841D). As a second best, he writes that sexual indulgence outside marriage with a woman can be sanctioned in custom and unwritten law, "provided there is privacy" (*Laws,* VIII, 841B). Plato angrily writes about

> making natural use of reproductive intercourse: on the one hand, one abstains from the male [when he acts] as if he were deliberately killing the human race, nor does he put his seed on stones and rocks where it cannot grow and increase; on the other hand, he does not put his seed in a female where he does not want the seed to grow. [*Laws,* VIII, 838E–839A]

8

Myth and the Womb of
Philosophy

The play of opposites in Hesiod's *Theogony* expressed a Greek method
of speculation not far removed from the intellectual constructs of
Greek philosophy. The genealogy of the gods, with its company of
abstracts, suggests that Greeks began to speculate about the nature
of the universe and the origins of that universe early in the history of
Greece. Soon Greek thinkers would discard the mythological surroundings of the speculations and drive their ideas about the physical
universe to logical endpoints. The creations of pure intellect based
on selected specific observations led eventually to the ethics of
Socrates and the ordered universe envisioned by Aristotle.

The process of development by accumulation, common in modern
scientific thinking, was rarely part of Greek philosophical concepts.
From the first, Greek thinkers displayed an exploring, ever questioning manner, and ideas took varying shapes according to the period
in which they were formed. Pre-Socratic philosophy took its mark
from an expansive, arrogant age that produced the lilting poems of
Sappho, the overweening lines of Archilochus, and the first hints of a
medicine other than that of the gods' whims, together with waves of
colonization in the western Mediterranean, consolidation of the *polis,*
and a hunger for new vistas, indicated by far-flung voyages of explor-
ation. Medicine was an important product of philosophy, but it had

a number of its own traits; other sciences in the Greek and Hellenistic world also grew from the base of the abstract intellect. To the Greeks, the abstract was more important than mere facts; the resulting intellectual construct was an acceptance of the reality of thought as a reflection of man and man's potential. If the mind could conceive, then reality bloomed, and studies like logic were born.

In philosophy and science, Greek thinking concentrated on known facts, although it explored the concept of experiment. The Greeks habitually took a single fact and probed and worried it from all angles until they could draw little more from it. They were interested in rational conclusions from a given fact, not in "verifying data." Hence, new facts were less important than new approaches to rationality. The collection of data did not enter the mainstream of Greek philosophy until the time of Aristotle and his students. But the practice of ignoring—or not seeking alternative facts—had an internal weakness. Greek philosophers relied on their own authority and assumed that their rationalism was better than other methods. This assumption led to dogmatic assertions and squabbling among the thinkers. Greek philosophy and science never freed themselves from this trap, and the slashing insolence of certain philosophers became legendary. Since the rational constructs were products from within the Greek mind, they incorporated so-called absurd ideas from the backlog of Greek myth and superstition. In spite of the fact that Greek philosophers denied such influence, many thinkers mirrored their own time. Pre-Socratic philosophy came when rapid change overtook the Greek world as a whole, but Plato and Aristotle set down their thoughts in a time when Greeks longed for the "good old days" of a smoothly functioning *polis*.

There are, on the other hand, distinct advantages in the methods of Greek philosophy. The ideas of each thinker were subject to ruthless criticism, and rounds of argument and counterargument resulted. In addition, the atmosphere of free exchange promoted the widespread knowledge of certain theories—denied by some, modified by others, accepted occasionally. Each philosopher pressed his conclusion as far as he desired, subject to critical examination by his colleagues, wherever they were in the Greek world.

Religion usually did not hamper philosophical speculation, although in 399 B.C., in an age not as free as earlier centuries, the Athenians charged Socrates and his teachings with impiety. Normally religion was the concern of the individual relating to his *polis;* each *polis* had a few organized religious festivals that emphasized the connection between certain gods or goddesses and the *polis*. (See chapter 6.) Otherwise, constant change was a hallmark of Greek philosophy; thinkers continued to refine their ideas or refute what they thought were nonrational conclusions.

The first stirrings of Greek philosophy came in the Greek cities of Asia Minor in the sixth century B.C. These *poleis* were not as bound by internal traditions as their kindred *poleis* on the mainland of Greece, and they were constantly in touch with ideas flowing in from points to the east. After philosophy took root in Greek Asia Minor, it next emerged in Greek Italy and Sicily, among the colonies of various cities in mainland Greece. The Greeks who lived in the new worlds of the West were very much like, and yet unlike, their brethren in the East. Breadth and massiveness were marks of Syracusan architecture in Sicily, and new comprehension and a kind of breathless optimism were characteristic in Greek philosophies from Sicily and southern Italy. The philosophers produced in Greece suggest a bubbling contact in the mother *poleis* with the colonies.

Hesiod disclosed that Greeks did not think of a creator god, but of deduced abstract forces explaining the gods. Like Hesiod, the earliest philosophers were concerned about the nature and origin of the universe. Aristotle later called these thinkers *physikoi:* those who hoped to understand *physis* ("the origin of things") (*Physics,* 193b12). Elsewhere (*Physics,* 184b17, 187a12, 205a5) Aristotle uses *physis* (pronounced "foosis") to mean nature; those who inquired into nature were natural philosophers. Practical observations led the first philosophers, like Thales and Anaximander, to conclusions, yet they combined rational conclusions with allegory. Their solutions were not exactly logical, as the term is usually understood, in the sense that the solutions were mathematical while the ideas were expressed in poetry.

The Pre-Socratic Philosophers

Thales of Miletus (*fl. c.* 585 B.C.) was recorded by tradition as the first of the natural philosophers in Greek Asia Minor. He was a practical astronomer, geometry expert, and all-around wise man, and he supposedly predicted an eclipse in 585 B.C. His knowledge of astronomy came from Babylonia, and Thales borrowed many astral techniques known for centuries among the successive cultures of

Mesopotamia. Looking for an explanation of natural origins, Thales postulated that water is the primeval substance and that the earth floats on water. Greek myths had spoken of water as part of the beginnings long before Thales, but his observation that water is necessary for the life of plants and animals led him to further speculation on the basic nature of water and its life-giving properties. More thought led Thales to suppose that a kind of soul permeated the world as a whole, since he noticed that certain stones had powers of movement. Aristotle describes (*Politics,* A 11, 1259a9) how Thales became a man of means when his observation of the stars foretold a coming heavy crop of olives. Thales cornered the market in olive presses long before his fellows were aware of the need for them, and he became rich hiring out the presses when more olives than had been expected arrived. Thales came to be regarded as the archetypal philosopher, and the stereotype obscures much of what we know about the actual thinking of many pre-Socratic philosophers.

Although the relative chronology of the Ionian philosophers is far from clear, Greek and Roman tradition spoke of Anaximander of Miletus (*c.* 550 B.C.) as the second philosopher, after Thales, on the list of philosophic speculators. There is proper skepticism about the story that he discovered the obliquity of the zodiac (as Pliny relates in *Natural History,* II, 31), but he is rightly credited with brilliant institutions about the origins of man and the universe around him. Anaximander thought the first animals arose from slime through the action of the sun, and his observations on the helplessness of undeveloped animals (the human baby, for example) led him to think that life developed protective devices in its weak stages. Thales had thought water was the primordial substance, and Anaximander elaborated that idea into slime. Other philosophers, however, suggested other possibilities in the search for beginnings. Anaximenes of Miletus (*fl. c.* 530 B.C.) believed air was primordial. To Anaximenes, air was the divine substance motivating the rest of the universe.

The ancients linked Anaximander with Anaximenes, and they may have known one another. It was Anaximander, however, who separated his thinking from the womb of Hesiod's abstract divinities. Anaximander wrote in prose, taking his speculation away from the poetry that smacked of Homer and Hesiod and earlier mythic concepts. Anaximander suggested a *to apeiron* ("infinite substance") that was unlimited in properties and indefinite, an all-encompassing matter in motion. The motion, and the quality of the infinite substance, gave rise to forces in opposition. Physical expression was found in the opposites of heat and cold; the cold was "packed together," while the heat occurred outside the cold. He thought the earth was shaped like a cylinder, and the opposites of heat and cold explained the relation of the earth to the rest of the universe. Heat was arranged in rings outside the earth, and the holes in the rings were stars. Rips in the rings were lightning. Further opposites were seen in wet and dry. Life emerged when the dry evaporated the wet (as the Milesians could see by walking on the seashore and noting the drying mud and the worms coming out of the slime). Anaximander's ideas were simple and had enormous impact. From the basic idea of change came the concept that the universe was not to last forever in the form one observed in the present.

Following Anaximander's lead, Anaximenes introduced another explanation of opposites. Thickening and thinning meant that air was the primordial life-force. The separation of opposites showed that the universe had an underlying unity, but that a mixture of the opposites was necessary for life. Eternal motion gave life, and the primal substance was the essence of condensation and rarefaction. Change was thus observed in seeking quantity, which controls specific kind. The primordial matter was alive, and the primal substance was the abstract, which explained all the features of the universe.

A reaction to such ideas was inevitable, and it came from Xenophanes of Colophon (*fl. c.* 500 B.C.), who was concerned with theology and unity rather than with matter. He was critical of polytheism and described his concept of deity positively, insisting that the study of theology (the gods, to most Greeks) was not something to be isolated from the observation of nature. The immorality of conventional gods was inconsistent with his concept of deity, and Xenophanes perceived that deity was not necessarily manlike. Noting that all races made their gods like themselves, he thought the accepted theology was subjective and of little value. He postulated a single, nonanthropomorphic deity that existed in man's perception and intelligence. Xenophanes stressed the limits of man's knowledge, but he could not prove that any belief was wrong—a problem unsolved by most philosophers. His interest in ethics had an influence much later, but his foreshadowing of monotheism did not go deeply into the Greek thought of his own day.

Other thinkers had brooded upon the theological implications of the intellectual construct of Greek thought. Pythagorean traditions were linked with the philosophy of Pherecydes of Syros (*fl. c.* 550 B.C.), who thought of Time (*kronos*) as a personal being. The universe devolved from personal conception, an idea extended by Pythagoras of Samos (*fl. c.* 535 B.C.). (He migrated to Croton in Italy, *c.* 530 B.C.) Pythagoras taught that all living things had a kinship, and he believed in the transmigration of souls. To improve their souls, men had to follow a religious fraternity that Pythagoras headed. The historian Herodotus thought Pythagoras' teachings were like those of the Orphics, but even as early as the fifth century B.C., traditions around Pythagoras had become muddled and confused. Rules of abstinence and prohibitions were important to the school of Pythagoras, but usual accounts of the school forbidding meat and the like are based on unreliable sources. Within Pythagoras' teachings the mystic became bound with the orderly, and objectives came through great learning and inquiry. The fate of the soul was a central theme, but religious speculation and inquiry were inseparable, forming a single way of life. Contemplation (*theoria*), the orderliness of the observed cosmos (*kosmos*), and purification (*katharsis*) motivated Pythagoras and his followers and gave rise later to extensions in music, medicine, and mathematics. There was a divine order in the universe, in the sense of harmony. Pythagoras visualized this order in mathematical terms and conceived numbers as dots.

By 500 B.C. some basic assumptions had been made. Philosophers thought there was a primary substance, and the world came into being by a process of "constant becoming." They disagreed on the results of the process and soon began to ask questions about the nature of "becoming." After such questions gained importance, "philosophy" became more "philosophic." Questions like "What is becoming?" and "What is the nature of being and existence?" went far below the seemingly whimsical ideas postulated by earlier nature philosophers. The question "Did a manifold world result from a basic unity?" could be answered better with philosophy than with the observation-speculation-conclusion chain followed in Greek Asia Minor.

Challenges to the older ideas were varied. Heracleitus of Ephesus (*c.* 500 B.C.) spoke with utter disdain of pure knowledge. Arrogant and dogmatic, he attacked other philosophers as simpleminded fact filers and expressed scorn for the ordinary man who was more impressed with facts than with thinking. He taught constant change,

a continual living and dying, and constant motion. Opposing forces balancing one another prevented chaos and anarchy. Change came from *logos,* a basic force, a "world reason" out of which the world was made. Later, Heracleitus thought of *logos* as fire and spoke of man's "life spark," a kind of inner burning flame. Moisture extinguished the flame, and too much moisture caused death, with the resulting dominion by the forces of chaos.

By contrast, Parmenides of Elea (*c.* 480 B.C.) believed there was no change. Motion that others detected was false. The world was static, although there might be apparent change. He taught that what is thought, existed, and that that which did not exist could not be conceived, and that the senses were inferior to the intellect. Parmenides' pupil, Zeno of Elea (*c.* 460 B.C.), spent his life proving his teacher right. Zeno is justly famous for a series of paradoxes logically proving that the senses have less value than the intellect. The tale of Achilles' race against a turtle is illustrative. Achilles will never be able to overtake the slower turtle if the turtle begins first. By the time Achilles reaches the point where the turtle began, the turtle has moved on to another point. When Achilles reaches the second point, the turtle has moved on again, and so on, indefinitely (Aristotle, *Physics,* Z9, 239b14).

Other questions and answers came from Empedocles, Anaxagoras, and Leucippus. Empedocles of Acragas, in Sicily (*fl. c.* 450 B.C.), wrote two poems, *On Nature* and *Purifications. On Nature* proposed disunity, and motion resulted from the opposition of the rule of love and the rule of strife. Attraction and repulsion among four materials (fire, air, water, earth) determined the nature of the physical world. The four materials were moved by the First Principles, love and strife. Thus material substances were changed through mixing, but their own natures did not change; change was a simple rearrangement of the four irreducible materials. In man, blood contained the most even mixture of the four materials; blood around the heart had Thought. Man's thoughts were fleeting because the mixture was temporary, like the physical mingling on which they rested.

Anaxagoras of Clazomenae (*fl. c.* 460 B.C.) spent much of his adult life in Athens and had some acquaintance with Pericles. The Athenians regarded Anaxagoras as an egghead (Plato, *Apology,* 26D), and they derided him for his notions that the sun was a molten rock and that the Nile's flooding came from snows melting in Ethiopia. In reaction to Parmenides and Zeno, Anaxagoras taught that the uni-

verse was made up of countless seeds, a mingling of a basic substance. The seeds were very small and the action of Mind (*nous*) explained their motion. He attempted to separate matter from the motive force, but Mind had a "fineness" that explained other qualities.

An "atomic" theory of the universe is jointly credited to Leucippus of Miletus (*fl. c.* 440 B.C.) and Democritus of Abdera (*c.* 460–*c.* 370 B.C.). Leucippus' atoms greatly resembled Parmenides' One, but his atoms were infinite and mobile. The world was created initially from a vortex (*dinē*), and creation was repeated numberless times within infinite space. Democritus added detail and cohesion to the theory, which has been so influential in the history of Western thought. Atoms and void were the two ultimate principles. Atoms were the real world, infinite in variety and shape, infinite in number, uniform in substance, immutable, and indivisible. Falling through the void, atoms attached themselves to one another, forming shapes. Varying combinations of shapes gave the secondary qualities, like color and sound, which were the results of men's conventions. Atoms were self-moving through the void, and true knowledge ensued from contact with Soul Atoms—a material force, round and fiery, distributed over the body.

These materialistic world systems were subject to chance and caprice, and so philosophers turned increasingly to questions of the ethical and spiritual nature of man. Cosmology seemed to be isolated in a lofty cleft with little connection to the life of Greeks in the *polis;* the intelligent citizen did not pretend to understand the theories, even when he parroted them. Often materialism seemed to threaten rather than elucidate, and some believed that materialistic cosmologies were grotesque and occasionally dangerous since they tended to explode conventional beliefs and the religious structure acceptable in fifth-century B.C. Greece.

The Sophists

Side by side with materialistic philosophy came the increasing influence and importance of the Sophists, who answered practical questions. As teachers, they wandered from *polis* to *polis* and gave instruction for fees. Their subject matter varied, but most taught the art of getting along in life, with an ultimate promise of success. Protagoras (*c.* 485–*c.* 415 B.C.) collected payment for teaching virtue (*arete*), what we would call efficient conduct. He doubted that study

gave any man more knowledge than another, but he taught the conventions that were to be learned and respected if one were to succeed within a *polis*. Gorgias (*c.* 483–376 B.C.) instructed students in how artistic speech best captured the *logos*. He hoped to make prose rival poetry and gave careful training in the devices of successful speech making. Eloquent oratory was the path to political influence in the democratic *polis,* and the Sophist teaching the art of oratory could become very rich. Hippias (*c.* 481–411 B.C.) claimed competence in oratory, mathematics, astronomy, grammar, poetry, music, and history, and he devised a memory system that allowed a person success in politics or in one of the skills. The Sophists' central purpose was to provide practical results rather than philosophic thought, but the trappings of philosophy often disguised the sorry products. The best of the Sophists taught their students to accept uncritically the conventions and traditions as they found them (that is, the best way to lead is to appear like those you want to lead), and the worst taught cynical disbelief in all moral restraints, in the quest of selfish, personal success. Thrasymachus (*fl. c.* 415 B.C.) believed justice always favored the strong, and Antiphon the Sophist (*fl. c.* 435 B.C.) opposed Socrates' notions that ethics was man's foremost concern. Many Sophists were unblemished in character and enjoyed great prestige, but their method led into an inevitable degeneration. As long as a man sounded as though he knew something, he could fool enough people to gain success in his community. On the other hand, the Sophists met a desire for higher education in a time when there were no formal universities that could inculcate the young in the mores of Greek culture. Many of the sciences came into students' ken through the Sophists, and a good teacher gave a grasp of intellectual complexities. Generally, however, the public regarded the Sophists with grave suspicion, and vitriolic attacks like Aristophanes' *Clouds* were also directed at philosophers.

Socrates

Socrates (470–399 B.C.) taught that ethic is the highest good, and he became infamous in Athens for his sharp and personally demeaning questions about Good and Evil. As an Athenian, he was devoted to his *polis* and served with distinction in the Peloponnesian War. A man of total intellectual honesty, he did not buckle under pressure from the rule of the Thirty Tyrants (404–403 B.C.), and as a teacher of genius, he gathered around him young men of good families looking forward to public careers, as well as serious thinkers hoping to gain from Socrates' insights. The list of students was impressive. Alcibiades, alternately the darling and pariah of Athens, received instruction for a time, although he failed to comprehend Socrates' concepts of higher goods. Xenophon, who later wrote a clear history of Greek affairs for the period 411 to 362 B.C., retained an incisive veneer derived from Socratic method. Plato became famous as a philosopher in his own right; his magnificent *Apology,* which gave a dramatic picture of Socrates' trial (399 B.C.), made Socrates one of the best-known figures in Greek history.

Socrates conceived a personal deity (*daimon*) to guide him throughout life, a notion his fellow citizens distrusted. He was charged with impiety and corruption of the youth in his trial, charges the philosopher denied, failing to refute direct accusations. Angered by Socrates' unrepentant attitude, the jury condemned him to death. A month later he drank hemlock, surrounded by his friends and students. They bitterly recalled Athens' misdeed time and time again; because of it, both Xenophon and Plato chose Sparta as their ideal state. Although Socrates wrote nothing, his systematic definitions to ethical questions seemed to attack the bedrock traditions of the *polis.* He gave voice to long-simmering discontent within the strictures of an Athens demanding conformity. The Peloponnesian War indicated in a glaring manner the faults of Athens' imperialistic democracy, but after losing to Sparta, Athens sought scapegoats to explain her downfall. Socrates' death remained a blemish that gave future thinkers pause about the inner brutality of democracy in defeat.

Plato

Plato (*c.* 429–348 B.C.) was looking forward to a career in politics when, at the age of twenty, he fell completely under the spell of Socrates' personality and his daggered questions, which always ended with "I know I don't know." Plato never went into politics, and he left Athens after Socrates' trial and death. Returning later, he founded his Academy, which gathered kindred spirits generally hostile to democracy. He hoped his ideas of the ideal ruler were practical; in an attempt to test his concepts, Plato became advisor to Dionysius II, tyrant of Syracuse, in Sicily. The effort was a dismal failure. Plato learned that tyrants did not like open criticism—even from a philosopher—and he may have had part in the coup of Dion in 357 B.C. The philosopher-king eluded Plato in real life, but in the meantime his ideas spread. His works became popular, something unusual for a serious writer of philosophy. Plato had the gift of style, writing in polished and clear prose that was often beautiful in its limpid simplicity.

His compositions are of two types: "progress reports on research" as he evolved an idea, and statements of positions he reached. Plato later changed his thinking on many points, so that the statements often varied from essay to essay. Following Socrates, his writing included the satiric, the amusing, and the homely, and it also included the honed essay, to move the reader emotionally. *Apology* is an example of the latter, an accurate summary of Socrates' ideas, although the words are Plato's. *Phaedo* is Plato's eloquent argument for the immortality of the soul. *Symposium* has gained more than its share of abuse from prudish scholars who lack a perception of Plato's ideal of love above the sensual levels. Plato's methods and impact are also well illustrated in his *Republic* and *Laws.*

In the *Republic,* Plato squarely faces the problem of proving the superiority of justice. Recalling instances like the sack of Melos during the Peloponnesian War, he set out to construct the ideal state, which would avoid or prevent slaughter and the abuse of power. He uses the form of the dialogue, with Socrates as the major speaker. Old age is the opening topic, but the discussion turns shortly to the definition of justice. The first definition is speaking the truth and paying one's debts. A second speaker suggests that conventional justice meant doing good to one's friends and evil to one's enemies. A third opinion notes that justice is in the interest of the strongest. Since the speaker is an extremist, Socrates cannot persuade him, but merely silence him. These definitions of justice are ones that give rewards; Socrates says he will defend justice in its own right and for its own sake.

By creating the ideal state, Plato can search for the true meaning of justice. His model is the *polis,* surrounded by Hellenic and barbarian settlements. Definitions begin with the principle of labor division, based in the order of things established in Nature, an order that best reflects inborn abilities. In the ideal *polis,* justice emerges when each man performs those duties for which he is best suited. Once the principle is defined, Plato (through the Socrates in the dialogue) applies it to his ideal state and divides its citizens into three classes:

at the top are the philosophers, who will govern; the second class is the soldiers, who will defend the *polis;* and at the bottom are the "producers"—the craftsmen, merchants, and farmers who will give the state its economic necessities. The three divisions correspond to men's Reason, Will, and Appetites. Reason must rule if justice of the Soul is to result. Only then can each of one's faculties do its destined tasks in a way that is best suited to it. This is true in the ideal state as well. Little change is in store for life among the lower class, but Plato focuses great attention on the philosophers and soldiers, whom he calls "guardians."

Plato would abolish private property for the top two classes, and a system of education would equip the philosophers for their task of governing. Soldiers would share the benefits of education, but to a lesser degree. To Plato, the role of gymnastics was a benefit for the soul as well as the body. Education would include gymnastics and music, but music would not retain any poetic myths and allegories. Later education would provide instruction in mathematics, geometry, harmonics, the study of Ideas (dialectic), and astronomy. Once mastery of dialectic had been attained, one could rule with justice, since the nature of the Good would be comprehended and understood.

Evil in the *poleis* resulted from the separation of philosophy and politics, and a solution would emerge when philosophers became rulers, or rulers became philosophers. In Book VIII of the *Republic,* Plato turns to the kinds of *poleis* that have forsaken the ideal. The *polis* devoted to honor (timocracy) is the least degenerate, while the state ruled by wealth or by cliques of the rich (plutocracy or oligarchy) deviates more from the ideal. Democracy, a state in which every man does as he pleases, is third on the list. Tyranny, rule by the tyrant alone in a slave state, is fourth, the type of *polis* farthest removed from the ideal.

Plato then contrasts the tyrant, the most unjust of men, with the philosopher, the most just, and contrasts the justice and injustice each state possessed. Now he can defend justice, stripped of all its rewards. Justice is to be preferred to injustice, just as health is craved more than disease or happiness is desired more than misery. Injustice is the internal conflict, the sickness of the soul, as disease is the sickness of the body. The tyrant suffers more than any other man. The *Republic* concludes with an attack on the popular image that the poets gave of the happiness of the soul after death, or of punishment after death. Plato thinks Homer did grave disservice to the concept of justice, particularly in his poetic portraits of the warrior-heroes.

Plato hoped to comprehend the basic world concept, the Idea. If man perceived the Idea, he could see the world more perfectly. Consequently, he taught that relativity was irrelevant. He found the Good through Reason; fundamental Reason allowed understanding of the highest Idea, Good. He discerned the Idea in a process similar to what a mystic undergoes in a trance, which implied the separation of the mind from the body. But Plato further states his mistrust of poets in *Laws*. Poets advocated life based on the irrational in man. In the ideal *polis,* strict censorship would check the influence of poets and musicians on the gullible.

Aristotle

Plato's Academy attracted many students, among whom was Eudoxus of Cnidos (*c.* 405-355 B.C.), a brilliant mathematician and astronomer. He later became close friends with Plato, turning the philosopher's thinking into new paths linked with astronomy. Eudoxus was skilled in geometry and had studied medicine with the renowned Philistion of Locri (*c.* 427-347 B.C.). Aristotle of Stagirus (386-322 B.C.), the son of a Macedonian physician, was also lured to the Academy. Aristotle arrived in Athens in 367 B.C. and remained with Plato for twenty years. Here the influence of his own background in biology combined with the impact of Eudoxus' mathematics and Plato's growing interest in astronomy and mathematics. Plato was never really interested in biology, but the young Aristotle retained his predilection for philosophy as it related to life in its myriad of forms.

Plato died in 348 B.C., but since Aristotle was a *metic* ("resident foreigner"), he was not made head of the Academy. Looking for a living, he became part of the small circle of intellectuals around the tyrant Hermeias of Atarneus (in Mysia, Asia Minor). Aristotle taught there until Hermeias' death in 345 B.C. Meanwhile, Aristotle had married Hermeias' niece, and he had begun his serious research into zoology. After 345 B.C., he went to the city of Mitylene on the island of Lesbos; there he met Theophrastus, who became Aristotle's best student. Theophrastus aided his mentor immeasurably in biological and zoological studies.

A little later, Philip II of Macedonia sent word around the Greek world that he wished to hire a tutor for his young son Alexander. Philip asked Aristotle to come to Pella, capital of the Macedonian kingdom, which was growing in power. Aristotle's influence on his royal pupil was slight, although later traditions enlarged on the connection between the budding military genius and the finest intellect from the *polis*. Alexander was anti-Persian when Aristotle arrived in Pella, and the philosopher intensified Alexander's fondness for Greek culture, which was already a part of the trappings in the Macedonian kingship. Alexander, however, disagreed with Aristotle over the question of rule. The philosopher thought Greeks should reign supreme, treating Persians and other Asiatics as inferiors, while Alexander hoped to unite the diverse peoples in his huge empire into an enormous whole.

With Macedonian support, Aristotle founded the Lyceum in Athens in 335 B.C. The Lyceum was a kind of research institution and gathering devoted to high-quality education. Students came to study varying subjects, and the Lyceum had a library with a fair collection of books. A spacious area provided teachers and students opportunities to withdraw and discuss problems as small groups. The Lyceum was laced with paths, and Aristotle occasionally delivered a lecture while walking (hence the name, Peripatetic). In the afternoons, he lectured on general topics like rhetoric. Once a month everyone met for a formal meal, but the major function of the Lyceum was intellectual, not social.

Aristotle and his pupils collected a vast body of facts of historical and scientific interest. Aristotle's amazing energy and activity funneled this huge collection of assembled facts into a series of ideas that formed an encyclopedia of knowledge. The facts were incorporated into the projected works through a systematic probing of the nature of knowledge. First came the collection and listing of data, which allowed the process of inductive logic to form a law (hypothesis). Next came application of that law. The development of logic was important to this chain of events, and Aristotle drew concepts from Parmenides and Zeno. Within this matrix, Aristotle structured the study of rhetoric, summarizing thinking on the subject. Logic then guided his attention to the structure of politics, and he collected facts about 158 constitutions in an attempt to determine successful political systems. The *Athenian Constitution,* recovered from the sands of Egypt in A.D. 1890, is one example of this study. This often jumbled document is of fundamental importance for knowledge of Athenian history, as well as of Aristotle's philosophy of politics.

Lists of facts and individuals associated with ideas shaped his histories of medicine, arithmetic, and philosophy. He compiled a list of victors in the Pythian Games and wrote an essay on the flooding of the Nile. Aristotle and his students assembled an enormous body of physiological facts, as well as an anatomical atlas, a superb example of the rational application of inductive logic to medicine. From Theophrastus (*c.* 369-285 B.C.) emerged a history of plants; the book remained the foundation-guide to curative plants and drugs until the beginnings of modern chemistry. After observing five hundred species of animals, Aristotle drew up a history of animals in ten books and attempted a scheme of classification for them that was the direct ancestor of Linnaeus' system.

Parts of Animals provides a clear illustration of Aristotle's method. The work is an account of why parts are what they are. First is the Motive Cause (the parent), then the Material Cause (the seed), third is the Formal Cause (the goal of following the development of a type), and last is a Final Cause (the aim to producing a perfected example of a type). This is a teleological view—i.e., that there is a purpose in nature. Through *Parts of Animals,* Aristotle's differences from and similarities to Plato become apparent. Plato sought his perfect Good in the sky, whereas Aristotle's perfect form was in matter and nature here on earth. He saw beauty in all of nature and took his ideas from the natural world. His *Politics* is a mixture of ideal generalization and facts. To him, the problem of *stasis* ("internal chaos") in the *polis* was paramount, and Aristotle again disagreed with Plato in emphasizing the biological rather than the mathematical qualities in man and his state. His *Prior Analytics* is an account of the deductive scheme of a syllogism, giving a masterful summary from point to point, but the *Metaphysics* and *Politics* are merely presentations of problems. All of his writings show Aristotle constantly searching for the truth, with a gradual shift in emphasis. But, as he became more of a scientist, he did not become any less a philosopher.

Hellenistic Philosophies

Alexander's conquests made classical philosophy obsolete. Aristotle's *Ethics* and Plato's *Republic* were out of date when they were written, since they defined goodness within the narrow limits of the *polis*. As a political force determining the fate of empires, the *polis* was finished, although Athens kept an aura of being a center for intellectuals and literary achievement. The swirling power of mercenary armies filled the new age of kingdoms that Alexander's talented generals had created; and the citizens of the *polis*-like cities that had been established as centers of Greek culture and control from Syria to India no longer lived under the time-honored customs, laws, and authority of the classical *polis*. The Greeks who migrated into the new kingdoms as part of the ruling class felt they were without guidance, even when they revived their heritages. Life for many was difficult and insecure, and the Hellenistic period was full of ethical bewilderment. Nihilism was a natural answer in such a time, as Pyrrho (*c.* 360–*c.* 270 B.C.) taught it, teaching that the only certainty was uncertainty. However, Pyrrho's negative philosophy brought little comfort to the spiritual exiles from the *polis*. Their growing needs included standards of values and a refuge from the fear of men or the whims of fate. Philosophers living in the *polis* viewed their search with a sense of intellectual doubt and perplexity. To the Hellenistic age and its Roman adapters, philosophy became a recognition of man's weaknesses and shortcomings, an art or guide in life, the "training or the healing of the soul" (Cicero, *Tusculan Disputations,* II, 13; III, 6; V, 5), or the "only medicine for diseases of the spirit" (Plutarch, *Education of Children,* 7D). Metaphysics lost importance, while individual ethics assumed prominence. Philosophy was no longer a pilot for a few diehard seekers after wisdom, but a force of rescue in man's struggle to exist. Many people living in the Hellenistic period replaced religion with philosophy, and most post-Aristotelian schools made no distinction in the social rank, sex, or nationality of their followers. They offered everyone a way to peace and happiness by varying roads, all promising relief from the ravages of fortune. Such philosophies tried to create a sage as an ideal person who could exist independently of the surroundings or circumstances.

Two systems that differed in their fundamental aspects and appealed to opposite sides of human nature were more or less successful in meeting the demands of the time. Both were materialistic and gave small hope of a pleasant afterlife. They sought to make each man an entity and taught independence through withdrawal or resignation, not through conquest. Epicurus avoided Evil, and Zeno denied it. Neither overcame it.

Epicurus' name conjures up false images of gross materialism or immoral pleasure seeking. Born in Athens (*c.* 341 B.C.), Epicurus lived on the island of Samos until the Athenians were expelled in 322 B.C. In fifteen years of homeless wandering, he displayed a genius for friendship and a strength of personality. He borrowed his concept of the universe from Democritus and added an improvement. Through a natural interpretation of the cosmos, man had little to fear from the gods, who lived remote from man in careless bliss and who had no reason to reward or punish men. Afterlife was of no concern, since the soul was as mortal as the body and death was sleep with no waking. Men made their own hells on earth, and they made civilization from savagery by natural means. Divine intervention had no place in the events of history; time and experience brought change. Thus fear of the gods or death was without intellectual foundation.

Like some later Romans, crude minds seized the aspects of Epicureanism most liable to perversion, winning for Epicurus the infamy associated with the epicure. Even the opponents of the new thinking, however, praised his charm and character. "In his lifetime his friends were numbered by whole cities" (Diogenes Laertius, *Epicurus* X, 9). Epicurus bought a garden outside Athens and settled down to receive his many admirers. He welcomed slaves and women, and children received some of his letters. He lived his own rule of seeking the greatest pleasure, which he defined as quiet intellectual contemplation, and he was faithful to his own dictum, "Live unobtrusively." His followers had little influence in politics, concentrating instead on the development of amiable home lives. Epicurus and his school fought superstition, while other philosophies (like Platonism and Stoicism) permitted superstition and astrology. Epicureans later became the unwitting companions of the early Christians because both were accused of atheism. After Epicurus' death in 270 B.C., his philosophy became popular among intellectuals in the Hellenistic kingdoms, and it later influenced many important leaders in the imperial Roman Republic. Epicureans represented the best qualities of the classical view of life, but they failed to meet the wide-ranging demands of their age and rarely appealed to the common man, who sought more than rational assurance that death was harmless.

Stoicism, which had many links with Cynicism and Near Eastern outlooks, emphasized a different ideal. It was reputedly founded by Zeno of Citium (in Cyprus), who arrived in Athens about 314 B.C. as a shipwrecked trader. Zeno became a teacher (*c.* 301 B.C.), giving lectures at the Stoa ("porch"), and he taught an intolerance for imperfection, an uncompromising idealism, and a resignation before an All Supreme. Such attitudes were common among Semitic peoples and are found in modern Islam, but they were new to Greece at the beginning of the third century B.C. Zeno introduced the ideas of duty and conscience, and he distinguished moral values (which were absolute) from practical values (which were relative and indifferent). Intention was everything and circumstances nothing, except as material to exercise the will and build character. Only one thing was good: Goodness, or Virtue.

Within Stoicism lurked a curious vagueness. There was no clear demonstration of how a man could rise from self-preservation to Virtue. The question "What is Virtue?" had no definite answer. To the student familiar with the *New Testament,* the Stoics seem similar to the Pharisees, who were fond of terminologies and distinctions, concerned with personal goodness, and harsh in their view of human nature. Love, pity, and the fate of friends were not essential to the sage, since they were emotions that distracted him from a central peace and were the companions of capricious fortune. The Stoic was totally detached.

Stoics tried to streamline Aristotle's views in ethics, metaphysics, and psychology. Zeno took Aristotle's four causes and reduced them to two, which were parts of one principle. Zeno postulated a unity of Soul, in contrast to Aristotle's division into the rational and irrational. Original Matter and Force were in the natural world (*physis*). Everything was Matter; however, the cause was Force, which was Creative Reason (*logos*), or God, and was always present in all Matter. Matter and Force were two aspects of an identical reality, parallel accounts of the same universe. One was the physical, the other the metaphysical, or theological. Highest reality was Fire (*pyr*), which was diversified in air currents of different tensions (*tonos*). Examples of material qualities were the "hardness in iron, thickness in stone, whiteness in silver" (Plutarch, *Stoic Contradictions,* 1053e). Reason, or God, was also Fire; Zeno pinned down the *logos* of the Socratics and joined it with the *logos* of Heracleitus. Reason ruled the universe and was the same Reason as that within men directing their lives. Thus the law in the universe was law in man's nature. Reason gained many labels—Necessity, Creator, Zeus, World-Soul, Fate; these were all attempts to describe the same thing. Necessity was also Virtue. Stoicism provided a sharp intellectual base for its brand of cosmopolitanism; it was not extraordinary in the Hellenistic world, but the Stoic summation gave it definition. Stoics retained what the Epicureans expressly denied, a faith in Providence. Stoics also admitted the power of superstitions and mythology as part of the ordinary, everyday world, unlike the Epicureans.

The Stoics were psychological monists. Reason alone ruled man's soul, not Reason in tension with the irrational, as Aristotle taught. Reason was subject to error in judgment through half-visions, called passions or impulses. Greed was based on the false notion that money is good, and pleasure came from mistaken ideas of the truly desirable. The Stoics avoided the passions, including pleasure, fear, pain, pity, desire, and love. As in Epicurean teachings, ethics was the center. Zeno fashioned a skilled simplification of ethics. Aristotle had taught three kinds of Good: good looks and health ("goods" for the body), prosperity and friendship (external "goods"), and "goods" of the soul. Zeno created the paradox of the unique goodness of Goodness; thus the most important thing in man was purpose or intent. "Therefore, it is not what is done or given that is important, but what is in the mind, because a benefit rests not upon what is done or given, but on the spirit of the giver or doer" (Seneca, *On Benefits*, I, 6. 2). Nothing was good (*kalon*) or had moral value except Virtue, and nothing performed was right (*katorthoma*) unless the intent was correct (Seneca, *Moral Letters*, 95. 57). Nothing was right or wrong in itself, but all actions badly motivated were sins (*hamartia*); and all acts "missing the mark" were equal, since drowning occurred as easily just below the sea's surface as in the depths. Life and death, reputation, pleasure and pain, wealth and poverty, health and disease were indifferent (*adiaphora*). Happiness rested solely on Virtue. Nature suggested appropriate acts, and such acts were obligations (*kathekonta*) or duties (*officia* in Latin).

Minor Philosophies

A series of dull moralists headed Plato's Academy until Arcesilas (d. 241 B.C.) revived its prestige. He argued against the Stoic theory of knowledge, noting Zeno's theory that some human sense perceptions (*phantasiai*) were so vivid that they immediately conveyed truth or reality. Arcesilas retorted that man had little means of knowing whether an impression came from a true object. He went beyond Socrates' "I know I don't know"; Socrates claimed he knew nothing, while Arcesilas did not admit even that. He went on to attack all dogma by posing arguments that evenly balanced opposing sides of a question. Followers of Arcesilas were called the Skeptics of the new Academy. The doctrines had extremely limited appeal and merely indicated the inherent anachronisms within Platonism.

Aristotle's Lyceum functioned for a time along the lines Aristotle laid down in the fourth century B.C. The Peripatetic school continued to collect data and write many books. Theophrastus put together works on botany, psychology, and philosophy and composed *Characters,* charming and biting vignettes of men's petty pretensions. Aristoxenus (*c.* 360-? B.C.) wrote a history of music, Duris (*c.* 340-260 B.C.) a history of art, and Menon (*fl. c.* 300 B.C.?) a history of medicine, and Dicaearchus (*fl. c.* 300 B.C.) brought geography up to date. The Lyceum's efforts petered out by 250 B.C.

Cyrenaicism, a minor Socratic school, was founded at Cyrene in Libya by Aristippus (*fl. c.* 400-365 B.C.) and was a forerunner of Epicureanism. Aristippus taught that the pleasures of the senses were the primary goals of life. His teachings exerted little influence, and the school died out after 275 B.C. On the other hand, the Cynics (*kunikoi,* from *kuon* ["dog"]) had an annoying impact for a long period. Diogenes of Sinope (*c.* 400-*c.* 325 B.C.), who lived in Athens after 362 B.C., laid down the principles. He rejected all conventions and traditions and lived in utter poverty, the life he taught. According to Diogenes, happiness resulted from the satisfaction of selfish needs in the cheapest and easiest way. Natural actions could not be considered dishonorable or indecent. Thus public urination was natural in spite of the convention that dictated otherwise. Diogenes rejected all conventional morality, and he outraged the Greek establishment as much as hippies have enraged our establishment. In turn, Diogenes taught that conventions contrary to nature should be ignored and ideally forgotten. Like Epicurus' doctrines, however, Diogenes' ideal was easily perverted by those seeking a life of ease, although the Cynics' model was *autarkeia* ("self-sufficiency"). The ideal man led a life of complete shamelessness, since all conventions were worthless. Crates of Thebes (*c.* 365-285 B.C.) taught simplicity and independence, which one achieved by avoiding all social entanglements or possessions. Remaining aloof, the Cynic lived well in the midst of war and disorder. Crates gave Cynic philosophy a popular image as he wandered over the Greek world, carrying a walking cane and living from a knapsack.

There were many itinerant Cynics in the third century B.C., when the Hellenistic kingdoms were falling apart under pressure from Roman meddling and internal weaknesses; but once greater stability came with Roman rule in the eastern Mediterranean, the Cynics faded from influence. To be sure, Cynicism gained revival in the first century A.D., but it appealled to those who opposed Roman imperial rule.

Greek philosophical systems defined an intellectual construct in several different patterns, but all stressed the search for an ideal, whether in the world of Idea or in the world around man. But with the politically unimportant exception of Cynicism, philosophical tenets did not touch the mass of ordinary men. Later Greek philosophy did reflect a gradual shift from the rational ideal to the accepted ideal represented by the Roman conquest of the Greek East; Stoicism and its kindred philosophical systems provided a language for an age moving toward greater syncretism in political systems and religion, particularly in mystery cults. The *logos* of Greek philosophy entered the new world of world-spanning empire and further cross-identifications in the Christian *New Testament*.

9

Magic, Science, and Disease

In all cultures, men have explained the world around them through forces, unknowns, and things they hoped to know. Forms of magic—in their own way precisely logical in prediction, once the correct formulae or charms are discovered—are almost universal among men, whatever their culture or age. Even in the rational and scientific West in the twentieth century, with its assumed sophistication, the method of science ("once we label it, we know it") suggests thinking surprisingly close to magic and voodoo. Both magic and science promise to predict the future, although science has a better probability of correct predictions through its experimental method. Its refusal to consider chance or inner, nonmeasurable qualities in human beings has led to a revolt against science and the formal disciplines that use the pseudojargon of science. Astrology, witchcraft, magic in its myriad colors, and the transmigration of souls compete for disciples in a time when one promising system after another is sampled for security. Magic provides some security by being completely unknown to the nonspecialist, who can take comfort that someone *must* know the secret riddles. All he need do is keep looking for that someone or something. The freedom of choice and uncertainty proffered by philosophy was too much to bear for most Greeks, and magic and its kindred disciplines diffused into medicine, astronomy, and religion. Always disguised, they retained a hold that persists today.

Greek Magic

The Pythagorean school slightly modified the magic numbers, and magic knots were known to have properties akin to given herbs and trees. From Assyria the Greeks inherited a hallowed tradition of voodoo whereby the tallow image of an enemy was bound with cords, particularly the face, so that the enemy was deprived of will-power and speech. Similar procedures with images took diseases from men, provided that the correct spells and words accompanied the ceremony, and occasionally the magician "killed" and "buried" the image. Sorceresses used magic knots as charms against lurking evil powers, and witches abound in Greek mythology and literature. The tales about Circe in the *Odyssey* and Medea in the story of the Argonauts show how Greeks conceived of spells, potions, and the women who changed men into beasts or who had knowledge of *pharmaka* ("magic powders" or "drugs"). Magicians could stop plagues, according to the *Iliad,* and Hesiod assures his readers of the lucky and unlucky days for planting in his *Works and Days*. Herodotus believes the tale of Telines of Gela in Sicily because Telines knew about unnamed Things akin to "the powers under the earth which produced wonders" (Herodotus, *Histories,* VII, 153). According to Thucydides' usual meticulous description, Nicias, one of the leaders of the grand Athenian armada against Syracuse (415 B.C.), was terrified of eclipses. Xenophon, who once sat at Socrates' feet, recorded dreams, sneezes, sacrifices, and divinations as a matter of grave importance, and Euripides and Plato take for granted the common knowledge of aphrodisiacs, charms, and magical sayings. Titles of Greek plays suggest an ever present awe of magic in a time of apparent rationalism; the magical Greek papyri and frequent allusions in the poems of Theocritus and in the Hellenistic romance tales give further support for this awe. Side by side with increased book learning in the fourth century B.C. came a mass of writing on magic and the occult studies; the Persian Ostanes first introduced this to the Greeks in the period of the Persian Wars (Diogenes Laertius, *Epicurus,* I, 2; Laertius' sources lump "philosophy" together with Druidism and the Persian Magi).

Plato writes that only doctors or seers understood the power of *pharmaka* ("spells," in this context), the power of matters that operate naturally, and the inner power of magical words, images,

and knots (*Laws*, XI, 933). His solution to their influence is to out-
law them, since the ordinary man could not be convinced to ignore
them. He "explained" liver divination through his idea that the liver
acted "like a mirror" for thoughts and thus recorded the images of
the soul (*Timaeus*, 71b6-8). The motion of the stars controlled
inferior creations in their search for "harmonious love," health, and
plenty. He termed all this "astronomy" (*Symposium*, 188B, in the
speech of the physician Eryximachus). Some stars were "divine and
eternal living beings," while others were "lesser gods," men who
returned to a happy state as stars after living a good life (Plato,
Timaeus, 40). In the *Republic*, he writes of the harmony and music
of the whorl-spheres of the seven planets with the eighth whorl-
sphere of the fixed stars, and he writes that "the spindle revolved on
the knees of Necessity" (*Republic*, X, 14. 617B). He shows his
belief in the doctrine of the Great Year (*magnus annus*) when he
writes, "The perfect temporal number as well as the perfect year are
completed at the time when all eight revolutions have gained their
total in relation to one another, marked by the regular and moving
revolution of the Same," as contrasted with the Different (*Timaeus*,
39). Scholars debate what this may mean in either astrology or
philosophy, but Plato's thoughts were firmly rooted in his own time,
which was steeped in star lore and semimagical attributions.

Aristotle's works contain bits and pieces from contemporary magic
and folklore, and the *Historia animalium* is filled with semilegendary
notations about magic or powerful properties of certain denizens of
the animal world. His student Theophrastus followed that path, and
even the most scientific of his writings, *On Fire*, has embedded
"observations" that were simple tales that everyone knew. His *History
of Plants* gives the expected list of herbs and medicinals in tandem
with the powers for each plant. The gap between magic and science
was small, and the bridge between philosophy and astrology well
traveled by the leading Greek thinkers. Nothing was forbidden to
their bubbling curiosity; for every subject that came within their ken,
they applied a kind of logic, and an attempt at system resulted.
Magic, mathematics, astronomy, physics, and medicine were fit
studies for the Greeks, and the Greek mind wrestled with each in its
own terms, terms supplied by the matrix of a time that took the
predictions of magic as seriously as it depended on the process of
logic in philosophy and mathematics.

Greek Science: Some Introductory Remarks

Designs similar in inquiry to those of magic and philosophy marked Greek science; the three were rarely distant. Modern science, by contrast, has developed an elaborate technology that allows man to apply discoveries in pure scientific research to the real world of problem solving. First comes the theoretical concept in the laboratory; then the scientist conducts experiments in light of his theory, which he verifies by observation in controlled experiments. Then the modern world takes the results and applies them to an aspect of science called technology, or environmental control. Western science and technology have also developed numerous instruments that help in understanding phenomena that the senses alone cannot perceive. The telescope was invented in the sixteenth century, while Greek astronomers (and astrologers) relied on their eyes and recorded tables. The microscope proved Harvey's circulation theory in the seventeenth century, but Hellenistic doctors noted what the pulse showed and what dissection proved—that veins in cadavers contained red blood, while arteries did not. The electron microscope enables the doctor, and his colleagues in biophysics and biochemistry, to make reasoned guesses about viruses, while Greek medicine observed the courses of diseases and speculated on the causes. Physicians in Thucydides' Athens were helpless against the great plague (430–429 B.C.), which, some modern medical historians conjecture, was caused by the half-virus, half-bacterium that engenders typhus. The most important difference between Greek and modern science is environmental control. Greek science collected observations and was occasionally linked to technology, but then only regarding the homely matters of agriculture, pottery manufacture, coinage, military hardware, ships, and the like. Philosophical systems, and their underlying assumptions, taught that the world was in essence a "living" thing, in its parts or whole.

Mathematics and Geometry

Like the Assyrians, who gave the Greeks some traditions in the practice of magic, Near Eastern ideas inspired the beginnings of Greek mathematics and geometry. This background indicates how Thales proved simple problems in geometry and the principles of similar triangles. Pythagoras studied geometric definitions and laid down a theory of proportion and means, the basis of harmonics. Musical intervals depended on arithmetic ratios. He also discovered the solution of a square that was the sum of two squares, and the proof for like properties of right triangles. The Pythagorean school invented the "application of areas," which solved the general quadratic equation by geometry. Democritus wrote on the irrationals, problems in which the ratio of two numbers could not be expressed exactly, and he knew of the infinitesimals (variables having zero as limits) when he wrote of cone and pyramid volumes.

Greek mathematics tended to be pure; the conclusions drawn were beautiful examples of logic, usually inapplicable in everyday life. There were well-known exceptions, however, illustrated by the stories surrounding Archimedes and Archytas of Tarentum. But for internal and psychologically diffuse reasons, Greek thought and its philosopher-spokesmen condemned the practical application of logic. Plato etched the reluctance to either experiment or apply science deeply into Greek and Roman thinking. Nonetheless, the Greeks' list of achievements in mathematics and geometry is impressive, and remained the apogee in those two fields until Newton demonstrated the calculus in the seventeenth century.

Hippocrates of Chios (*fl.* 440 B.C.) discovered how to reduce the duplication of the cube to find two mean proportionals; he also squared three kinds of lunes (crescent-shaped plane figures bounded by two arcs of circles, either on a plane or a spherical surface). He compiled a book of elements, made famous by Euclid's later summation. Plato's friend Archytas of Tarentum (*fl. c.* 380 B.C.) was learned in mechanics. He build a wooden dove capable of flight and invented a rattle to distract destructive babies. (Both were merely toys.) He distinguished four types of mathematics: arithmetic, geometry, astronomy ("spherics"), and music. Mathematics fascinated Plato because it gave limits in definitions (e.g., line, straight line, circle). Eudoxus (405–355 B.C.) discovered the general theory of proportion, set out in Euclid. Menaechmus, one of Eudoxus' students, wrote on conic sections, which Euclid also borrowed.

Euclid (*fl. c.* 300 B.C.) became famed for his textbook, *Elements* (*stoicheia*). No other book than the Bible was more widely read and studied from the Renaissance through the first half of the twentieth century. A magnificent piece of Greek logic applied to mathematics and geometry, *Elements* was a synthesis in two ways: it incorporated much of earlier geometry and it was a synthesis of logic. Euclid proceeded from the known and simple to the unknown and complicated. Analysis reduced the unknown and demonstrated the complex, a process that underlay the discovery of proofs. He labeled the method *reductio ad absurdum,* since analysis began with reduction of the proposition. The truth of the proposition was assumed, and the student reduced the proposition to a less complex form, recognized as true or false. Sometimes reduction led to patently incorrect conclusions, but *reductio ad absurdum* was an invaluable analytical method. Before 1955, American schoolchildren were familiar with Euclid's corollaries, or *porismata* ("porisms")—"provided" or "ready made" matters that were incidentally revealed as results while demonstrating the major proposition.

Archimedes of Syracuse (*c.* 287–212 B.C.), remembered for inventing the *kochlias* ("waterscrew") and discovering the principle of specific gravity, was the most original thinker. Closer in concept to the modern notion of mathematical research than were most of his contemporaries, he studied for a time in Alexandria and spent the rest of his life in mathematical and mechanical investigation. His fame rested on ingenious machines, but Archimedes conceived of them as "appendages of geometry at play" (Plutarch, *Marcellus,* 14. 4). So uninterested was he in practical applications that only one book on mechanics, *On the Making of Spheres,* has survived from his efforts. Yet on persuasion by the king of Syracuse, Archimedes offered him his services in 212 B.C. against the besieging Romans. His devices for hurling rocks on Roman ships and troop formations were so effective and frightening that Roman soldiers retreated in panic at the hint of a wooden projection or rope above the wall (Polybius, *Histories,* VIII, 7–8). The Romans took Syracuse in spite of Archimedes' clever machines, and he was slain by an unknown soldier, but his repute lived on.

Many of the tales about Archimedes were semilegendary, like the stories around medical men at the Alexandrian Museum. Hieron, the king of Syracuse, had given Archimedes a crown claimed to be of gold, and the king wanted to find out whether silver was concealed in greater proportion than stated. Archimedes later recognized the principle of specific gravity when he sat down in his bath and it overflowed. Dashing out into the street without putting on his clothes, he shouted "Eureka! Eureka!" ("I have found it!") to stupified bystanders (Vitruvius, IX, 3). He also claimed that he could move the earth if he had a place to stand while "moving a weight by a given force" (Pappas, VIII, 1060). He proved "any weight could be moved by a given force," to the amazement of King Hieron and his court. Archimedes beached a large ship with a compound pulley and then moved it back into the sea after dozens of men had huffed and strained and could not move it (Plutarch, *Marcellus*, 14). His waterscrew aided irrigation; both the owners of large Roman plantations and Egyptian farmers borrowed the device. The latter still use it. He devised a planetarium that showed the motions of the sun, moon, and five planets with surprising accuracy, even indicating the apparent movement of the sun and the periods of the moon (Cicero, *Tusculan Disputations*, I, 63; *On the Nature of the Gods*, II, 88). He borrowed Eudoxus' "method of exhaustion" and performed calculations to find the area of a parabola and of a spiral, the surface and volume of a sphere and any segment of it, and the segments of the conicoids of revolution. In *Measurement of a Circle*, he found by pure arithmetics the upper and lower limits (3 1/7 and 3 10/71) to *pi*. His *Sandreckoner* gave an original system for expressing large numbers. *On Method* illustrated methods of Greek mathematics and became a handbook.

The abstract book learning at the Alexandrian Museum produced the great geometer Apollonius of Perga (*c.* 262–190 B.C.), who studied with Euclid's successors. In 1710 Edmund Halley, the English astronomer, first made known Apollonius' *Conics*, which had survived in four Greek books and three Arabic. Curves were called parabola, ellipse, and hyperbola. Apollonius believed that eccentric circles were valid in astronomy; other curves with familiar terms came from his students: the cissoid, conchoid, and spiric. Hipparchus (*c.* 190–*c.* 126 B.C.) studied trigonometry and spherical trigonometry; medieval Arabs and Hindus used Hipparchan theory and developed the trigonometry used today. Claudius Ptolemy (*fl.* A.D. 121–151) purloined Hipparchus' trigonometric theory and fashioned a table of chords of arcs, followed by solutions for spherical triangles. Diophantus of Alexandria (*fl. c.* A.D. 250) originated limited algebraic notation; even with the handicap of having to express algebra in linguistic terms, he conceived minus as a *leipsis* ("wanting") and plus as a *huparxis* ("forthcoming"). Thus he gave solutions to simple quadratic equations. Diophantus was the inspiration for Pierre de Fermat (1608–1665) in arriving at his theory of numbers and his important theories on light speeds in varying media. Pappas of Alexandria (*fl. c.* A.D. 300) wrote commentaries on Euclid and was a source of intuition for René Descartes (1596-1650) in formulating coordinate geometry.

Immanuel Kant (1724-1804) observed that Newtonian theories were based on necessities of thought about time and space. Kant thought geometry, in particular, indicated how minds work; his idea clarifies differences and similarities between Greek and modern concepts in mathematics and geometry. Euclid maintained a stranglehold on geometry well into the nineteenth century, even after other geometrical systems had been postulated. Euclid's axioms were accepted as proven, except for one. He said that only one line could be drawn through a point in space parallel to a given straight line, and that the two lines will never meet, no matter how long they are made. The loophole bothered mathematicians for a long time, until a radical change in thinking made it possible to construct systems in which the parallel axiom did not apply. Hyperbolic geometry, which Nicholas Lobachevsky (1793-1856) first conceived, was the result: space extends indefinitely in all directions (as in Euclid), but the sum of the angles of a triangle is less than the sum of two right angles, the difference depending on the size of the triangle. Later another geometry was surmised in which there were *no* parallel lines and space had no boundary. A plane in this later system is like the surface of a sphere in Euclid. In spherical geometry the sum of the angles in a triangle exceeds that of two right angles, the difference again depending on the size of the triangle. The three geometries have much in common. All state that space is homogeneous and geometrically the same everywhere. In small areas the differences among the three are diminished; within the solar system, Euclidean geometry worked so well that Newton and Kant thought it substantially correct. But outside the solar system, distances and time become immense, and Euclidean concepts are not satisfactory. The turnover in thinking has occurred in modern astronomy, and the view of the cosmos is far from that of the pre-Socratic Greek thinkers. Yet the base on which modern mathematics and astronomy build is simple logic, derived from observation and the collation of various theories on the observations.

Physics and Astronomy

Until Plato and Aristotle arrived, physics was part of philosophy, forming sections of philosophers' considerations of nature as a whole. Anaxagoras and Empedocles thought air had corporeal qualities, and

Empedocles proved it by filling a vessel with water only after the air had escaped. Leucippus taught that nothing existed or came into being for nothing. Scattered throughout Aristotle's works were views on physics, particularly in *Physics* and *Meterologica*. Physics was a theoretical subject concerned with bodies in nature having qualities of movement and rest. He considered matter and form, their four causes, three kinds of motion (increase and decrease, change, and self-movement), and space. He noted something moving in a void will remain moving until something stronger stops it (*Physics,* IV, 8. 215a20-22). Archimedes speculated on forces and bodies as well as hydrostatics.

Theories in optics became prominent after the atomist philosophers. They thought atoms went from the object to the eye, carrying "copies." Aristotle taught that the eye was a simple receptive organ, and that the object acted on the eye only through a transparent medium (*De anima,* II, 7). In *Optica* Ptolemy considered the principles of refraction, choosing ideas of his Hellenistic predecessors. Acoustic theory was a by-product of Pythagoras' discovery of harmonic intervals, and many writers took up the subject. Euclid wrote an *Elements of Music,* and Aristoxenus' *Principles and Elements of Harmonics* survives in part.

Like mathematics and geometry, Greek astronomy also had sources in the Near East. The Egyptian year divided into 365 days became common in Greek Asia Minor, and Thales thereby noted the inequality of the astronomical seasons. He advised sailors to sail by the Little Bear rather than by the Great Bear and learned from the Babylonians how to predict eclipses. Anaximander knew about the sundial, brought from Babylonia (Herodotus, II, 109), and he proposed theories about the distances from earth and mass of the sun and moon. Pythagoras and Parmenides thought the earth was a sphere, and Pythagoras believed in antipodes. Anaxagoras taught that the moon received its light from the sun (Plato, *Cratylus,* 409a), and Plato's astronomy was partly rooted in Pythagoras. Later Plato changed his mind about placing the earth in the middle of the universe, citing irregularities in planetary movements. Eudoxus formulated an explanation of Plato's odd motions with an elaborate system of simultaneously revolving spheres, and Aristotle turned the theoretical system into a mechanical one (Aristotle, *Metaphysics,* 1073b17-1074a15).

Aristarchus of Samos (*c.* 310-230 B.C.) put forth a heliocentric hypothesis and said that the sun and stars remained fixed while the earth revolved around the sun in a circle (Archimedes, *Sandreckoner,* preface). The idea was not only contrary to common notions about the earth and heavens but also did not match further observation by astronomers (they proved that the motion of the earth in a circle was wrong). Hipparchus of Bithynia (*fl. c.* 145 B.C.) finally put together a theory that both explained the irregularities and reasserted Greek reluctance to accept an earth freely moving in space. He proposed a system of epicycles and eccentric circles and varying combinations of each, and put the whole into a geocentric theory. Ptolemy made the concept canonical in his *Syntaxis,* and all astronomical theory until Copernicus and Kepler was based on Hipparchus, through Ptolemy. Hipparchus also discovered the precession of the equinoxes.

Astrology

Greater learning than ever before was part of the environment of the unstable Hellenistic kingdoms, and many of the physical and astronomical discoveries became common knowledge among the upper classes. Poetical allusions to technical theories in mathematics, physics, and astronomy were commonplace, but in cosmopolitan life, education assumed a role that included necromancy, astrology, and a welter of occultism perhaps connected with internal fear of the awesome freedom that philosophy and science offered. The crusty traditions of the ancient Near Eastern cultures, then under a flimsy Hellenic veneer, underwent a diffusion in Greek guise. Egypt became the land of wisdom, whence issued arcane esoterica in lost tongues. Knowledge resulted from the reunderstanding of the most ancient writings, and longing for old books containing secret formulae became commonplace after 200 B.C. Thus any text worth copying had to have the pedigree of antiquity, and in the plethora of circulated treatises on magic, astrology, curatives, savior gods, and rebirth formulae, all claimed inspired and hoary authorship. The teachers of astrology enjoyed enormous popularity after 200 B.C., and it was known that the magi of the East had used the signs of the zodiac to predict the future. By 100 B.C. astrology had been garbed in Greek dress and armed with Greek astronomy. The old Babylonian series of star charts then became intelligible in Greek as horoscopes, considered infallible in predicting happiness, disease, everyday actions, and the movements of empires.

Hipparchus' theory of the precession of the equinoxes found a home in astrology, since it gave meaning to variations in observations in astrological tables. By the time of Theon of Alexandria (*fl.* A.D. 370), the precession of the equinoxes had passed into astrological lore attributed to "ancient astrologers" like Hipparchus (Theon, commenting on Ptolemy, *Manual Tables,* ed. Halma, p. 53). The array of calculations, degree variations, and lists of observations collected in Theon was harnessed into astrology, which immediately related to men in a troubled world. An astrologer assured order and reason in a seemingly capricious world, and ordinary citizens and educated specialists alike accepted astrology with few qualms. The overwhelming mass of literature, including that of the late Stoic Posidonius (*fl. c.* 80 B.C.), who openly espoused astrology and kindred studies, drowned voices raised in opposition.

Greek and Hellenistic Medicine

Greek farmers were hardy, but they occasionally became sick from causes they knew as part of the unfavorable powers around them. They had an armory of amulets and charms, so Hesiod notes, and childbirth—always risky before antiseptic hospital facilities became standard—had its practitioners among the numerous midwives and elderly women in the local community. Wounds received in battle were treated, except those in the head and abdomen. The poor soldier with this condition was given up as dead. If he recovered, his fellows duly respected a miracle or suspected a visit to one of the village amulet sellers. Most often sickness came, so the Greeks believed, from a kind of common pollution (*miasma*), resulting from some individual's offense against a deity or the powers beyond man. As a consequence, Greeks banished disease and plague either by exile of the guilty from the community or through a complicated set of propitiatory rituals performed by priests knowing the correct formulae. A new planting season that was free from plague normally rewarded belief in the cleansing ritual (*katharsis*), and Greeks had no doubt why the plague had departed. An assurance dominated the theory and practice of plague chasing, midwifery, and magic medical charms, and optimism characterized the Greeks' general outlook, even though modern standards would make life in early Greece seem brutal and crude.

Achilles had powers of healing, and several of the Greek gods became renowned for their potency in healing sickness. Apollo, the giver of light, had many shrines at which the sick would gather in hopes of a divine visitation. However, a later entry into the Greek pantheon became more important than the other gods for divine cures; the newer god's shrines dotted the Hellenistic kingdoms by the fourth century B.C. As the healer deity, Asclepius appeared to the sick in dreams, prescribing methods and rituals for cure. The testimony of votives that festooned the walls of Asclepian temples was proof of the god's miraculous visitation to thousands who went away healed; friends of the formerly ill received the individual back as one who had been brought back literally across the threshold of death by the intervention of the god. As important as the Asclepian shrines were for late Greeks and the Hellenistic kingdoms, the real heyday for the temple visits and enormous popularity of Asclepian medicine came in the days of the Roman Empire.

Philosophy and Medicine

Philosophy suggested another path for the study of sickness, and Greek medicine originated in the principles of pre-Socratic thought. The study of nature was applied to the study of man's nature; Alcmaeon of Croton (*fl. c.* 500 B.C.) indicated the promise inherent within philosophy of medical speculation and rational approaches to disease. From speculation about the distant universe, man turned to his own body. Under the influence of Pythagoras, Alcmaeon taught the application of philosophical conclusions to health and disease. Tradition recorded that he was the first to dissect, and he investigated what he could within the boundaries of the philosophical mold. Facts in themselves did not form the basis for such an investigation; it was the verification of the philosophical construct in relation to the questions at hand that formed the basis. The seed of the rational approach to health is of cardinal importance to Western medicine, and Greek rationalization of disease provides a keystone of modern medicine.

From Pythagoras' teaching of opposites in the universe, Alcmaeon borrowed the principle of balance for the human body, and he believed in a proper proportion of "the powers, wet and dry, cold and hot, pungent and sweet, and the remainder" (Aetius, V, 30. 1). He taught that the soul was immortal (Aristotle, *De anima,* A2, 405a29) and that divinity was in continual motion. He also investigated sense perception in man and may have dissected the eye. His conclusions, however, emerged in forms like philosophical tenets: "Man understands while other animals perceive but do not understand" and "The senses are in some way associated with the head" (Theophrastus, *De sensu,* 25–26).

Although philosophic speculation never left Greek and Hellenistic medicine, the practice of medicine soon became identified with the more practical end of enabling man to maintain good health. Of the Greek sciences, medicine alone took its place beside gymnastics as an answer to health, and medical theoreticians were as common as athletic experts in Greek gymnasia. While the oil was being scraped from the gleaming bodies of athletes in training for one of the Pan-Hellenic festivals, medical theoreticians and their gymnastic colleagues stood around and declaimed on balances within the healthy body, pointing to the epitomes of youthful vibrancy produced on the exercise fields. Among educated Greeks, diet and pruned exercise became crucial for the successful life, and medical theory was attached as a philosophical justification for fervent activity in athletics.

Hippocrates

Hippocratic medicine (named after the semilegendary Hippocrates of Cos, *fl. c.* 425 B.C.) indicated the Greek genius in the organization and synthesis of systems. Medicine was a *techne* ("art") whose doctrine developed from rules of practical application. Ordination appeared in the terse Hippocratic works on the doctor's proper deportment and correct attitude toward patients. Advice was given according to the social mood of the times, but cast in terms borrowed from earlier philosophy (like the Hippocratic Oath, which was founded on Pythagorean principles); these terms, in turn, specified the physician's unique approach within philosophical thought. The activity of Diocles of Carystos (*fl. c.* 360 B.C.) directed this psychological subtlety, proposed in the Hippocratic *Right Way to Behave,* into another groove. Diocles was a man of an "inquiring and subtle mind who says something about nature and claims to derive principles therefrom" (Aristotle, *De respiratione,* 480b22). He studied anatomy, but his conclusions probably arose from examining and dissecting animals, also true in Aristotle's study of zoology. Dietetics and its corollary of proper food for athletes appeared as a handbook specialty from Diocles' study and speculation about "right" anatomy and "proper" diet. Later practitioners of dietetics and Hippocratic medicine plied their skills on many planes, ranging from the sublime and lofty to the fraudulent and foolish.

Hippocratic medicine taught understanding of the human body within the context of nature as a whole. The approach probed the question, "Is the body a simple structure, or is it made up of varying parts?" and put it into a logical focus. Then the Hippocratic physician determined the relationship between the body and the rest of nature—how nature acted on the body and how the body effected nature. Greek medicine chose to think that the body was an organism, and Hippocratic medicine taught medical philosophy, which rose from compacting various particulars of the body into one system. Once the single system was clear, the medical philosopher divided it up again into its natural kinds. Plato termed this buildup and re-separation "dialectic" (Plato, *Phaedrus,* 270c–d). Later Meno wrote how Hippocrates explained disease: it rose from undigested food that exuded air or gases, and illness came when air entered the body ("Meno," *Anonymus Londinensis,* 6). Yet medical philosophy was fit for dispute, like the other branches of philosophy, and Plato did not accept the Hippocratic notion of "good medicine" without argument:

> Indeed, the mode of the skill of medicine is very similar to that of rhetoric . . . in both, one ought to analyze nature; for the one, the nature of the body, and, for the other, the nature of the soul, if one goes about it in a skillful way, not simply by habit and practice, to give health by suggesting drugs and diet, or with correct discourses and training to endow the soul with desired knowledge and goodness . . . one should not be satisfied with the words of Hippocrates but to look and see if reason agrees upon inquiry. [Plato, *Phaedrus,* 270b–c]

The works in the traditional Hippocratic *Corpus* do not mirror what Plato said Hippocrates taught; indeed, the Hippocratic *Corpus* did not record Hippocrates, but was a collection of medical literature that scholars in the Alexandrian Museum assembled. The *Corpus* covered all aspects of medicine. The whole took the name of the "ideal" doctor, Hippocrates. The art of prognosis, dietetics, surgery, use of drugs, health and disease in balance, and differing medical philosophies (the Coan, Cnidian, atomistic, and others) form the *Corpus.*

Hippocratic medicine embodied modifications of pre-Socratic

thought on the "balances" within the human body, expressed as the Doctrine of Humors. Usually the four humors (body fluids) were phlegm, blood, bile, and water (Hippocratic *Corpus, On Diseases,* 4); however, other works within the *Corpus* indicated an unlimited number of humors (like *On Ancient Medicine*), while *The Nature of Man* (another work in the *Corpus*) proposed that the black bile was the major humor. According to the author of this "Hippocratic" work, the proper mixture of black bile, yellow bile, phlegm, and blood produced health; the strength, temperament, and quantity of each was important for the correct proportions. Yellow bile was characterized as fire, black bile was earth, phlegm was water, and blood was air. To clarify the whole notion, the author added that the qualities of hot-dry and moist-cold were important for the health-giving blend.

Plato's view of Greek medicine showed a struggle between the mechanistic and nonmechanistic philosophical approaches as they spilled over into medical theory. Although Hippocrates tried to combat materialistic tendencies in medical philosophy, further medical studies did not necessarily follow Hippocratic guidelines. Medicine in the Hellenistic period took the direction Aristotle suggested, and state endowment of research and collection of data determined its mood. Aristotle and his school suggested separating philosophy from the study of nature by distinguishing between different areas of knowledge. Speculation entered those subjects that were suited for abstraction, but natural history emerged from the enormous mass of observations, with greater attention to detail and common patterns than before. The Aristotelians recorded the life, mating habits, and morphology of over five hundred kinds of animals, and they pondered the developing chick and produced a classic history of embryology. The school investigated squids, formulated accurate concepts of mammalian sex organs, noted that whales were warm-blooded, and observed developmental morphology among fish, particularly sharks. Aristotle stressed comparative anatomy in order to study the relationships of structures; these relationships, in turn, defined a scale of creation in animals. The system held until the nineteenth century.

Medicine at Ptolemaic Alexandria

State support of scholarly research (more like the "study of collected things" than the modern concept of "research") provided the atmosphere for the work Aristotle advised. Especially famous was the

Ptolemaic "Museum" in the metropolis of Alexandria in Egypt. In an attempt to rival the other Hellenistic kings' courts, the first Ptolemies (Ptolemy I, 305-283 B.C., and Ptolemy II, 283-245 B.C.) established a Temple to the Muses (the museum), with a priest to direct the efforts of the scholars who flocked to Egypt. Most work in the museum consisted of gaining reliable texts of classic authors like Homer and the great Athenian tragedians. Some "Hippocratic" works were included in scholarly collation, but poetry remained the queen of the scholars, who reminded one poet of a group of "well-fed bookish birds in a gilded cage" (Timon of Phlius in Athenaeus, *Deipnosophistae,* I, 22d). Well paid for the acquisition of erudition, the literary pedants indulged in long-winded quibbling over tidbits in obscure lines; these lines could only be found in the huge storehouse of scrolls that formed the library attached to the museum. Yet, occasionally, startling discoveries—such as mathematical theories and a few matters related to the study of astronomy and medicine—were made in the context of the museum. For a time, Alexandria provided unique opportunities for cadaver dissection, and later tradition noted that "criminals given by Ptolemy" were dissected (Celsus, *On Medicine,* pr. 23-27). Little genius emerged from the medical investigations in the museum, but patient and painstaking observation added many details in anatomy. Alexandrian doctors pursued their craft with firmer assurance than their Hippocratic predecessors, who had only rough information and shrewd guesses.

Two names stand out in the accounts of Alexandrian medical research. Nothing is known about either the anatomist Herophilus or the physiologist Erasistratus except that Herophilus arrived in Alexandria about 285 B.C. and Erasistratus was slightly younger than Herophilus. Their writings vanished after antiquity, and only quotations in Celsus, Soranus, Rufus, and Galen (all from Roman imperial times) remain.

Herophilus was a careful observer in the Hippocratic mold and wrote some commentaries on Hippocratic works in response to orders from the priest who ran the museum. He taught the Doctrine of Humors and believed in a humoral pathology to explain disease. Following his teacher, Praxagoras of Cos (*fl. c.* 320 B.C.), he noted the importance of the pulse in diagnosis. Drugs were important, but Herophilus believed they were "the hands of the gods" (quoted in Galen, ed. Kühn, *Opera Omnia,* XII, 966). He studied the brain, nerves, liver, and sexual organs, and he thought the brain was the seat of intelligence, linked to the body with cords labeled *neurai.*

Most of his dissection work was with animals indicated by the description of the *rete mirabile,* a complex of blood vessels at the base of the brain in certain ungulates (hoofed animals), but not in man. He may have intuited the basic difference between what are now known as motor and sensory sensations, correctly joining his observations with those on the *neurai.* He performed postmortem examinations and saw the ventricles of the brain, made the distinction between cerebrum and cerebellum, named the duodenum, and described the uterus.

Erasistratus threw out humoral pathology and substituted his own doctrine of *pneuma* (roughly rendered as "life-giving air"), the material of the blood necessary for life. Thus there was a *pneuma* for each of the bodily functions, and combinations of the *pneumata* were essential for health. He was disgusted at the prevailing fondness for bleeding as a cure-all and rejected the treatment that favored meager diets. He knew the haphazard result of drug therapy and used only the mildest *pharmaka*—and those only sparingly, hearkening back to the Hippocratic admonitions against dependence on drugs. He invented a catheter, but archaeology proves he was not the first to do so.

Improved knowledge of anatomy meant improved surgery, and the Alexandrian Museum produced newly designed surgical tools. There is doubt that many of the traveling sophist doctors knew how to use their flashy instruments, but they were the forerunners of standard tools like the scalpel. Cupping vessels, most useful for bleeding treatments, reached a level of sophistication unexcelled even in the revival of medical bleeding in the seventeenth and eighteenth centuries.

Medical philosophies received names of their own, like the schools connected with given philosophers. The medical "schools" or "sects" meant "those who followed a way of interpretation in medical philosophy" and did not mean an organized center of medical studies similar to the large medical educational complexes of the twentieth century. Certain cities, like Alexandria, Ephesus, and Pergamon, became famous for their medical philosophies, but no Greek, Hellenistic, or Roman city ever contained an organized medical school. Occasionally resident philosopher-physicians delivered public lectures, but they were given in the usual style of sophistic exercises to impress the ignorant, and oratorical technique was more important than knowledge of anatomy, surgery, or drugs.

Nonetheless, given sects had differing approaches to medical

studies. Herophilus and Erasistratus were classed among the ration-
alistic philosopher-physicians or, as they were commonly known, the
Dogmatic sect of medicine (Galen, *On the Natural Faculties,* passim).
The Dogmatic school placed value on the study of the causes of
diseases with the aid of anatomy and some understanding of body
functions (physiology). The Empiric sect emerged about 280 B.C. as
a reaction to medical speculation. The Empiricists discarded anatomy
and physiology and held that medicine was concerned only with the
cure of diseases, not with their causes. Thus doctors could discern
whatever treatment banished any particular set of symptoms, guided
by personal observation, analogy, and relevant previous traditions.
The sect prized the discovery of new drugs and opposed meaningless
speculation in medicine.

The study of anatomy ended at Alexandria about 200 B.C., although
numerous commentaries on previous work were written after that.
No truly satisfactory explanation of the demise of medical research
after 200 B.C. has been offered, but factors often cited are that the
presence of slaves discouraged scientific effort, or that some kind of
prevailing religious prohibition led the Ptolemies to stop the practice
of dissection in the museum. As it was, dissection became easily
confused with vivisection (a heinous crime to the ancient mind), and
later sources recorded the tradition of "vivisection of humans" from
Ptolemaic Alexandria.

Greek and Hellenistic science and medicine made extraordinary
headway in an age permeated by astrology and a host of irrational
explanations for the natural and unnatural universes. Greeks craved
instant answers and solutions that required little mental effort, and
they increasingly sought out "experts" that the Hellenistic age
produced in prolific numbers. Sophistic teachings gave the specialty
approach, which became the bane of the time, much as it has become
a troublesome feature of the twentieth century. Self-taught experts
in magic, necromancy, medical philosophy, astrology, the theory of
mathematics and geometry, and alchemy wandered like the swarms
of Cynic thinkers from town to town, performing their wonder-
working stunts before gaping crowds that always gathered in the
agora. Except at known centers of higher learning and stifling
pedantry—such as Alexandria, Antioch in Syria, Pergamon and
Ephesus in Asia Minor, and, later, Rome—the itinerant orator-
scholars were semifrauds who sported a little learning and layers of
glib oratorical technique. Disgust at learned pedantry may have

turned potential minds back into the time-tested grooves of magic, mystery cults, and the pseudolearned Hellenistic invention of astrology, which still has a wide following. At least it had the terms and jargon of astronomy, and that was enough to convince most of those who heard astrological doctrines. If that was not sufficient, then the long data lists of recorded portents persuaded many doubters. But the germ of scientific research remained embedded in Greek scrolls, and the rational approach to disease provided the kernel for the beginnings of Western medicine, which flourished after Vesalius re-examined classical anatomy in light of actual cadavers, and after chemistry displaced alchemical theory in the late eighteenth century. Antiquity chose the reliable answers of magic and religion, witchcraft and occultism, perhaps in fear of the incredible freedom offered by both science and philosophy.

10

On the Poetic and the Sublime

Modern psychology has confirmed what poets have instinctively
known since the dawn of mankind. According to the research report
on "poetry therapy" by a team of psychologists from Southern
Methodist University, appropriate rhythms underneath a poem are
far more important in evocation of mood than are the words in the
poem (in *Psychological Record,* 22 [1972], no. 3). The psychologists
asked 129 students to react to recordings of drums beating different
rhythms. The students heard two drums of dissimilar timbres beating
rhythms and sequences at fast and slow speeds, integrated with
"syllables" of two and three "feet." The subjects were asked to rate
lightness or heaviness of sound and feelings of happiness or sadness
that might spring to their mind in response to the rhythms. The
faster rhythms were thought to be "light" and "happy," while the
slower ones were "heavy" and "sad." The psychologists remark that
"the major difference between feet appears to be in the number of
syllables per foot, with placement of accent having little effect."
And traditional two-syllable feet (trochees and iambs) "evoke feelings of heavy, sad, earnest, and tragic, along with the sensation of
the outdoors." Continuing, the researchers write that three-syllable
feet (anapests and dactyls) "evoke the cluster of light, happy, playful, and humorous, as well as indoors." They also suggest why so
much of modern poetry, which contains little understanding of
underlying rhythm, often jars rather than evokes mood. "The mood

evoked by the structure may occasionally conflict with the content"
(*Psychological Record*).

Homer's *Iliad* and *Odyssey*

Greek poetry began (as far as the Greeks were concerned) with
Homer and his magnificent *Iliad,* honed into 15,693 lines of dactylic
hexameter, lines of six "feet" that always summoned images of the
tragedy of war, the flawed valor of Achilles, and the poignancy of
Hector. The bard "sang" his poem, but the music of the Greeks was
not melodic in the sense of modern counterpoint and octaves.
Rather, Greeks witnessed a single bard in the great halls where the
poets sang of deeds in days past. He sometimes accompanied himself
on a lyre or had an assistant playing a few, very measured tones on
an *aulos* (which resembled the modern oboe more than a "flute," as
aulos is often translated). More important to the recitation of poems
among the Greeks, however, was the nature of the Greek language
itself. The structure of Greek, and the usual pronunciation of most
of the dialects, was something our Western ear would label "musical." In English, speakers place stress on words, syllables, or phrases
they wish to emphasize, but the Greeks spoke in pitches, a singsong
that would sound quite strange to listeners in the twentieth-century
United States. Thus Greek poetry depended much more on the
flowing "sound" of music, sometimes suggested by a cadence or
marked rhythm that went with the poem as the bard sang it. The
occasional "poetry reading," depicted in shoddy novels about the
ancient world, is far from reality.

According to the accepted story among later Greeks and Romans,
Homer was a blind bard who had the genius to put together the first
great poem in the Greek language. The Greek of his *Iliad,* and its
sequel, the *Odyssey* (named for the hero, Odysseus, and his many
adventures on his ten-year return journey from the Trojan War), is
normally labeled homeric Greek, since its structure and vocabulary
are somewhat different from later Attic, Doric, or Ionian Greek
dialects. The poem does not tell about the Trojan War as much as it
does about Achilles and his temper tantrums. As the ideal warrior,
Achilles is the superhero of the *Iliad,* and he is flawed—as humans
generally are. The consequences of his anger affect the fortunes of
war, particularly as his sulking leads to near disaster for the Achaeans,
who depend on him for the model of valor in battle. The leader of

the Achaean forces is Agamemnon, king of Mycenae, but he has his own flaws in his conduct with his fellow kings. On the Trojan side, Homer depicts Hector as the supreme model of the defender of home and family, engaged in a valiant but losing contest against the foreign invaders.

The *Iliad* gives a clear look at the early Greek genius for peering at men and their gods. The poem emphasizes an unadorned homeliness, a nobility of spirit, and the balance of language. The lines of the *Iliad,* precisely fitting into the motion of the dactylic hexameter, define simplicity and dignity by the rhythm and music of their structure. The epic delineates nobility in men struggling in war, but it also makes noble the humble matters of everyday life, such as cooking a meal or taking a bath. The *Iliad* does not consist of words strung together, but of groups of words and phrases—epithets—that, when repeated, unify the whole poem. Consequently, the epithets in the *Iliad* are not only conventional or proper names but also part of the glue that holds one section of the epic to another, succeeding section. For example, Homer calls Achilles "Swift of Foot" throughout the poem, and the sea is usually "loud-roaring."

Just as Greek artists strove for an ideal in their work, so Greek poets portrayed their own version of several ideals. In the *Iliad,* Achilles is youthful, enormous in strength, superior to all others in manly beauty, and superbly skilled and brave in battle. His presence strikes dismay into the Trojans, and his oratorical cunning in persuading his fellow Achaeans to a given action has no peer. Achilles' flaw is the violence of his anger, but he dampens his emotions when the gods expressly command it. His initial wrath at Agamemnon is rationalized by the king's conduct in the affair of the slave girl Briseis. Both want her as a mistress. In the course of the argument, Achilles almost kills Agamemnon, but Athena forbids him, and he jams his great sword back into its sheath. The great warrior's anger seethes and makes him reject Agamemnon's apologies and gifts with scorn. In so doing, Achilles loses his status as champion of the Achaeans. Blinded by his arrogance and desire for revenge, he has spurned his obligations to the Greek army. Forgetting even his duty to his closest comrade and friend, he allows Patroclus to go into battle in his place. Patroclus is slain, and Achilles' grief is as moving as his anger was excessive.

> The black mist of grief closed over Achilles. With both hands
> he gathered up the gritty dirt, raining it upon his head and

befouling his face of beauty. And he grayed his deathless tunic
with ashes black. He lay in the dust, all mighty in his might,
prostrate, tearing his hair with his hands. [*Iliad,* XVIII, 21–27]

His great sorrow propels him back into battle, but he barbarously
refuses Hector's dying request for a proper burial. Achilles abuses
the body of the dead Trojan hero in a manner that is both savage
and uncouth, and Zeus has to restrain the wrath of Achilles, who
finally gives the corpse over to the weeping Trojans. The flawed
ideal is clear. Achilles is noble, but clouded by his turbulent
emotions, he is led into mistaken judgments and ultimately into
an unhappiness that overwhelms him.

The tragedy of Troy is the tragedy of Hector. Like his home
city, he is destroyed in a quarrel quite unworthy of him. Hector
does not believe fair Helen justifies the war; nor does he revel in
the froth of battle. His sister Andromache begs him to refuse to
fight, but his reply gives his true feelings:

> I would yet have deep shame before the Trojans, and before
> the women of Troy with cloaks trailing, if like a coward I
> shrank away from battle. The force within will not allow me to
> flee, since I have drunk of valor and learned to struggle always
> in the front ranks of the men of Troy. [*Iliad,* VI, 441–445]

His flaw is his fear of being called a coward, and this clouds his judgment from stopping a war that he knows has little reason or justice.

Each Greek ("Achaean" in Homer) hero is a king, but Agamemnon
is most kingly among the Achaeans, a lord who works while the rest
slumber, a general who inspires his troops before battle, a bull in a
herd of cattle. He is a skillful warrior and an excellent fighter in a
group of doughty soldiers. His first concern is for the welfare of the
allied army, but he suffers from a lack of confidence. He drifts more
in his thinking than would other men, so Homer suggests, and is
helpless in the face of the confusion that results from his indecision.
With the help of Athena and Hera, Odysseus (in the Latin versions,
Ulysses) pulls many of the problems back from chaos into order.
Panic strikes Agamemnon, and each time he attempts to see the end
of the war, he plummets into despair after he has floated up to tri-
umphant overconfidence. The wise Nestor, king of Pylos, and
Odysseus, king of Ithaca, often must undergird their leader, since
they are formed of tougher matter. Agamemnon was a great ruler
through his blood ties and kinship lines with many of the assembled

Greek heroes, and he was mighty in his lordship of Mycenae. His uncertainty is the quandary of a great king, a mortal faced with too many decisions at once.

Odysseus is important in the *Iliad,* but particularly in the romantic adventure "The Return of Odysseus," or *Odyssey*. The Western tradition embedded him as *the* Greek, crafty and daring, ruthless and resourceful. Homer stresses his *sophron* rather than his guile. The term has no good equivalent in English, but it means that quality in a man which allows him to employ what brains he has to their fullest capacity. Consequently, Odysseus is the opposite of Achilles. Achilles is brilliant, but his uncontrolled emotions cause faulty judgment. Odysseus has the mighty passions fitting a Greek hero, but his intellect keeps them under firm guidance and control. He has one goal in the *Iliad:* the Greeks must win. In the *Odyssey,* he is the man of direct action: he must get home and set his household aright. Homer makes Odysseus his "complete" man, although he is not the most noble of the Achaeans. He is able to plow with the same practiced ease as he builds a bed, or as he skillfully makes a raft and then sails it. By squelching his joy when he sees his faithful Penelope after twenty years, by ignoring tempting offers from beautiful women and goddesses in his lengthy wanderings, and by coldly controlling his anger at the suitors sponging off his wife, he survives. His enemies underestimate his intellect and cunning, and thus he outlasts all the dangers and pleasures that he meets.

Hesiod's Outlook

The homeric poems were sung before audiences of aristocrats living in the shadow of chaotic times just before the emergence of the *polis*. Here local nobles gathered to hear the tales about the Great War and the great warrior. Aristocratic ideals permeate the *Iliad* and *Odyssey;* there is little evidence of cooperative effort in terms of phalanx warfare or *polis* armies made up of citizens. Although Homer's poems might have given Greek civilization its first depiction of Greek values, they were the values of a nobility that was passing from history, to be replaced by the more widely based citizen governments of the city-state.

Hesiod of Ascra (*fl. c.* 700 B.C.) spoke more to a class of disgruntled farmers, irritated at the corruption of the kings. His *Theogony* and

Works and Days became standard in Greek literature, but in a greatly differing way from the dignified hexameter of Homer. The homeric poems assumed myth as a common background, and it was expected that the aristocratic audiences would fully know all of the folktales and myths behind the pedigrees of the heroes. Hesiod, on the other hand, pulls myth into his poems, and he uses it to illustrate the basic value of work and the good life a farmer could expect if he worked hard, was frugal, and respected the gods. His *Theogony* probably summarizes most of the commonly held conceptions of the gods in the Greek states of the seventh century B.C. He speaks to the citizens of a newly emerging *polis* and calls on the Muses to give his song poetic power. "O Pierian Muses, who grant glory in song, come forth, speak of Zeus your Father and sing in his praise" (*Works and Days,* 1-2). Hesiod's audiences would know the myth telling of the nine Muses, daughters of Zeus and Mnemosyne. The Muses sang and danced for the Olympians, giving sweet sounds and gossamer feeling to festivities and important gatherings.

Poetry and the State

In their written works, the Greeks continually stress their excellence as "musicians." A man was not considered educated, according to Plato, unless he could function as both a singer and dancer and "take his place in a chorus" (*Laws,* II, 645a-b). The ideal citizen in the *polis* remained a person who could compose poetry, understand the meaning of art, and be a gentleman in politics. The culture of the *polis* was expressed initially in poetry and art—signifying that Greek education was artistic, as opposed to the "scientific" teaching in modern schools, and that Greek artistic endeavor was in poetry and music long before it took on literary or sculptured forms. "Constant joy with the lyre, the light-footed dance, and sparkling song" summarized civilized life, in the words of Theognis (*fl. c.* 542 B.C.), an elegiac poet from Megara. He sings further, "I would have no other desire come to me to replace this lovely, sensual art . . . it keeps my wits sharp in companionship of good men" (Theognis, I, 789-792).

Poetry provided a model for education in the developed *polis,* but the young man who would participate in the best social circles of the Greek state had to "know" more than a few quotations from Homer, Hesiod, and the elegiac poets. He learned the songs of tradition, the folk songs that preserved the distillate of cultural values, from childhood, and the chants or cheers that wafted over the great athletic festivals were often milked from the common heritage of a certain *polis*. At home, cultural life centered on the "men's club"— the *hetairea* in Athens, the *sussition* as rigidly defined in Sparta, and otherwise called the *andreion* from the old Dorian (Spartan and Cretan) gathering. Here conversation sparkled among the gentlemen during the *symposion,* the drinking party that normally followed an extended evening meal. As with the eating, strict rules of etiquette applied to the drinking. Every one of the drinkers received in turn a branch of myrtle when it was his time to sing to his comrades, in a song that went from guest to guest, "singing one to another in time to the *aulos,* clear and liquid in voice" (Theognis, I, 241-243). The Greeks called this poetic and singing ritual the *scholion,* and it was the essential literary exercise around which other artistic accomplishments clustered—namely, dancing and musical interludes on the *aulos* and lyre. The man of excellence

> wisely nursed his riches, and did not harvest the bloom of his youth in violence or with lack of justice. Rather he winnowed poetry in the peaceful covert of the Pieridian Muses. . . . as a dear companion, he was sweeter, more succulent, finer than the honey in the intricate bees' combs. [Pindar, *Pythian Odes,* VI, 46-54]

Solon, *archon* of Athens (594 B.C.) and venerated statesman in the legend, proposed many of his maxims and rules of proper government in poetry. Later Athenians believed he embodied the wisdom of their *polis,* and they long quoted him as the major moral authority behind oratory and law. He reminded his people of the moral obligations sons owed their fathers. Aristotle records how Cleophon (an Athenian orator, died 404 B.C.) cited Solon "and his elegiac verse to show that discipline was long lacking in the family of his enemy Critias, or Solon never would have written "Tell Critias of the flaming hair to do what his father commands'" (Aristotle, *Rhetoric,* I, 1375b32-37).

Likewise, Tyrtaeus, the Spartan poet who composed martial lines to inspire soldiers in the drawn-out wars with Messenia (see chapter 4), gave his messages about community and good government in poetry, although his emphasis was different from that of Solon. Tyrtaeus' ideal was *eunomia,* a balance within the state required by justice. The Spartan thought the greatest danger to the *polis* came from within, from clan feuds, social injustice, and constant dissension. Embedded in his dire warnings about the future of the *polis* are expressions of the unadorned joys of life, which exist for man in spite of all the problems that beset his organized political actions. He sings of the ecstasies of wine, song, friendship, and love. His "Happy is the man who loves children and horses, dogs of the hunt, and strangers" (Fragments 12–14) became a Greek proverb.

Plato, on the other hand, was fierce in his attack on poetry and poets, since (as he saw it) the poetic myths were lies that gave a pernicious picture of the gods and heroes, quite unworthy of their divine perfection. As a philosopher, he believed the art of poetry to be founded on illusion, which, by definition, was inconsistent with the quest for truth. Plato thought the seeking of truth meant the attainment of rational knowledge, and he broke with the Greek tradition that venerated Homer as the beginning of moral and ethical precepts. He so vigorously contrasted poetry with philosophy that the Western dichotomy between the arts and sciences still persists. It is quite significant that Plato and Aristotle chose to view with disdain the poetic lines of early pre-Socratic philosophers, particularly Xenophanes of Colophon (*fl. c.* 545 B.C.). The extant fragments of Xenophanes' philosophical thinking—written as poetic exercises— suggest that he was most concerned with the poor depiction myths gave to the gods, and that he thought the accepted conventions of society were in error. Excellence (*arete*) founded on athletic or military prowess was less important than refinement of the intellect, according to Xenophanes, and he argued for a divine and eternal Mind to replace the gods of myth.

History and Historians

Myth, tales of heroes, and a growing sense of difference from other groups of peoples produced more literary works as Greek civilization developed. Poetry was made for "singing" and the commemoration of special events, as Pindar's difficult lyrics exemplified. Alongside the poets arose some writers who recorded the tales of each state; these stories were told in company with the myths known by all Greeks. Local traditions were linked specifically with limited geographic areas, but it was not until prose writing became important that "history" was delineated as a particular kind of writing. Behind the first historians of Greek life and achievements stood a long line of tale collectors, local stories, and quasi myths accepted as part of the "history" of a particular people.

The civilizations of the ancient Near East had a clearly defined sense of time, but they made little effort to give a history beyond the deeds of kings. Hesiod's concepts of time and space, especially in *Theogony,* frequently reflect Near Eastern ideas. Indeed, the Hebrews had developed a kind of historical chronicle, but the first books of the *Old Testament* did not attempt a history as much as they defined the relationship of a particular god with a special people over a period of time. In contrast, the Greeks began to collect chronological data during the age of colonization, and they dimly conceived historical ages in generations or numbered them by Olympic festivals (traditionally beginning in 776 B.C.). Thus Herodotus of Halicarnassus (*c.* 485 B.C.–*c.* 428 B.C.) did not compose his *Histories* in a vacuum, but garnered an enormous store of local memories in his epic about the struggle between the Greeks and the Persians. Herodotus well understood the universal Hellenic fascination for heroic themes, which all Greeks shared in the homeric lays. Consequently, by one definition the *Iliad* and *Odyssey* were the first great histories of the Greeks, according to C. G. Starr, *The Awakening of the Greek Historical Spirit* (New York: Knopf, 1968). Homer and poets of his time sang of the returns of the heroes from Troy, and the mood and tone of the epic dominated. The epic was the form, poetry its expression. In writing his *Histories,* Herodotus was steeped in the epic tradition, and his theme—Persia against Greece—was of epic proportions. His aim was to measure the Greeks against Persian and other non-Hellenic cultures.

Herodotus

Herodotus was born on the western coast of Asia Minor, where Greeks, Persians, Lydians, Phoenicians, and many other peoples mingled, bringing variety and color to everyday markets and political affairs. A natural curiosity, not unlike that of the philosophers hailing from Miletus on the same coast, drove Herodotus to address his inquiries to the various barbarian traditions known to the Greeks living in the coastal cities of Asia Minor. To this accessible backlog, he added knowledge gathered from widely ranging travels. Everything Herodotus heard or saw filled him with questions. He was intrigued with the burial customs of the Scythian kings, nomadic chieftains living north of the Danube River who swept the plains of southern Russia with their herds of horses. He puzzled over the fat-tailed sheep of northern Arabia, wondering why Arabian sheep were dif-

ferent from the varieties he knew. He listened to the legends about
the origins and spread of the Phoenicians, and he was fascinated by
their piratical practices. Sea voyages to the limits of the earth, as
told by crusty mariners over good wine, became part of his accumu-
lated data, though he expressed doubt at some of the more extrava-
gant claims. The color of Libyan salt, the religion and customs of
Egypt, the question of the Nile source, and a host of related matters
fill the pages of the *Histories* in such profusion that it remains a basic
source for folkways, chronology, life-styles, customs, skills, political
systems, and general legends for the sixth and fifth centuries B.C. In
collecting his material, Herodotus sorted out everything into the
form most familiar to Greeks of his time, the hoary *logoi* ("tales")
similar to those of his predecessors in Ionia (the so-called logographers).
Then he wove the stories into a unified tapestry in the manner of the
homeric poets. Herodotus composed an epic in prose, following the
poetic models.

The prose in the *Histories* ("Inquiries") is flowing and limpid,
factors that allow Herodotus' charm and enthusiastic sparkle to come
across fairly well in an English translation. Although readers of a
translation can catch the verve and liveliness of the Greek original,
Herodotus put down the *Histories* as a long story meant to be read
aloud in several lengthy installments. The span of time was all of
human memory and the geographic limits were the frontiers of the
known world. Herodotus' intellect was of a high order. Where others
recorded, he inquired. Why were the priestesses at Dodona called
Doves? Why did the Nile flood? Why were the Scythians nomadic in
habit? Why did the Greeks and Persia go to war with one another? In
his questioning, he writes why he has put down his findings. The
work was written "in order that the deeds of men should not be
expunged by time, nor the great and wonderful acts done both by
Greeks and barbarians be denied fame. And for the remainder, why
they waged war on each other" (*Histories,* I, preface).

Even though the meaning of "history" is questioning and inquiry,
and written history is the result of inquiry, simple questioning and
inquiry are not sufficient. To judge the reliability and accuracy of
information, one also needs some standards. Herodotus thought his
capacity of reason provided the best judge, and he thus tried to be a
direct observer or a listener to a direct observer of events. However,
he often had to rely on hearsay, but he believed several varying
accounts were useful in making judgments on hearsay. He conse-

quently relates as many of these kinds of tales as he can gather together, marks the one he thinks the most probable, but does not assume the most probable to be necessarily true. Sometimes—like his fellow Greeks—he was overcredulous about events far away in time and space, and he seems awed with large numbers of troops. Generally, he shows a sturdy common sense in his choice of sources, and the wide experience in foreign lands supplies a delightful irony from time to time as he was led around as a Greek tourist. For example, Book II contains an extended summary of Egypt and its plethora of legend, custom, and religions. Herodotus did gaze in some wonder at the sphinx and the pyramids, and his guides regaled him with stories, showing him an inscription "on the pyramid in the Egyptian charac-ters. It listed how much was expended in radishes, onions, and garlic, fed to the workmen. The guide and interpreter, as I seem to recall, read the inscription, and related to me that it totaled sixteen hundred *talents* of silver." He continues by remarking, "If this is really true, then much more was spent on the tools of iron, on bread, and cloth-ing for the workers" (*Histories,* II, 125). Herodotus apparently has some doubts about the guide's competence, which, according to the standard W. W. How and J. Wells, *Commentary on Herodotus* (Oxford: Oxford University Press, 1928), were well founded. How and Wells note that

> the royal inscription was mistranslated; the onion plant was the heiroglyph for *nesut* ("king"), and the papyrus and the lotus were used in spelling his titles as Lord of Upper and Lower Egypt . . . Herodotus' guide was as unable to read hieroglyphics as Herodotus himself . . . he concealed his igno-rance by a complete invention, which he meant also to be a joke. [*Commentary,* 1:229]

The epic is the clash of two cultures. Herodotus thought *Histories* was a comprehensive account of the Greek and the barbarian, what each thought about the other, and how each lived in distinction from the other. He defined the collision in political terms: between the ideal of Greek freedom and the despotic rule of Persian kings. He sharply focused for Greece the result of the quarrel, and his final question explores the causation of history itself. He thought chance was important for the individual, and he constantly repeats the prevailing Greek sentiment that no man could be happy until death put him beyond the caprice of fortune. He believed that the gods punish vain ambition, conceit, and impiety in kings and statesmen

as well as in ordinary men. Unlike Aeschylus (*c.* 525–456 B.C.), however, he did not measure the gods in terms of human justice, believing that law is man-made and that the exercise of justice in the *polis*
lies within the control of human beings.

Thucydides

Little more than twenty-five years separate Herodotus from Thucydides (*c.* 460–*c.* 400 B.C.), but they show the moods of completely
different times. Herodotus mirrors the exuberance and fresh dawn-
ing of the Greek victory over Persia and of the promise in the Athens
of Pericles. Thucydides has seen every ideal of his time ground into
the dust. He witnessed Athens, beacon of Greece, fall into total ruin,
and the vaunted democracy revealed as cacophonous folly. In his
day, Persia had again become a feared power and even an ally of
Sparta, who had callously bargained away the freedom of Greeks in
Asia Minor as the price of her victory over Athens in 404 B.C.
Thucydides' concern is with the gloomy present, and he takes little
interest in the rather uncertain events of a distant past. This present—
the course of the great war between Athens and Sparta—he thinks
should be considered without prejudice for the general education of
mankind. The war

> was without doubt the greatest event that ever transpired
> among the Greeks, and among a portion of the barbarians, and
> extended, as one may put it, even to most of mankind. For the
> events that went before this, and those even more ancient, it
> seems impossible, through the length of time, to view them
> with certainty. From such evidence, however, as I am prone to
> trust, looking back as far as possible, I am not of the opinion
> that they were great, either in regard to wars or in other mat-
> ters. [*History*, I, 1]

Thucydides quickly sketches the events that led to the conflict
between Athens and Sparta (431–404 B.C.), and then he meticulously
narrates the war to 411 B.C. He employs the annalistic method, recording the happenings of summer and winter in chronological order.
He achieves complete clarity in sequence of events, but the account
is marred when Thucydides jumps from one theater of the war to
another to tell of simultaneous events. From time to time, as he sees
fit, he has his major characters make speeches, which adhere "as
closely as possible to the general sense of what really was said" (I,

22). A. W. Gomme, the author of the standard *Commentary on Thucydides*, 4 vols. to date (Oxford: Oxford University Press, 1956-1970), believed that speeches covering times when evidence was scanty were to cover "what would be likely to happen—poetry in Aristotle's sense of the phrase" (A. W. Gomme, *The Greek Attitude to Poetry and History* [Berkeley: Univ. of California Press, 1954], 141-142). Furthermore, Thucydides "frankly writes in his own style, making no attempt to imitate the oratory of the different speakers" (Gomme, *Commentary*, I, 141). The speeches allow Thucydides to make a kind of commentary on his own, the sort of historical material modern scholars put into footnotes or appendices. The speeches show individual hopes as they emerged on both sides of the conflict. The soaring funeral oration that Pericles delivered over the Athenian dead of the first year of the war gives the general gist of the actual oration (Thucydides, II, 35-46). Contained in the speech are the ideals of Athens and her democracy, enunciated by her greatest citizen. In the speeches of the generals before battles, Thucydides summarizes strategic and tactical problems.

His work gives translators headaches, since his language and style are often unique. Sometimes he uses straightforward narrative, although even in these passages, his chosen words are compact, succinct, and rapid. In his introspective passages (for example, the Periclean Oration) he packs as much content as he can into a limited number of words. His brevity is so extreme that it exasperated ancient commentators as much as modern scholars. The choice of words apparently is intended to "sound" harsh in the setting of terseness. Thucydides' tone and manner are fairly clear in the Greek, but English renditions cannot capture the total of Thucydides' brooding or the sound of occasional battle clatter any more than modern translations can isolate the wispy smoke in Pindar's poems.

Thucydides took the recorded facts as being accurate. He examined their relationships and then gathered them together to form an idea of their origins. To do this he first chopped away myth and legend encrusted from the past, then deduced the core of reality. For example, he writes that no greater war ever occurred in Greece, a premise he makes on the basis of the war's power and activity. Then, step by step, he shows the development of Athenian power after the Persian Wars, relating these facts to the immediate causes of the Peloponnesian War. These facts also illustrate and buttress his analysis of state policy as it relates to power, and they give Thucydides opportunities to comment on both the motives and psychology of power. Thus, in the speeches, two "arguments" appear: the opinion of the purported speaker, and the comment of Thucydides. This method of analysis is lucid in the "Melian Debate" (*History,* V, 85–113), where he examines the advantages to Athens of a generous policy toward a defenseless island people. Unfortunately, he comments, the brutal power of Athens and her democracy is used to slaughter in the name of "might makes right."

The crisis surrounding important decisions reveals the inner psychology of each *polis*. The speech of Pericles over Athens' dead depicts the relationship between statesmen and their people. Statesmen make decisions and the people follow them. Thucydides submits that there is an intimate link between power and morality, and between morality and disaster. Further, there is a close relationship between factions inside a *polis* and morality, and then between morality and potential disintegration. Boldly, Thucydides draws the connections between successes and failures abroad and attitudes at home in Athens.

Thucydides believed economic and geographic factors were no more than circumstances of chance, similar to religions and ideologies. These matters were indeed beyond the control of men, but they were not important. However, the responsibility for war certainly rested with men's actions, not on divine will. Consequently, wise men and wise *poleis* could avoid war by taking care that a situation did not develop to a crucial point. Men, therefore, make history by their choice of actions toward one another, and the wise leader needs an understanding of human nature. Thucydides thought certain qualities in human conduct were constant: the strong will instinctively dominate the weak; men will defend themselves against intruders; they will fight to keep what they have taken by force to save face; self-interest will direct human actions; and fear will remain a constant. Wise leaders assume these qualities both in themselves as well as in other men, and exercise their power to formulate policy in the light of this understanding. Above everything else, wise statesmen and their *poleis* will see the essence and effects of war. Reason and the intellect prove that neither right nor wrong guarantees victory and that the gods have little to do with the outcome of war. War is always unpredictable. The dangers of war and the eventual defeat or victory will emerge from men's judgments. Thus mistakes in judgment will determine defeat more than margins of strength.

Particularly in a democracy, extended or prolonged war produces unrestrained passion, unchecked brutality, and the disintegration of values and standards of conduct. Thucydides' *History of the Peloponnesian War* is a remarkable guide to the understanding of power, policy, and the uncertainties of war.

The Theatre

Epic poetry led to the epic of Herodotus and the speeches of Thucydides. Similarly, the function of "acting" derived from that of the poet. Originally, the poet who wrote lines for a recitation was the "actor." According to tradition, Thespis won the prize for tragedy at the first Dionysia in Athens (probably 534 B.C.) for inventing an "actor." The poet put an answerer and response-giver (*hypokrites*) opposite the leader of the normal chorus of singers; the *hypokrites* and chorus leader wore masks or costumes that contrasted wildly from one another. Disguised as the god or hero he was to play, Thespis stepped forward as the *hypokrites* to reply to the chorus, simultaneously creating the first actor and the first tragedy.

The poetic genius of tragedy found unique expression in Athens. Although Thespis and his victory of 534 B.C. appear fully grown like Athena from the brow of Zeus, behind the institution of the Dionysia as a festival celebrating Athens' religious bonds lay a long history. Earlier, groups of poets sometimes gathered to sing works in unison, a custom that may have led to the chorus in Attic tragedy and comedy. Side by side with the formal poetic exercises were the skits of the countrymen; these were most often bawdy burlesques about the gods' sexual chases after mortal women, but sometimes they considered more serious themes about the gods and their problems, as suggested in the homeric poems.

Modern plays are social events where one goes to view famous actors (and, if one is wealthy, to be viewed in public). Commercial aims dominate, and when a given play fails to attract paying audiences, it "folds," after being repeated nightly for a week or so. This situation is far different from that of the plays presented in ancient Athens, put on only once in conjunction with a religious celebration. The plays were presented at the Festival of Dionysus, the god of wine associated in art and legend with the *tragos* ("goat"), both wine and goats being appropriate symbols of Athens' commercial and agricultural life. The City Dionysia, held in late spring, gave poets an opportunity to "publish" their work (in the ancient definition). Three tragic poets and five comic poets entered their plays in competition for the prizes that the judges, selected from the *demes* of Attica, awarded for excellence. The Rural Dionysia in the *demes* might provide other chances for publication; occasionally the plays presented there were repeats from the City Dionysia, but more often they were different plays. Even though the plays were generally performed once, the scripts were preserved.

The City Dionysia lasted about six days. Before the opening of the celebration, the poets proposed their subjects. Later people brought the statue of Dionysus into the city, and on the first day of the City Dionysia a joyful procession winding into Athens celebrated the coming week. Then, still on the first day, the people went to the theater to take in ten dithyrambs (lyric narratives and dances set to musical accompaniment). The Athenians sat for five hours—thirty minutes for each dithyramb—and voted for a prize winner at the conclusion of the performances. From the second through the sixth day, the people watched plays. On the sixth day, the assembly made sure the form and procedure of the festival had been carried out according to correct custom.

The assembly required each tragic poet wishing to present his work to compose three tragedies (a trilogy) plus a satyr play as an afterpiece. (Comic poets wrote only one play.) The poet turned in the trilogy and the satyr play to the *archon,* who selected from all the submissions what he thought to be the best three trilogies. The *archon* then appointed a *choregus* ("producer"), who agreed in the name of civic patriotism to foot the bill for training the actors and paying for their costumes. To avoid constant bickering among playwrights, each of whom wanted the best actors in *his* play, the *archon* chose the actors for each play.

At dawn, the Athenians assembled at the Theater of Dionysus on the south slope of the Acropolis, paying two *obols* a head to get in, and took their places on wooden seats. Men were segregated from women, but both sexes watched the comedies, as well as the tragedies. The permanent set consisted of a circular orchestra with an altar to Dionysus, around which the actors and chorus performed, and a backdrop depicting the front of a palace or temple. The chorus opened the play with an introductory statement sung to an *aulos* playing somewhere in the background. Early Attic tragedy used the chorus as the "actor," but later the chorus became the group observing, commenting, or replying. Actors came, gave performances, and went away. In later tragedy, only two or three men were on stage at once, and the actors usually doubled in their roles. Only men acted on the stage, and the audience quickly identified the well-known roles from the standard masks—"king," "queen," "the god so-and-so," and several others. Generally the actor engaged in a recitative, but on occasion he would give something like an operatic aria. Music was quite important in the Attic plays, but unfortunately, little firm evidence remains about the part music had in tragedy or comedy. The rhythms of the poetic lines provide some clues, and ancient commentators sometimes indicate instruments behind the plays. When one attends a modern revival of Greek tragedy or comedy without the musical setting, which will be lost until scholars decipher Greek musical notations, it is like hearing opera spoken in monotone.

After the plays were completed, the ten judges voted for the best. These judges were, in effect, "drama critics" elected from each of the ten tribes of Attica. Each judge wrote out his decision and put it into a pot. Only five votes were drawn from the ten cast. The winning poet received a wreath, the *choregus* gained the privilege of setting up a triumphal memorial to himself, and the best actor in the winning play had his name inscribed on an official list displayed in full view in the main *agora*.

The Tragedies

The subjects of tragedy came from legend and myth, but some were historical plays that focused on a set of ideals rather than events in time. Characters in tragedy were larger than life, often blending in with the gods who moved the world and showed the tragic consequences from mortal misdirection. None of the subjects were of the "trash can school" common in the modern theater. Athenian plays did not narrate a myth or tell a story; rather, they explored man's defects and limitations, illuminating a flaw that led to tragedy. Events were explained in divine terms, and the gods securely ruled men. Overweening pride (*hybris*) ultimately preceded disaster, but this pride was checked with a balance (*sophrosyne*) between pride in mortal achievement and perception of human limits and weaknesses. The Athenians were proud of their *polis,* but they recognized the peril of fattened and static contentment. They believed the gods gave to men what they fashioned for themselves.

Aeschylus (*c.* 525–456 B.C.) molded and perfected the literary, dramatic, and poetic developments of early Attic tragedians. His play *Prometheus Bound* has many links with Hesiodic thinking as expressed in *Theogony.* Aeschylus portrays Zeus as a crude despot, but, like men, gods can apparently improve in character. There is little byplay in the seven Aeschylus plays that have survived (out of eighty plays written). Rather, Aeschylus poses a probing intellect, sharpened into pointed concentration. The power of the gods is overwhelming and ruthless, yet tempered with kindness. Zeus is

> whatever he might be, if this name called do please, and there-
> fore I call him, call him forth. I have brooded about all things,
> but I am unable to see a path, a road, only Zeus, to eject the
> dead, dread weight of ignorance from my mind. . . . Zeus, o
> god who pointed men into the paths of thought, who has
> ordained wisdom, arrives alone with agony, with suffering
> [*Agamemnon,* 160–178]

Agamemnon, Libation-Bearers, and *Eumenides* are tragedies guiding man to the final end, where he finally learns the price of widsom. In his *Persians,* he reveals Athens' exultation in her victory over mighty Persia. The theme is Athens' achievement in the face of Xerxes' *hybris.* Athens' ambition is clear (the play being produced in 472 B.C.): driving toward supremacy and expansion in the Greek world. *Persians* is a patriotic ode cast in the setting of *polis* religious cele-bration, an Athenian thanksgiving for her greatness.

Sophocles (496–406 B.C.) learned the art of poetry and tragic com-position in times of open joy and confidence. He built up the crea-tion of his older contemporary, Aeschylus, and in many ways, Sophocles was the greatest Athenian playwright, surpassing both Aeschylus and the younger master poet Euripides. Sophocles received a good education as education went in Athens, and at age sixteen, he was chosen leader of the chorus, which was dancing in celebration over the naval victory at Salamis. By 471 B.C. he was writing tragedies. In 468 B.C. his play won a prize over one of Aeschylus' plays, and thirty years later, he gained poetic victory over Euripides. Over a long and productive life, Sophocles wrote 123 dramas, 7 of which survive.

Unlike the plays of Aeschylus, which show an irregular and uneven style, the Sophoclean tragedies indicate a uniformity in method, approach, and content. In *Ajax,* the earliest surviving play, produced about 445 B.C., the dialogue among three persons has a few imperfections. However, the dialogue in the remaining six plays is smooth and lucid, whether there are the traditional two actors or (Sophocles' innovation) three. He had the quality of genius as he depicted powerful characters in delicate strokes of words and phrases. Like Shakespeare, he could vary his structure, and his flexibility encompassed weight and dignity, rapidity and floating lightness, and sometimes that rarest of successful stage devices, a casualness that is really casual. In the Greek, Sophocles' verse is remarkable. He will employ four-word and five-word lines that have great weight but no trace of rigidity or stiffness. Likewise, he can squeeze twenty-one words into twenty-four syllables, as he does in *Oedipus the King* (370 f.); and his simple passages are utterly simple. He can also use music and the chorus with stunning and moving effect, marked in the Greek texts by snapping changes in rhythms, indicating that the dancing must have been vivid. Rhetorical flourishes in his plays are some of the finest illustrations of Greek rhetoric, and scholars argue whether the rhetoricians learned their art from Sophocles, or he from them.

Many of Sophocles' tragedies stand at the top of any list of great works of Western literature. *Oedipus the King* is a striking summary of an honorable and sensitive man, caught within a web of misfortune he himself set in motion. The play is a model of characterization and skilled employment of tense moments and soothing interludes. Like Homer's Agamemnon, Oedipus makes a poor decision in good faith and then encounters opposition he does not understand that makes him persist in his mistake. Oedipus' theme is that a man can break divine law unknowingly, and his tragic doom will follow from divine law and its counterpart within the *polis*. Oedipus violates law in complete innocence, but his guilt is without question. In *Oedipus at Colonus*, Sophocles brilliantly delineates the results of violating divine law. The blind and aged Oedipus, cursed for the crime of incest when he unwittingly married his mother after killing his father, is akin to a monster, and people avoid him wherever he goes. Cursed by men for his double crime, he is a total outcast. Yet he bears an innocence on which the gods will rule. The gods give Oedipus the marks of their favor at the end, since the last place he is seen is ordained lucky and blessed. Sophocles' poetry makes a point Athenians could well appreciate in the years immediately following their disaster of 404 B.C. (*Oedipus at Colonus* was produced posthumously about 401 B.C.) The consequences of error in decisions and rational judgment are inevitable: isolation from men, personal neglect, and years of wandering and suffering. But Oedipus' rational innocence and his shame, coupled with his will and effort to understand the error, prove the measure of his mistakes. "At last, let tears cease to flow, let no one be in mourning again. These things rest in the hands of the gods" (*Colonus,* 1776–1778). At the end, man is vindicated.

Sophocles' *Antigone* (produced in 441 B.C.) harnesses passion to the ideal of balance. Antigone is torn between duty to her brother (who must be properly buried) and the commands of the *polis,* which forbid her to do so. At first glance, this seems like a simple conflict between an undeniable right and an unmistakable wrong, but Sophocles wants to examine the premise that "tragedy is not an imitation or reproduction of persons but of an action" (as Aristotle noted, *Poetics,* 1449b24, 1450a16, and 1450b3). In *Antigone,* the fate of the heartless Creon appears natural after what he has done to the body of Antigone's brother and what he inflicts on Antigone herself. "Lastly she cursed you as the murderer of her children. . . . she knew your guilt in the death of him before you, and even the elder dead" (*Antigone,* 1303–1304, 1311–1312). To Creon's cry of shame and entreaties for a swift death, the chorus replies, "That lies in the future. We must see the present. What is to be rests in hands other than ours . . . no mortal man is able to escape the fated doom for him prepared" (1332–1333, 1338–1339). The action of Creon is accompanied by the action of the wrathful gods; the actions of men and gods go together. To Sophocles and his Athenian audience, the interaction of divine will with human action, explained in human circumstances, implied the operation of a divine law. Thus the action would be more important than the persons, and Sophocles wished to portray the persons and their actions as clearly and vividly as he could. "The gods must receive their debted respect. Great words by prideful men cause greater calamities for them. Thus wisdom arrives to the aged" (1349–1352).

When Euripides (*c.* 485–*c.* 406 B.C.) became a prominent tragic poet, he generally perfected the external and internal form of tragedy. After much struggle and disappointment, however, he succeeded in changing drama in yet another way, leaving his particular mark on Attic tragedy of the late fifth century B.C. He altered the beginning and end of the tragedy. In his plays the prologue suggests preceding events, whereas Sophocles' prologue suggests the opening of action. Euripides' endings often employ the much-lampooned *deus ex machina* ("god from a machine"), an actor lowered from a crane who arrives to unravel knotty questions. The innovations of Euripides' drama were firmly rooted in the philosophical, sophistic, religious, and social changes current in Athens, and those innovations became the butt of comedy, like the jabs at flighty sophists.

An open fascination with the problems of rampant emotion distinguishes Euripides' plays from those of Sophocles and Aeschylus. He allows open anger and passion full expression in his attempt to understand the origins of irrational behavior that doom the human being. *Hippolytus* (produced in 428 B.C.) observes sexual passion openly and—what is most unusual for tragedy—from the vantage point of a woman. A turbulent desire for her stepson Hippolytus possesses Phaedra; the model may be Helen's erotic attraction for Paris in the homeric poems. Women portrayed as senseless monsters, ruled by their uninhibited emotions, were familiar to Athenian theatergoers; they recalled the vivid characters of Aeschylus and Sophocles—Clytemnestra, Cassandra, Electra, and Antigone. But Euripides is not concerned with the issues of incest or the violation of trust bonds between father and son. He seeks to probe the perversion of the relationship in its own terms. When Hippolytus rejects Phaedra, she is compelled to kill herself from shame. When Hippolytus' father, Theseus, plans revenge on his son after he learns of the matter, Hippolytus' defense is simple: even an immoral man would have shrunk from such an involvement. The full power of her sexual passion drove Phaedra into the crime, not merely to desire for her stepson but more importantly to complete disregard for rational action. Perversion is also a key to understanding Hippolytus' loudly proclaimed purity. Euripides uses him as the ironic foil to Phaedra, guilt-ridden with lust. She craved the one man noted for his absolute continence.

Euripides' *Alcestis* and *Medea* (produced in 438 B.C. for a second prize and 431 B.C. for a third prize, respectively) are occasionally revived on the modern stage; *Medea* is one of the most famous Attic tragedies. *Alcestis* is a more complicated piece, an inverted tragedy in which the hero Admetus is saved at the end by the one redeeming quality he has: respect for the rights of guest-friends (Homer's *xenia*). Once again, the leading lady, Alcestis, is full of passion, but she reserves her emotions for her children and remains icy toward her husband, Admetus. The question of the play is whether a man of high character will let his wife die for him. Even though Admetus loves his wife and children (superficial qualities according to Euripides), he lacks the courage to face death, or what is worse, he cannot admit to himself that he should die in place of Alcestis. In a reversal of the normal plotting of tragedy, this "virtue" saves Admetus from ruin, but the play is not intended to be humorous. As a drunk, Heracles (Admetus' father-in-law) is indeed droll, but the appended quarrel between Admetus and Heracles is gross and all too familiar. The words of anger between Apollo and Death are warped and grotesque, linking back (one presumes) to the passion Alcestis has for her offspring. In this play Euripides puts forth a recognizable and important theme: a weak man who sees the small fragment of "virtue" in himself can persevere with it and overcome the power of cowardice.

In *Medea*, Euripides takes a well-known myth to illustrate a woman's irresponsible rage when she has been wronged. The story of Jason and his band of adventurers sailing to distant Colchis to capture the fabulous Golden Fleece was a favorite of the time. The audience would know that Jason gained his goal with the help of the sorceress *Medea*, who had fallen in love with him. She had murdered her brother to aid Jason, but he abandoned her once they came back to Corinth. He thus releases all of the fury of Medea's jealousy. Medea schemes to destroy as many of her supposed enemies as she can with her black arts. Jason had married the daughter of Creon, the Corinthian king, and so Medea kills Creon and his daughter with a robe that clings and burns, a fitting and agonizing manner of death. To injure Jason with the most grievous wound, she murders her children by him and then escapes. Her vengeance dominates, and her hatred for Jason swamps her maternal instincts. After Jason has discovered her horrible act, she says these words:

> No, it was not foreordained that you could disdain me, scorning my love, living the rest of your life calmly, mocking me, laughing at me. Nor would the king's daughter, nor the king who tempted you with her, expel me without paying for the insult . . . I also, as I was compelled to do, have grasped and seized your heart [*Medea*, 1354–1360]

Attic Comedy

The City Dionysia included comedies that took their subjects from everyday life, in contrast with the storehouse of myth and legend that lay behind the tragedies. Attic comedy colorfully illustrates what Athenian audiences considered amusing, funny, and hilarious, and the poetic genius of tragedy is matched by the rollicking lines of the comedy writers. The origins of comedy are a little more clear than for those of tragedy. Bawdy burlesques were common in the Peloponnesus after 750 B.C. These "mimes" had simple plots (man chases woman, woman chases man, huffing and panting) that emphasized the awkward moments and buffoonery of sex. By 450 B.C. comedy was part of Athenian playwrighting; the comedies had better plots and choral organization than their predecessors, the inherited sexual puns, and warm, boisterous, and blustering obscenity calculated to convulse the mixed audience in fits of laughter.

Attic comedy was a hodgepodge—a mixture of wit, puns, farce, and serious lampoons of political figures and national decisions. An actor began by giving a prologue, which was followed by a choral entrance. The argument between actor and chorus became an *agon* ("contest") that set the scene for the play. Occasional "patter songs," similar to the staccato songs from the Victorian light operettas of Gilbert and Sullivan, carried the lines along. For example, the twitting description of an oracle in Aristophanes' *Knights* (195-201) is like the ironic "Model of a Modern Major General" in *Pirates of Penzance,* produced in 1879. The clipped, rapid movement of the speaker's mouth in both cases keeps the audience anticipating the lyricist's skill and the ability of tooth and tongue of the actor. Compare *eu ne tous theous kai poikilos pos kai sophos enigmenos* ("Swelling well with the divine promises, well wrapped and with wisdom mysterious") (*Knights,* 195-196) with the second verse of "Major General":

> I quote in elegiacs all the crimes of Heliogabalus. . . . I know
> the croaking chorus from the *Frogs* of Aristophanes. . . . Then
> I can write a washing bill in Babylonic cuneiform, And tell
> you ev'ry detail of Caractacus's uniform. In short, in matters
> vegetable, animal and mineral I am the very model of a modern
> Major General. [Gilbert and Sullivan, *Pirates of Penzance*]

The comedies stressed the absurd (like the comic antics of the Marx Brothers' movies of the 1930s and 1940s), with a loose structure of puns, jokes, and dancing. Unlike tragedy, the actors in a comedy sometimes addressed the audience directly to involve them in the jests and mirth, and the actor wheedling the audience ("aw, c'mon, laugh at it!") added to the merriment.

Although Cratinus (*c.* 484-419 B.C.) and Eupolis (*fl.* 430-410 B.C.)

were regarded as comic writers of genius, only fragments of their works remain. However, eleven of Aristophanes' plays survive. Aristophanes (*c.* 450–*c.* 385 B.C.) was the most famous comedy writer of ancient times, a writer of genius who could take obscenity and make it simply funny. In fact, most Attic comedy is laced with sex, but sexual references that indicate what Athenians thought amusing: the grotesque, the bumbling lust of horny old men, and the loudly praised chastity of Greek women. The comedy writers used pornography as humor and attached little prudery to sex, which Greeks took for granted as an everyday part of life. (See chapter 7.)

Aristophanes loved the ideal of the poor, frugal farmer, an ideal well illustrated in *Acharnians* (produced in 425 B.C.). The ignorant and simple farmer is highly patriotic, but he suffers from the exploitation of city slickers and from the arrogant disrespect of the younger generation. War certainly did not aid the farmer in tilling his small plot, and the play is a plea for peace. The audience must have sympathized, since *Acharnians* was awarded first prize. The astute combination of farce and reality was Aristophanes' mark; he openly revealed his personal and political opinions, especially when he referred to contemporary events. In 424 B.C., in *Knights,* the playwright struck hard at the overweening pride and political buffoonery of the demagogue Cleon, just returning from his astounding victory over some Spartans at Pylos. Cleon was sitting in the front row of the audience, and he later filed suit for libel against Aristophanes. On the other hand, the Athenians were delighted with the play's lampooning, and it won first prize. The audience understood that *Knights* was not antidemocratic, but an attack on the gullible masses misled by demagogues, Cleon in particular. *Clouds* (423 B.C.) was a sharp attack on the "new learning" of the time. Socrates received the butt of joking, as the "philosopher" sat aloft in a basket hoping to understand the cosmos better than men who merely walked around. As a diatribe against the Sophists, *Clouds* was unsuccessful, winning only third prize, but it shows that Aristophanes and his audience were well acquainted with sophistic techniques and teachers. *Birds* (414 B.C.) was a farcical fantasy on the Athenian dream of empire, produced a year after the Sicilian expedition had set sail for Syracuse. *Lysistrata* (411 B.C.) has been revived in modern times. Another plea for peace, it shows how much women could influence men at war. The ban on sex that the women of Greece proposed leads to hilarious problems, especially when some of the women have difficulty keeping their agreement. Peace finally arrives when the Spartans discover they are having the same problems with their women as are the Athenians. The play ends in general confusion when the parties signing the peace treaty have trouble keeping their minds on the business of diplomacy. The women wait, while the men pant.

In Aristophanes' last play, *Plutus* (388 B.C.), a new world intrudes. Politics does not dominate, and the mood is less secure even though the play shows greater urbanity and sophistication. The playwright looks longily into a past when virtue had meaning and people knew and accepted values. The *polis* hovers like a shadow, but there is little devotion to it except as a symbol of the "good old days."

Suggested Further Reading

Books with paperback editions are marked*

General Works on Greek History and Life-styles

Andrewes, Antony. *The Greeks*. London: Hutchinson, 1967. A thought-provoking, lucid, and clear survey, reflecting scholarship in Greek history to 1965.

Botsford, George W., and Robinson, Charles A., Jr. *Hellenic History*. 8th printing. New York: Macmillan, 1965. The best brief history of Greece from prehistoric times to the Roman conquest of the Greek East.

Bowra, C. M. *The Greek Experience*.* New York: Mentor MP 349, 1957. Stylistic masterpiece, with a certain prudish opinion on sexual matters, which reflects Bowra more than the Greeks.

Burn, A. R. *The Pelican History of Greece*.* Harmondsworth: Penguin A792, 1966. Solid, well-written history, which includes the period down to the Roman conquest.

Bury, J. B. *A History of Greece*. 3d ed., rev. by R. Meiggs. London: Macmillan, 1963. An updated version of the traditional type of history text. Names and battles abound, but in a way that makes for good reading.

Frost, Frank J. *Greek Society*.* Lexington, Massachusetts: D. C. Heath, 1971. Lively rendering of the different aspects of Greek life, from the farm to the *polis*. Chapter 6, "Some Greek People," is excellent.

Hammond, N. G. L. *A History of Greece to 322 B.C.* 2d ed. Oxford: Oxford University Press, 1967. The most complete and detailed of the general histories of Greece, especially sound for drawing conclusions from source material, but somewhat overtrusting of semi-legendary materials like Homer. Sections on warfare and economics are particularly strong. Hammond pens memorable portraits of the great figures in Greek literature and art.

Kitto, H. D. F. *The Greeks*.* Many reprintings. Harmondsworth: Penguin A220, 1957. One of the best single volumes ever written on the Greeks.

Quennell, Marjorie and Quennell, C. H. B. *Everyday Things in Ancient Greece*. 2d ed., rev. by Kathleen Freeman. New York:

Putnam, 1954. This is the book for all those little details, from locks in Homeric times to lyres. There are fine line drawings.

Webster, T. B. L. *Life in Classical Athens.** New York: Capricorn CG 362, 1969. Strong on drama, literature, and what we can gain from source material from the Persian Wars to Alexander.

For more extensive accounts of any particular era, see the appropriate volumes of the *Cambridge Ancient History.* Volumes 4 through 8 cover Greek history from the beginnings of classical times to the Roman take-over of Pergamon in 133 B.C., with Roman Republican history intermeshed. The new edition of volume 2—part 1 appeared in 1973—gives updated accounts of Minoan and Mycenaean matters. Summary accounts of most subjects can be located conveniently in H. H. Scullard et al., eds., *Oxford Classical Dictionary,* 2d ed. (Oxford: Oxford University Press, 1970).

Chapter 1   Greeks in Settlements

All of the works cited under "General Works on Greek History and Life-styles" have sections devoted to the *polis.* To begin, I would recommend the works of Burn, Frost, and Kitto. In addition, I would suggest the following:

Ehrenberg, Victor. *The Greek State.** New York: Norton N250, 1964. Part 1 covers the *polis* in its classical form; part 2 gives an analysis of the Hellenistic *polis.* This is one of the best inclusive books on the subject. Students have noted that it is difficult reading, but rewarding in the long run.

Freeman, Kathleen. *Greek City-States.** New York: Norton N193, 1963. Short, vivid sketches of the *poleis* not found in most volumes. This is an excellent source for mythological settings (Thourioi, Acragas, Corinth, Miletus, Cyrene, Seriphos, Abdera, Massilia, and Byzantium).

Jones, A. H. M. *The Greek City.* Oxford: Oxford University Press, 1940. The history of the *polis* from Alexander the Great to Justinian. It indicates the persistence of the earlier institutions and is good reading.

Aristocracies and Tyrannies

Andrewes, Antony. *The Greek Tyrants.** New York: Harper Torch-

book TB1103, 1963. By far the best book on the origins and
importance of tyrannies and much praised by students.

Finley, M. I. *The World of Odysseus.** New York: Viking Compass
C184, 1965. The aristocrats who emerge from the homeric period
and lead to the rise of the *polis.*

The Rise of Hoplites

Snodgrass, A. M. *Arms and Armour of the Greeks.* London: Thames
and Hudson, 1967. The section on archaeology is a great help in
understanding the early period of Greek history. Further listings
for warfare are included under chapter 4.

Early Greek Coinages

Kraay, C. M. *Greek Coins.* London: Thames and Hudson, 1966,
p. 325. A listing on this page includes two beneficial articles by
Kraay: "The Archaic Owls of Athens: Classification and Chronology," *Numismatic Chronicle* (1956); and "The Early Coinage of
Athens," *Numismatic Chronicle* (1962).

Ravel, O. "The Colts of Ambracia." *Numismatic Notes and Mono-
graphs* 37 (1928). An article to give the reader an introduction to
Corinthian coinage.

Seltman, C. T. *Athens: Its History and Coinage before the Persian
Invasion.* Cambridge: Cambridge University Press, 1924. Good
selection of materials. But specialists do not now accept the views
put forth in the text.

Would-be Greek numismatists should begin their study by becoming
familiar with the following:

British Museum Department of Coins and Medals. *A Guide to the
Principle Coins of the Greeks.* London: The British Museum, 1965.
A basic catalogue.

Head, Barclay V. *Historia Numorum: A Manual of Greek Numismatics.* 1911. Reprint. Chicago: Argonaut, 1967. A massive guide.
However, recent research has changed many details.

Athens

Most books about Greece are actually about Athens. Consequently, there are many volumes about Athens. Volume 5 of the *Cambridge Ancient History* still offers a good account, although recent research has challenged many details in the text. I recommend the following books, presuming that the reader will be led where he wishes through their notes and bibliographies:

Forrest, W. G. *The Emergence of Greek Democracy.* * New York: McGraw-Hill, 1966. Controversial retelling of the Greek story against the backdrop of corollary developments in Corinth and Sparta. This well-written book is a favorite of students.

Gomme, A. W. *The Population of Ancient Athens.* 1933. Reprint. Chicago: Argonaut, 1967. The key book for statistics, as known in 1932.

Hignett, C. *A History of the Athenian Constitution.* Oxford: Oxford University Press, 1952. The standard work on the topic.

Jones, A. H. M. *Athenian Democracy.* Oxford: Blackwell, 1964. Collection of stimulating essays written by a master scholar. Chapter 5, "How did the Athenian Democracy Work?" is especially illuminating.

Kounas, Dionysius A. *Perikles Son of Athens.* * Lawrence: Coronado Press, 1970. Handy collection of the biographical materials about Pericles from Plutarch, Thucydides, Aristophanes, and Pliny, with a good introduction and up-to-date bibliography.

Zimmern, Alfred. *The Greek Commonwealth.* * 5th ed. 1931. Reprint. New York: Oxford University Press, 1961. Traditional account, written in the enviable British manner.

Sparta

Forrest, W. G. *A History of Sparta.* * London: Hutchinson, 1968. Terse, controversial summary of the evidence. Students enjoy Forrest's brevity.

Huxley, G. L. *Early Sparta.* London: Faber, 1962. Archaeology and other matters. Mycenaean heritages are emphasized.

Michell, H. *Sparta.* * Cambridge: Cambridge University Press, 1964. Lucid and hotly debated among scholars.

The Spartan Rhetra. * Lawrence, Kansas: Coronado Press, 1970. Convenient collection of the literary source materials from Xenophon and Plutarch.

Thebes

Larsen, J. A. O. *Greek Federal States.* Oxford: Oxford University Press, 1968, pp. 26-40 and 175-180. Rugged reading for the beginner, but well worth the effort.

Corinth

Graham, A. J. *Colony and Mother City in Ancient Greece.* 1964. Reprint. New York: Barnes and Noble, 1971, pp. 118-153, 218-223, and 233-235. Stimulating and well written. It emphasizes colonial efforts, but social and economic matters form part of the analysis.

Colonization

Boardman, John. *The Greeks Overseas.** Harmondsworth: Penguin A581, 1964. The best general survey, with good coverage of the early Greek contacts in the East. Every beginning student should read chapter 1, "The Nature of the Evidence," which applies to much more than the colonies.

Carpenter, Rhys. *The Greeks in Spain.* Bryn Mawr: Bryn Mawr College, 1925. Unique book on the subject.

Cook, J. M. *The Greeks in Ionia and the East.* London: Thames and Hudson, 1962. Good plates in the back. The title indicates the scope.

Dunbabin, T. J. *The Western Greeks.* Oxford: Oxford University Press, 1948. Archaeologically detailed account down to 480 B.C.

Freeman, E. A. *History of Sicily.* 4 vols. Oxford: Oxford University Press, 1891-1894. Fundamental for material later than 480 B.C.

Graham, A. J. *Colony and Mother City.* Cited under "Corinth." Solid and readable.

Woodhead, A. G. *The Greeks in the West.* London: Thames and Hudson, 1962. A short survey.

Argos

Tomlinson, E. A. *Argos and the Argolid.* Ithaca: Cornell University Press, 1972. Necessarily dependent on the archaeological evidence and stiff, but well woven with literary fragments.

Megara

Highbarger, E. L. *The History and Civilization of Ancient Megara.*
Baltimore: Johns Hopkins Press, 1927. A comprehensive survey.
Kagan, Donald. *The Outbreak of the Peloponnesian War.* Ithaca:
Cornell University Press, 1969, chap. 15, "Megara." The details
behind Megara's quarrel with Athens.
Legon, Ronald P. "The Megarian Decree and Greek Naval Power,"
Classical Philology 68 (1973): 161-171. A supplement to Kagan.

The Oracle at Delphi

Parke, H. W., and Wormell, D. E. W. *The Delphic Oracle.* 2 vols.
Oxford: Blackwell, 1956. The history of the oracle, with a collec-
tion of responses from the shrine.
Whittaker, C. R. "The Delphic Oracle: Belief and Behavior in
Ancient Greece—and Africa." *Harvard Theological Review* 58
1965): 21-47. Wide-ranging and suggestive.

Sources

Translations of authors cited in the text can be found in the Loeb
Classical Library or the Penguin Classics,* except for *The Hellenica
Oxyrhynchia.* The Greek text is best edited by B. Bartoletti (Leipzig:
Teubner, 1959), while the reader without Greek will appreciate the
indications of controversy and context in I. A. F. Bruce, *A Historical
Commentary on the Hellenica Oxyrhynchia* (Cambridge: Cambridge
University Press, 1967). Efforts to identify the anonymous author
with one of the known Greek historical writers have proven fruitless.

Chapter 2 The Plow and the Mind

Geography

Cary, Max. *The Geographic Background of Greek and Roman History.* Oxford: Oxford University Press, 1949, chaps. 2 and 3. Clear
summary of the peculiar physical features of Greece. Climate,
vegetation, and so on are all here, with bibliographical leads.

The Minoans and the Mycenaeans

Of the plethora of books on this topic, I recommend the following:

Chadwick, John. *The Decipherment of Linear B.** New York: Modern Library P65, 1958. The fascinating account of how Michael Ventris cracked the script used in late Mycenaean times.

Desborough, V. R. d'A. *The Last Mycenaeans and their Successors.* Oxford: Oxford University Press, 1964. The meat of archaeology. This will be heavy going for the general reader, but will correct many romantic myths about Mycenae and her archaeology.

Hutchinson, R. W. *Prehistoric Crete.** Harmondsworth: Penguin A501, 1962. The best introduction to the history and archaeology of Minoan civilization.

Luce, J. V. *The End of Atlantis.* London: Thames and Hudson, 1969. Good reading in vulcanology, general geology, and myth debunking and a favorite with students. Volcanic eruptions and the Island of Thera bring Plato's Atlantis home to the Aegean.

McDonald, William A. *Progress into the Past.** Bloomington: Indiana University Press, 1969. Clear and accurate account of how Schliemann, Dörpfeld, and others unearthed the Mycenaeans. It is lengthy and complete and a good bibliographical guide.

Mylonas, George E. *Mycenae and the Mycenaean Age.* Princeton: Princeton University Press, 1966. Controversial interpretation of Mycenaean civilization, firmly based on archaeology.

Taylour, Lord William. *The Mycenaeans.* London: Thames and Hudson, 1964. Solid summary by one of the leading excavators.

Vermeule, Emily. *Greece in the Bronze Age.** Chicago: University of Chicago Press, 1964. Lucid account of the Mycenaeans. It is especially good on matters concerning art and commerce.

From Mycenae to the Rise of the Polis

Starr, Chester G. *The Origins of Greek Civilization.* New York: Knopf, 1961. Dark Age Greece through its pottery. Students have found this thought-provoking book intriguing.

Webster, T. B. L. *From Mycenae to Homer.** New York: Norton N254, 1964. A bit broader coverage than Starr, with emphasis on poetic links and Eastern contacts.

The Homeric Myths and History

Carpenter, Rhys. *Folk Tale, Fiction, and Saga in the Homeric Epics.* *
Berkeley: University of California Press, 1962. Provocative and
well-written account of Indo-European myths and the Greeks.

Lord, Albert B. *The Singer of Tales.* * New York: Atheneum 76,
1965. A plausible picture of poets and their world views before
writing.

Page, Denys. *History and the Homeric Iliad.* * Berkeley: University of
California Press, 1963. A sifting of the "historical" Trojan War
and the epic portrait in the *Iliad* through the strainer of modern
archaeology.

Solon

Woodhouse, W. J. *Solon the Liberator.* Oxford: Oxford University
Press, 1938. Readable volume with the bias that the title indicates.
The Greek quotations do not intrude too much.

Horses and Dogs

Anderson, J. K. *Ancient Greek Horsemanship.* Berkeley: University
of California Press, 1961. The book for equine enthusiasts.

Hill, Denison B. *Hounds and Hunting in Ancient Greece.* Chicago:
University of Chicago Press, 1964. The book for dog lovers.

Details of Greek Farming and Crops

Ehrenberg, Victor. *The People of Aristophanes.* * New York: Schocken
SB27, 1962, chap. 3. Drawn from the pages of Athenian comedy.

Glotz, Gustave. *Ancient Greece at Work.* * 1927. Reprint. New York:
Norton N392, 1967, chap. 4. Colorful and overblown. This is a
favorite with students, although many note that Glotz fails to tell
where he got his evidence.

Michell, H. *The Economics of Ancient Greece.* * 1940. Reprint. New
York: Barnes and Noble, 1963. Good rendition, stuffed with
minutiae. The information is here, but little life. Chapter 2 covers
agriculture.

Sources

I have given fresh translations for the quotations from the Greek. English translations are found in the Loeb Classical Library (Cambridge, Massachusetts: Harvard University Press) or in paperback in the Penguin Classics.

Chapter 3   Who Bought What, and Why

Generally, the best guide to Greek technology is C. Singer et al., *A History of Technology,* vol. 2. *The Mediterranean Civilizations and the Middle Ages* (Oxford: Oxford University Press, 1956). References to the various sections of volume 2 will be made as Singer. *History.* Chapter 6 of Henry Hodges, *Technology in the Ancient World* (New York: Knopf, 1970) is particularly strong on the common crafts of leatherworking and throwing pottery, and the ship drawings are some of the clearest to be found anywhere. Johannes Hasebroek, *Trade and Politics in Ancient Greece,* trans. L. M. Fraser and D. C. MacGregor. (Reprint ed., New York: Biblo and Tannen, 1965) is a tight and controversial account of how trade and politics mixed together. H. Michell, *The Economics of Ancient Greece** (1940; reprint ed., New York: Barnes and Noble, 1963) offers more detail; references to these works appear as Hasebroek, *Trade* and Michell, *Economics.*

Piracy

Ormerod, H. A. *Piracy in the Ancient World.* 1924. Reprint. Chicago: Argonaut, 1967. This rambling book remains the only monograph on the subject in English.

Slavery and the Slave Trade

Of the vast literature on this topic, I suggest the following sources which will lead to further books and articles listed in the bibliographies and footnotes:

Finley, M. I., ed. *Slavery in Classical Antiquity.** Cambridge: Heffer, 1960. This collection contains the following writings on Greek slavery: W. L. Westermann, "Slavery and the Elements of Freedom in Ancient Greece"; M. I. Finley, "Was Greek Civilization Based on Slave Labour?"; Robert Schlaifer, "Greek Theories of Slavery from Homer to Aristotle"; Gregory Vlastos, "Slavery in Plato's Republic."

Westermann, W. L. *The Slave Systems of Greek and Roman Antiquity.* Philadelphia: American Philosophical Society, 1955, chaps. 1–8. The best summary of sources, with the added bonus of late Greek and Hellenistic inscriptions and papyri. As the Englished version of the author's lengthy German discussion in Pauly-Wissowa, *Real-Encyclopädie der classischen Altertumswissenschaft,* the account is rough going and somewhat tedious for the general reader.

Traders

Hasebroek. *Trade.* Chap. 1.
Michell. *Economics.* Chap. 8.

The Phoenicians

Baramki, Dimitri. *Phoenicia and the Phoenicians.* * Beirut: Khayat, 1961. A good beginning by a Lebanese scholar. It includes art, archaeology, and some history.
Harden, Donald. *The Phoenicians.* * New York: Praeger, 1962. Readable and quite lucid, a rarity among books that deal with the specifics of archaeology. It has good plates in the back and includes a section on Carthage.

Gold

Michell. *Economics.* Chap. 3.
Rosenfeld, A. *The Inorganic Raw Materials of Antiquity.* New York: Praeger, 1965, chap. 5. The physical and chemical data for the ancient refining processes.
Singer. *History.* Pp. 40–43.
Sutherland, C. H. V. *Gold,* 2d ed. London: Thames and Hudson, 1969, chap. 4. A vivid account of Greeks, Persians, and gold, by one of the leading scholars in ancient numismatics.

Amber

Michell. *Economics.* Pp. 216 and 246.

Spekke, Arnolds. *The Ancient Amber Routes and the Geographical Discovery of the Eastern Baltic.* Stockholm: M. Goppers, 1957. Unique narrative from the Northern viewpoint.

Thomson, J. Oliver. *History of Ancient Geography.* Cambridge: Cambridge University Press, 1948, pp. 52–54. A learned summary of the sources.

Exploration and Explorers

Bolton, J. D. P. *Aristeas of Proconnesus.* Oxford: Oxford University Press, 1962. A delightful book about one of the earliest adventurers (*c.* 675 B.C.), who went into the hinterlands beyond the Black Sea.

Cary, M., and Warmington, E. H. *The Ancient Explorers.** Harmondsworth: Penguin A420, 1963. An absorbing book that should be required reading for all would-be novelists treating Greek sailing and ships.

Thiel, J. H. *Eudoxus of Cyzicus.** Groningen: Wolters, 1967. Although Eudoxus lived later than the period treated in "Who Bought What, and Why," this booklet reveals much about earlier traditions.

Mycenaean Art and Artifacts

See listings under "The Minoans and the Mycenaeans" of chapter 2.

Olives and Olive Oil

Brothwell, Don, and Brothwell, Patricia. *Food in Antiquity.* London: Thames and Hudson, 1969, pp. 153–157. This book is generally one of the best on ancient foodstuffs.

Michell. *Economics,* pp. 192–193 and 284–286.

Rostovtzeff, M. *Social and Economic History of the Hellenistic World.* 3 vols. Oxford: Oxford University Press, 1941, index entries, vol. 3, p. 1716. A masterpiece of detailed scholarship. The olive trade and manufacture that existed in the Hellenistic era were generally like that of earlier Greek times.

Singer. *History.* Pp. 112–113.

Tyrian Dye

Michell. *Economics.* Pp. 189–190.

Iron

Singer. *History.* Pp. 55–61.

Leather

Singer. *History.* Pp. 147–174.

Mining of Ores

Hopper, R. J. "The Mines and Miners of Ancient Athens." *Greece and Rome.* 2d series, 8 (1961): 138–151. Updates earlier accounts.
Singer. *History.* Pp. 1–6 with appended bibliography.

Solon

Hammond, N. G. L. "Land Tenure in Athens and Solon's Seisach-theia." *Journal of Hellenic Studies* 81 (1961): 76–98. A clear argument that Attic land was inalienable until late in the fifth century B.C. Woodhouse, *Solon,* cited under "Solon" of chapter 2, proposes this for Archaic Greece.

See also listing under "Solon" of Chapter 2.

Silver

Forbes, R. J. "Silver and Lead in Antiquity." *Jaarbericht ex Oriente Lux* 8 (1942): 747–751. Technical.
Forbes, R. J. *Studies in Ancient Technology.* Vol. 8. Leiden: Brill, 1964. Also technical. Neither of these sources is recommended for casual reading.
Strong, D. E. *Greek and Roman Silver Plate.* London: Methuen, 1966, chap. 1. An excellent summary of craftsmen and their metals.

Grain

Hyams, Edward. *Soil and Civilization.* London: Thames and Hudson, 1952, chap. 8, "The Soils of Attica and the Rise of Athens." Of great interest in the setting of Greek history as a whole.

Moritz, L. A. *Grain-Mills and Flour in Classical Antiquity.* Oxford: Oxford University Press, 1958, chaps. 1–9. Sources and details for this neglected aspect of Greek life.

Ships

Singer. *History.* Pp. 563–569. See further listings under "Ships and Triremes" of chapter 4.

Athenian Empire

Meiggs, Russell. *The Athenian Empire.* Oxford: Oxford University Press, 1972. The most complete and readable book on the subject in English.

Athenian Coinages

Kraay, C. M., and Hirmer, Max. *Greek Coins.* London: Thames and Hudson, 1966. Magnificent plates and solid commentary.

Starr, Chester G. *Athenian Coinage 480–449 B.C.* Oxford: Oxford University Press, 1970. Puts some order into the numismatic confusion of the period.

Wood and Timber Transport

Michell. *Economics.* Pp. 235, 244, 278–280, and 283.

Sources

English renditions of all cited authors can be found in the Loeb Classical Library or the Penguin Classics,* with a few exceptions.

The best Greek text of Dioscorides, M. Wellmann, ed., *De materia medica,* 3 vols. (Berlin: Weidmann, 1958), has not been utilized for a complete English translation. There is also the redacted, re-edited, English Dioscorides, R. T. Gunther, ed., *Greek Herbal,* from the 1655 translation by John Goodyer. (1933; reprint ed., New York: Hafner, 1959). I have drawn my citations for Dioscorides from the Wellmann text.

No translation exists for the *Geoponica.* The text is edited by H. Beckh (Leipzig: Teubner, 1895).

The *Zenon* reference comes from: Campbell C. Edgar. *Zenon Papyri in the University of Michigan Collection.* Ann Arbor: University of Michigan Press, 1931.

The Periplus of the Erythryaean Sea has been rendered into English by W. H. Schoff (New York and London, 1912). The notes are copious and keep the reader well informed, but they are occasionally disputable. The Greek text is edited by J. I. H. Frisk (Göteburg, 1927).

Chapter 4   War

Greek Warfare in General

Adcock, F. E. *The Greek and Macedonian Art of War.* * Berkeley: University of California Press, 1962. Clipped and lucid and the best summary.

Fuller, J. F. C. *A Military History of the Western World.* * Vol. 1. New York: Minerva Press, 1967, chaps. 1-3. The traditional tome, modeled after the classic E. S. Creasy, *Decisive Battles of the World* (New York: Colonial Press, 1899). Often very dry.

Pritchett, W. Kendrick. *Ancient Greek Military Practices.* * Berkeley: University of California Press, 1971. Minutiae about booty, pay, the marching song, scouts, and so on. It is difficult reading.

Homeric Warfare and the Rise of Hoplites

Lorimer, H. L. "The Hoplite Phalanx." *Annual of the British School at Athens* 42 (1947): 76-138. The thesis that heavily armed soldiers lead to tyrannies.

Snodgrass, A. M. "The Hoplite Reform and History." *Journal of Hellenic Studies* 85 (1965): 110-122. The thesis opposing Lorimer.

The Chigi Vase

Arias, P. E., and Hirmer, M. *A History of Greek Vase Painting.* London: Thames and Hudson, 1962, plates 16 and 17 (black and white) and plate IV (color), with text, pp. 275–276. An artistic masterpiece.

Tyrtaeus, the Spartans, and the Paean

Hudson-Williams, T. *Early Greek Elegy.* Oxford: Oxford University Press, 1926, pp. 106–115. An instructive commentary on the fragments of Tyrtaeus.

Pritchett, W. Kendrick. "The Marching Paian." In W. Kendrick Pritchett, *Ancient Greek Military Practices.** Pp. 105–108. Berkeley: University of California Press, 1971. A collection of the evidence.

Athletic Contests and Warfare

Gardiner, E. Norman. *Athletics of the Ancient World.* Oxford: Oxford University Press, 1930, chap. 3, "Homer." (From the abbreviated version of his *Greek Athletic Sports and Festivals* [1910].) Pointed writing for the necessity of athletics.

Harris, H. A. *Sport in Greece and Rome.* London: Thames and Hudson, 1972, chaps. 1 and 7. Lively and balanced account by a long-time enthusiast. It uses the sources liberally.

Robinson, Rachel Sargent. *Sources for the History of Greek Athletics.** Cincinnati: Rachel Sargent Robinson, 1955, chaps. 1 and 2. Translated source materials from the time of Homer through the late Roman Empire.

Persia

Cambridge Ancient History. Vols. 4 and 5.

Olmstead, A. T. *History of the Persian Empire.** 1959. Reprint ed. Chicago: University of Chicago Press, 1959. The standard history. I recommend chapter 5, "Life Among the Subject Peoples," and chapter 11, "Problems of the Greek Frontier."

Ships and Triremes

Lionel Casson has published a number of articles and books on this topic. I recommend the following:

The Ancient Mariners. New York: Macmillan, 1959, chaps. 6-8. Readable summary and a favorite with students.

Illustrated History of Ships and Boats. Garden City: Doubleday, 1964, chaps. 3 and 4. "Popular" and accurate summary, with self-explanatory drawings and photographs.

"Ancient Shipbuilding: New Light on an Old Source." *Transactions and Proceedings of the American Philological Association* [cited hereafter as *TAPA*] 94 (1963): 28-33. A discussion of keels, planks, and underwater archaeology.

"The Emergency Rig of Ancient Warships." *TAPA* 98 (1967): 43-48. An explanation of substitutes for the mainsail.

"Galley Slaves." *TAPA* 97 (1966): 35-44. None before the Renaissance.

"Hemiolia and Triemiolia." *Journal of Hellenic Studies* 78 (1958): 14-18. The workings of pirate vessels.

"Speed Under Sail of Ancient Ships." *TAPA* 82 (1951): 136-148. The data telling "how long it took."

Following are other books and articles on ships and triremes:

Gomme, A. W. "A Forgotten Factor of Greek Naval Strategy." In A. W. Gomme, *Essays in Greek History and Literature,* Oxford: Oxford University Press, 1937, pp. 190-203. The sharp limitations of Greek fleets.

Morrison, J. S. "The Greek Trireme." *The Mariner's Mirror* 27 (1941): 14-44.

Morrison, J. S. "Notes on Certain Greek Nautical Terms. . . ." *Classical Quarterly* 41 (1947): 122-135. Two essays that demonstrate the three superimposed banks of oarsmen on the trireme.

Morrison, J. S., and Williams, R. T. *Greek Oared Ships.* Cambridge: Cambridge University Press, 1968. The texts and details for all aspects of these ships. This is not casual reading.

Torr, Cecil. *Ancient Ships.* 1894. Reprint. Chicago: Argonaut, 1964. Still useful for rigging and plates; the writings by Morrison and Casson generally make it outdated.

The opposing scholarly view (that there were not three banks of oarsmen) is represented by:

Amit, M. *Athens and the Sea.* Collection *Latomus.* Vol. 74. Bruxelles-Berchem, 1965, pp. 99–102. Full citation of sources and secondary works.

Marathon

Hammond, N. G. L. "The Campaign and Battle of Marathon." *Journal of Hellenic Studies* 88 (1968): 13–57. A detailed reconstruction. I recommend part 4, pp. 43–47, for the beginner.

Xerxes' Invasion

Green, Peter. *Xerxes at Salamis.* New York: Praeger, 1970. Smooth, literate account; Green has full command of the source materials.
Hignett, C. *Xerxes' Invasion of Greece.* Oxford: Oxford University Press, 1963. Complete and readable.

Salamis

Hammond, N. G. L. "The Battle of Salamis." *Journal of Hellenic Studies* 76 (1956): 36–54. A convincing reconstruction, but rough going for the nonclassicist.

The Athenian Empire

Meiggs, Russell. *The Athenian Empire.* Oxford: Oxford University Press, 1972. Should be used in company with volume 3 of B. D. Meritt, H. T. Wade-Gery, and Malcolm F. McGregor, *Athenian Tribute Lists* (Princeton: American School of Classical Studies at Athens, 1950).

The Peloponnesian War

Many sources exist. I suggest three more recent books (but further reading can be easily gleaned from footnotes and bibliographies):

Ste. Croix, G. E. M. de. *The Origins of the Peloponnesian War.* Ithaca: Cornell University Press, 1972. Thick, but highly readable tome. It defends Thucydides' work against his numerous scholarly (modern) critics.

Kagan, Donald. *The Outbreak of the Peloponnesian War.* Ithaca: Cornell University Press, 1969.

Kagan, Donald. *The Archidamian War.* Ithaca: Cornell University Press, 1974. Both Kagan's books give arguments against Thucydides' assertions that the Peloponnesian War was inevitable.

The Athenian Plague

Littman, Robert J., and Littman, M. L. "The Athenian Plague: Small-pox." *TAPA* 100 (1969): 261–275. An argument that the plague was smallpox.

Scarborough, John. "Thucydides, Greek Medicine, and the Plague at Athens: A Summary of the Evidence." *Episteme* 4 (1970): 77–90. An argument for epidemic typhus. It includes a full bibliography.

The Expedition against Syracuse

Green, Peter. *Armada from Athens.* Garden City: Doubleday, 1970. History written for enjoyable reading, with a full command of sources.

Alcibiades

Raubitschek, A. E. "The Case against Alcibiades." *TAPA* 79 (1948): 191–210. Sober analysis of a romantic subject.

Sources

Translations of Greek and Latin sources cited in the chapter may be procured in the Loeb Classical Library or the Penguin Classics,* with the following exceptions: the

Inscr. Sparta Museum. 400. In H. A. Harris, *Sport in Greece and Rome* (London: Thames and Hudson, 1972), p. 104, together with note 63, p. 266, citing an article by M. N. Tod, "Sparta Inscriptions," in the *Annual of the British School at Athens.*

Justin/Trogus. No English translation has been rendered from up-dated texts. The standard text is O. Seel, ed., *Iustini epitoma historiarum Philippicarum Pompei Trogi* (Leipzig: Teubner, 1972).

The bits and pieces that have survived from Trogus are in O. Seel, ed., *Pompeii Trogi Fragmenta* (Leipzig: Teubner, 1956); it includes extracts from the quotations of Trogus as found in later works (generally Greek, as well as Latin), along with a comparison of given passages of Trogus to Justin's abridgment. Trogus was also the author of a work entitled *On Animals,* lost except for the fourteen fragments that Seel collected. The welter of the fragments of lost Greek historical writers is admirably summarized in Truesdell S. Brown, *The Greek Historians** (Lexington, Massachusetts: D. C. Heath, 1973), chapter 5, "Ephorus; Theopompus; the Alexander Historians," and chapter 6, "Megasthenes and Timaeus."

Pindar. There is one volume of the Loeb Classical Library. However, I have employed the text in A. Turyn, *Pindari Carmina* (Oxford: Blackwell, 1948).

Pseudo-Aristotle, *Mechanica.* The citation is drawn from Morrison and Williams, *Greek Oared Ships* (Cambridge: Cambridge University Press, 1968), p. 323, No. 41 under "Handling."

The Byzantine encyclopedia, *Suda.* The standard text is Ada Adler, ed., *Suidae Lexicon* (Leipzig: Teubner, 1933–1938; rptd. 1967–1971 in 5 vols. [Partes I–V]). The Tyrtaeus entry appears in Pars IV (Pi–Psi) [ed. 1935, rptd. 1971]).

Tyrtaeus. Part of a volume is devoted to him in the Loeb Classical Library (*Elegy and Iambus,* Vol. 1). I have used the text in E. Diehl, ed., *Anthologia lyrica Graeca* (Leipzig: Teubner, 1954), Fasc. 1 (Poetae elegiaci), 6–22.

The *Greek Anthology* comprises five volumes in the Loeb Classical Library.

Chapter 5   More War

Sparta's Victory and Hegemony

Forrest, W. G. *A History of Sparta.** London: Hutchinson, 1968, chap. 13, "Sparta's Empire." Succinct, with a short bibliography.

Xenophon

The best introduction to Xenophon is his own writing. Good translations of the *Anabasis* ("March up Country") and the *Hellenica* are in the Penguin Classics*; *Hellenica* appears as *A History of My Times.* Other works will be found among the Xenophon volumes in the Loeb Classical Library. See also J. K. Anderson, *Military Theory and Practice in the Age of Xenophon* (Berkeley: University of California Press, 1970).

Mercenaries

Parke, H. W. *Greek Mercenary Soldiers* (Oxford: Oxford University Press, 1933). Chapters 4–13 cover the fourth century B.C.

Pay and Rations

Pritchett, W. Kendrick. *Ancient Greek Military Practices.* * Berkeley: University of California Press, 1971, chaps. 1 and 2. A collection of the evidence.

The Second Athenian Confederacy

Larsen, J. A. O. *Representative Government in Greek and Roman History.* * Berkeley: University of California Press, 1966, chap. 3, especially pp. 58–65. Technical.

Marshall, F. H. *The Second Athenian Confederacy.* Cambridge: Cambridge University Press, 1905. Badly in need of replacement.

The Peltasts

Best, J. G. P. *Thracian Peltasts and their Influence on Greek Warfare.* Groningen: Wolters-Noordhoff, 1969. Straightforward. However, the text suffers from a number of errata, corrected on a loose sheet that the Dutch publishers supply.

Cavalry

Anderson, J. K. *Ancient Greek Horsemanship.* Berkeley: University of California Press, 1961, chap. 12, "Military Equipment and Tactics." Based on Xenophon and carefully documented.

Horse Races

Harris, H. A. *Sport in Greece and Rome.* London: Thames and Hudson, 1972, chaps. 7 and 8. Lively and packed with enthusiasm. Chapters 10 and 13–15 do much to correct the myths of *Ben-Hur.*

Robinson, Rachel Sargent. *Sources for the History of Greek Athletics.* * Cincinnati: Rachel Sargent Robinson, 1955, pp. 82–83, 96,
   and 220. Sources in translation.

Pelopidas and Epaminondas

In spite of the importance of these two military leaders, there is little
modern literature about them in English. Thus the best introduction
remains Plutarch's semibiographical treatment in *Pelopidas,* which
Ian Scott-Kilvert has freshly translated as a section of *Plutarch: The
Age of Alexander* * (Harmondsworth: Penguin L286, 1972). Pausan-
ias, *Description of Greece,* ix: 13–15, gives excerpts from the lost
Epaminondas by Plutarch. In the Penguin Classics Pausanius' work
appears as Peter Levi, trans., *Pausanius: Guide to Greece,* * 2 vols.
(Harmondsworth: Penguin L225 and L226, 1971); the section about
Epaminondas appears in Volume 1, pages 332–339.

Philip II of Macedonia

Pickard-Cambridge, A. W. "The Rise of Macedonia" and "Macedonian Supremacy in Greece." In *Cambridge Ancient History.* Vol.
   6. Cambridge: Cambridge University Press, 1933, pp. 200–271.
   Comprehensive.
Wilcken, Ulrich. *Alexander the Great.* * Translated from the German
   edition of 1931. New York: Norton N381, 1967, trans. by G. C.
   Richards, chap. 2. Sober account that deftly wends its way among
   quasi legends.

Demosthenes

Pickard-Cambridge, A. W. As cited above under Philip II. Good for
   general coverage. It does not dwell on the numerous controversies
   that are the subject of most journal essays. Plutarch's biography
   Demosthenes also appears in the Scott-Kilvert translation refer-
   enced under Pelopidas.

The Battle of Chaeronea

Hammond, N. G. L. "The Victory of Macedon at Chaeronea." In

N. G. L. Hammond, *Studies in Greek History*. Oxford: Oxford University Press, 1973, pp. 534–557. Of some interest are the remarks on pages 553–557 in "Note on the Lion of Chaeronea."

Alexander the Great

Of the enormous amount of literature extant, I suggest two collections of essays and four biographies, presuming that the reader will chase after those topics that are particularly interesting. The fundamental account of Arrian has been reissued in the Penguin Classics as A. de Selincourt, trans., and J. R. Hamilton, ed., *The Campaigns of Alexander** (Harmondsworth: Penguin L253, 1971); Plutarch's biography *Alexander* is part of the Penguin series *Plutarch: The Age of Alexander** (listed under Pelopidas).

The entire October 1965 issue of *Greece and Rome,* second series, vol. 12, no. 2, is devoted to Alexander. Included are the following articles: J. R. Hamilton, "Alexander's Early Life"; A. K. Narain, "Alexander and India"; P. A. Brunt, "The Aims of Alexander"; E. Badian, "The Administration of the Empire"; C. Bradford Welles, "Alexander's Historical Achievement."

G. T. Griffith, ed., *Alexander the Great: The Main Problems* (New York: Barnes and Noble, 1966), includes these essays in English: E. Badian, "Harpalus" and "Alexander the Great and the Unity of Mankind"; Lionel Pearson, "The Diary and Letters of Alexander the Great"; W. W. Tarn, "Alexander's Foundations," "Alexander's Deification," and "Alexander the Great and the Unity of Mankind"; Truesdell S. Brown, "Callisthenes and Alexander."

Fox, Robin Lane. *Alexander the Great: A Biography*. New York: The Dial Press, 1974. A splendid account, refreshingly accurate and solidly buttressed by the various types of source materials. This makes captivating reading.

Fuller, J. F. C. *The Generalship of Alexander the Great.** New Brunswick: Rutgers University Press, 1960. For military buffs.

Tarn, W. W. *Alexander the Great.** Boston: Beacon BP 26, 1956. Idealistic portrait.

Wilcken, Ulrich. *Alexander the Great.** New York: Norton N381, 1967. Sober and balanced. But students have favored Tarn over Wilcken.

Hellenistic History in General

For this vastly complicated and rich period, there are few readable summaries. Most textbooks offer lists of names, dates, and battles, but here are some worthy exceptions:

Peters, F. E. *The Harvest of Hellenism.** New York: Simon and Schuster, 1970, chaps. 1-9. Readable and accurate and particularly good on the cultural setting. Students have lavished praise on this book.

Rostovtzeff, M. *Social and Economic History of the Hellenistic World.* 3 vols. Oxford: Oxford University Press, 1941. The encyclopedia for the era.

Tarn, W. W., and Griffith, G. T. *Hellenistic Civilisation.** Cleveland: Meridian 121, 1961. The best general survey, except for chapter 1 (in which the names and numbers syndrome is at its worst, making the chapter a virtually unreadable Hellenistic "phone directory").

Ptolemy

Bell, H. Idris. *Egypt from Alexander the Great to the Arab Conquest.* Oxford: Oxford University Press, 1948, chaps. 1 and 2. Brilliant summary by a leading specialist in papyrology.

Bevan, Edwyn R. *The House of Ptolemy.* 1927. Reprint. Chicago: Argonaut, 1968. The most comprehensive account, but outdated by recent research in papyri and numismatics.

Fraser, P. M. *Ptolemaic Alexandria.* 3 vols. Oxford: Oxford University Press, 1972. Encyclopedic.

The Antigonids

Duggan, Alfred. *Besieger of Cities.** New York: Pyramid Books, 1967. Semifictional and colorful book about Demetrius Poliorcetes, based on thorough knowledge of the limited sources.

Tarn, W. W. *Antigonus Gonatas.* 1913. Reprint. Oxford: Oxford University Press, 1969. Plodding account of the dynasty's founder.

Walbank, F. W. *Philip V of Macedon.* 1940. Reprint. New York: Archon, 1967. The book about the king who learned firsthand, in defeat in 197 B.C., about the Roman legions.

Seleucus and Seleucid Rule

Bevan, Edwyn E. *The House of Seleucus.* 2 vols. 1902. Reprint. New York: Barnes and Noble, 1966. Still the most connected summary, but now rather dated by recent research in archaeology and numismatics.

The Greek Leagues

Larsen, J. A. O. *Greek Federal States.* Oxford: Oxford University Press, 1968, pp. 173–497. The standard volume and complex.

Pergamon

Hansen, Esther V. *The Attalids of Pergamon.* 2d ed. Ithaca: Cornell University Press, 1971. Detailed materials and clear prose.

McShane, Roger B. *The Foreign Policy of the Attalids of Pergamum.** Urbana: University of Illinois Press, 1964. Pergamon bearing the flag of Greek freedom. Students have found the writing uneven— from lucid to awful.

Rhodes

Fraser, P. M., and Bean, G. E. *The Rhodian Peraea and Islands.* Oxford: Oxford University Press, 1954. Technical, with the Greek untranslated. It is worth the effort for general readers who can skip the Greek.

Casson, Lionel. "The Grain Trade of the Hellenistic World." *TAPA* 85 (1954): 168–187. About Rhodes and ships. This could provide meat for novels.

Greek Bactria and India

Narain, A. K. *The Indo-Greeks.* Oxford: Oxford University Press, 1957. Difficult book, based on coinages.

Tarn, W. W. *The Greeks in Bactria and India.* 1951. Reprint. Cambridge: Cambridge University, 1966. Very speculative. It gives a good development of the eastern extension of Seleucid rule. Students have been fascinated by this thick tome.

Woodcock, George. *The Greeks in India.* London: Faber, 1966. The best beginning book.

Elephants and Hellenistic Warfare

Adcock, F. E. *The Greek and Macedonian Art of War.** Berkeley: University of California Press, 1962. Tempered humor.

Griffith, G. T. *The Mercenaries of the Hellenistic World.* 1935. Reprint. Groningen: Bouma's Boekhuis, 1968, pp. 214–225. About Carthage and her use of Greek soldiers. It is written in the style of dusty military annals and provides food for the war game companies.

Scullard, H. H. *The Elephant in the Greek and Roman World.* London: Thames and Hudson, 1974, chaps. 2, 3, 5, and 6. Fascinating reading about Aristotle, biology, and military applications among the Hellenistic successors and Carthage.

Tarn, W. W. *Hellenistic Military and Naval Developments.* 1930. Reprint. New York: Biblo and Tannen, 1966, pp. 92–100. A terse summary.

Diplomatic Marriages and Hellenistic Queens

Macurdy, Grace Harriet. *Hellenistic Queens.* Baltimore: Johns Hopkins Press, 1932. The strength and ruthlessness of Greek dynasts' wives.

Volkmann, Hans. *Cleopatra.* London: Elek, 1958. The best of the many books on Antony's mistress. In looks and action, history's Cleopatra was far different from Elizabeth Taylor.

Sources

With the exception of the following, translations of all sources cited in the text can be found in the Loeb Classical Library or the Penguin Classics:*

The Hellenica Oxyrhynchia. It is listed under "Sources" for Chapter 1. Justin-Trogus. It is listed under "Sources" for Chapter 4. Polyaenus. I have employed E. Wölfflin, ed., *Polyaeni strategematon libri VIII.* Stuttgart: Teubner, 1970.

Sparta Inscriptions: Inscriptiones Graecae, V, 1. 213. This is found in H. A. Harris, *Sport in Greece and Rome* (London: Thames and Hudson, 1972), p. 161, with note 109, p. 268, citing L. Moretti, *Iscrizioni agonistiche Greche* (Rome, 1953), 16.

Chapter 6   Greeks and Myth

Handbooks and General Treatments of
Greek Mythology

Many sources are available. I recommend the following, since they are in paperback editions:

Graves, Robert. *The Greek Myths.** 2 vols. Harmondsworth: Penguin A508 and A509, 1955. Cryptic and complete, sometimes speculative, generally stimulating. It provides brief source references.

Morford, Mark P. O., and Lenardon, Robert J. *Classical Mythology.** New York: McKay, 1971. A good primer. There are many translated sources under three categories: The Myths of Creation, The Gods, and Greek Sagas and Greek Local Legends. Added is The Survival of Classical Mythology. Chapters 22–24 offer a rarity in books of this kind, evinced by "Roman Mythology" and "Classical Mythology in Music."

Rose, H. J. *A Handbook of Greek Mythology.** New York: Dutton, 1959. More prosaic than Graves, but a solid introduction.

Warner, Rex. *The Stories of the Greeks.** New York: Noonday 355, 1967. Tales retold for the modern reader. It is well executed and suited for casual reading.

Greek Religion in General

One book will suffice here, since it surpasses any contenders:

Guthrie, W. K. C. *The Greeks and their Gods.** Boston: Beacon BP 2, 1950. A rare synthesis of the scholarly with the enjoyable. It will be cited henceforth as Guthrie. *Gods.*

Minoan Religion

Finley, M. I. *Aspects of Antiquity.** New York: Viking C252, 1969, chap. 1, "The Rediscovery of Crete." A cogent warning about what is known in this mysterious realm.

Hutchinson, R. W. *Prehistoric Crete.* * Harmondsworth: Penguin
A501, 1962, chap. 8. Securely based on art and archaeology.

Mycenaean Religion

In addition to the listings under "The Minoans and the Mycenaeans"
for chapter 2, see:

Nilsson, Martin P. *The Mycenaean Origin of Greek Mythology.* *
1932. Reprint. New York: Norton N234, 1964. A book with a
definite axe to grind: Nordic origins and sources.

Gods, Myths, History, and Homer

To the listings under "The Homeric Myths and History" in Chapter
2, I would add these books:

Finley, M. I. *Aspects of Antiquity.* * New York: Viking C252, 1969,
chap. 2, "Lost: The Trojan War." Lucid and puckish. It will give
the beginner a good insight into the bloated scholarly war that
occasionally reaches the pages of the newspapers.
Kirk, G. S. *Homer and the Epic.* * Cambridge: Cambridge University
Press, 1965. A layman's version of his more technical *The Songs
of Homer* (Cambridge, 1962).

Troy (Archaeology)

Blegen, Carl W. *Troy and the Trojans.* London: Thames and Hudson,
1962. The best general survey.

Pylos and the Linear B Tablets

Dow, Sterling. "The Linear Scripts and the Tablets and Historical
Documents." In *Cambridge Ancient History.* Vol. 2, part 1. 3d ed.
Cambridge: Cambridge University Press, 1973, pp. 582–626.
Chadwick, John. "The Linear B Tablets as Historical Documents."
Ibid., pp. 609–26. Discussions, with some tablets in diagram illus-
tration. These two sources are for linguistic enthusiasts.
Nilsson, Martin P. *A History of Greek Religion.* * 2d ed. New York:
Norton N289, 1964. A shortened work for the nonspecialist reader.
Two other volumes by Nilsson are listed, respectively, under

"Mycenaean Religion" and "Indo-European Links and Older Myths" (to come).

Heracles

Guthrie. *Gods.* pp. 231–241.

Hesiod

Rose, H. J. *A Handbook of Greek Literature.** New York: Dutton, 1960, pp. 57–79. Clipped survey of the poet and his times.
Solmsen, F. *Hesiod and Aeschylus.* Ithaca: Cornell University Press, 1949. The connections between the two poets.

Indo-European Links and Older Myths

Campbell, Joseph. *The Masks of God.* New York: Viking, 1959.
Campbell, Joseph. *Hero with a Thousand Faces.** Cleveland: Meridian Books M22, 1956. Plausible arguments from anthropology for the cross-identification of primitive myths.
Frazer, Sir James George. *The Golden Bough: A Study in Magic and Religion.** A one-volume abridgment of the 12-volume original work. New York: Macmillan, 1963. A gigantic hodgepodge of data and ingenuous arguments, incredibly readable and fascinating in detail. Volume 4, *Adonis Attis Osiris,* 3rd ed. (London: Macmillan, 1907) is perhaps the most provocative volume.
Graves, Robert. *The White Goddess: A Historical Grammar of Poetic Myth.** New York: Farrar Straus and Giroux, 1966. The shimmer of poetic understanding and the language of myth. The Great Earth Mother emerges with power. However, the general reader may have some difficulty with the linguistic gymnastics.
Nilsson, Martin P. *Greek Folk Religion.** New York: Harper Torchbooks TB78, 1961. A brilliant evocation of the common people and their fears and hopes.

Aesop

Introduction to *Fables of Aesop.** Translated by S. A. Handford. Harmondsworth: Penguin L43, 1964.

Zeus

Cook, A. B. *Zeus.* 3 vols. Cambridge: Cambridge University Press, 1914-1940. Standard reference.

Parke, H. W. *The Oracles of Zeus.* Cambridge, Mass.: Harvard University Press, 1967. A discussion of Dodona, Olympia, and Ammon.

Hera

Guthrie. *Gods.* Pp. 66-72.

From Poseidon through Hestia and Hephaestus

Farnell, L. R. *Cults of the Greek States.* 5 vols. Oxford: Oxford University Press, 1896-1909. The usual beginning point. Each god or goddess has a separate entry.

The Eleusinian Mysteries

Mylonas, George E. *Eleusis and the Eleusinian Mysteries.* * Princeton: Princeton University Press, 1969. Historical narrative. Good plates show the physical remains.

Delos

Ferguson, W. S. *Hellenistic Athens.* 1911. Reprint. Chicago: Ares Publishers, 1974, chap. 9, "Athens and Delos." Still the best short account.

Orphism

Guthrie. *Gods.* Pp. 307-332.

Oracles of Delphi and Dodona

Parke, H. W. *The Oracles of Zeus.* Cambridge, Mass.: Harvard University Press, 1967, chaps. 1 and 3-7. Coverage of Dodona.

Parke, H. W., and Wormell, D. E. W. *The Delphic Oracle.* 2 vols. Oxford: Blackwell, 1956. Standard reference.

Asclepius and Temple Medicine

Edelstein, Emma J., and Edelstein, Ludwig. *Asclepius.* 2 vols. Baltimore: Johns Hopkins Press, 1945. A presentation of the great majority of the testimonia, with translations and commentary.

Jayne, Walter A. *The Healing Gods of Ancient Civilizations.* 1925. Reprint. New York: University Books, 1967, chap. 6. A trifle naïve and simplistic, but with a solid base in German scholarship.

Dionysus

Otto, Walter F. *Dionysus: Myth and Cult.** Bloomington: Indiana University Press, 1965. The methods of Freud (especially those in *Totem and Taboo*) and, on occasion, Jung, applied to Greek mythology. Termed fanciful by some classical scholars, a few students have called *Dionysus* a "mind bender."

Hellenistic Religion in General

Grant, Frederick C. *Hellenistic Religions.** Indianapolis: Bobbs-Merrill, 1953. Sources in translation.

Hadas, Moses. *Hellenistic Culture.** 1959. Reprint. New York: Norton N593, 1972, chap. 14, "Cult and Mystery." Synoptic account leaning on Jewish interpretations.

Rose, H. J. *Religion in Greece and Rome.** New York: Harper Torchbooks TB55, 1959, chap. 5, "The Gods on Trial," and chap. 6, "The Gods of the Wise." Full command of source materials without citation. This is a steady favorite with students.

Greeks and Jews

Hadas, Moses. *Hellenistic Culture.** 1959. Reprint. New York: Norton N593, 1972, chap. 15, "Prayer and Confession," and chap. 16, "Blessed Landscapes and Havens." A sketch of the background of messianic Judaism and its general impact.

Peters, F. E. *The Harvest of Hellenism.** New York: Simon and Schuster, 1970, chap. 7, "Hellenes and Jews." Succinct and well written. Students have remarked that this chapter "puts some order into the mess."

Tcherikover, Victor. *Hellenistic Civilization and the Jews.** Trans-

lated from the 1959 Hebrew edition. New York: Atheneum, 1970.
Packed with data.

Isis, Serapis, and Religious Life

Fraser, P. M. *Ptolemaic Alexandria.* 3 vols. Oxford: Oxford University Press, 1972, vol. 1, chap. 5, "Religious Life." Complete, with extensive notation in vol. 2, pp. 323-461.

Kurtz, Donna C., and Boardman, John. *Greek Burial Customs.* London: Thames and Hudson, 1971, chaps. 8 and 16. A volume that employs art and archaeology with unusual effectiveness. The images shine brilliantly in oversized tombs and displays.

Witt, R. E. *Isis in the Graeco-Roman World.* London: Thames and Hudson, 1971. A book with magnificent plates, as is usual with Thames and Hudson books.

Magic and Astrology

Cumont, Franz. *Astrology and Religion among the Greeks and Romans.* * 1912. Reprint. New York: Dover, 1960. A short summary.

Dodds, E. R. *The Greeks and the Irrational.* * Berkeley: University of California Press, 1951, chap. 8, "The Fear of Freedom." A modern classic of its kind. Specialists agree with my students that Dodds' points are thought-provoking and beautifully expressed.

Halliday, W. R. *Greek Divination.* 1913. Reprint. Chicago: Argonaut, 1967. The answer to how the Greeks took their omens.

Holmyard, E. J. *Alchemy.* * Harmondsworth: Penguin A348, 1968, chaps. 1, 2, and 4. A summary of Greek ideas on the subject.

Hughes, Pennethorne. *Witchcraft.* * Harmondsworth: Penguin A745, 1967, chaps. 1-3. A complete demonstration of the long history and interest in the topic.

Lindsay, Jack. *The Origins of Alchemy in Greco-Roman History.* London: Muller, 1970. A morass of facts, quasi facts, and speculations—ancient and modern—and the mysterious Bolos of Mendes, Ostanes, Hermes Trismegistos, Maria the Jewess, et al. It is impossible to use for source hunting.

Neugebauer, O., and Hoesen, H. B. van. *Greek Horoscopes.* Philadelphia: American Philosophical Society, 1959. Technical. If you ever wondered from where all those bits of "scientific" data for star charts in astrology emerged, late Hellenistic times had them as well.

Scarborough, John. "Gnosticism, Drugs, and Alchemy." *Pharmacy in History* 13 (1971): 151-157. The mixture of mysticism and drug lore.

Thorndike, Lynn. *A History of Magic and Experimental Science.* New York: Columbia University Press, 1923, vol. I, chap. 1. Still the best work on magic and related matters.

Inscriptions

Inscriptional evidence becomes important toward the end of the chapter. Students have found these introductions to epigraphy illuminating:

Lattimore, Richmond. *Themes in Greek and Latin Epitaphs.* * Urbana: University of Illinois Press, 1962. An excellent selection of religious and other feelings from grave memorials. Greek is translated, but not Latin.

Woodhead, A. G. *The Study of Greek Inscriptions.* * Cambridge: Cambridge University Press, 1967. A discussion of how the historian of ancient civilization uses inscriptional evidence, from which the general reader will benefit. A little Greek is required, but not that much.

Sources

With the exception of the Galen passage, all other sources are available in the Loeb Classical Library or the Penguin Classics.*

The Greek text of the Galen quotation is in C. G. Kühn, ed., *Claudii Galeni Opera Omnia,* 20 vols. in 22 (1821-1832; reprint ed., Hildesheim: Olms, 1964-1965), 12: 207.

For Pausanias, *Description of Greece,* the rich offerings of James G. Frazer's commentary are still unmatched. Recently, the six volumes of translation and commentary were reprinted (New York: Biblo and Tannen, 1965).

Chapter 7   Proper Conduct and Sexual Mores

In contrast to the plentiful literature on most particulars of Greek civilization, there is little available in English about Greek sexual mores. The topic is usually relegated to pseudoscholarly works, most often masking as pornography. When one looks up these references, hoping to uncover source materials on "what the Greeks themselves *really* thought about this" (as one student grumbled in a pique of irritation), he finds that the "sources" are either fabrications or "interpretations" of particular materials to suit a modern message. The following form the most trustworthy accounts in English:

Hyde, H. Montgomery. *A History of Pornography.** London: New English Library Four Square Books, 1966, chap. 2, "Pornography in the Ancient World." A rapid survey, drawing on the diverse materials in the *Song of Solomon,* Athenaeus, and other sources. Hyde claims objectivity, while writing to condemn the vestiges of Victorian prudery in modern England. His more basic flaw is assuming that cited sources were considered "pornographic" in antiquity.

"Licht, Hans," (P. Brandt). *Sexual Life in Ancient Greece.* Translated first by J. H. Freese from the German in 1932. London: The Abbey Library, 1971. A semianalytical approach, putting Greeks and Romans "on the couch." Here ancient Greece means Greek sources from the entire span of classical times, including the Roman Empire. Source references are not always reliable.

Lacey, W. K. *The Family in Classical Greece.* London: Thames and Hudson, 1968, chap. 7, "Women in Democratic Athens." The best approach in English, with full citation of sources. An occasional prostitute peeps through in her historic context.

Marrou, H. I. *A History of Education in Antiquity.** New York: Mentor MQ552, 1964, chap. 3, "Pederasty in Classical Education." Good balance and the best short narrative available on the subject. The sources have detailed notations, including those for Sappho.

Pottery

Beazley, J. D. *Attic Red-Figure Vase-Painters.* 2d ed. Oxford: Oxford University Press, 1963. The basic reference work.

Corpus Vasorum Antiquorum. In many volumes. Illustrations of the vases, giving an indication of vase-painting as a whole and some concept of painting styles. A good university library will usually have a set of this multilanguage series.

Arias, P. E., and Hirmer, M. *A History of Greek Vase Painting.*

London: Thames and Hudson, 1962. A convenient summary of both Red-Figure and Black-Figure painting and the significance of scenes that might aid in historical interpretation, and a magnificent book.

Henle, Jane. *Greek Myths: A Vase Painter's Handbook.** Bloomington: Indiana University Press, 1973. A classification of mythological themes on the vases.

Pickard-Cambridge, A. *The Dramatic Festivals of Athens.* 2d ed., rev. by J. Gould and D. M. Lewis. Oxford: Oxford University Press, 1968, chap. 4, "The Costumes," especially pp. 210-231. Illustrations from the pottery of Athenian comedy, with its sexual overtones in costuming.

Aristophanes and Sexual Allusions

Dover, K. J. *Aristophanic Comedy.* Berkeley: University of California Press, 1972. Unassuming and powerful in depth of understanding. This is the best book by far on Aristophanes, especially for the puns, jokes, allusions, and contexts. Dover makes it all fit together, as the Greeks might have done. He provides chapters on each extant play of Aristophanes, with original translations, but without the usual blushing over "obscenities."

Attic Law

Harrison, A. R. W. *The Law of Athens.* 2 vols. Oxford: Oxford University Press, 1968-1971. Clear and succinct. One may stumble over the unrendered Greek.

Sources

With the exception of the following, materials cited from the Greek can be obtained in the Loeb Classical Library or the Penguin Classics:*

Herodas. Walter Headlam and A. D. Knox, eds., *Herodas: The Mimes and Fragments* (Cambridge: Cambridge University Press, 1922). Mime VI is given in translation (with Greek text), pp. 274-316, along with commentary.

Hesychius. M. Schmidt, ed., *Hesychii Alexandrini Lexicon* (Jena: Duftius, 1867). This is the complete text. The new edition, Kurt

Latte, ed., *Hescychii Alexandrini Lexicon* (Copenhagen: Munksgaard, 1953-1966) has only been completed up to Omicron.
Pollux. E. Bethe, ed., *Pollucis Onomasticon,* 3 vols. (1900-1937;
reprint ed., Stuttgart: Teubner, 1967).
The "Follow Me!" Sandals. W. Krenkel, "2. Profane Prostitution,"
in *Der Kleine Pauly* (München: Alfred Druckenmüller Verlag,
1964-), vol. 4, cols. 1192-1194 [1193]. The reference comes
from part of Krenkel's article. He cites Clement of Alexandria and
an illustration in the older Daremberg-Saglio, *Dictionnaire des
antiquités grecques et romaines* (Paris, 1877-1919) [B, Abb.
4968].

Chapter 8   Myth and the Womb of Philosophy

Of the many volumes on Greek philosophy, I suggest those that
combine reasonability with solid expertise. The philosophers are
never easy to read, and Plato and Aristotle deserve concentration and
consideration over a long time. There is no short, glittering, and
simple method by which to approach the philosophers.

All of the philosophers from Thales to Socrates are contained in
W. K. C. Guthrie, *A History of Greek Philosophy*. Three volumes
have so far been printed: Volume 1, *The Earlier Presocratics and the
Pythagoreans* (Cambridge: Cambridge University Press, 1967), vol-
ume 2, *The Presocratic Tradition from Parmenides to Democritus*
(Cambridge: Cambridge University Press, 1965), and volume 3, *The
Fifth-Century Enlightenment* (Cambridge: Cambridge University
Press, 1969). Sections of volume 3 are available as paperbacks from
Cambridge University Press ("Socrates" and "The Sophists"). This is
a brilliant work that supercedes all other general narratives. Guthrie
is judicious in writing about the puzzling fragments of the pre-
Socratic thinkers, and he provides bibliographical leads that are sig-
nificant and up to date, and (most important to the professional
philosopher) include several varying viewpoints on the fragments.

Equally brilliant, but from another angle, is Bruno Snell, *The Discovery of the Mind** (New York: Harper Torchbook TB 1018,
1960). He makes full connections between the poets and philosophers, the *polis* and the intellectual construct.

Other general accounts

Bréhier, Emile. *The Hellenic Age.** Chicago: University of Chicago
Press, 1963.

Bréhier, Emile. *The Hellenistic Age.* * Chicago: University of Chicago Press, 1965. A noted French scholar's views. In both books he presumes that the reader has some knowledge of the basic tenets.

Guthrie, W. K. C. *The Greek Philosophers from Thales to Aristotle.* * (New York: Harper Torchbooks TB 1008, 1960). Chapters 1-4 are synopses of his more extensive *History*. Chapters 5-8 provide one of the clearest summaries of Plato and Aristotle in English.

Jaeger, Werner. *Paideia.* 3 vols. (Oxford: Blackwell, 1945). The ideals preached by all intellectuals, from poets to politicians. Volume 1 has appeared as an Oxford University Press paperback. Volume 3 has the excellent section for "Greek Medicine as Paideia."

The Pre-Socratics

Vogel, C. J. de. *Pythagoras and Early Pythagoreans.* Assen: van Gorcum, 1966. Controversial collection of the evidence, real and otherwise.

Furley, David J. *Two Studies in the Greek Atomists.* Princeton: Princeton University Press, 1967, especially pp. 44-103. Clear summary of what is known of Greek atomism from the Pythagoreans through the Eleatics.

Furley, David J., and Allen, R. E. *Studies in Presocratic Philosophy.* London: Routledge Kegan Paul, 1970, vol. 1. A collection of essays from the professional journals. I recommend Gregory Vlastos, "Equality and Justice in Early Greek Cosmologies," "On Heracleitus," and "Theology and Philosophy in Early Greek Thought"; and W. A. Heidel, "The Pythagoreans and Greek Mathematics."

Jaeger, Werner. *The Theology of the Early Greek Philosophers.* Oxford: Oxford University Press, 1947. Splendid overview of cosmography, cosmogony, and theogony of the early thinkers.

Lloyd, G. E. R. *Polarity and Analogy.* Cambridge: Cambridge University Press, 1966. The structure of thinking and theories. This is a well-written account with Greek medical thinking interwoven.

O'Brien, D. *Empedocles' Cosmic Cycle.* Cambridge: Cambridge University Press, 1969. The somewhat technical book on love and strife.

Stokes, Michael C. *One and Many in Presocratic Philosophy.* Washington: Center for Hellenic Studies (Harvard University), 1971. The struggle for definition. Although heavy going for the novice, it indicates the difficulties the pre-Socratics had in gaining a conceptual framework. It is an important book.

Wheelwright, Philip. *Heraclitus.* Princeton: Princeton University Press, 1959. Stimulating introduction. Several students praised it.

Socrates

Guthrie, W. K. C. *Socrates.* * Cambridge: Cambridge University Press, 1972. Without peer.

Plato

Friedländer, Paul. *Plato.* * New York: Harper Torchbook TB 2017, 1964. The soundest introduction for the beginner.

Koyré, Alexandre. *Discovering Plato.* * New York: Columbia University Press, 1960. Short book emphasizing Platonic dialogues and their political/philosophical unity. It sends one back to the dialogues themselves.

Levy, G. R. *Plato in Sicily.* London: Faber, 1966. Popular work on Plato's misadventures in Sicily.

Taylor, A. E. *A Commentary on Plato's Timaeus.* Oxford: Oxford University Press, 1928. The first step for Atlantis enthusiasts. The Greekless reader can follow passages in a good translation.

Taylor, A. E. *Plato the Man and His Work.* 1926. Reprint. London: Methuen, 1966. Still the best summary in one volume.

Aristotle

Allen, D. J. *The Philosophy of Aristotle.* Rev. ed. Oxford: Oxford University Press, 1963. A good beginner's summary.

Cherniss, Harold. *Aristotle's Criticism of Presocratic Philosophy.* 1935. Reprint. New York: Octagon, 1971. Significant book that demonstrates Aristotle's acuity in historical analysis.

Grene, Marjorie. *A Portrait of Aristotle.* London: Faber, 1963. A solid popular account.

Jaeger, Werner. *Aristotle.* * Oxford: Oxford University Press, 1962. The thesis that Aristotle's concepts developed gradually, as he moved slowly away from Plato.

Lloyd, G. E. R. *Aristotle.* * Cambridge: Cambridge University Press, 1968. Delicious clarity without a sacrifice to learning.

Randall, John Herman, Jr. *Aristotle.** New York: Columbia University Press, 1962. A standard reference, often cited without comment in general histories. It will be difficult for the beginner.

Ross, Sir David. *Aristotle.* 1949. Reprint. London: Methuen, 1966. The best introduction to pull the disconnected strands into a perceivable whole, by one of the great scholars of Greek philosophy.

Eudoxus

Dicks, D. R. *Early Greek Astronomy to Aristotle.* London: Thames and Hudson, 1970, chap. 6. The best short account.

Theophrastus

Eichholz, D. E., ed. and trans. *Theophrastus: De lapidibus.* Oxford: Oxford University Press, 1965. Emphasis on Greek mineral-formation theories.

Hellenistic Philosophies

Bailey, Cyril. *Epicurus: The Extant Fragments.* Oxford, 1926. Reprint. Hildesheim: Olms, 1970. Still the most useful collection and brief commentary.

Rist, J. N. *Stoic Philosophy.* Cambridge: Cambridge University Press, 1969. Examination of the ethical paradoxes. It sometimes suffers from *hamartia* ("missing the mark").

Posidonius

The remnants of Posidonius have never been fully rendered into English, although Ludwig Edelstein was working on such a project until his death in 1956. His papers on the topic were re-edited and have appeared as:

Edelstein, L., and Kidd, I. G., eds. *Posidonius,* Vol. 1, *The Fragments.* Cambridge: Cambridge University Press, 1972. Introduction and Greek texts.

Since several students through the years have indicated an interest in the "Posidonius behind Cicero," I suggest these good essays from the professional journals:

Baldry, H. C. "Zeno's Ideal State." *Journal of Hellenic Studies* 79 (1959): 3-15. Good summary of the long-range impact of Stoicism.

de Lacy, P. "Some Recent Publications on Hellenistic Philosophy." *Classical World* 52 (1958): 8-15, 25-27, 37-39, and 59. Bibliographical guide, with multilingual contributions.

Dobson, J. F. "The Posidonius Myth." *Classical Quarterly* 12 (1918): 179-195. Outdated by recent scholarship, but still useful as a cogent warning.

Edelstein, Ludwig. "The Philosophical System of Posidonius." *American Journal of Philology* 57 (1936): 286-325. The basic essay in English.

Gould, J. B. "Chrysippus." *Phronesis* 12 (1967): 152-161. Technical article about Stoic truths and conditional propositions, but well worth the mental wrestling.

Jones, R. M. "Posidonius and Solar Eschatology." *Classical Philology* 27 (1932): 113-135. About the sun and the stars.

Nock, A. D. "Posidonius." *Journal of Roman Studies* 49 (1959): 1-16. The later impact of Posidonius.

Solmsen, F. "Greek Philosophy and the Discovery of the Nerves." *Museum Helveticum* 18 (1961): 150-163 and 169-197. The context for the Alexandrian dissections.

Sources

Most of the works by Plato and Aristotle will be found in either the Loeb Classical Library or the Penguin Classics.* For the pre-Socratic fragments, the fundamental work is H. Diels and W. Kranz, *Die Fragmente der Vorsokratiker* 3 vols. 6th ed. 1951-1952. Reprint. Zürich: Weidmann, 1966-1967. Kathleen Freeman, *Ancilla to the Pre-Socratic Philosophers* (Oxford: Blackwell, 1962), provides an English rendering of the major fragments; her *The Pre-Socratic Philosophers* (Oxford: Blackwell, 1946) adds historic and philosophical context. G. S. Kirk and J. E. Raven, *The Presocratic Philosophers** (Cambridge: Cambridge University Press, 1964) provide selected fragments, with text, translation, contextual commentary, and good bibliographical data. Students have found Kirk and Raven of great help in understanding Greek history and Greek medicine.

Chapter 9   Magic, Science, and Disease

The following references are in addition to the listings under "Magic and Astrology" of Chapter 6.

Magic and Religion

Guthrie, W. K. C. *The Greeks and their Gods.* * Boston: Beacon, 1955, pp. 270-277. The vivid power of magic and witchcraft.

Magical Amulets and Papyri

Bonner, Campbell. *Studies in Magical Amulets Chiefly Graeco-Egyptian.* Ann Arbor: University of Michigan Press, 1950. Discussion of the amulets and their presumed use. The collected diagrams and photographs point up how common such objects were.

Eitrem, S. *Magische Papyri.* In *Münchener Beiträge für Papyrusforschung,* vol. 19. 1933. Fundamental for information on the papyri.

Drugs

Schmidt, A. *Drogen und Drogenhandel im Altertum.* Leipzig, 1924. The basic work.

Urdang, G. "Pharmacy in Ancient Greece and Rome." *American Journal of Pharmaceutical Education* 7 (1943): 160 ff. An English version of some of the German work and source material.

Sonnedecker, Glenn, ed. and rev. *Kremers and Urdang's History of Pharmacy.* 3d ed. Philadelphia: Lippincott, 1963, pp. 11-20. A very general account of Greek and Roman drug lore.

Cohen, Morris R., and Drabkin, I. E., eds. *A Source Book in Greek Science.* Cambridge, Mass.: Harvard University Press, 1958, pp. 509-521. Suggested reading. This volume will be cited as Cohen/Drabkin. *Source Book.*

Watson, G. *Theriac and Mithridatium.* London: The Wellcome Historical Medical Library, 1966, chap. 1. Of great interest.

Theophrastus

Cohen/Drabkin. *Source Book.* Pp. 509-510 and 514-517.

Loeb Classical Library. *Inquiry Into Plants* is translated with an introduction.

Greek Mathematics and Machinery

Brumbaugh, Robert S. *Ancient Greek Gadgets and Machines.* * New York: Crowell, 1966. Nontechnical.

de Camp, L. Sprague. *The Ancient Engineers.* * Cambridge, Mass.:
  MIT Press, 1970, chaps. 4 and 5. Glib and readable.
Heath, Sir Thomas. *A History of Greek Mathematics.* 2 vols. Oxford:
  Oxford University Press, 1921. The standard account, and detailed.
  A shortened version appeared as *A Manual of Greek Mathematics.* *
  (1931; reprint ed., New York: Dover, 1963). This version is recom-
  mended to mathematics majors as a primer on the subject.
Klein, Jacob. *Greek Mathematical Thought and the Origin of Alge-
  bra.* Cambridge, Mass.: MIT Press, 1968. Key work that argues
  against the origins of algebra in Plato and Diophantus.
Lasserre, François. *The Birth of Mathematics in the Age of Plato.* *
  Cleveland: Meridian, 1966. Strong book about the philosophic/
  mathematical accomplishments in Plato's time. Students in mathe-
  matics and other fields have remarked on Lasserre's clarity.
Neugebauer, O. *The Exact Sciences in Antiquity.* * New York: Har-
  per Torchbooks TB 552, 1962, pp. 145–228. The best in English.
  It is technically oriented.
Waerden, B. L. van der *Science Awakening.* * Translated from the
  Dutch. New York: Wiley, 1963, chaps. 4–8. Clear and synoptic.
  He makes entries by the biographical system. This is a favorite
  with students who appreciate memory aids.

Euclid

Heath, Sir Thomas L. *The Thirteen Books of Euclid's Elements.* 3
  vols. Cambridge: Cambridge University Press, 1925. The standard
  historical introduction and commentary.

Archimedes

Dijksterhuis, E. J. *Archimedes.* Copenhagen: Munksgaard, 1956. The
  best volume in English on his life and works.
Drachmann, A. G. *The Mechanical Technology of Greek and Roman
  Antiquity.* Copenhagen: Munksgaard, 1963. A treatment of Greek
  and Roman machines.

Apollonius of Perga

Heath. *History.* II. Pp. 126–196.

Physics and Astronomy

Cohen/Drabkin. *Greek Science.* Pp. 89–350. Lengthy representation. of the sources, with some clipped notes.

Clagett, Marshall. *Greek Science in Antiquity.** New York: Collier, 1963, chaps. 6 and 7. Clear and stimulating account by a leading scholar in medieval science.

Dicks, D. R. *Early Greek Astronomy to Aristotle.* London: Thames and Hudson, 1970. The best book in English. Especially recommended is chapter 1, "General Principles."

Farrington, Benjamin. *Greek Science.** Harmondsworth: Penguin A142, 1961, pp. 90–111. Despite the emphasis on economic determinism, worth reading for its power of synthesis.

Aristarchus

Heath, Sir Thomas L. *Aristarchus of Samos.* Oxford: Oxford University Press, 1913. Complete translation with commentary.

Heath. *History.* II. Pp. 1–15.

Hipparchus

Dicks, D. R., ed. and trans. *The Geographical Fragments of Hipparchus.* London: University of London Athlone Press, 1960. Replaces all earlier works on the subject.

Ptolemy on Astronomy and Geography

Bunbury, E. H. *A History of Ancient Geography.* 2 vols. 1883. Reprint. New York: Dover, 1959. Vol. 2, chaps. 28 and 29. Still the best summary, almost a century after its appearance.

Neugebauer, O. "The Early History of the Astrolabe." *Isis* 40 (1949): 240–256. The representation of the spherical universe.

Price, Derek J. DeS. "An Ancient Computer." *Scientific American* 200 (June 1959): 60–67. Account of an ancient Greek astronomical calculator found in a shipwreck near the Aegean island of Antikythera.

The Ptolemaic System

Neugebauer, O. *The Exact Sciences in Antiquity.* * New York: Harper Torchbooks TB 552, 1962, pp. 191-207. A clear descriptive summary.

Astrology and Medicine

In addition to the references listed under "Magic and Astrology" of Chapter 6, I recommend:

Budge, E. Wallis. *Syrian Anatomy, Pathology and Therapeutics, "The Book of Medicines."* 2 vols. London: Oxford University Press, 1913. A rich collection of materials, including aspects of Hellenistic astrological medicine and Syriac sources. Many materials go back into Assyrian and Babylonian times.

Asclepian Medicine

See listings under "Asclepius and Temple Medicine" of chapter 6.

Greek Medicine

Phillips, E. D. *Greek Medicine.* London: Thames and Hudson, 1973. (The American edition bears the title *Aspects of Greek Medicine* [New York: St. Martin's Press, 1973]). Solid account. It is noteworthy for depicting Greek medicine without apology and for an understanding of the difference between modern approaches and those the Greeks used.

Sigerist, Henry E. *A History of Medicine.* Vol. 2. Oxford: Oxford University Press, 1961, chaps. 1 and 4. Generally the clearest writing in English on the topic, particularly on the nettling questions of the Hippocratic *Corpus.*

Alcmaeon of Croton

Guthrie, W. K. C. *A History of Greek Philosophy.* Vol. 1. Cambridge: Cambridge University Press, 1967, pp. 341-359. The best summary.

Kirk, G. S., and Raven, J. E. *The Presocratic Philosophers.* * Cam-

bridge: Cambridge University Press, 1964, pp. 232-235. Some
texts, translations, and commentary.

Vlastos, Gregory. "Isonomia." *American Journal of Philology* 74
(1953): 337-366. A brilliant synopsis.

Hippocrates and the Hippocratic "Corpus"

Levine, Edwin B. *Hippocrates.* New York: Twayne, 1971. Pedestrian
but complete survey of life and times. It suffers from a lack of
firsthand knowledge of medicine in its specialized setting.

Phillips. *Greek Medicine.* Chaps. 2 and 3. The best updated account.

Sigerist. *History.* Chap. 4. Learned and occasionally profound. It
includes a healthy skepticism about the "genuine" Hippocrates.

Temkin, Owsei, and Temkin, C. Lilian, eds. *Ancient Medicine:
Selected Papers of Ludwig Edelstein.* Baltimore: Johns Hopkins
Press, 1967. A collection of Edelstein's more important essays. I
recommend "The Hippocratic Oath"; "The Hippocratic Physician";
"Greek Medicine in its Relation to Religion and Magic"; "The
Relation of Ancient Philosophy to Medicine."

Praxagoras of Cos

Steckerl, Fritz. *The Fragments of Praxagoras of Cos and his School.*
Leiden: Brill, 1958. Texts with translations.

Hellenistic Medicine and the Alexandrian Museum

Dobson, J. F. "Herophilus of Alexandria." *Proceedings of the Royal
Society of Medicine* [Sect. History] 18 (1924-1925): 19-28.

Dobson, J. F. "Erasistratus." Ibid. 20 (1927): 825-832. Collection
and translation of fragments in both articles.

Fraser, P. M. *Ptolemaic Alexandria.* 3 vols. Oxford: Oxford University Press, 1972, I: 338-376 and II: 495-551. Extended collection
of the literary materials and commentary on this topic. It is the
most complete account in English of the Alexandrian Museum.

Phillips. *Greek Medicine.* Cited under "Greek Medicine." Chap. 6.
Good for context and very readable.

Scarborough, John. *Roman Medicine.* London: Thames and Hudson,
1969, chap. 2. A summary, with emphasis on later influences.

Sources

Some source materials in translation for Greek science and medicine can be found in the Cohen/Drabkin *Source Book* or in scattered volumes of the Loeb Classical Library. The Penguin Classics have no purely medical or scientific works, but a new translation of Hippocrates is due soon from G. E. R. Lloyd for their series. Sources cited from the original include:

Aetius. *Placita.* V, 30. 1. Ed. H. Diels in *Doxographi Graeci.* Aetius is an otherwise unknown compiler who lived sometime in the second century A.D. See also Kirk and Raven, *Presocratic Philosophers,* page 5.

Galen. XII, 966, from the Greek text of C. G. Kühn, ed., *Opera Omnia,* vol. XII, p. 966. See also full listing under "Sources" of chapter 6. Only Galen's *Natural Faculties* is a volume in the Loeb Classical Library.

Pappas. VIII, 1060. Ed. F. Hultsch. Pappas probably lived in Alexandria about A.D. 284–305, where he put together *Synagoge* ("Collection"). See also Heath, *History,* II, pages 427–439; this summarizes the contents of Book VIII.

Ptolemy. The text of the *Almagest* is best edited by J. L. Heiberg, 2 vols. (Leipzig: Teubner, 1898–1903). *Tetrabiblos,* Ptolemy's canonical work on astrology and its relations with astronomy, is available in English (Loeb Classical Library in the volume listed as Manetho and Ptolemy). Ptolemy lived in Alexandria *c.* A.D. 127–148.

Theon. *Commentary on Ptolemy, Manual Tables.* Ed. B. Halma. *Tables manuelles astronomiques de Ptolemée et de Théon.* Paris, 1822–1825, p. 53. Theon lived in Alexandria (*fl. c.* A.D. 364), and he contributed nothing original in mathematics or astronomy, but his work is valuable for the historical data he preserved. See also Heath, *History,* I, page 58, and II, page 526.

Theophrastus. *De sensu.* 25–26. Ed. G. M. Stratton. *De sensibus.* London: Allen and Unwin, 1917. This has translation and commentary.

Chapter 10   On the Poetic and the Sublime

Homer as Poet

In addition to the listings under "The Homeric Myths and History" of chapter 2 and under "Gods, Myths, History, and Homer" of chapter 6, I recommend:

Lattimore, Richmond. *The Iliad of Homer.** Chicago: University of Chicago Press, 1961. Introduction, pp. 1-55. A fine summary of the content, meter, and so on, by a scholar who fully comprehends poetry. The translation is one of the best.

Hesiod as Poet

See listings under "Hesiod" of chapter 6.

Music, Musical Instruments, and Dancing

Anderson, Warren D. *Ethos and Education in Greek Music.* Cambridge: Harvard University Press, 1966. A needed volume on how music permeated most aspects of Hellenic life.

Clements, E. "The Interpretation of Greek Music." *Journal of Hellenic Studies* 42 (1922): 133-166. The vexing questions of what and how.

Feaver, D. D. "The Musical Setting of Euripides' *Orestes.*" *American Journal of Philology* 81 (1960): 1-15. Tragedy, rhythm, and sounds. It puts the plays in a three-dimensional world.

Higgins, R. A., and Winnington-Ingram, R. P. "Lute-Players in Greek Arts." *Journal of Hellenic Studies* 85 (1965): 62-71. What the lutes looked like.

Lawler, Lillian B. *The Dance in Ancient Greece.** Seattle: University of Washington Press, 1967. Lucid. She provides full citation of sources, including numerous vase paintings.

Shirlaw, Matthew. "The Music and Tone Systems of Ancient Greece." *Music Review* 4 (1943): 14-27. A clipped discussion.

Winnington-Ingram, R. P. He has written a number of essays on these topics. I recommend: "Ancient Greek Music 1932-1957." *Lustrum* 3 (1958): 6-57 and 259-260. Bibliographical guide.

"Aristoxenus and the Intervals of Greek Music." *Classical Quarterly* 26 (1932): 195-208. Interweaving of philosophy, theory, and history.

"The Pentatonic Tuning of the Greek Lyre: A Theory Examined." *Classical Quarterly* s.s. 6 (1956): 169-186. Technical.

Wright, F. A. "The Technical Vocabulary of Dance and Song." *Classical Review* 30 (1916): 9-10. The special terms and their setting.

Chronology and History

For this difficult subject, the most complete one-volume survey is E. J. Bikerman, *Chronology of the Ancient World* (London: Thames and Hudson, 1968). Do you ever wonder how historians really know when events occurred? Within it are reviews of Greek calendars and the Athenian calendar, along with tables of Olympic years, Athenian *archons,* and a host of other time-tracking data.

Herodotus, Thucydides, and Writing of History

Brown, Truesdell S. *The Greek Historians.* * Lexington, Mass.: D. C. Heath, 1973. A long-awaited book that treats the subject through Hellenistic times and gives the student a clear introduction to the fragmentary sources.

Bury, J. B. *The Ancient Greek Historians.* * 1909. Reprint. New York: Dover, 1958, chaps. 2-4. Students have found this short account most helpful.

de Selincourt, Aubrey. *The World of Herodotus.* * Boston: Little, Brown, 1962. Fluid narrative by the gifted translator of Herodotus in the Penguin Classics.*

Finley, John H., Jr. *Thucydides.* Cambridge: Harvard University Press, 1942. One of the better books on the convoluted problems of Thucydides' approach, language, sources, and style.

Gomme, A. W. *A Historical Commentary on Thucydides.* Oxford: Oxford University Press, 1956, vol. 1, pp. 1-87. Gomme's memorable introduction to his remarkable commentary has aided students greatly as they begin to read Thucydides, both in the Greek and in translation.

How, W. W., and Wells, J. *A Commentary on Herodotus.* Oxford: Oxford University Press, 1912, vol. 1, pp. 1-51. Although badly dated, still one of the best introductions.

Starr, Chester G. *The Awakening of the Greek Historical Spirit.* New York: Knopf, 1968. Good analysis of how the epics and histories emerged from the same strands. Chapters 2, 3, and 6 are recommended.

The Plays

Bieber, Margarete. *The History of the Greek and Roman Theater.*
Princeton: Princeton University Press, 1961. Replete with drawings
and photographs. Chapters 1–7 cover the Greek period. Chapter 5,
"The Development of the Theater Building in the Classical Period,"
will warm architects' hearts.

Thespis

Pickard-Cambridge, A. W. *Dithyramb, Tragedy and Comedy.* 2d ed.,
rev. by T. B. L. Webster. Oxford: Oxford University Press, 1962,
pp. 69 ff. The best summary of what is known.

The Festival of Dionysus

Bieber, *History.* Pp. 51–53. Excellent short summary, with full
bibliographical leads.
Pickard-Cambridge, A. W. *The Dramatic Festivals of Athens.* 2d ed.
Oxford: Oxford University Press, 1968, pp. 1–126. Basic guide to
literary and archaeological sources.

Aeschylus, Sophocles, and Euripides

From the vast literature on the three playwrights, I suggest two
volumes: the first for its intrinsic merits, the second for its unusual
interpretations:

Kitto, H. D. F. *Greek Tragedy.** Garden City: Doubleday A38, 1954.
One of the finest overviews of the plays between two covers, and a
small volume.
Thomson, George. *Aeschylus and Athens.* New York: Grosset and
Dunlap, 1968. Well written and a fine example of the principles of
historical materialism applied to Greek history and artistic effort.

Aristophanes

Dover, K. J. *Aristophanic Comedy.* Berkeley: University of California Press, 1972. Finally, a book that does not pussyfoot about
what the plays were meant to do. Dover begins with the state of

the texts and their emergence from Byzantine holdings. This is good reading in history, mores, culture, and what people like to laugh at.

Ehrenberg, Victor. *The People of Aristophanes.** New York: Schocken, 1962. One of the better books about the people of fifth-century B.C. Attica. The major flaw—taking the stage portraits literally—does not dim its readability. Students have thoroughly enjoyed this volume.

Murray, Gilbert. *Aristophanes.* Oxford: Oxford University Press, 1933. A sensitive, though guarded, survey of the comedies. I urge producers who wish to revive the *Lysistrata* in modern guise to read pages 179-180.

Sources

All cited materials are available in either the Loeb Classical Library or the Penguin Classics.* Both the Modern Library (New York) and the University of Chicago Press have complete editions of the Athenian tragedies in translation.

Index